The Courts of Philip II and Alexander the Great

The Courts of Philip II and Alexander the Great

Monarchy and Power in Ancient Macedonia

Edited by
Frances Pownall, Sulochana R. Asirvatham
and Sabine Müller

DE GRUYTER

ISBN 978-3-11-135279-4
e-ISBN (PDF) 978-3-11-062294-2
e-ISBN (EPUB) 978-3-11-062364-2

Library of Congress Control Number: 2021949832

Bibliographic information published by the Deutsche Nationalbibliothek
The Deutsche Nationalbibliothek lists this publication in the Deutsche Nationalbibliografie; detailed bibliographic data are available on the Internet at http://dnb.dnb.de.

© 2023 Walter de Gruyter GmbH, Berlin/Boston
This volume is text- and page-identical with the hardback published in 2022.
Cover image: silver tetradrachm with head of Alexander, minted posthumously at Amphipolis, 323–320 BC. Reproduced by kind permission of the W.G. Hardy Collection of Ancient Near
Eastern and Classical Antiquities, University of Alberta (photo Colin Ash).
Printing and binding: CPI books GmbH, Leck

www.degruyter.com

Preface

The genesis of this volume was a conference by the same name, held at the University of Alberta in Edmonton in May of 2018, which attracted 44 papers. This conference, the first devoted to the courts of Philip and Alexander, was the ninth in a semi-regular but informal series of international symposia, the first held at the University of Calgary in 2002, followed by a second in Calgary in 2005, and then New Zealand (2006), South Carolina (2008), Spain (2010), Sydney (2013), Salt Lake City (2014), and Milan (2015). The earliest conferences focused upon the larger-than-life figure of Alexander the Great, but subsequent organizers incorporated the reigns of his father, Philip II, as well as the Successors, in order to achieve a fuller understanding of the historical context and significance of Alexander's achievements. Similarly, the traditional questions which dominated the earlier conferences on Alexander have now largely given way to thematic approaches that offer new insights and open up complementary avenues of research. These conferences have attracted the leading scholars on Ancient Macedonia, who are usually scattered throughout the world, offering them the ability to engage with one another, as well as with emerging scholars, students, and the general public. From the beginning, the "Alexander conferences" (as they have affectionately come to be known) have been characterized by intense and spirited (although always collegial) discussions, often continued long after the formal program has drawn to a close. This spirit of debate is evident in the published collections of revised papers from these conferences, which have begun to revolutionize the study of Alexander the Great.[1] We offer up this volume, a collection of selected papers originally presented at the conference, in the hopes that it will provide a fresh look at the significant roles that Philip II and Alexander the Great played in the emergence of a new kind of Macedonian kingship and court culture that was spectacularly successful and transformative.

I owe many debts of gratitude. First of all, to all those who presented, chaired the sessions, or were members of the audience at the 2018 Edmonton conference; it is thanks to you that the conference was such an outstanding success. Thank you to the (then) Chair of the Department of History and Classics, David Marples, and the (then) Dean of Arts, Lesley Cormack, for your support

---

[1] Heckel and Tritle (2003); Heckel *et al.* (2007); Wheatley and Hannah (2009); Carney and Ogden (2010); Alonso Troncoso and Anson (2013); Bearzot and Landucci (2016); Walsh and Baynham (2021). Full references to these works can be found in the bibliography to the introduction.

and for your kind words of welcome to our truly international group of guests. Thank you to our office staff (Barb Baker, Shufen Edmondstone, Lindsey Rose, and especially Lia Watkin) for your patient and cheerful administrative assistance. The tireless work behind the scenes of University of Alberta graduate students ensured that all went smoothly; special thanks to Gino Canlas, Kat Furtado, Adam Wiznura, and especially Beatrice Poletti (Event Manager) and Kristen Spencer-Millions (Research Assistant). Thanks are also due to my husband Joe Pownall for ferrying some of the speakers to a post-conference trip to Banff and helping me act as tour guide; the Canadian Rockies provided a stunning backdrop for reflection on the insights arising out of the papers. Funding for the conference was generously provided by the Department of History and Classics, the Faculty of Arts, and the Kule Institute for Advanced Study at the University of Alberta, the Social Sciences and Humanities Research Council of Canada, the Scott R. Jacobs Fund (special thanks to Lindsay Adams), the *Ancient History Bulletin* (special thanks to Tim Howe), and the Department of Classics and Religion, University of Calgary (special thanks to John Vanderspoel). And last but not least, I thank my wonderful co-editors, Sulochana Asirvatham and Sabine Müller, without whom this volume would not have been possible.

Proper names are generally given in their Latin forms, although there are some exceptions in the cases of unfamiliar names in accordance with the wishes of individual authors.

Frances Pownall
Edmonton, Alberta
June 2021

Contents

Frances Pownall
Introduction —— 1

I The Transformation of Royal Authority: Personal Relationships at the Macedonian Court

Edward M. Anson
Philip and Alexander and the Nature of Their Personal Kingship —— 17

Waldemar Heckel
Storm Clouds over Three Hellenistic Courts: Observations on the Life and Death of Ptolemy Ceraunus —— 33

II The Courts of Philip and Alexander in the Eyes of Contemporary Greeks

Jeremy Trevett
Diplomatic Activity at the Court of Philip II —— 57

Craig Cooper
Kairos, Mistrust of Tyranny and the Rhetoric of Court in Demosthenes' *Olynthiacs* —— 79

Thomas C. Rose
The Exile of Demochares of Leuconoe Revisited —— 97

Sabine Müller
Philip II, Alexander III, and Members of Their Court in Greek Comedy —— 125

III The Influence of Persia and the Ancient Near East on Alexander's Court

Elizabeth Baynham
Bosworth on Alexander and the Iranians Revisited: Alexander's Marriages to Persian Brides at Susa: A Study of Arrian, *Anabasis* 7.4.4–8 —— 149

Philip Bosman
Two Conceptions of Court at Persepolis —— 169

Rolf Strootman
***Pothos* or Propaganda? Alexander's Longing to Reach the Ocean and Argead Imperial Ideology —— 189**

IV Raising a Prince in the Macedonian Court: Stories of Alexander's Birth and Education

Daniel Ogden
The Serpent Sire of Alexander the Great: A Palinode —— 211

Christian Thrue Djurslev
Educating Alexander: High Culture in the Argead Court through Ancient Texts —— 233

V Alexander's Court in Retrospective

Rebecca Frank
"The Best Man Among the Dead:" Alexander son of Ammon in an Alexandrian Inscription —— 255

Steven E. Hijmans
Alexander or not? The Problem of Alexander-like Portraits in Roman Art —— 275

Index —— 299

Frances Pownall
Introduction

The aim of this volume is to explore the pioneering effect of the reigns of Philip II and Alexander the Great, who transformed Macedonia into the most important power in the Mediterranean world, "the ancient equivalent of a superpower," in the words of Paul Millett.[1] It is our hope that it will generate new avenues through which to assess the continuing impact of Philip and Alexander on court culture through the ages.

Recent years have witnessed an outburst of excellent interdisciplinary comparative research on court culture in the ancient and medieval worlds,[2] in the wake of the seminal study of Norbert Elias.[3] There has also been a new and welcome focus upon the Argead monarchy that set the stage for the transformative reigns of Philip and Alexander.[4] It is now widely recognized that Philip and Alexander adopted carefully selected-elements of their self-fashioning and court ceremonial from previous empires in the Ancient Near East, and that the Achaemenid Persian empire was highly influential upon their predecessors in the Argead monarchy as early as the reign of Alexander I.[5] Nevertheless, the court culture of Philip and Alexander themselves has received comparatively little attention as a system,[6] and it is generally assumed that the advent of the Macedonian royal court as the locus of politics and culture occurred only in the post-Alexander landscape of the Hellenistic world, when his empire was fractured into independent kingdoms ruled by his commanders (the so-called Successors).[7]

Philip II successfully consolidated his kingdom, implemented major institutional, social, and military reforms, and gained hegemony over the Greek *poleis*, laying the foundation for his son, Alexander III, to conquer most of the known world. Of course, the spectacular military achievements of Philip and Alexander

---

[1] Millett (2010) 488.
[2] See e.g. Hekster and Fowler (2005); Spawforth (2007a); Duindam *et al.* (2011); Llewellyn-Jones (2013); Mitchell and Melville (2013).
[3] Elias (1983). For the ancient court, see Winterling (1999).
[4] Carney (2015); Müller (2016); Müller *et al.* (2017); Heckel *et al.* (2020).
[5] E.g., Bosworth (1980); Brosius (2003); Spawforth (2007b); Briant (2010) 101–138; Olbrycht (2010); Müller (2014) esp. 224–242; Wiesehöfer (2017); Heinrichs (2020).
[6] Notable exceptions are Spawforth (2007b) and Weber (2009); some of the essays in D'Agostini *et al.* (2020) examine the interpersonal dynamics of the courts of Philip and Alexander.
[7] On Hellenistic courts, see esp. Herman (1997); Ma (2011); Strootman (2014); Erskine *et al.* (2017); D'Agostini *et al.* (2020).

have attracted attention since antiquity, naturally enough, as military success was the primary criterion for legitimation in Ancient Macedonia,[8] as is reflected in the ideology of the Argead court and is remarked upon (with a certain amount of chagrin) by the contemporary Greek sources. It is only relatively recently, however, that scholarly attention has begun to focus upon the institutional, social, ideological, and iconographical aspects of the reigns of Philip and Alexander, and their efforts to be viewed as legitimate monarchs by their Greek and (eventually) Asian and (North) African subjects. The time has come for a fuller examination of the role of Philip and Alexander in the development of a court culture and royal ideology that were responsible for the efflorescence of fully-fledged monarchies in the Successor kingdoms. The Hellenistic courts in turn served as inspirations and models for Roman imperial culture, and through Roman transmission ultimately exerted a profound influence upon later periods of history.

In a study of the social dynamics of Alexander's court, Gregor Weber describes it as an "extended house" (*oikos*), in which he identifies two separate (although somewhat permeable) categories: an "inner court," comprising those with "real or titular proximity to the ruler," and an "outer court," comprising guests, foreign ambassadors, and civil servants (i.e., those not normally attached to the court).[9] The analogy of the *oikos* has been further developed in a volume examining affective relations at the courts of Alexander and the Hellenistic Successors, where a distinction is made between the ways in which intra-familial ("The Restricted *Oikos*") and extra-familial ("The Extended *Oikos*") networks influenced the exercise of power.[10] However one precisely categorizes the social structure of the courts of Alexander and the Hellenistic Successors, it is clear that the king served as the nucleus of the Macedonian court, situated at the center of a complicated web of relationships radiating outward from his royal authority.

What has not been sufficiently examined, however, is the extent to which Philip and Alexander transformed what had once been a relatively simple court dynamic into one that was much more elaborate, international, and multi-dimensional. Prior to the reign of Philip II, the king essentially was the state, serving as the chief commander of the army and enacting foreign policy on his own behalf. Because his power was largely personal, there was no real apparatus of court bureaucracy, except for the (often fraught) relationship be-

---

8 Cf. Müller (2020).
9 Weber (2009) 85. Cf. Winterling (1999) and Butz *et al.* (2004) on the general conception.
10 D'Agostini *et al.* (2020) esp. 1–12.

tween the king and the landed Macedonian elite (the *hetairoi* or "Companions"), who served as the king's counsellors and comrades-in-arms.[11] As part of his ambitious program of reformation, Philip made far-reaching changes to the dynamics and structure of the Argead court, singlehandedly transforming it into a complex entity where decisions were made that governed not only Macedonia, but ultimately Illyria, Paeonia, Epirus, Thrace, and Greece as well. He consolidated the central authority of the Argead dynasty, in particular incorporating into the ranks of the Companions the Macedonian elite from all regions of the kingdom (including the formerly independent cantons of Upper Macedonia), thus preventing them from allying with the Balkan groups who were perennially poised for incursion across Macedonia's borders as well as neutralizing the threat of possible assassination by rival factions (a fate that had befallen a number of his predecessors). Advancement at court could only be achieved by winning the king's favor, and Philip encouraged the Companions to vie for social position and prestige through intense competition, the hunt and royal symposia providing occasions where status could be displayed and contested.[12] Another method of finding the elite more closely to himself was Philip's reorganization of the institution of the *basilikoi paides* (often misleadingly translated as Royal Pages), according to which sons of the landed aristocracy were sent to be educated at court and to act as personal attendants of the king; in effect, they served as guarantors of their families' continued loyalty.[13]

Philip's rapid expansion of Macedonian territory beyond its traditional boundaries set in motion a more intensive internationalization of the Argead court. Although some previous Argead rulers had been polygamous (e.g., Amyntas III), Philip married an extraordinary seven times, the first six of which were dynastic marriages to foreign women intended to consolidate his military conquests, according to the Peripatetic biographer Satyrus (*FHG* 3.161 fr. 5 = F 25 Schorn). Similarly, although his predecessors patronized Greek intellectuals and cultural luminaries as a component of their royal self-legitimation,[14] Philip widened the range of the Greek literati that he invited to his court beyond the traditional poets, musicians and artists to include intellectual heavyweights as part of a systematic attempt to ground his rule in current intellectual discourse

---

[11] On Macedonian kingship prior to Philip, see King (2010) 375–379 and Anson (2020) 15–44, both with earlier bibliography.
[12] On the institutional role of the hunt at Philip's court, see Carney (2002); on that of symposia, see Pownall (2020c).
[13] On the *basilikoi paides*, see Pownall (2020a).
[14] See Carney (2003) and Pownall (2017).

and showcase his regime as a center of culture and learning.[15] One of Philip's court intellectuals was the philosopher Aristotle (whose family already had a longstanding connection with the Argead court), whom he commissioned to educate his son and heir Alexander, along with other Macedonian elite youths. Philip was the first of the Argead kings whose military strength meant that he had to be taken seriously by the Greek *poleis*, resulting in the arrival at court of a wide array of Greek diplomats, ambassadors, literary and cultural figures, mercenaries, and fortune-seekers. Philip appointed many of these newly-arrived Greeks and other non-Macedonians to the ranks of the *hetairoi* and the upper echelons of his court administration,[16] which allowed him further to dilute the influence of the Macedonian landed aristocracy. Under Philip, the Argead court was truly transformed into "a venue for international display of royal style" (as Elizabeth Carney has put it).[17]

The creation of a truly international Macedonian court continued and intensified under Alexander. Naturally, as Alexander spent most of his reign on active campaign, his court was a travelling one, associated with his person rather than with any particular location, the king's royal tent (a borrowing from the Achaemenid Persians) serving as the center of the empire on ceremonial occasions.[18] Despite its itinerant and temporary nature, literally thousands of Greeks flocked to Alexander's court in search of fame and fortune.[19] In order to legitimize his rule to the elites of his new subjects in his multi-ethnic empire, Alexander incorporated carefully-selected Achaemenid royal garments, insignia, and court ceremonial,[20] and adopted certain elements of traditional Babylonian and Egyptian kingship.[21] Although Alexander had not yet fully implemented his vision of a new style of Macedonian monarchy integrating the various ethnic groups of his vast and freshly-conquered empire at the time of his premature death in 323 BC, the Hellenistic Successors adopted the model of an intellectually vibrant and cosmopolitan court centered around the personal authority of the king that Philip and Alexander bequeathed to them, and transmitted it through the Romans to later periods of history.

---

15 Pownall (2020b).
16 On Philip's introduction of non-Macedonians into his inner circle, see Paschidis (2006) 252–253; Strootman (2020).
17 Carney (2007) 131.
18 Alonso Troncoso and Álvarez Rico (2017); cf. Spawforth (2007b).
19 Tritle (2009).
20 Collins (2012); cf. Bowden (2021).
21 Babylonian kingship: Collins (2013); Egyptian kingship: Pfeiffer (2014); cf. Collins (2009).

The volume opens with an examination of the ways in which Philip and Alexander transformed royal authority. Edward M. Anson ("Philip and Alexander and the Nature of Their Personal Kingship") offers an overview of the changes that they made to the traditional Macedonian notion of kingship. Philip extended the bond that the king traditionally held with his *hetairoi* to his heavy infantry, using land grants to transfer their loyalty to him personally, thereby diminishing the regional authority of the landed aristocracy. Through the judicious use of royal patronage, Philip enhanced his royal authority by increasing the complexity of his chancellery, appointing loyal non-Macedonians such as Eumenes to key positions at court, and creating new institutions such as the *basilikoi paides* and the *somatophylakes* (royal bodyguards) to safeguard the king's preeminent status vis-à-vis the Macedonian elite. Alexander continued Philip's efforts to offset the influence of the old-guard *hetairoi*, gradually replacing his father's commanders with those of his own generation and outlook. Eventually, as he progressed deeper into the heartland of Asia, Alexander began to incorporate Iranian elites as well, with a view to creating a new Achaemenid-style empire. Nevertheless, despite the far-reaching innovations of Philip and Alexander, the fundamentally personal nature of Macedonian kingship remained largely unchanged.

In the second paper in the opening section, Waldemar Heckel ("Storm Clouds over Three Hellenistic Courts: Observations on the Life and Death of Ptolemy Ceraunus") examines how the ongoing importance of personal power in the changes that Philip and Alexander made to the nature of traditional royal authority played a decisive role in the final years of the Diadochi. Through a re-assessment of the polarizing figure of Ptolemy Ceraunus (the aptly-named "Thunderbolt"), he illustrates how the serial polygamy practiced by (especially) Philip (but also Alexander, as illustrated in the marriages at Susa) as a deliberate part of dynastic politics resulted in amphimetric strife and bloody conflicts over succession in the courts of the Hellenistic kingdoms. Born to Ptolemy I when he was still nominally satrap of Egypt ruling on behalf of Alexander's heirs, Ceraunus was the offspring of a dynastic marriage to Eurydice (one of Antipater's daughters). After Eurydice was supplanted as Ptolemy's favorite wife by her cousin Berenice and Ptolemy's position as *basileus* in Egypt was secure, Ptolemy I passed over Ceraunus as his heir and successor in favor of his younger half-brother Ptolemy II Philadelphus. It is likely at this point that Ceraunus left Alexandria for the courts of the rival successors, where similar dynastic conflicts offered tantalizing possibilities of intrigue and intervention. Heckel argues convincingly against the common supposition that Ceraunus sought refuge at the court of Lysimachus, who was the most closely tied of the Successors to Ptolemy I and (the future) Ptolemy II; this assumption probably arises from a confusion in the sources between Ptolemy Ceraunus and his homonym, the son of Lysimachus and Arsinoë (the daughter of Ptolemy I and Berenice). Instead, it is more likely that Ceraunus went directly to the court of Seleucus, and was in his entourage when the latter defeated Lysimachus at the Battle of Corupedium. Ceraunus fell out with Seleucus when he made it clear that his intention was to pursue the kingship of Macedonia rather than restore his protégé to the throne of Egypt, whereupon Ceraunus murdered his erstwhile benefactor and had himself proclaimed king in his place. As part of an attempted reconciliation with his half-brother Philadelphus, Ceraunus renounced his claim to the Ptolemaic throne and entered into a dynastic marriage with his half-sister Arsinoë. The continuing attempts of her eldest son Ptolemy to foment revolution likely precipitated Ceraunus' assassination of her two younger sons by Lysimachus (an event that has been sensationalized by hostile sources). Ceraunus was not necessarily a bad or unpopular ruler; the short duration of his kingship should be attributed to an error in judgement (choosing military action against the Gauls over diplomacy) rather than to any putative lack of capability or virtue. Nevertheless, his relentless drive for personal power proved to be the final nail in the coffin of the re-uniting of Alexander's empire.

The second section moves to the diplomatic relations of Philip and Alexander with the Greek *poleis* and, conversely, how they and their courts were portrayed by their (often hostile) Greek contemporaries. As Jeremy Trevett ("Diplomatic Activity at the Court of Philip II") observes, it is under Philip II that the Macedonian court became the *locus* of diplomatic interactions with the Greeks. The opposing speeches of Demosthenes (19) and Aeschines (2) reflecting the events that led to the Peace of Philocrates in 346 BC offer a particularly detailed and informative window into the conduct of diplomatic visits at the Macedonian court, written as they are by participants and published within three years of the negotiations that they describe. Nevertheless, they must be treated with caution for their aim as law-court speeches was to be persuasive rather than truthful and each speaker was concerned to defend his own actions in respect to a peace that quickly fell into disfavor in Athens. Although we must exercise caution in making generalizations from these speeches about diplomacy at the Macedonian court, they do provide useful information about how Philip wished to present himself in the particular context of his broader political aims at that moment (when he was in a position of strength). The speeches make it clear that diplomacy was the personal responsibility of the king, and Philip's *hetairoi* and senior advisers were markedly subordinate to him in his negotiations with the Greek ambassadors. Furthermore, Philip attempted to forge personal ties with the visiting diplomats through lavish hospitality at court symposia and royal largesse (possibly deliberately intended to embroil the hapless ambassadors in political hot water with the Athenian democracy upon their return), designed to bind a few influential Athenian citizens to him through the granting of favors, in much the same way he cemented the bond between himself and the Macedonian elite. Nevertheless, it was not necessarily a one-way street, for there were benefits to the Athenians and other Greek *poleis* to having "friends" at the Macedonian court, a practice that continued in the Hellenistic courts of the Successors. As Trevett concludes, "the Macedonian court was not just the place where diplomacy happened but also the mechanism by which it was conducted."

Craig Cooper ("*Kairos*, Mistrust of Tyranny and the Rhetoric of Court in Demosthenes' *Olynthiacs*) examines how Demosthenes exploits descriptions of the Macedonian court in his *Olynthiacs* and connects them to his broader rhetorical strategy on *kairos* ("opportunity"). Demosthenes uses the concept of *kairos* as a sustained metaphor in his *First Olynthiac*, where he attempts to make the case that the distrust of tyrants by the Olynthians in particular and constitutional forms of government in general offers a *kairos* for the Athenians against Philip. Demosthenes builds on this theme in the *Second Olynthiac*, in which he illustrates how the weaknesses of Philip's tyranny can be found in his depraved court, where Philip's perfidy has engendered distrust even among his own courtiers, endowing the Athenian with a golden opportunity to stop prevaricating and take decisive action against him. The Greeks' willingness to write Philip off as a stereotypical tyrant (with all the connotations of enervation and dissipation that term conveyed), however, had the unfortunate result of blinding them to Philip's real source of power, his creation of a network of personal alliances at the Macedonian court that solidified his royal authority and enabled him to defeat the Greek *poleis* both on the diplomatic and (eventually) the military fronts.

Thomas C. Rose ("The Exile of Demochares of Leuconoe Revisited") explores how the figure of Demochares, the nephew of Demosthenes, illustrates how even the most strident opponent of Macedonian interference in Athenian political affairs was forced to reconcile himself to the necessity of maintaining cordial diplomatic relations with the Macedonian court. In his youth, Demochares was a passionate defender of the Athenian democracy and as fiery a critic of the Macedonians as his uncle had been. Despite his polemical attacks on the other Successors, he showed himself willing to co-operate with Demetrius Poliorcetes, who ostentatiously restored the democracy when he gained control of Athens in 307 BC and expelled Demetrius of Phalerum, who was ruling the city on behalf of Cassander. After his return from exile, Demochares became an active participant in embassies to the royal courts of the Hellenistic Successors. Therefore, in order to achieve a full understanding of Demochares' resignation to the new political reality, it is crucial to determine the date and reason for his exile. Plutarch dates it to 303 BC and implies that it was due to agitation against Poliorcetes. As

Rose demonstrates, however, Plutarch's chronology is not trustworthy, and Demochares' exile fits better into the political context of a nascent anti-Antigonid alliance in central Greece and the open revolt of the Boeotians against Poliorcetes in 293 BC. Poliorcetes' swift military response ensured that the Greek coalition organized against him never came to fruition, and Demochares was collateral damage for his role in attempting to forge an alliance with the Boeotians when the Athenians hastily backpedaled in an attempt to placate Poliorcetes. If Rose's hypothesis is correct that Demochares was exiled for advocating an anti-Macedonian alliance with the Boeotians, his career is ironically parallel to that of his famous uncle. Their fates, however, could not be more different: Demosthenes was martyred for his anti-Macedonian activities, whereas Demochares not only organized embassies to the courts of the Successors but was willing to accept royal gifts. By time of the final years of the Diadochi, seeking financial help from the courts of the Successors had become not only acceptable, but was even considered praiseworthy behavior by the Athenian democracy.

In the final paper in this section, Sabine Müller ("Philip II, Alexander III, and Members of Their Court in Greek Comedy") turns to the portrayal of the court of Philip and Alexander in contemporary Greek comedy, which in turn reflects how they were widely perceived by a heterogeneous Greek audience. Macedonians do not appear on the Greek stage until the Peloponnesian War, when Perdiccas II was forced to walk an uneasy tightrope of calculated diplomacy between the competing interests of the Athenian and the Spartan alliances to preserve the integrity of his kingdom. The representation of Perdiccas in comedy as uncultured and duplicitous confirms that the negative image preserved by Thucydides reflects the view of the wider Greek public. The stereotypical depiction of the Macedonians as uncouth and dishonest brutes persisted, even after Philip began to dominate the political and military scene in Greece, although a new strand emerged mocking his bellicosity and the widely-alleged corruption, decadence, and depravity of his court. Despite the efforts of the comic poets and the wider Greek public to dismiss Philip and the Macedonian court as their cultural and moral inferiors, the fact remained that the Greeks seriously underestimated Philip's military strength and political acumen. In the end, they lost their political autonomy and Philip had the last laugh.

The papers in the third section examine the influence of Achaemenid Persia and the Ancient Near East on the court of Alexander in particular. In a tribute to the late Brian Bosworth, who was one of the first to recognize significant Achaemenid influence on Alexander's court policy,[22] Elizabeth Baynham ("Bosworth

---

22 Bosworth (1980).

on Alexander and the Iranians Revisited: Alexander's Marriages to Persian Brides at Susa: A Study of Arrian, *Anabasis* 7.4.4 – 8) further develops Bosworth's own rethinking on the mass marriages at Susa. As she rightly notes, the issue of marriage was a critical one for Alexander's court (as for any court society), as it offered not only the opportunity to make powerful alliances, but also underpinned the future of his court through the provision of heirs. In this unprecedented set of mass marriages, Alexander, like Darius I, married more than one wife precisely in order to consolidate Achaemenid royal blood lines and legitimize himself (and his future children) as rightful Achaemenid rulers. The marriages also served as an instrument of policy, allowing Alexander to reward the loyalty of certain prominent Persians, to indicate favor to certain members of his inner circle, and (possibly) to create a future court composed of a blended aristocracy to strengthen his own sovereignty. But with Alexander's sudden and premature death, his vision of an amalgamated court was left to be fulfilled by Seleucus, which explains his prominence in Arrian's narrative of the Susa marriages, despite the fact that he was still a relatively junior officer at the time.

Philip Bosman ("Two Conceptions of Court at Persepolis") argues that the conflicting accounts in the ancient sources on the motives for the looting and burning of the royal Achaemenid palaces at Persepolis reflect at their heart a clash between the traditional Macedonian conception of court and the Achaemenid Persian one. The Macedonian elite found it increasingly difficult to accept the elaborate hierarchical structure of the Achaemenid court and the deliberate inaccessibility of the king, both of which (in their view) threatened their own carefully-negotiated basis of power. These conflicting ideologies came to a head during the unexpectedly long sojourn of Alexander and his army at Persepolis, where the royal palaces embodied the Achaemenid court. Although Alexander conceded to the wishes of his elite on this occasion by condoning the burning of the palaces at Persepolis, his concession was short-lived, and he soon afterwards began openly to incorporate Achaemenid aspects of royal rule into his court despite the ongoing opposition of the Macedonian elite.

In the final paper in this section, Rolf Strootman (*Pothos* or Propaganda? Alexander's Longing to Reach the Ocean and Argead Imperial Ideology") reconsiders the famous notion of Alexander's *pothos* (yearning to reach the limit of the known world). As he argues, although Alexander did not use the term himself (it comes from later Hellenistic imperial cosmography), his *pothos* was historical rather than a later literary construct and can be traced to contemporary Argead universalistic imperial ideology. This ideology was not new to Alexander, however, but was a common tool employed to create cohesion in the multi-ethnic and culturally-diverse empires of the Ancient Near East, and likely represents a direct borrowing from the Achaemenid Persians by the Argeads, the fruit of a longstanding familiarity with their concepts of monarchy and empire. The ideology of world conquest and universal empire in turn was transmitted to the Seleucids and Ptolemies, and ultimately through them to the Romans, who preferred to credit it to the idealized figure of Alexander rather than to the Achaemenid Persians or the Hellenistic kingdoms which they had conquered.

The fourth section of the volume focuses upon the birth legends and the stories that aggregated around Alexander's education at the Argead court. Daniel Ogden ("The Serpent Sire of Alexander the Great: A Palinode") catalogues the principal references in the ancient sources to Alexander's serpent sire. He revises his previous view that the evidence represents a unitary tradition that Alexander's divine sire was identified with Zeus-Ammon in serpent form, arguing instead that there are in fact two distinct traditions, Zeus-Ammon and a divine serpent, which have occasionally been contaminated. Without the necessity of reconciling the serpent sire with the Zeus-Ammon tradition, Zeus Meilichios (with his associations with the Macedonian court) is no longer a suitable candidate for the original identity of the snake sire, whose affinities, if they were not intended to be deliberately mysterious, are emphatically Asclepian. Further refinement of the complex tradition on Alexander's siring snake is crucial in light of Ptolemy's efforts to legitimize his own dynastic claim to Egypt by associating Alexander with Zeus-Ammon,[23] a tradition that continued to hold ideological significance in Alexandria even after the Ptolemaic empire had been defeated by the Romans (as Rebecca Frank demonstrates in her contribution in the next section).

In the second paper in this section, Christian Djurslev ("Educating Alexander: High Culture in the Argead Court through Ancient Texts") focuses upon the literary traditions of Alexander's education at the Argead court. Although it is often thought that Plutarch's *Alexander* offers the only useful account of Alexander's upbringing, Djurslev identifies a range of other literary sources (in particular the oft-dismissed *Alexander Romance*) that are consistent with Plutarch's biography and complement it; it is clear that all draw from a much larger storehouse of anecdotal material that was circulating in antiquity, much of which originated in the first generation of Alexander historiographers. Similarly, there were many alternatives to Aristotle as Alexander's teacher in the literary tradition, and these stories form part of a rich tradition that also has an early genesis, originating in the often cutthroat competition between the intelligentsia at Philip's court to win the king's favor. Djurslev concludes with case studies of three topics (training in physical education, warfare, and medicine) that corrob-

---

[23] Ogden (2009) esp. 161–162 and Pownall (2021).

orate the general tendencies found in the literary traditions on Alexander's upbringing at court. Despite the early genesis of many of these stories, it is necessary to approach them with caution, for later writers have embroidered them and manufactured content to fit their own contemporary *milieux*.

The theme of the manipulation of the ideologies of the courts of Philip and Alexander in later periods is further developed in the final section of the volume. Rebecca Frank ("'The Best Man Among the Dead:' Alexander son of Ammon in an Alexandrian Inscription") examines how the competing narratives of Alexander's filiation as the son of a god and the son of Philip II, which engendered considerable opposition at his own court, were exploited in the context of Alexandria in the early Roman imperial period. A funerary tablet commemorating the premature death of a young man in the first or second century AD refers to Alexander as the son of Ammon whom the god sired while in the form of a snake. As Frank argues, the reference to Alexander is the narrative linchpin of the epitaph, and reflects his enduring importance as an explicitly *Egyptian* ruler, the divine founder of Alexandria, and the king of the Macedonians even in the post-Ptolemaic landscape of Roman Egypt. This epigram offers valuable insight into the complexity and multi-faceted nature of the figure of Alexander as well as the ongoing popularization and romanticization of Alexander and his rule in the Roman imperial period.

The exploitation of the image and ideology of Alexander by the Romans is the topic of the final paper in the volume. Alexander carefully controlled his public image, including the way he was depicted in the original Alexander portraits, commissioned at his court and almost certainly subject to his direct approval. As Andrew Steward has shown,[24] the image of Alexander eventually devolved into a series of clichés that represented not so much his actual likeness as the ways in which the idea of Alexander was remembered and manipulated by subsequent Hellenistic rulers. It is in this context that Steven Hijmans ("Alexander or not? The Problem of Alexander-like Portraits in Roman Art") examines how the Romans in turn appropriated many of the stereotypical features of the image of Alexander, which makes it very difficult to determine whether a portrait was actually of Alexander himself, or was merely borrowing from Alexander iconography in service to a different agenda. This study of the enduring significance of the image of Alexander to the Roman imperial court and the fluidity through which its stereotypical features could be adapted to other political, religious, and cultural contexts is a fitting conclusion to our volume that

---

24 Stewart (1993).

highlights the crucial importance of the courts of Philip and Alexander to later periods.

The overall goal of the original conference was to open up new avenues of research into the courts of Philip and Alexander, reshaping how we view their court culture and leading to a new recognition of their lasting influence on later court society. Many of the features that are typically associated with the Hellenistic courts—the personal authority of the ruler, the importance of royal hospitality and largesse, the use of courtiers to facilitate diplomacy, dynastic marriage as an instrument of legitimation, the creation of a royal ideology justifying world conquest, the invocation of divine support—can already be seen at the courts of Philip and Alexander. The papers in this volume treat the Macedonian court not only as a historical reality, but also as an object of fascination to the contemporary Greeks that will eventually become a *topos* in later reflections on the lives and careers of Philip and Alexander.

Bibliography

Alonso Troncoso and Anson (2013): Victor Alonso Troncoso and Edward M. Anson (eds.), *After Alexander: The Time of the Diadochi (323–281 BC)*, Oxford and Oakville, CT.

Alonso Troncoso and Álvarez Rico (2017): Víctor Alonso Troncoso & Mauricio Álvarez Rico, "Alexander's Tent and Camp Life", in: Müller *et al.* (2017), 113–124.

Anson (2020): Edward M. Anson, *Philip II, the Father of Alexander the Great: Themes and Issues*, London.

Bearzot and Landucci (2016): Cinzia Bearzot and Franca Landucci (eds.), *Alexander's Legacy*, Rome.

Bosworth (1980): A.B. Bosworth, "Alexander and the Iranians", in: *Journal of Hellenic Studies* 100, 1–21.

Bowden (2021): Hugh Bowden, "The man who would be king: Alexander between Gaugamela and Persepolis", in: Walsh and Baynham (2021), 129–149.

Briant (2010): Pierre Briant, *Alexander the Great and his Empire*, trans. A. Kuhrt, Princeton and Oxford.

Brosius (2003): Maria Brosius, "Alexander and the Persians", in: Joseph Roisman (ed.), *Brill's Companion to Alexander the Great*, Leiden and Boston, 169–193.

Butz *et al.* (2004): Reinhard Butz, Jan Hirschbiegel, and Dietmar Willoweit (eds.), *Hof und Theorie. Annäherungen an ein historisches Phänomen.* Cologne.

Carney (2002): Elizabeth Carney, "Hunting and the Macedonian Elite: Sharing the Rivalry of the Chase (Arrian 4.13.1)"; in: Daniel Ogden (ed.), *The Hellenistic World: New Perspectives*, London and Swansea, 59–80; reprinted in Carney (2015), 265–282.

Carney (2003): Elizabeth D. Carney, "Elite education and High culture in Macedonia", in: Heckel and Tritle (2003), 47–63; reprinted in Carney (2015), 191–205.

Carney (2007): Elizabeth Carney, "Symposia and the Macedonian Elite: The Unmixed Life", in: *Syllecta Classica* 18: 129–180; reprinted in Carney (2015), 225–264.

Carney (2015): Elizabeth Carney, *King and Court in Ancient Macedonia*. Swansea.
Carney and Ogden (2010): Elizabeth Carney and Daniel Ogden (eds.), *Philip II and Alexander the Great: Father and Son, Lives and Afterlives*, Oxford and New York.
Collins (2009): Andrew W. Collins, "The Divinity of Alexander in Egypt", in Wheatley and Hannah (2009), 179–206.
Collins (2012): Andrew W. Collins, "The Royal Costume and Insignia of Alexander the Great", *American Journal of Philology* 133, 371–402.
Collins (2013): Andrew W. Collins, "Alexander the Great and the Kingship of Babylon", in: *The Ancient History Bulletin* 27, 130–148.
D'Agostini *et al.* (2020): Monica D'Agostini, Edward M. Anson, and Frances Pownall (eds.), *Affective Relations and Personal Bonds in Hellenistic Antiquity: Studies in Honor of Elizabeth D. Carney*, Oxford and Philadelphia.
Duindam *et al.* (2011): Jeroen Duindam, Tülay Artan, and Metin Kunt (eds.), *Royal Courts in Dynastic States and Empires: A Global Perspective*, Leiden and Boston.
Elias (1983): Norbert Elias, *The Court Society*, trans. Edmund Jephcott, Oxford (originally published as *Die höfische Gesellschaft* in 1969).
Erskine *et al.* (2017): Andrew Erskine, Lloyd Llewellyn-Jones, and Shane Wallace (eds.), *The Hellenistic Court: Monarchic Power and Elite Society from Alexander to Cleopatra*, Swansea.
Heckel and Tritle (2003): Waldemar Heckel and Lawrence A. Tritle (eds.), *Crossroads of History: The Age of Alexander*, Claremont, CA.
Heckel *et al.* (2007): Waldemar Heckel, Lawrence A. Tritle, and Pat Wheatley (eds.), *Alexander's Empire: Formulation to Decay*, Claremont, CA.
Heckel and Tritle (2009): Waldemar Heckel and Lawrence A. Tritle (eds), *Alexander the Great: A New History*, Malden, MA.
Heckel *et al.* (2020): Waldemar Heckel, Johannes Heinrichs, Sabine Müller and Frances Pownall (eds.), *Lexicon of Argead Makedonia (LexAM)*, Berlin.
Heinrichs (2020): Johannes Heinrichs, "Achaimenids", in: Heckel *et al.* (2020), 32–37.
Hekster and Fowler (2005): Olivier Hekster and Richard Fowler (eds.), *Imaginary Kings: Royal Images in the Ancient Near East, Greece and Rome*, Stuttgart.
Herman (1997): Gabriel Herman, "The Court Society of the Hellenistic Age", in: Paul Cartledge, Peter Garnsey, and Erich Gruen (eds.), *Hellenistic Constructs*, Berkeley, 119–211.
King (2010): Carol J. King, "Macedonian Kingship and Other Political Institutions", in: Roisman and Worthington (2010), 371–391.
Llewellyn-Jones (2013): Lloyd Llewellyn-Jones, *King and Court in Ancient Persia*, Edinburgh.
Ma (2011): John Ma, "Court, King, and Power in Antigonid Macedonia", in: Robin J. Lane Fox (ed.), *Brill's Companion to Ancient Macedonia*, Leiden, 521–543.
Millett (2010): Paul Millett, "The Political Economy of Macedonia", in: Roisman and Worthington (2010), 472–504.
Mitchell and Melville (2013): Lynette Mitchell and Charles Melville (eds.), *Every Inch a King: Comparative Studies on Kings and Kingship in the Ancient and Medieval Worlds*, Boston.
Müller (2014): Sabine Müller, *Alexander, Makedonien und Persien*. Berlin.
Müller (2016): Sabine Müller, *Die Argeaden: Geschichte Makedoniens bis zum Zeitalter Alexanders des Großen*. Paderborn.
Müller (2020): Sabine Müller, "Legitimization", in: Heckel *et al.* (2020), 311–313.

Müller et al. (2017): Sabine Müller, Tim Howe, Hugh Bowden, and Robert Rollinger (eds.), *The History of the Argeads: New Perspectives*, Wiesbaden.

Ogden (2009): Daniel Ogden, "Alexander's snake sire", in: Wheatley and Hannah (2009), 136–178.

Olbrycht (2010): M.J. Olbrycht, "Macedonia and Persia", in: Roisman and Worthington (2010), 342–369.

Paschidis (2006): Paschalis Paschidis, "The Interpenetration of Civic Elites and Court Elite in Macedonia", in: Anne-Marie Guimier-Sorbets, Miltiades B. Hatzopoulos, and Yvette Morizot (eds.), *Rois, cités, nécropoles. Institutions, rites et monuments en Macédoine*, Athens, 251–268.

Pfeiffer (2014): Stefan Pfeiffer, "Alexander der Große in Ägypten: Überlegungen zur Frage seiner pharaonischen legitimation", in: Volker Grieb, Krzysztof Nawotka, and Agnieszka Wojciechowska (eds.), *Alexander the Great and Egypt: History, Art, Tradition*. Wiesbaden, 221–240.

Pownall (2017): Frances Pownall, "The Role of Greek Literature at the Argead court", in: Müller et al. (2017), 215–229.

Pownall (2020a): Frances Pownall, "*Basilikoi paides*", in: Heckel et al. (2020), 137–139.

Pownall (2020b): Frances Pownall, "Sophists and Flatterers: Greek Intellectuals at Alexander's Court", in: D'Agostini et al. (2020), 243–265.

Pownall (2020c): Frances Pownall, "Symposion," in: Heckel et al. (2020), 481–483.

Pownall (2021): Frances Pownall, "Ptolemaic Propaganda in Alexander's Visit to Ammon", in Walsh and Baynham (2021), 33–53.

Roisman and Worthington (2010): Joseph Roisman and Ian Worthington (eds), *A Companion to Ancient Macedonia*, Malden, MA and Oxford.

Spawforth (2007a): A.J.S. Spawforth (ed.), *The Court and Court Society in Ancient Monarchies*, Cambridge.

Spawforth (2007b): T. Spawforth, "The Court of Alexander the Great between Europe and Asia", in: Spawforth (2007a), 82–120.

Stewart (1993): Andrew Stewart, *Faces of Power: Alexander's Image and Hellenistic Politics*, Berkeley.

Strootman (2014): Rolf Strootman, *Courts and Elites in the Hellenistic Empires*, Edinburgh.

Strootman (2020): Rolf Strootman, "*Philoi*", in: Heckel et al. (2020), 423–426.

Tritle (2009): Lawrence A. Tritle, "Artists and Soldiers, Friends and Enemies", in: Heckel and Tritle (2009), 121–140.

Walsh and Baynham (2021): John Walsh and Elizabeth Baynham (eds.), *Alexander the Great and Propaganda*, London and New York.

Weber (2009): Gregor Weber, "The Court of Alexander the Great as Social System", in: Heckel and Tritle (2009), 83–98.

Wheatley and Hannah (2009): Pat Wheatley and Robert Hannah (eds.), *Alexander & His Successors: Essays From the Antipodes*, Claremont, CA.

Wiesehöfer (2017): Josef Wiesehöfer, "The Persian Impact upon Macedonia: Three Case Studies", in: Müller et al. (2017), 57–64.

Winterling (1999): Aloys Winterling, *Aula Caesaris. Studien zur Institutionalisierung des römischen Kaiserhofes in der Zeit von Augustus bis Commodus (31 v. Chr.–192 n. Chr.)*. Munich.

The Transformation of Royal Authority: Personal Relationships at the Macedonian Court

Edward M. Anson
Philip and Alexander and the Nature of Their Personal Kingship

Philip II transformed the power of the office of King in Macedonia in many ways, but the fundamental aspect of royal authority remained unchanged. While there was slightly more bureaucracy than with previous holders of the office, monarchy under the reigns of both Philip II and Alexander III was still largely personal. Though the king might in theory be an absolute autocrat,[1] the reality was quite otherwise. Macedonia traditionally was a land with a powerful aristocracy who historically made up the true government of the state. Much of the kingdom was composed of large noble estates peopled by a dependent peasantry. These aristocrats were the king's *Hetairoi*, his companions. The more youthful adults of this class made up the principal arm of the Macedonian army, its cavalry. More senior and prominent representatives became the king's advisors and his generals. Regional government was mostly and practically in the hands of these *Hetairoi*. Theopompus (*BNJ* 115 F 225b) reports, probably with some exaggeration, that 800 of Philip's *Hetairoi* possessed as much land as 10000 of the richest Greeks. The ancient *hetairos* relationship between king and nobles was built on camaraderie, not on the basis of royal absolutism, and their relationship with the king often reminds historians of that described in the *Iliad*.[2]

Philip's bureaucratic innovations were indeed minimal. He likely introduced a more complex chancellery which was headed by the Cardian Greek, Eumenes. Eumenes was one of many "Greek" *Hetairoi*.[3] Royal authority in what was a personal relationship could be enhanced through appointing loyal individuals to the ranks of the *Hetairoi*, and non-Macedonians' status was entirely tied to the king. Their lands in Macedonia were given to them by the king; not due to hereditary possession. The fluidity of the *hetairos* institution was such that many were *Hetairoi* because of their power, while others had power through their selection as *Hetairoi*. As Waldemar Heckel has emphasized, actual power was indirectly negotiated often on the basis of powerful personalities and shifting coalitions.[4]

Philip II clearly strengthened his position vis-à-vis the aristocrats in Macedonia by achieving greater control over the resources of his kingdom and these re-

---

1 See Anson (1985a); (1991).
2 Anson (2013) 24–25.
3 On the establishment of the chancellery by Philip, see Anson (1996) 501–504.
4 Heckel (2003) 198.

sources gave him great advantages as a patron. The mines he had acquired in Thrace gave him 1000 talents of gold a year (Diod. 16.8.7; Dem. 18.235), he collected a tithe from the Thracians (Diod. 16.71.2), and the import/export duties in Thessaly (Dem. 6. 22; 19.89). However, the nature of the Macedonian government remained personal. Indeed, the greatest increase in royal power came from an extension of this personal bond. Philip changed the nature of the Macedonian military by creating a new infantry force. Prior to Philip the national military of Macedonia was an excellent cavalry, but only a light and ill-trained infantry. Philip redesigned the Macedonian infantrymen from javelin to pike carriers. Beginning with an enlarged infantry guard of perhaps 300 men, which eventually grew to 3000, there were many thousands more equipped as pikemen.[5] As the king regularly gave his *Hetairoi* vast tracts of land (Theopomp. *BNJ* 115 F 225b; Plut. *Alex.* 15.3–6),[6] Philip employed a diminished aspect of this tradition when he extended it to the heavy infantry. Philip did not just give land to his aristocratic companions, but he made viritane distributions to his infantrymen as well, creating a middle class where only peasants and dependent pastoralists had existed previously.[7] With land he rewarded his supporters and built his new army. But, this bond went well beyond the gratitude and self-interest that came from lavish patronage. Philip through extensive grants of land to Macedonian commoners had created a large manpower pool for recruiting heavy infantry. After his victory on the Granicus, Alexander granted to the parents and the children of the slain "remission of land taxes, and of all other personal services and property taxes" (Arr. *Anab.* 1.16.5).[8] As Brian Bosworth observed, these taxes were on property granted by the king, the personal services may have been military, and the property taxes likely on capital assets.[9] Additionally, Philip early in his reign extended the traditional *hetairos* relationship to infantry soldiers, at first to his infantry "bodyguard," but later to his entire heavy infantry, thus strengthening the personal bond with these troops. The identity of the king actually extending the relationship to the infantry is disputed,[10] since there are few direct references to the *Pezhetairoi* in the surviving sources, and the majority of these are from scholiasts and lexicographers.[11] In the *Second Olynthiac* (2.16–17) Demosthenes differentiates between the Macedoni-

---

[5] Anson (1985b) 246–248; (2010) 51–68; (2013) 46–51.
[6] Stagakis (1962).
[7] Anson (2008) 17–30; (2009) 88–98; (2013) 50–51.
[8] As noted by Bosworth (1980) 126, this is basically repeated in his speech at Opis.
[9] As argued effectively by Bosworth (1980) 126.
[10] Anson (2009) 88–98.
[11] These are collected by Erskine (1989) 385–388.

ans, Philip's mercenaries, and the *Pezhetairoi*.¹² The scholiast commenting on this passage and quoting Theopompus (*BNJ* 115 F 348) makes it clear that perhaps as late as 340 B. C. this term only referred to Philip II's royal guards: "Theopompus says that picked men from all the Macedonians, the largest and the strongest, served as the King's guards, and they were called the *Pezhetairoi*." Demosthenes' and Theopompus' description of these foot-companions as an elite guard is supported by all but one of the later commentators. A fragment from Anaximenes' history of Philip (*BNJ* 72 F 4 = Harpocration, *Suda* s.v. *Pezhetairoi*) has most often been interpreted as supporting the broadening of the relationship between that king and his infantry to include all of his heavy infantry. Anaximenes had accompanied Alexander on his invasion of Asia (*Suda* s.v. *Anaximenes*). The fragment is as follows:

> Anaximenes in Book 1 of his *Philippica* when talking of Alexander states: "Then, after training the most renowned men to serve as cavalry, he gave them the name of *Hetairoi*; but the majority, that is, the foot, he divided into *lochoi* and *dekades* and other commands, and designated them *Pezhetairoi*. He did this in order that each of the two groups, by sharing in the royal Companionship, should be always exceedingly loyal to him."

The association of these changes with an unspecified Alexander has produced all manner of speculation. Some commentators believe that Alexander the Great is being referenced,¹³ others have suggested Alexander I,¹⁴ Alexander II,¹⁵ and even Archelaus.¹⁶ Since the citation reportedly comes from Anaximenes' first book of his history of Philip II, that fact and the context of the Demosthenic passage would make it less likely that, if the attribution to an Alexander is correct, Alexander III, and not one of Philip's predecessors, was being referenced.¹⁷ However, there are those who argue it could be none other than the great conqueror himself, arguing that the companion status then was broadened both

---

12 Griffith (Hammond and Griffith (1979) 439 n. 1, 705) believes that Demosthenes is here confusedly referring to the *Hetairoi*, but Demosthenes gave this speech in 349. The Athenians had been at war with Philip since 357. Even though this passage is followed by clear allusions to Philip's *Hetairoi*, it is unlikely that after three years of conflict Demosthenes would be unaware of the true nature of the *Pezhetairoi*. Moreover, this speech would have been edited by its presenter prior to publication.
13 Develin (1985) 493–96; Hammond and Griffith (1979) 707–709; Errington (1990) 243–44; Hatzopoulos (1996) 269–270.
14 Brunt (1976) 151, 153.
15 Hammond (1980) 26; Greenwalt (2017) 80–89.
16 Lock (1974) 18–24.
17 This is a point strongly made by Brunt (1976) 51, who believes the reference must be to Alexander I, but that the fragment itself as evidence is "worthless."

to include the entire infantry and the entire aristocratic Macedonian cavalry, suggesting that previously the status had applied solely to an infantry guard and only to the most prominent aristocrats.[18] That the term *hetairos* during Philip's reign applied only to those prominent aristocrats of his court would appear to be unlikely given Theopompus's diatribe (F 225b = Ath. 260d–261a) against the king's companions. Theopompus clearly identifies these individuals as soldiers by profession, "man-slayers," though proclaiming that they do not live up to this standing. Demosthenes (11.10) also implies the military nature of the *Hetairoi*, stating that they "have some repute for valor." The wealth of these *Hetairoi* and their military nature suggest that these were cavalrymen. One of the ways the Page Hermolaus was degraded was that his horse was taken from him (Arr. *Anab.* 4.13.2), and Amyntas, the son of Andromenes, an infantry battalion commander and *Hetairos*, was outraged when ordered to give some of his horses to those who had lost theirs, and threatened the individual making the request (Curt. 7.1.15). These are indications of the close connection between an aristocrat and his horse. The position of *Hetairos* as both courtier and cavalryman appears to have been ancient, even though the first confirmed reference comes from the reign of Archelaus (Ael. *VH* 13.4).

With respect to the foot-companions, certainly, if one of Philip's predecessors was responsible for their creation, they existed only as a small infantry guard. Every tribal chief had his own personal armed retinue, troops who attended the monarch on a permanent basis. Langaras, the king of the Agrianians, possessed his own personal guard, "the finest and best armed troops he possessed" (Arr. *Anab.* 1.5.2). If it is to such a personal guard that Anaximenes is referring, then whatever its original size, Philip expanded the corps to 1000 men and later to 3000.[19] Demosthenes in the *Second Olynthiac* (2.16–17) differentiates the Macedonian military into a tripartite division of Macedonians, mercenaries, and the *Pezhetairoi* and the scholiast who comments on this passage and quotes Theopompus (*BNJ* 115 F 348) clearly associates the term *Pezhetairoi* with Philip II's royal guards.

The best evidence that Philip was the individual most likely to have established this relationship with the Macedonian heavy infantry in its entirety is that he was the individual who created the first effective and numerous Macedonian heavy infantry. While the exact timing of this expansion is unclear, such an expansion of the companion relationship to the heavy infantry could only occur after such a force came into existence. Therefore, this expansion could only

---

18 Develin (1985) 493, 496.
19 Anson (1985b) 248.

have occurred during the reign of Philip or that of his son Alexander with it most likely that it was the father who created the companion heavy infantry. He had years to accomplish this transformation, while Alexander only a bit more than a year. Moreover, it was Philip who freed thousands of the native Macedonians from their dependence on the aristocratic class. As the passage from Arrian (*Anab.* 7.8.2–3), ostensibly quoting Alexander concerning his father indicates, many new landholders came from the landless class of Macedonia.[20] Philip's liberation of these individuals from their landlords bound them to him as their benefactor. Given these actions by this king, the likelihood that, if he did not create the concept of foot companions, he at the very least expanded to the entire infantry the status of *Pezhetairoi*, appears certain. When Philip extended the relationship to his entire Macedonian infantry, the 3000-member guard acquired the name Hypaspists.[21]

In any case, the Anaximenes passage offers a number of additional problems besides its lack of clarity regarding which Alexander is meant. It is a citation in the *Suda* from Harpocration, making it twice removed from its original author. The context is a gloss on the Demosthenic reference to the *Pezhetairoi* earlier discussed from the *Second Olynthiac* (17), but the fragment associates the passage with the *Philippics* instead. Additionally, there were attacks in antiquity on Anaximenes' integrity. Since he had a quarrel with Theopompus, he wrote a treatise abusing the Athenians, the Spartans, and the Thebans, imitating the style of Theopompus and ascribed that author's name to this spurious production. Theopompus then became a hated figure throughout the Greek world (Anaximenes *BNJ* 73 T 6). Dionysius of Halicarnassus (*De Isaeo* 19) remarks that Anaximenes was "feeble and unconvincing," "a jack-of-all-trades, and a master of none."

Perhaps, the most common bond between the Macedonian king and his subjects involved the king as commander of the army, and here Philip's connection to his new infantry was much closer than that of his son's. In Macedonia, the king literally led his troops into battle. In the days prior to Philip's innovations, it was as commander of the aristocratic cavalry that the king shared the dangers

---

20 Carney (1996) 33; see also Brunt (1983) 532–533, who argues, "We need not believe a word of any of the speeches included in our surviving sources ... like most speeches preserved in ancient historical writers, these deserve little credence," and A. B. Bosworth (1988) proclaims this particular speech is "an absurdity" (108). D. B. Nagle (1996) has declared that "the substance of the speech was spoken by Alexander at Opis" (152), but that it was a piece of propaganda summarizing the "official version of Philip's reign," and hence not necessarily reflective of reality (153, 169–170). While the actual words probably do owe much to Arrian, what it claims for Alexander's father is accurate; Anson (2013) 44–52, 66–71.
21 Anson (1985b): 246–248.

and hardships of war (cf. Thuc. 1.61.4, 62.2–3, 63.2; 4.124. 1), but with the creation of the *Pezhetairoi*, the king now shared this same bond with the foot soldiers. It is interesting that Philip is most often associated with direct leadership of the infantry. Philip led the "pick of his foot soldiers" on his right wing (Diod. 16.4.5; Front. 2.3.2) in the battle in the Erigon River valley, and at Chaeronea again he was in control of the infantry (Polyaen. 4.2.2). This association with his new model infantry further cemented his ties to this group.

The heavy infantry, now the *Pezhetairoi* or "foot-companions," formed a third rail in the political structure of Philip's Macedonia, a counterbalance to the aristocratic cavalry and clear supporters of the king. The infantry would no longer be the dependents of the great landlords, but holders of the king's land. These new companions would be especially loyal to the king who was not just their paymaster, but also the source and protector of their new status. As Richard Billows notes with respect to the later Hellenistic monarchs, the granting of land was "a powerful inducement to future loyalty."[22] Billows, however, sees this loyalty as stemming from the inherent revocability of the royal grants, which may also be true of Philip and Alexander's grants, but with respect to these particular kings, the allegiance seems one of devotion rather than of fear. The importance of land to a rural population has not changed from antiquity to the modern day. The desire for land on the part of the landless or the small landowner encumbered by debt or obligation has sparked revolution across the centuries. Peter Brunt has demonstrated that it played a significant role in the so-called Roman Revolution that saw the overthrow of the Republic and the installation of the regime of Augustus,[23] and it has become a truism among commentators on modern rural revolutions that what the peasants want is unencumbered land, and that they very often employ violence to obtain it.[24]

Other innovations likewise emphasized the personal nature of the monarchy. Philip's introduction of the Pages,[25] young men who were personally to serve the

---

[22] Billows (1995) 132–137.

[23] Brunt (1988): 240–275.

[24] Huntington (1968) 375; Prosterman and Riedinger (1987) 10; Migdal (1974) 158–159, 201. For specific studies, see especially Harvey (1998) and Wiegersma (1988).

[25] The Pages were modeled on a similar institution in the Persian Empire. Xenophon (*An.* 1.9.3–6) describes the Persian pages as performing many of the same tasks as their Macedonian counterparts. Even though there are those who doubt that Philip was the institution's initiator, Kienast's claim that the program was initiated by Philip II appears most likely; Kienast (1973) 264–266. Arrian (*Anab.* 4.13.1) clearly states that the institution was introduced by Philip. Claims that the institution may not have arisen with Philip routinely claim that it was Philip who dramatically changed the institution. G. T. Griffith (Hammond and Griffith (1979) 401) suggests

king while revolutionary in his relationship with his aristocratic companions, was still personal. The "Pages" were the sons of prominent aristocratic Macedonians (Arr. *Anab.* 4.13.1; Ael. *VH* 14.48; Curt. 5.1.42; Diod. 17.65.1). The likely purpose for the creation of this institution was to hold the sons as guarantors of their fathers' good behavior and secondarily to forge the loyalty of the next generation of aristocrats to the Macedonian king, his heir, and the nation. That aristocrats would willingly surrender their sons as potential hostages would only make sense if the status of the relationship of the king and nobles had become strongly in favor of the king and attendance at court had become desirable in order to maintain power and prestige.

With Philip, the source of power, wealth, and increasingly of honor, was the king. Most of Alexander's elite officers had started their careers with his father.[26] Much of the countryside, however, was still dominated by the king's aristocratic *Hetairoi*. The position of the *Hetairoi* was not then entirely or, perhaps, even majorly tied to the king. They had political power already and continuously in Macedonia. In Macedonia then power even in the reign of Philip II was an interplay of royal patronage and regional authority. The best insights into the actual workings of the Macedonian state are to be found in the operations of the traditional Macedonian court, which, as Frances Pownall has shown,[27] was more a symposium than a court in the Persian or the early modern European sense. In anthropologic jargon the term feast is probably even more appropriate than symposium,[28] since in addition to the drinking that categorized the traditional Greek symposium, food was most often a part of these Macedonian get-togethers. It was a way to strengthen the ties between the Macedonian king and his *Hetairoi*.[29] This was the exercise of the traditional shared government between king and *Hetairoi*. In this court/feast atmosphere the aristocrats as companions exercised free speech and deferred to the king as the ruler of the feast (cf. Polyb. 5.27.6), not as sovereign lord, even though with the accession of Philip II and the institution of Pages and *Somatophylakes* suggest a growing preeminence of

---

that, while the institution was ancient, Philip "developed the institution as no king had done before," and Waldemar Heckel ((1986) 281), while stating that no firm conclusion can be drawn as to the origin of the institution, suggests that at the least the recruitment of the sons of Upper Macedonian nobles should be attributed to Philip.

26 Heckel (1992) 243–244.
27 Pownall (2010) 55–65.
28 Dietler and Hayden (2001) 3; Wright (2004) 133.
29 Pownall (2010) 55–65.

the monarch in this setting,[30] the tradition of speaking freely remained, but no longer entirely free from repercussion. When Cleitus in 326 vociferously objected to Alexander's flatterers comparing the king favorably with the gods, Alexander killed him and although subsequently expressing great remorse, the incident clearly put a damper on such expressions (Arr. *Anab.* 4.8.6–8; Curt. 8.1.28–2.2; Plut. *Alex.* 50–51). It was only the year before that Callisthenes "spoke with too much freedom" in objecting to the attempt to introduce the ceremony of *proskynesis* and was later accused of participating in the Pages conspiracy and imprisoned and executed (Diog. Laert. 5.1.5; Arr. *Anab.* 4.11.2–4; Curt. 8.5.13; *Suda* s.v. *Callisthenes*).

The most famous example of this freedom of speech in the court of Philip is found in the feast arranged to celebrate Philip's last of his seven marriages (Plut. *Alex.* 9.6–10, Athen. 13.557d–e). During the drinking, Attalus, the uncle of the bride Cleopatra, insulted Alexander the apparent heir to Philip's throne by proclaiming his hope that a legitimate heir might come from this new union. Alexander immediately rose exclaiming "do you then take me for a bastard" and hurled a cup at the offender. Philip angrily drew his sword and approached his son but fell. Alexander then declared "here is the one who was preparing to cross from Europe to Asia and he is upset in attempting to cross from one couch to another" (Plut. *Alex.* 9.5). The situation was clearly the result of too much wine, but there is some truth to the phrase *in vino veritas*, when inhibitions are loosened by drink. Attalus was also the indirect cause of Philip's later murder. He had caused a young Macedonian aristocrat, Pausanias, to be made drunk and turned over to be molested by some muleteers. When the young man appealed to Philip for redress, nothing was done, and Pausanias came to blame Philip for the grave insult and subsequently assassinated him (Plut. *Alex.* 10.4).[31] Both incidents involving Attalus show that Philip gave special deference to important aristocrats. Now, this may indeed have been because the king had married this particular *Hetairos*' niece, but Attalus was also one of the commanders sent with the vanguard of troops preparing for Philip's impending invasion of Asia.

---

[30] Philip II's establishment of the *Somatophylakes* (Arr. *Anab.* 4.13.1), the seven elite, ceremonial, bodyguards, was in part to guard the king in his bedchamber. In a warrior world where the king is simply the first among equals, guarding the king's bedchamber is not esteemed an honor. Perhaps, in origin the *Somatoplylakes* were young men associated with the court for whom it was so regarded.

[31] The turning of hostility towards Philip may have been heightened, since Attalus was in Asia Minor leading Philip's advance force in Asia and unavailable for retribution.

Alexander made few changes in the basic structure of government inherited from his father. Here again the importance of the *Hetairoi* is apparent. His second-in-command was Parmenio, two of whose sons also enjoyed prominent positions in the army that did cross to Asia with Alexander. Nicanor commanded the Hypaspists and Philotas the Companion Cavalry. As Alexander progressed deeper into Asia, his relationship with the *Hetairoi* changed increasingly in his favor. These individuals were now quite distant from their bases of power back in Macedonia. Also, Alexander over time replaced his father's old commanders with men of his own age and confirmed in their loyalty to him personally. Moreover, Alexander by his actions and successes was increasingly cementing his relationship with his other companions, the Macedonian infantry. He shared their burdens and fought at the front in his battles, although unlike his father, most often in command of the cavalry *Hetairoi*. The camp had become for all intents and purposes the new Macedonian homeland. While Alexander increasingly took on autocratic airs, his direct involvement with the army enhanced his status with his troops. While grumbling, complaints, and even attempted assassination plots arose in the ranks of his aristocratic companions, until late in his reign there is scarcely a complaint from the common soldiers concerning his more autocratic behavior. In fact, when at a symposium/feast in Maracanda the king in a drunken rage killed the *Hetairos* Cleitus, the army actually and spontaneously met and declared that Cleitus had been justly put to death.[32] Even later the Macedonian troops were not that concerned with Alexander's behavior at court, a place only members of the guard regularly attended, but rather were displeased with his increasing incorporation of Asiatic troops not only into his grand army but also into Macedonian units. As Waldemar Heckel has stated,[33] at Opis where there were slurs hurled at Alexander by some of his troops[34] in the end the opposition from his infantry crumbled and Alexander's domination emerged stronger than ever. The meeting of the Macedonians at Opis was summoned by Alexander initially to announce the discharge of many of his Macedonian veterans (Curt. 10.2.8, 19; Arr. *Anab*. 7.8.1; Diod. 17.109.1–3; Just. 12.11.4–8), an action long sought by the veterans themselves. Many of the soldiers, however, now interpreted this discharge as an insult; they believed that they were to be replaced by Asians (Arr. *Anab*. 7.8.2; Curt. 10.2.12; Plut. *Alex*. 71.3), a conclusion not without merit. Alexander reacted quickly arresting thirteen of the most vocal protest-

---

[32] Arr. *Anab*. 4.8.8–9.1; Curt. 8.1.49–2.12; Plut. *Alex*. 51. 9–11; Just. 12.6.3.
[33] Heckel (2009) 81.
[34] Curt. 10.2.12–4.3; Arr. *Anab*. 7.8.1–11.9; Diod. 17.109.2–3; Just. 12.11.1–12. 12; Plut. *Alex*. 71.2–9.

ers, who without any sort of hearing were executed that same day.[35] This quick action along with the general regard most of his troops felt for their king saved the situation.[36] With the disturbance quelled, Alexander proceeded with his plans to demobilize many of these veterans.[37] Subsequently, Alexander in order to restore his relationship with his soldiers banqueted the entire army paying special attention to his Macedonians who dined in an inner circle with their king (Arr. *Anab.* 7.11.8). Those who were initially to be dismissed and sent back to Macedonia were still sent.

As Alexander proceeded deeper into Asia the power of the *Hetairoi* diminished. His court was soon peopled by the elite from the conquered, and many of his father's companions replaced by those of Alexander's generation and outlook. While the power of the *Hetairoi* at court diminished, the importance of the infantry companions amplified, and increasingly after Gaugamela and the subsequent death of Darius, Alexander had to resort to cajoling his troops to proceed further east, in what Errington refers to as checking his *auctoritas* before exercising his *potestas*.[38] On the Hyphasis, the troops' reluctance to continue deeper into India convinced Alexander not to order them to do so and he turned south, sailing and fighting his way down the Indus.[39] Alexander's relationship with his Macedonians increasingly was becoming one of commander and commanded, not king and faithful subjects.

The result of Alexander's attempt to establish a new relationship with his subjects angered the Macedonians, both noble and commons. However, there was a distinction between the two classes with respect to their concerns. For

---

[35] Curt. 10.2.30; Arr. *Anab.* 7.8.3; Diod. 17.109.2–3; Just. 12.11.8; according to Arrian the ringleaders were seized before Alexander spoke, but in Curtius, Diodorus, and Justin, they are apprehended after his speech. Also in Arrian Alexander points out those to be arrested, while Curtius, Diodorus and Justin have Alexander himself seizing the troublemakers. It should also be noted that these individuals were not given a show trial before the army, but were summarily executed (Arr. *Anab.* 7.8.3; Curt. 10.3.4; Diod. 17.109.2; Just. 12.11.8).

[36] Even though many factors contributed to the Opis confrontation (see Bosworth (1988) 160), Callines, an officer of the companion cavalry, afterwards told Alexander that the ill-feeling derived from the perception that Alexander no longer regarded the Macedonians as his kinsmen (Arr. *Anab.* 7.11.6–7).

[37] Bosworth ((1986) 1–12; (1988) 267) estimates that at Opis there were 18,000 Macedonian veterans of which Alexander eventually dismissed 10,000 (Arr. *Anab.* 7.12.1). Bosworth's estimate of the number of Macedonian veterans present at Opis is generally regarded by scholars as on the high side. R. D. Milns ((1976) 127) believes that the total before discharge at Opis was 13,000; both Griffith ((1935) 141) and Hammond ((1980) 245) estimate that at Alexander's death the grand army contained around 10,000 Macedonians.

[38] Errington (1978) 87–90.

[39] Arr. *Anab.* 4.15.6; 5.26.1–2; Curt. 9.2.2–12; Just. 12.7.4; Plut. *Alex.* 62.2, 5.

the Macedonian infantry were concerned that they were losing their place of prominence in the army to Asians, while the aristocrats were concerned that their king was turning into an autocrat, as opposed to their leader and companion. The distinction is clear in the Opis affair. While one of the soldiers' stated concerns was Alexander's adoption of Persian dress, clearly they were far more concerned with the entrance of Persians into their ranks. The common soldiers were not often present in the king's symposia where most of the changes in leadership style would be apparent. Alexander never attempted to introduce *proskynesis* to the rank-and-file, but only in his court. Therefore, in the so-called Pages Conspiracy, when Hermolaus accused Alexander of treating the Macedonians as slaves and not free men he was expressing an aristocratic concern (Curt. 8.7.1). Alexander certainly by the time he had subdued the Persian heartland was attempting to transform his government from what it had been traditionally to one more reflective of his new Asian domains, more bureaucratic and with a ruler with true autocratic power. With respect to the army, however, Alexander was still their commander-in-chief. He was always in the forefront of the fighting and risking his life along with those of his troops. He had been wounded six times and had his leg broken in battle. However, the rapprochement with the Persians angered his Macedonians both aristocratic and common. Moreover, many, if not most Macedonian rank-and-file, had been continuously on campaign since they left Macedonia. Even though Demosthenes states (8.11) that Philip's army was always in the field, the truth is otherwise. Those troops not specifically needed for a particular campaign were able to return home. Home during Alexander's expedition was the camp. The connection to Macedonia was diminishing with each year and these troops were acquiring the characteristics of mercenaries.[40] This was an army tied directly to their king as their king, but also as their patron, colleague, and victorious commander. Part of Alexander's ability to maintain his control of his infantry was that he would appear to his soldiers as the only individual capable of playing this complex role. In Asia they were not willing to trust in any other commander. Therefore, as Philip had used the *Pezhetairoi* as an off-setting power opposed to his aristocratic *Hetairoi*, Alexander increasingly was using his new Asiatic *Hetairoi* and soldiers as counterpoises to his Macedonians. After Opis, with his Macedonian troops well under his control, the king continued to use the Asiatic troops as a manpower pool to supplement his Macedonians.[41] These troops, while sharing the equipment and often the name of a parallel Macedonian unit, did not share the privilege of

---

40 Anson (1985a) 309–310.
41 Bosworth (1980) 20.

being companions to the king. Their role was as it would have been in the previous Achaemenid army. These troops were to act as Alexander's third rail, the counter to his Macedonians, both common soldier and aristocratic companion.

Had he lived the actual structure of both his court and his army might have been quite different and his legacy to his Successors perhaps very different as well, but he died and we will never know what might have come of his innovations. Alexander clearly was moving towards creating his own court and his own army. The result of Alexander's campaign was to create a new dynamic of king and ruled. The court would resemble more that of the Achaemenid Empire than the traditional Macedonian relationship. After Opis with the collapse of the infantry's opposition and the incorporation of the Iranians, the army had become the true partner in this nomadic military state created by Alexander. The state had become the military camp. While Macedonians still retained some of their traditional loyalty to their national monarch, they were also becoming increasingly mercenary in their behavior. As Alexander progressed further into Asia the king frequently had to give pep talks to his troops most often emphasizing the plunder to be had by further campaigning (for example, Arr. *Anab.* 5.26.8; Curt. 9.2.27).

In the Successor period, as long as the commander maintained a close relationship with what had become under the Conqueror and would continue under his Successors basically a mercenary force, paying well and being successful, his power would hold. Lack of success in battle, inability to pay troops, and/or an aloofness in his relationship with them, meant that a general's longevity would be short.[42] The Successors also followed Alexander's treatment of conquered populations. Those not involved in the army or court would be treated as at best second-class citizens, but direct interference in their lives would be minimal. The great weakness in these Successor states apart from Macedonia was that the native population was never fully integrated into these societies.[43] Officers and administrators in these kingdoms, while not exclusively Greek and Macedonian migrants, were predominantly those attracted from these lands by grants of landed estates.[44] Philip's greatness was in creating a Macedonian nation. The Macedonians in Asia and Egypt were always a foreign ruling class. Even with the accretions of Greeks and some encultured natives, the majority of the native population remained a subject population.

---

[42] See Austin (1986) 456–462 for the most extreme view.
[43] See Anson (2014) 190–195.
[44] Billows (1995) 137.

The society that Alexander created was a military one. The bond between commander and troops was not extended to the majority of the people in the areas of Alexander's conquest, and this bond with the army was basically one between employer and employed. This relationship so dependent on pay and success could only be improved by establishing a sense of trust and even empathy with one's soldiers. Loyalty to homeland was now subordinated to personal interest. The evolution of Alexander's army into a characteristically mercenary force made it necessary that his Successors have the authority to control such a force. As noted, outside of Macedonia the non-military civilian population became second-class citizens and often ethnically distinct from their military counterparts. While by tradition the Argeads were a foreign ruling clan, whatever the truth of this claim, they identified themselves with their Macedonian subjects and that relationship was reciprocated. Alexander's Successors in Asia and Egypt did not come to be identified with the people they ruled. Only in Macedonia was a national state reborn in the persons of the Antigonid kings. For those states in Asia and Egypt it might almost be said that with the death of Alexander they remained in a state of arrested development.

Bibliography

Anson (1985a): Edward M. Anson, "Macedonia's Alleged Constitutionalism", in: *Classical Journal* 80, 303–316.
Anson (1985b): Edward M. Anson, "The Hypaspists: Macedonia's professional citizen-soldiers", in: *Historia* 34, 246–248.
Anson (1991): Edward M. Anson, "The Evolution of the Macedonian Army Assembly (330–315 B. C.)", in: *Historia* 40, 230–247.
Anson (1996): Edward M. Anson, "The 'Ephemerides' of Alexander the Great", in: *Historia* 45, 501–504.
Anson (2008): Edward M. Anson, "Philip II and the Transformation of Macedonia: A Reappraisal", in: Tim Howe and Jeanne Reames (eds.), *Macedonian Legacies: Studies in Ancient Macedonian History and Culture in Honor of Eugene N. Borza*, Claremont, CA, 17–30.
Anson (2009): Edward M. Anson, "Philip II and the Creation of the Macedonian *Pezhetairoi*", in: Pat Wheatley and Robert Hannah (eds.), *Alexander in the Antipodes,* Claremont, CA, 88–98.
Anson (2010): Edward M. Anson, "The Introduction of the *Sarisa* in Macedonian Warfare", in: *Ancient Society* 40, 51–68.
Anson (2013): Edward M. Anson, *Alexander the Great: Themes and Issues,* London.
Anson (2014): Edward M. Anson, *Alexander's Heirs: The Age of the Successors,* Malden and Oxford.
Austin (1986): Michel M. Austin, "Hellenistic Kings, War and the Economy", in: *Classical Quarterly* 36, 450–466.

Billows (1995): Richard A. Billows, *Kings and Colonists: Aspects of Macedonian Imperialism*, New York.
Bosworth (1980): A. Brian Bosworth, *A Historical Commentary on Arrian's History of Alexander*, Vol. 1, Oxford and New York.
Bosworth (1986): A. Brian Bosworth, "Alexander the Great and the decline of Macedon", in: *Journal of Hellenic Studies* 106, 1–12.
Bosworth (1988): A. Brian Bosworth, *Conquest and Empire: The Reign of Alexander the Great*, Cambridge.
Brunt (1976): Peter A. Brunt, "Anaximenes and King Alexander I of Macedon", in: *Journal of Hellenic Studies* 96, 151–153.
Brunt (1983): Peter A. Brunt, *Arrian. Anabasis of Alexander, Books V-VII, Indica*, Cambridge, MA.
Brunt (1988): Peter A. Brunt. *The Fall of the Roman Republic and related essays.* Oxford.
Carney (1996): Elizabeth D. Carney, "Macedonians and Mutiny: Discipline and Indiscipline in the Army of Philip and Alexander", in: *Classical Philology* 91, 19–44.
Develin (1985): R. Develin, "Anaximenes (FGR HIST 72) F 4", in: *Historia* 34, 493–496.
Dietler and Hayden (2001): Michael Dietler and Brian Hayden, "Digesting the Feast: Good to Eat, Good to Drink, Good to Think: An Introduction", in: M. Dietler and B. Hayden (eds.), *Feasts: Archaeological and Ethnographic Perspectives on Food, Politics, and Power* Washington, D.C., 2001, 1–20.
Errington (1978): R. Malcolm Errington, "The nature of the Macedonian state under the monarchy", in: *Chiron* 8, 77–133.
Errington (1990): R. Malcolm Errington, *A History of Macedonia*, trans. C. Errington, Berkeley and Los Angeles.
Erskine (1989): Andrew Erskine, "The ΠΕΖΕΤΑΙΡΟΙ of Philip II and Alexander III", in: *Historia* 38, 385–394.
Greenwalt (2017): William Greenwalt, "Alexander II of Macedon", in: Tim Howe *et al.* (eds.), *Ancient Historiography on War & Empire*, Philadelphia and Oxford, 80–91.
Griffith (1935): Guy T. Griffith, *The Mercenaries of the Hellenistic World*, Cambridge.
Hammond (1980): Nicholas G. L. Hammond, *Alexander the Great, King, Commander and Statesman*, Park Ridge, N. J.
Hammond and Griffith (1979): Nicholas G. L. Hammond and Guy T. Griffith, *A History of Macedonia*, Vol. 2. 550 B. C—336. B. C., Oxford.
Harvey (1998): N. Harvey, *The Chiapas Rebellion: The Struggle for Land and Democracy*, Durham.
Hatzopoulos (1996): Miltiades B. Hatzopoulos, *Macedonian Institutions under the Kings*, Vol. 1, Athens and Paris.
Heckel (1986): Waldemar Heckel, "*Somatophylakia:* A Macedonian Cursus Honorum", in: *Phoenix* 40, 279–294.
Heckel (1992): Waldemar Heckel, *The Marshals of Alexander's Empire*, London and New York.
Heckel (2003): Waldemar Heckel, "King and 'Companions': Observations on the Nature of Power in the Reign of Alexander", in: Joseph Roisman (ed.), *Brill's Companion to Alexander the Great*, Leiden, 197–225.
Heckel (2009): Waldemar Heckel, "Alexander's Conquest of Asia", in: Waldemar Heckel and Larry Tritle (eds.), *Alexander the Great: A New History*, Chichester and Malden, MA, 26–52.

Huntington (1968): Samuel P. Huntington, *Political Order in Changing Societies*, New Haven.
Kienast (1973): Dietmar Kienast, *Philipp II. von Makedonien und das Reich der Achämeniden*, Munich.
Lock (1974): Robert Lock, *The Army of Alexander the Great*, Unpub. PhD diss., University of Leeds.
Migdal (1974): Joel S. Migdal, *Peasants, Politics, and Revolution; Pressures Toward Political and Social Change in the Third World*, Princeton.
Milns (1976): Robert D. Milns, "The Army of Alexander the Great", in: Ernst Badian *et al.* (eds.), *Alexandre le Grand: image et réalité*, Fondation Hardt, Geneva, 87–130.
Nagle (1996): D. Brendan Nagle, "The Cultural Context of Alexander's Speech at Opis", in: *Transactions and Proceedings of the American Philological Association* 126, 151–172.
Pownall (2010): Frances Pownall, "The Symposia of Philip II and Alexander III of Macedon: The View From Greece", in: Elizabeth D. Carney and Daniel Ogden (eds.), *Philip II and Alexander the Great: Father and Son, Lives and Afterlives*, Oxford and New York, 55–65 and 256–260.
Prosterman and Riedinger (1987): Roy L. Prosterman and Jeffrey M. Riedinger, *Land Reform and Democratic Development*, Baltimore.
Stagakis (1962): George J. Stagakis, *Institutional Aspects of the Hetairos Relation*, Unpub. Ph.D. diss., University of Wisconsin. Madison.
Wiegersma (1988): Nancy Wiegersma, *Vietnam: Peasant Land, Peasant Revolution. Patriarchy and Collectivity in the Rural Economy*, New York.
Wright (2004): Jacob L. Wright, "A Survey of Evidence for Feasting in Mycenaean Society", in: *Hesperia* 73, 133–178.

Waldemar Heckel
Storm Clouds over Three Hellenistic Courts: Observations on the Life and Death of Ptolemy Ceraunus

Ceraunus.[1] The nickname implies sudden, unexpected, and irrational behavior. It was used of (and by) others,[2] but none more aptly than the son of Ptolemy Soter and murderer of Seleucus Nicator. What we know about his life with relative certainty spans just over half a decade. To the world at large, he was all but unknown; and by those who knew him his death was generally unlamented.[3] Even within the tight-knit, incestuous circles of Alexander's Successors, his activities brought family politics to a level so low that only rumor could add further debasement. Yet, his story illuminates the problem of royal succession during the final years of the Diadochi, when marriage alliances and amphimetric strife dominated the courts of the Hellenistic kingdoms.

I

Born the son of Ptolemy son of Lagus,[4] at that time satrap of Egypt in the dysfunctional and ill-starred empire of the last Argeads, the boy's mother was

---

All translations of Justin are based on those by Yardley (1994). I wish to thank Sabine Müller, Frances Pownall, and Konrad Kinzl for their helpful comments on this paper.

1 Heinen dedicated 94 pages (roughly half of his Historia Einzelschrift) to Ptolemy Ceraunus. This remains the most detailed and sensible guide (see also Müller (2009) 67–84). I offer only a few points of disagreement and some speculation—since the dearth of evidence does not allow for greater certainty—on the motives of, and background to, Ceraunus' actions. At the same time, this is not an attempt at rehabilitation, even though modern scholarship is almost unanimously hostile to the subject of this study. The epithet, like the *epiklesis* Philadelphus, and the references to Arsinoë I and II, used (in most cases prematurely), are intended to make it easier for the reader to distinguish the two Ptolemies (indeed, even Ptolemy I, who is often identified as Soter, though in this case not anachronistically) and Arsinoës.
2 Clearchus, the tyrant of Pontic Heraclea, deliberately named his son Ceraunus, which because of its associations with Zeus was thought to be a positive thing (Just. 16.5.11).
3 The consternation of the Macedonians, described by Just. 24.5.11, was for the kingdom's fate, for which they blamed Ceraunus: *quos furor et temeritas Ptolomei regis perdidisset* ("whom King Ptolemy's mad recklessness had brought to ruin").
4 Heckel (2021) no. 1011.

Eurydice, a daughter of Antipater, who had arranged her marriage for the sake of stability and *koinopragia*.[5] It soon became clear that the two concepts were not compatible. Intended to blunt the ambitions of Perdiccas son of Orontes, the move was nevertheless accompanied by other marriage offers that used the bonds of kinship to further centrifugal policies to the detriment of the father-in-law who sought to bind them to a more modest (and honorable) cause.[6] Three sisters, daughters of the man who had ruled Macedon during the absences of Philip II and Alexander III, and a cousin, who until the 320s had languished in obscurity, produced in the space of little more than a decade a brood of children who would rule—seldom amicably—territories they had done nothing to conquer and very little to maintain.[7] The greatest conflagration of their time was sparked by the Thunderbolt, whom dynastic strife had cast into their midst.

The founder of the Ptolemaic line was a man of considerable experience when he won, either on the basis of merit or negotiation, appointment as satrap of Egypt and the adjacent Libyan lands,[8] territorries that were agriculturally rich, had ready access to raw materials, and were blessed by geography with natural defenses.[9] Although his pedigree was far from impressive—so much so that rumors of illegitimacy enhanced rather than detracted from his reputation[10]—he was some ten years older than Alexander, whose "boyhood friend" he is often mistakenly thought to have been.[11]

---

5 *Koinopragia:* working together to achieve a common goal, as opposed to *idiopragia*, acting in one's own interest. See Heckel (2002).
6 Seibert (1967) 11–18. Antipater: Heckel (2021) no. 127; Grainger (2019) 3–128. His daughters: Landucci (2003) 58–69; also Heckel (1989).
7 For Ptolemy's marriages and offspring, see the discussions in Ogden (1999) 67–80 and Ager (2018).
8 Diod. 18.3.1 (Egypt); Just. 13.4.10: *prima Ptolomeo Aegyptus et Africae Arabiaeque pars sorte venit* ("first of all, Egypt and part of Africa and Arabia were allotted to Ptolemy"); App. *Syr.* 52.264 (Egypt).
9 For the natural defenses see Kahn and Tammuz (2008).
10 Ellis (1994) 3: "it is possible that Ptolemy, or one of his admirers, deliberately encouraged the rumor to enhance his reputation and his claim to the title of king by allowing people to believe that he was Alexander's half-brother." On this question see Collins (1997); Ogden (1999) 67–68; Worthington (2016) 8–9. *Suda* Λ 25 claims that he was the son of Arsinoë, but not by Lagus, who exposed the child on a shield only to have it protected and nourished by an eagle. Plut. *Mor.* 458a–b; Porphyr. *BNJ* 260 F 2 §2; Theocr. 17.26 with Gow (1950) 2.331; cf. Curt. 9.8.22. The question of the father's paternity appears to have had no impact on Ceraunus, unless the thunderbolt and the eagle are meant to suggest a connection with Zeus (but see Heinen (1972), 84).
11 For his birthdate: [Lucian.], *Macrob.* 12. For the view that Ptolemy, Nearchos, Harpalos, Laomedon and Erigyios were not coeval with the king, see Heckel (1985) 288 and Heckel (2016) 231.

The personal relationship between Ptolemy son of Lagus and Perdiccas son of Orontes is portrayed by our sources as a hostile one, deriving virtually without exception from the events that followed the death of Alexander the Great. How they felt about each other during the King's lifetime is impossible to say, but the close relationship between Perdiccas and Hephaistion suggests that Ptolemy may have been jealous of Perdiccas, a younger man whose career was undeniably more accomplished than his own.[12] Whatever Perdiccas' shortcomings as a colleague, these were doubtless exaggerated by his political enemies, not least by Ptolemy. That man's insubordination was transmogrified, by a wave of the historiographical wand, into justifiable fear of Perdiccas' ambitions. What we do know is that very soon after Alexander's death, Antipater attempted to secure the support of Perdiccas and Craterus by offering them Nicaea and Phila respectively, and it appears that, around the same time, another daughter, presumably Eurydice, was intended for Leonnatus. The political aim of these unions was conciliatory and constructive. By contrast, the second set of marriage proposals—following the deaths of Leonnatus, Craterus, and Perdiccas—was designed to create a coalition (*koinopragia*), serving the private interests of Antipater, Antigonus, Lysimachus, and Ptolemy.[13] Hence, marriages to Antipater's daughters—the sisters of Cassander—took on added importance, both for the members of the coalition and for the individual bridegrooms.[14] Eurydice, we may speculate, came to Egypt soon after the meeting at Triparadeisos, if she was not already in her father's camp in early 320, and the birth of a son—if we believe that Ptolemy (Ceraunus) was the first of Eurydice's children (cf. Porphyr. *BNJ* 260 F 3 §9, who calls him son of "Lagus" and Eurydice)—took on special meaning. If he was born in 319, one would have expected to find him at Ipsus in 301, if only his father had sent an army to assume his share of the burden. But, in truth, we know virtually nothing about him: the year of his birth, both in absolute terms and in relation to Soter's other children; his father's plans for him; his education and military-administrative training. When he comes onto the scene he is a dispossessed, angry, and scheming man intent on taking for himself what had either not been granted or else offered and then withdrawn.

---

12 On Perdiccas and Hephaistion see Heckel (2016) 161. See also Müller (2012).
13 See Seibert (1967); Ogden (1999); Cohen (1973). For the limitations of such marriage alliances see Heckel (1986).
14 For Ceraunus himself, in a bid for the Macedonian throne, the fact of being Cassander's nephew proved to be a valuable asset.

II

Of the children of Eurydice, we know that Lysandra was old enough to marry Alexander V, the son of Cassander and Thessalonice, a marriage that may have been arranged before Cassander's death in 297.[15] Hence it is likely that Lysandra was born before 310 and that she was at least in her mid-twenties when her second husband Agathocles was murdered in Lysimachea. Alexander V was killed by Demetrius Poliorcetes in 294/3,[16] and it is surprising that we do not hear of Lysandra returning to her father's house or being offered by him to another. All we know is that by the mid-280s she had been married to Lysimachus' son Agathocles for some time and had children by him; but clearly it was Agathocles himself who was a threat to Arsinoë and her children (Paus. 1.10.3: Ἀρσινόην φοβουμένην ἐπὶ τοῖς παισί, μὴ Λυσιμάχου τελευτήσαντος ἐπ' Ἀγαθοκλεῖ γένωνται). This part of the story is natural enough, since Agathocles had clearly been designated Lysimachus' heir (Just. 17.1.4: *Agathoclem, filium suum, quem in successionem regni ordinaverat, per quem multa bella prospere gesserat*).[17] But the story is somewhat distorted by Plutarch, who carelessly implies that, when Seleucus agreed to marry Stratonice very soon after Ipsus, both Lysimachus and his son Agathocles had married daughters of Ptolemy (*Demetr.* 31.5)—thus antedating the marriage to Lysandra by at least five or six years. Pausanias adds to the confusion by saying that Lysimachus married Arsinoë, even though Agathocles had children by Lysandra (1.10.3: Ἀγαθοκλεῖ παίδων ὄντων ἐκ Λυσάνδρας). In truth, Lysandra must have had equal concerns for the fate of her children in the event of something happening to her husband. She was, after all, merely the wife of the King's heir—and this status, as the case of Ptolemy Ceraunus shows, could be revoked—whereas Arsinoë was Lysimachus' queen.

The details of the happenings in Lysimachea are vague and contradictory; and, indeed, the chronology is far from certain. But we must begin by noting that Arsinoë (the one who would later became known as Philadelphus) was Ptolemy's daughter by Berenice, who came to Egypt with her cousin, Eurydice, and later supplanted her as the favorite wife. The exact time frame of this transition is unclear but we do know that, after the great confrontation at Ipsus

---

[15] Euseb. *Chron.* 1.232. Carney (2000) 160–161. See also Beloch (1927) IV² 2.179.
[16] The fact that Demetrius did not take Lysandra as his wife (marriage by levirate) suggests that Lysimachus had deliberately kept her out of the Besieger's clutches.
[17] Paus. 1.10.3: "Arsinoë, fearing lest, upon Lysimachus' death, her children should fall into the hands of Agathocles." Just. 17.1.4: "his son Agathocles, whom he had appointed successor to the throne and through him won many victories in war."

(301), Soter began to pursue a foreign policy that bound potential rivals to him by marriages to Berenice's children. Arsinoë, the oldest of Berenice's children by Ptolemy, was given to Lysimachus probably in 300/299, a move countered by Demetrius, who offered his daughter Stratonice to Seleucus.[18] Not much later Soter procured two sons-in-law in the West, marrying Theoxena to Agathocles of Syracuse and Antigone to Pyrrhus the Molossian (both were children of Berenice by her first husband, an obscure individual named Philip).[19] The fact that Pyrrhus, when he was restored to his kingdom, was forced to share it with Neoptolemus II, suggests that Cassander was still alive and needed to be conciliated; perhaps it was at this time that Soter arranged for Cassander's youngest son Alexander (V) to marry Lysandra, his daughter by Eurydice. Where this was intended to lead is unclear: by 295/4 Neoptolemus had been executed on a (perhaps false) charge of conspiracy; Antigone had died, leaving Pyrrhus free to marry Lanassa of Syracuse without offending his benefactor; Agathocles of Thrace had suffered a "near miss" in his dealings with Dromichaetes, ruler of Getae; and Cassander's heirs—the King himself had died in 297—were on the verge of being consigned to the footnotes of Diadochic history.

III

Most scholars have assumed that Ptolemy Ceraunus, when he learned that this father was going to leave the kingdom to his younger half-brother, fled to the court of Lysimachus, where he expected to find help for his cause from Agathocles, the Thracian king's heir and husband of his sister Lysandra. Thus, Niese writes: "Der verdrängte Ptolemäos Keraunos hatte sich an den Hof des Lysimachos begeben, wo seine Schwester mit Agathokles vermählt war."[20] Here, accord-

---

18 Plut. *Demetr.* 31.5–6.
19 The story of Pyrrhus' marriage to Antigone is heavily romanicized, with the Epirote prince (who had gone to Alexandria as a hostage after Ipsus) impressing Berenice with his manhood and his charm (Plut. *Pyrrh.* 4.5–7; cf. Pyrrhus' respect for his in-laws: Plut. *Pyrrh.* 6.1); the marriage to Antigone was, furthermore, the only one of Pyrrhus' unions that was monogamous (Plut. *Pyrrh.* 9.1: γυναῖκας (...) πλείονας ἔγημε μετὰ τὴν Ἀντιγόνης τελευτήν). For Agathocles' marriage to Theoxena (Just. 23.2.6). For Theoxena's uncertain parentage, see Beloch (1927) IV² 2, who on p. 179 makes her a daughter of Eurydice but lists her in his stemma on p. 186 as Berenice's child.
20 Niese (1893) I 389: "The ousted Ptolemy Ceraunos had gone to the court of Lysimachus, where his sister was married to Agathocles." Heinen (1972) 12: "Die Gegenpartei, darunter Lysandra und Keraunos, sah sich zur Flucht zu Seleukos genötigt." ("The opposition party, including Lysandra and Ceraunos, found it necessary to flee to the Seleucus.") Cf. Lund (1992) 186: "some

ing to the most sensational accounts, he became embroiled in the power struggle between Lysimachus' wife, Arsinoë, and his oldest son, Agathocles. Droysen offers a picture of events which, although based on the worst evidence, has until fairly recently captured the imagination of modern writers.

> Der älteste und zum Erben des Reiches bestimmte Sohn des Lysimachos war Agathokles, derselbe, der den Feldzug gegen Demetrios mit ebensoviel Mut wie Besonnenheit geführt hatte, ein edler und ritterlicher Fürst, der am Hofe, im Heere, vor Allem aber in Kleinasien, wo er mehrere Jahre commandirt haben mochte, außerordentlich beliebt war; man freute sich, in ihm und seinen Kindern die Erben des Reiches zu sehen. Nur Arsinoë sah das Alles mit bittrem Neid; sollten denn diesem Sohn der Odryserin ihre, die Königstochter Kinder nachstehen? Sollten sie einst von Agathokles' und seiner Kinder Gnade leben? Sollte sie selbst dann dieser Stiefschwester Lysandra, die sie im väterlichen Hause schon verachtet, den Rang abtreten und sich mit dem armseligen Wittwensitz Heraklea begnügen müssen? Ihre Kinder nahten dem Alter der Mündigkeit; es war die höchste Zeit zu handln, wenn ihnen der thrakische Thron werden sollte. Auch noch Geheimeres mag in ihrer Seele vorgegangen sein; Agathokles war schön und ritterlich, was half es der Königin, des alten Mannes Bette zu theilen? Lysandra war die Glücklichere; man erzählt sich, die Königin habe den jungen Fürsten zu gewinnen versucht; er liebte seine Gemahlin, er vermied die zweideutige Gunst seiner Stiefmutter, er wandte sich verachtend von ihr. Arsinoë sann die gräßlichste Rache. Der flüchtige Ptolemäus Keraunos war gen Lysimachia gekommen, mit ihm schmiedete sie Pläne.[21]

The oldest son of Lysimachus, and the designated heir to kingdom, was Agathocles, the same man who in the campaign against Demetrius had led with as much courage as prudence, a noble and chivalrous prince, who was inordinately loved at the court, in the army, but particularly in Asia Minor, where he might have held command for several years; one was pleased to see in him and his children the heirs to the kingdom. Only Arsinoë viewed all this with bitter envy. Were her children, born to a King's daughter, to take a back seat to this son of an Odrysian woman? Was she to live by the grace of Agathocles and his children? Was she herself to yield rank to this stepsister, whom she had disdained in her father's house, and be forced to content herself with the miserable widow's residence, Heraclea? Her children were nearing the age of maturity. It was high time to act, if the Thracian throne was to become theirs. She may have harbored even more secret thoughts in her heart. Agathocles was handsome and chivalrous, and what good was it for the queen to share an old man's bed? Lysandra was the happier one. The story goes that the queen had attempted to win over the young prince, but he loved his wife and he avoided the am-

---

time after 287 BC, Lysimachus had welcomed to his court Ptolemy Ceraunus, dispossessed son of Ptolemy I." But, beyond this statement, Lund has nothing to say about his presence in, and later departure from, Lysimachea. Carney (2013) 42–43, and 53: "Ptolemy Ceraunus, as we have seen, traveled first to the court of Lysimachus where his full sister Lysandra was married to Agathocles, probably hoping for some kind of preferment and help to overturn his brother's rule in Egypt." But Landucci (1992) 212 n. 166, following Heinen (1972), expresses serious doubts.

21 Droysen (1836) 635–636, preserving the wording and orthography of the original publication.

biguous favors of his stepmother and contemptuously turned away from her. Arsinoë plotted hideous revenge. The fugitive Ptolemy Ceraunus had come to Lysimachea and with him she devised plans.

Droysen goes on to describe how Arsinoë persuades Lysimachus that Agathocles has been plotting against him, bringing in Ptolemaios Ceraunus as a reliable witness:

> Endlich nannte sie Agathokles Namen, berief sich auf Ptolemaios Zeugnis, "dem in Wahrheit zu glauben sei, da Agathokles Gemahlin seine rechte Schwester; der habe, für seines edlen Beschützers Leben besorgt, ihr Alles entdeckt." Der König glaubte; er eilte, einem Verbrechen zuvorzukommen, dessen der edle Agathokles nicht fähig gewesen wäre. Der Sohn ahnte die schauderhaften Ränke der Königin; als ihm an seines Vaters Tisch Vergiftetes gereicht war, nahm er Gegengift und rettete sein Leben. Er ward ins Gefängniss geworfen, Ptolemäus übernahm es, ihn zu ermorden.[22]

> At long last she mentioned Agathocles by name, invoking the testimony of Ptolemy, who was in truth worthy of belief, since Agathocles' wife was his legitimate sister; he, out of concern for the life of his noble protector, revealed everything to her. The King believed [what he heard]: he hastened to forestall a crime which the noble Agathocles would not have been capable of committing. The son suspected the queen's dreadful intrigues. When poison was offered him at his father's table, he took an antidote and saved his life. He was thrown into prison and Ptolemy undertook the task of murdering him.

The story is filled with inherent improbabilities, most of all the unlikelihood that Ceraunus sought refuge in Lysimachea. What appears to place him securely at Lysimachus' court is Memnon of Heraclea's assertion that it was Ceraunus who murdered Agathocles (*BNJ* 434 F 1 §5.6: ὁ δὲ Πτολεμαῖος, ὃς αὐτόχειρ τοῦ μιάσματος ἐγεγόνει, ἀδελφὸς ἦν Ἀρσινόης, καὶ ἐπώνυμον διὰ τὴν σκαιότητα καὶ ἀπόνοιαν τὸν Κεραυνὸν ἔφερεν).[23] Pausanias (1.16.2) also says that Ptolemy fled from Lysimachus' court to Seleucus (παρὰ Λυσιμάχου παρ'αὐτὸν [sc. Σέλευκον] πεφευγώς), but he claims that the epithet Ceraunus had its origins in Ptolemy's murder of Seleucus. Heinen, in a lengthy and persuasive discussion, concludes that Memnon (or his source) confused Ceraunus with Arsinoë's own son, also named Ptolemy.[24] Indeed, it is hard to know what Ceraunus hoped to accomplish at Lysimachus' court. Nevertheless, Heinen, after absolving him of the crime, believes that he was present in Lysimachea and went from there

---

22 Droysen (1836) 636.
23 "Ptolemy, who by his own hand became the author of this defilement, was the brother of Arsinoë, and he bore the epithet, "the Thunderbolt," on account of his mad and sinister nature."
24 Heinen (1972) 7–17.

—after Agathocles' death—to the court of Seleucus. There is, in fact, good reason to doubt that he went to Lysimachea at all. Appian tells us that

> Ptolemy Ceraunus was the son of Ptolemy Soter and Eurydice, the daughter of Antipater. He had been driven from Egypt by fear, because he learned that Ptolemy the was going to leave the kingdom to his youngest son. Seleucus welcomed him as the unfortunate child of a friend and he nourished and indulged in every way his own murderer.[25]

The chronology of Ceraunus' flight from Egypt is difficult to determine. It must have occurred no later than 285, when Ptolemy Soter formalized his decision to make Philadelphus his heir by giving him the crown. But it is likely that, by the time his father's plans were realized, Ceraunus had already left Alexandria, possibly in the company of his mother Eurydice, who was escorting her daughter Ptolemais to Miletos, where she would at last consummate the marriage to Demetrios that had been arranged soon after Ipsus.[26] It is doubtful that Eurydice brought her daughter to Miletos without her husband's approval—the defiance of Cynnane in bringing Adea to marry Arrhidaeus in 322/1 does not provide a parallel, since Cynnane was a widow and without a guardian—but this does not mean that Eurydice's departure from Egypt was intended to be temporary. Indeed, it appears that Miletos, which had long been in Lysimachus' hands but had gone over to Demetrius,[27] may have become Eurydice's temporary home and Ptolemais remained there with her mother when the Besieger continued his ill-fated campaign in Asia Minor. Soter had little to fear from Demetrius at this point and he may have thought that taking him as a son-in-law—notably this was the first and only marriage alliance involving Demetrius and Ptolemy Soter—would make cooperation between Demetrius and Seleucus less likely.[28]

---

25 *Syriaca* 62.330: υἱὸς ἦν ὁ Κεραυνὸς ὅδε Πτολεμαίου τοῦ Σωτῆρος καὶ Εὐρυδίκης τῆς Ἀντιπάτρου. καὶ αὐτὸν ἐκπεσόντα Αἰγύπτου διὰ δέος, ὅτι νεωτάτῳ παιδὶ Πτολεμαῖος τὴν ἀρχὴν ἐπενόει δοῦναι, ὁ Σέλευκος οἷα φίλου παῖδα ἀτυχοῦντα ὑπεδέξατο καὶ ἔφερβε καὶ περιήγετο πάντῃ φονέα ἑαυτοῦ.

26 Plut. *Demetr.* 32.6; 46.5. Wheatley and Dunn (2020) 451 date the marriage to 286. If the betrothal is not reported out of context, the delay may be due to the girl's age or, what is more likely, the changing fortunes of Demetrius: immediately after Ipsus he appeared weak, but his power grew when he regained Athens and then seized Macedonia. It is no concidence that the marriage alliance was revived when Demetrius was once again at a very low point in his career.

27 See Wheatley and Dunn (2020) 409–410 with nn.; cf. Tarn (1913) 99.

28 There were limits to which Seleucus was prepared to cooperate with Demetrius. Certainly, after driving the Antigonids out of Asia after the battle of Ipsus, he had no desire to see the Besieger reestablished there, even after making a marriage alliance with him in 299 (see Plut. *Demetr.* 31.5–32.3, 38.1).

He himself had formed a very close bond with Lysimachus, who had married Berenice's daughter, Arsinoë (II), and whose son was the husband of Eurydice's daughter, Lysandra; Soter was probably already negotiating the marriage of Arsinoë (I), daughter of Lysimachus and Nicaea, to the younger Ptolemy (Philadelphus). So it appears that Soter was content to make a pact with Demetrius, now hardly a threat, and at the same time defuse the dynastic (amphimetric) strife at his own court by removing Eurydice and her children from Alexandria. In the process, he became Demetrius' only ally, and the extent of his support was surely dependent upon the Besieger's good faith.

All this makes the assumption that Ceraunus, disinherited by his father and eager to find support against his younger brother, went to Lysimachea—the one place most closely tied to his father and the newly elevated Ptolemy II—difficult to accept.[29] His only option was to take refuge with Seleucus, and even he would not act (at least, on the question of the Egyptian inheritance) as long as Soter lived. Memnon's claim (*BNJ* 434 F 1 §8.2) that Seleucus planned to help Ceraunus recover Egypt once his father died is anachronistic (since at the time of Corupedium, Ptolemy Soter had already been dead for over a year) but not otherwise factually wrong:

> Ptolemy Ceraunus, when the affairs of Lysimachus had come under Seleucus' control, was in his entourage, not looked down upon like a prisoner-of-war but worthy of honor and consideration as the son of a king. And, furthermore, he was emboldened by promises, which Seleucus held out, that if his father should die, he would restore him to Egypt, his paternal kingdom.[30]

The word αἰχμάλωτος (meaning a prisoner-of-war) is troublesome, and W. W. Tarn went to some length to explain it: "It is obvious from Memnon 12 (after Corupedium Ceraunus ὑπ' αὐτὸν (Seleukos) ἐτέλει, οὐχ ὡς αἰχμάλωτος κτλ) that Ceraunus *was* Seleucus' prisoner, that is, that he stayed with Lysimachus to the end; as is required, too, to explain his acceptance later by Lysimachus' old army. He was presumably Lysimachus' right hand after Agathocles' death, holding high command."[31] But this interpretation flies in the face of all other evidence. The only plausible way of explaining Ceraunus' position as αἰχμάλωτος, besides dismissing it as an error on the part of Memnon or his source, is to sup-

---

29 Nevertheless, Carney (2013) 53 writes: "He had no better place to go."
30 Πτολεμαῖος δὲ ὁ Κεραυνός, τῶν Λυσιμάχου πραγμάτων ὑπὸ Σελεύκῳ γεγενημένων, καὶ αὐτὸς ὑπ' αὐτὸν ἐτέλει, οὐχ ὡς αἰχμάλωτος παρορώμενος, ἀλλ' οἷα δὴ παῖς βασιλέως τιμῆς τε καὶ προνοίας ἀξιούμενος, οὐ μὴν ἀλλὰ καὶ ὑποσχέσεσι λαμπρυνόμενος, ἃς αὐτῷ Σέλευκος προύτεινεν, εἰ τελευτήσειεν ὁ γεινάμενος, ⟨εἰς⟩ τὴν Αἴγυπτον, πατρῴαν οὖσαν ἀρχήν, καταγαγεῖν.
31 Tarn (1913) 125 n. 26. οὐχ ὡς αἰχμάλωτος ("not as a prisoner-of-war").

pose that Ceraunus accompanied his sister Ptolemais to Miletos and then joined his new brother-in-law on his campaign in Asia Minor. When Demetrius surrendered to Seleucus, Ceraunus was among the captives but was treated well by his father's longtime friend. This is, however, speculative at best.

Finally, there is a problematic passage in Pausanias (1.10.4): ὡς γὰρ δὴ τότε ὁ Λυσίμαχος ἀνελεῖν τὸν Ἀγαθοκλέα Ἀρσινόῃ παρῆκε, Λυσάνδρα παρὰ Σέλευκον ἐκδιδράσκει τούς τε παῖδας ἅμα ἀγομένη καὶ τοὺς ἀδελφοὺς τοὺς αὑτῆς, οἳ περιελθὸν τοῦτο ἐς Πτολεμαῖον καταφεύγουσι. The final clause is corrupt. W. H. S. Jones, in the Loeb edition, translates: "Since Lysimachus, then, overlooked Arsinoe's murder of Agathocles, Lysandra fled to Seleucus, taking with her her children and her brothers, who were taking refuge with Ptolemy and finally adopted this course." Peter Levy's Penguin translation ((1979) 1.34) is less helpful: "When Lysimachos had permitted Arsinoe to destroy Agathokles, Lysandra ran away to Seleukos with her children and her brothers." Seleucus and Ptolemy Ceraunus were in the same place at this time, that is, at the former's court in Antiocheia. Lysandra sought support from Seleucus, who had the power to avenge the murder of her husband and protect her children; the brothers fled to join (and become fellow exiles) with their brother. As is often the case in Greek, the plural need not necessarily be taken literally, referring in this case to Meleager.[32] It is, in fact, unusual that Pausanias would say that the brother(s) had fled "to Ptolemy" (meaning Ceraunus) when he had not previously mentioned Ceraunus at all.

IV

The instabililty at Lysimachus' court had repercussions that were felt in Asia Minor. Docimus, who had earlier abandoned Antigonus in favor of Lysimachus now defected to Seleucus, together with Philetaerus. This was probably a reaction to the flight of Agathocles' friends, along with his wife and children, as well has his half-brother Alexander, to Seleucus.[33] With a plausible *casus belli* and the support of dynasts in Asia Minor, Seleucus crossed the Taurus and attacked Sardis before Lysimachus could mobilize his forces (Polyaen. 4.9.4); many scholars believe that it was at this time that Alexander son of Lysimachus

---

[32] Heckel (2021) no. 698.
[33] Paus. 1.10.4.

captured Cotiaeium by trickery (Polyaen. 6.12).[34] Lysimachus appears to have sailed directly to Ephesos, where he left Arsinoë behind and advanced with his army to Corupedium,[35] just to the west of Sardis; there he was felled by a javelin thrown by the Heracleot Malacon (Memnon *BNJ* 434 F 1 §5.7). Although no source speaks of Ceraunus' participation in the battle itself, it is virtually certain that he was in Seleucus' entourage, as was Lysimachus' younger son Alexander.[36] On the other hand, the assumptions that Ptolemy son of Lysimachus was in Ephesos with his mother or with Lysimachus at Corupedium are pure speculation.[37] Polyaenus (8.57) claims that, after the battle, the pro-Seleucid party (οἱ σελευκίζοντες) rose up in the city and Arsinoë fled alone (καθ' ἑτέραν θύραν ἐξῆλθε μόνη καὶ δραμοῦσα ἐπὶ τὰς ναῦς ἀπέπλευσε), which suggests that she had no children with her.[38] Perhaps he remained in Lysimachea as (nominal) regent in his father's absence. Given the instability at Lysimachus' court and the alarming series of defections, it would have been unwise not to leave a symbol of authority behind to oversee the kingdom. Indeed, the fact that the pro-Seleucid party in Ephesos intended to kill Arsinoë suggests that the avenging of Agathocles extended beyond the punishment of Lysimachus.[39] If Ptolemy had remained in Thrace, he must have taken up residence in Cassandrea after his mother's flight from Ephesos/Arsinoea; for there is no reference to an attempt to defend the Chersonese or Lysimachea itself some seven months later.

Once the affairs of Asia Minor had been ordered to his satisfaction, Seleucus crossed the Hellespont and landed not far from Lysimachea. He no doubt claim-

---

34 Heinen (1972) 29–30; Lund (1992) 202; Walbank (1988) 241. The identification of Alexander as son of Lysimachus and (incorrectly) Amastris, with no mention of his being in Seleucus' service, suggests that the event described probably belongs to the period before Alexander's flight from his father's court. He may have commanded a force that was detached from Agathocles' army. See Heckel (2021) s.vv. Alexander, Arsinoë nos. 52, 221.
35 The location of the battle is not entirely clear. App. *Syr.* 62.329 suggests it was in Hellespontine Phrygia (περὶ Φρυγίαν τὴν ἐφ' Ἑλλησπόντῳ), but a funerary inscription for a Bithynian named Menas (see Heinen (1972) 28 n. 89) mentions Korou Pedion in Lydia.
36 Cf. Grainger (1990) 183.
37 Ptolemy son of Lysimachus: Heckel 2020 no. 1013. In Ephesos: Tarn (1928) 98. With Lysimachus at Corupedium: Heinen (1972) 38 n. 120.
38 "She exited alone by another door, ran to the ships, and sailed away." Cf. Carney (2013) 47–48, who raises the question—to which there is no clear answer—of why Lysimachus took her to Asia Minor. It may be that Lysimachus believed that her presence might be influential.
39 That the intention was to kill Arsinoë is clear from the "fact" that Menecrates killed the servant girl who had disguised herself as her mistress (Polyaen. 8.57: Μενεκράτης, εἷς τῶν ἡγεμόνων, (…) κατεκέντησε τὴν θεράπαιναν οἰόμενος Ἀρσινόην φονεύειν). Admittedly, it is not certain that the order came from Seleucus himself.

ed Thrace by right of conquest,⁴⁰ but there is no good evidence that he was officially proclaimed King of Macedon; for this he would have needed the acquiescence of the assembled Macedonians, and these appear, at the time, to have supported Arsinoë and her son Ptolemy.⁴¹ The prospect of living out his life as ruler in the homeland he had not seen in over fifty years was difficult to resist. He left his Asian possessions to be administered by his son Antiochus,⁴² and it became clear to all that he had enhanced his own position in the guise of a benefactor. We hear nothing more about Lysandra, and it may be that she had not given Agathocles a male heir. Alexander too disappears from historical accounts, and we must assume that he was never a serious candidate for the throne but a faithful supporter of his half-brother. As far as Ptolemy Ceraunus was concerned, if Seleucus had any intention of restoring him to Egypt, that had clearly taken a back seat to the prospect of the Macedonian kingship. Lysimachus, Arsinoë, and Ptolemy Ceraunus have all received a bad press from the historical sources, but Seleucus' opportunism must have been regarded as betrayal.⁴³

A conspiracy was quickly formed (Memnon *BNJ* 434 F 1 §8.3: ἐπιβουλὴν γὰρ συστήσας) and Seleucus was murdered by Ceraunus (Just. 17.2.4: *a Ptolomeo ... per insidias circumventus occiditur*: "he was trapped and killed by Ptolemy"). We do not know who his accomplices were but there were clearly supporters both within the army and in Lysimachea.⁴⁴ Memnon (8.3) tells us that Ptolemy, after he had murdered Seleucus, rode to Lysimachea where he assumed the diadem and surrounded himself with a splendid bodyguard and then returned to

---

40 Polyb. 18.51.4: Σελεύκου δὲ πολεμήσαντος πρὸς αὐτὸν καὶ κρατήσαντος τῷ πολέμῳ πᾶσαν τὴν Λυσιμάχου βασιλείαν δορίκτητον γενέσθαι Σελεύκου. ("When Seleucus waged war against him and conquered him in the war, all Lysimachus' kingdom became Seleucus' by right of conquest.")
41 The subject was debated vigorously by Reuss (1907), (1909) and Lehmann-Haupt (1905), (1907), (1909) (discussed by Heinen (1972) 46–48); see Walbank (1988) 241–242, with n. 8.
42 Memnon *BNJ* 434, F 1 § 8.1: κἀκεῖ τοῦ βίου τὸ λεῖπον διανύσαι, γηραιὸς ἤδη ὤν, διανοούμενος, τὴν δὲ Ἀσίαν Ἀντιόχῳ παραθέσθαι τῷ παιδί.
43 The ancient sources are generally favorable in their treatment of Seleucus. See Plut. *Demetr.* 51.3–4, where Seleucus rejects Lysimachus' offer of money if he killed Demetrius. Cf. Cassander's offer of 200 talents to Glaucias if he surrendered Pyrrhus (Plut. *Pyrrh.* 3.5). His betrayal is, however, not unprecedented: according to Nepos, *Eum.* 5.1, he was one of those who murdered Perdiccas in Egypt.
44 Will (1984) 113 ignores the conspiracy, as if Ceraunus had given no forethought to consequences of his actions. Instead, "he ... assassinated his benefactor Seleucus with his own hand and fled to Lysimachea, where, posing as the avenger of the leader defeated at Corupedium, he managed to have himself acclaimed king of Macedon by the army." The sentence, as it is formulated, implies that the army was that of the Lysimacheans and not Seleucus' former forces, as Memnon *BNJ* 434 F 1 § 8.3 makes clear.

the army (διάδημα περιθέμενος μετὰ λαμπρᾶς δορυφορίας κατέβαινεν εἰς τὸ στράτευμα). There he was proclaimed king by Seleucus' erstwhile supporters. But clearly the assumption of the diadem in Lysimachea was accompanied by Ceraunus' recognition as king by what remained of the Lysimacheans in Thrace; when the Seleucid army declared for him, this was confirmation of the decision made in Lysimachea. Although the army was made up of many of Lysimachus' troops who surrendered at Corupedium, and probably also a fair number of mercenaries, it is implausible, as Heinen notes,[45] that Seleucus conducted a campaign against Macedonia without an army that was loyal to him.[46] Memnon says that the leaderless army had little choice: δεχομένων αὐτὸν ὑπὸ τῆς ἀνάγκης καὶ βασιλέα καλούντων. In Lysimachus' kingdom, Ceraunus was received favorably because of his lineage and because he was the old king's avenger (Just. 17.2.6). Whatever grievances Lysimachus' subjects had concerning the fate of Agathocles, it was clear that they preferred to maintain the bond that the old king had forged with the house of Ptolemy to annexation by a foreign ruler.[47] Nevertheless, it is difficult to know whether Ceraunus had initially planned to act in the interests of Lysandra and her supporters. The fact that Lysandra disappears from the historical record and that Ceraunus quickly pursued a marriage with his half-sister Arsinoë, posing as the protector of her sons, suggests once again that Lysandra had no son on whose behalf he could have assumed the regency.[48]

V

His position was strengthened by a victory over Antigonus Gonatas, who brought his forces north on the news of Seleucus' death. Many of Gonatas' troops were placed on transports, but Ceraunus attacked them with Lysimachus' fleet (anoth-

---

45 Heinen (1972) 61–63.
46 Mercenaries: Bouché-Leclercq (1903) 1.149. Paus. 1.16.2 says the army was made up of Greeks and barbarians: στρατιὰ μὲν καὶ Ἑλλήνων καὶ βαρβάρων ἦν παρὰ Σελεύκῳ. Ex-Lysimachean forces: Grainger (1990) 191. See also Ogden (2017) 250.
47 Welles (1970) 70 notes that the Macedonians did not want a king who would "plan to use Macedonia merely as a base of operations for further conquests." In effect, Seleucus would have ruled Macedonia as an appendage of his Asian kingdom.
48 *Contra* Tarn (1913) 129: "Ptolemy saw that with Seleucus' decision to occupy Macedonia his chance of getting anything out of the wreck of Lysimachos' fortunes, whether on his own account *or as regent for Lysandra's son, the rightful heir*, was at an end" (emphasis added). The sources never speak of a son of Agathocles. On Lysandra, Tarn (1913) 130 comments: "How Keraunos dealt with Lysandra and her children we do not know, but perhaps may guess...."

er indication of the loyalty of the troops), which included a contingent of Heracleot ships (Memnon *BNJ* 424 F 1 § 8.4–6). The victory allowed Ceraunus to move into Macedonia, where his authority was being challenged by Arsinoë's son (Memnon 8.6: Πτολεμαῖος δὲ ἐπὶ Μακεδονίαν διέβη, καὶ βεβαίως ἔσχε τὴν ἀρχήν).[49] The last stage of Ceraunus' rise to power involved an attempted reconciliation with Philadelphus. Facing opposition from Antiochus, whose father he had murdered, and Antigonus Gonatas, who claimed the kingdom of Macedon as his patrimony, and possibly even Pyrrhus, Ceraunus offered to marry Arsinoë, giving her the title of queen (*basilissa*) and adopting her sons; at the same time, he wrote to his half-brother promising to relinquish all claims to the Egyptian throne. Justin (17.2.9–10) recounts Ceraunus' approach to his half-brother but does not say how Philadelphus reacted. If he took a "wait and see" attitude, this was, at least, a partial victory for Ceraunus.[50] How this shift in policy could have been acceptable to his fellow-conspirators, who had placed their faith in Ceraunus and were about to see their own ambitions thwarted a second time, is baffling. One can only speculate.

By the time Seleucid forces landed on the Gallipoli peninsula, Arsinoë and her sons had taken refuge in the Macedonian heartland. When Arsinoë fled from Ephesos, she appears to have gone directly to Cassandrea. Her son Ptolemy, after the defeat and death of his father, may have found it necessary to abandon Thrace, where the Agathocles party was emboldened by the events at Corupedium. Justin (17.2.6–8) reports that Ceraunus hoped to gain control over Lysimachus' sons by marrying their mother: *ut cum in locum patris eorum successisset, nihil illi moliri vel verecundia matris vel appellatione patris auderent.*[51] The story is reiterated in Book 24: Ceraunus agreed to swear an oath "that it was in total sincerity that he sought the hand of his sister, that he would name her as his queen, that he would not insult her by taking another wife or recognizing children other than hers as his sons" (Just. 24.2.9). The eldest son, Ptolemy, warned his mother

---

[49] Just. 24.1.8: *nam Ptolomeus pulso Antigono cum regnum totius Macedoniae occupasset, pacem cum Antiocho facit.* ("for Ptolemy, putting Antigonus to flight, seized control of all Macedonia. Ptolemy then made peace with Antiochus"). Nevertheless Macedonia was not securely in his power, and many regarded Ceraunus has having usurped the kingdom of Arsinoë's sons (Just. 24.1.2: *sororis filios, quorum regnum occupaverat*).

[50] Bouché-Leclercq (1903) 153 assumes that Philadelphus was more interested in gaining control of Koile-Syria. Certainly, he was not prepared to risk the stability of his own kingdom for the sake of his sister's claims. That was the kind of thing that could serve as a pretext for a desired action but not as a motive for an unfeasible one.

[51] Just. 17.2.8: "[The reasoning behind this was] that, once he had taken their father's place, the boys would not venture to work against him, either out of respect for their mother or because he was, in name at least, their father."

that Ceraunus had treacherous motives, but to no avail. The marriage was celebrated in Cassandrea and soon afterwards, when Ceraunus had gained control of the city, the two younger boys—the eldest did not participate in the ceremony—were killed and Arsinoë went into exile on Samothrace (Just. 24.3.1–9).

We must be careful not to confuse outcome with intent. It is simplistic to assume that Ceraunus approached Arsinoë with the aim of gaining control of Cassandrea—indeed, all of Macedonia—and murdering his stepsons. That is not say that they might not have been eliminated in due course, but at the time Ceraunus was making what appears to be the most politically astute move.[52] Furthermore, Justin's sensational account, which saw Arsinoë's hopes fulfilled and then dashed on the very same day, the day of the wedding, probably conflates a series of events that occurred over a longer period in order to highlight the perfidy and wickedness of Ceraunus. In all likelihood, it was the fact that Ptolemy son of Lysimachus refused to play a part in his new stepfather's scheme but rather continued to foment rebellion that forced Ceraunus' hand.[53] C. Bradford Welles presents a plausible account of events; if only it were supported by the ancient sources:

> Ptolemy the Thunderbolt established his mother in Cassandreia under the protection of a certain Apollodorus as garrison commander and moved on to Pella with Arsinoe and her sons when he met with his first setback. The eldest of these sons, also named Ptolemy, escaped to Monunius of the Illyrian Dardanians and presently returned with an army to seize the kingdom of his father Lysimachus. The attack was repulsed, but the Thunderbolt realized the danger. He put to death the other two boys and consequently was abandoned by Arsinoe, who took refuge in Samothrace.... For the Thunderbolt ... this probably unavoidable act of eliminating rivals has given him in the tradition a chracter of wanton cruelty. It can hardly have hurt the scruples of the Macedonians at the time, for they were well used to dynastic murders.[54]

It is noteworthy that we have no evidence that Lysimachus, after Agathocles' death, designated Arsinoë's son as the new heir. The backlash that followed the crown prince's murder, both at court and in Asia Minor, may have prevented

---

[52] But see Carney (2013) 14: "Ceraunus probably planned the murders from the start, just as he had probably planned the elimination of Seleucus. This was a trick marriage all along."
[53] Trogus, *Prol.* 24: *bellum quod Ptolemaeus Ceraunus in Macedonia cum Monunio Illyrio et Ptolemaeo Lysimachi filio habuit, utque Arsinoen sororem suam imperio Macedonicarum urbium exuit.* ("the war by Ptolemy Ceraunus against Monunius the Illyrian and Ptolemy, son of Lysimachus, and how Ptolemy stripped his sister Arsinoe of her rule over the cities of Macdonia.") If this summary preserves the order of events, Ceraunus was reacting to a serious threat from Lysimachus' son.
[54] Welles (1970) 70–71.

him from making such a move. Ptolemy was barely sixteen when his mother married Arsinoë and neither was particularly dear to the Macedonian people. Justin's claim that Ceraunus was "eager to exploit the memory of his father, Ptolemy the Great, amongst the people" (17.2.6) is unconvincing. The very fact that Ceraunus was able to neutralize the power of Arsinoë's (and the young Ptolemy's) faction with relative ease and force the queen into exile suggests that the Macedonians had no strong attachment to Berenice's daughter. By contrast, Ceraunus boasted a closer degree of kinship to Cassander and his line;[55] he was also a man, mature and recently tested in battle, and thus a more stable choice to manage the kingdom's affairs, whether as regent or king in his own right. Sabine Müller rightly notes that the marriage to Arsinoë served another important purpose: it took her "off the market" and prevented rivals from exploiting her status for their own political gain ("Eine zusätzliche Überlegung wird gewesen sein, dass er Arsinoë als heiratspolitischen Machtfaktor neutralisierte, indem er möglichen Konkurrenten um ihre Hand zuvorkam").[56] The continued opposition of Ptolemy son of Lysimachus was counterproductive. When Ceraunus took the final steps to secure his power neither the Macedonians nor the Thracians turned away from him. It was only the fact that he foolishly waged war on the Gauls that led to his downfall and death. But again it is doubtful that his contemporaries, or at least the majority of them, regarded it as just punishment for his "crimes," as the thoroughly negative narrative of Justin implies (*sed nec Ptolomeo inulta scelera fuerunt; quippe diis inmortalibus tot periuria et tam cruenta parricidia vindicantibus brevi post a Gallis spoliatus regno captusque vitam ferro, ut meruerat, amisit*).[57] His reign as King of the Macedonians lasted from September 281 until about February 279.

---

[55] His claims were surely strengthened by settling his mother Eurydice, Cassander's sister, in Cassandrea (Polyaen. 6.7.2).

[56] Müller (2009) 72. "One additional consideration will have been that he neutralized Arsinoë as potent factor in the realm of political marriage, inasmuch as he anticipated possible rivals for her hand."

[57] Just. 24.3.10: "But Ptolemy's crimes did not go unpunished. A short time afterwards, the immortal gods exacted vengeance for all his treacherous actions and his bloody murders–he was stripped of his throne by the Gauls and taken prisoner, to perish by the sword, as he deserved.") For Ceraunus' encounter with the Gauls (which need not be discussed in detail here) see Just. 24.3.10 – 5.11, esp. 5.1– 6; Diod. 22.3; Plut. *Pyrrh.* 22.2.

VI

Any attempt to make sense of Ceraunus' brief rise to power is methodologically perilous: one is forced to view events through the wrong end of the telescope, and the hostile judgments of the few surviving ancient sources have been reinforced by modern accounts that accept the ancient evidence uncritically. Ceraunus is branded as "a man in whom no trace can be discovered of humanity or gratitude,"[58] who "seems to have had the gift of short-term plausibility, the attribute of the confidence trickster at all times and places."[59] Indeed, so villainous was he that the ancients could not even agree on which act it was that earned him the epithet Ceraunus. But, although his story has clearly been misrepresented by sensational writers, such as Duris and Phylarchus, and Heracleot historians whose bias is unmistakable, there is next to nothing in the sources that is explicitly favorable.[60] Hence, we can do little more than resort to what is probable, plausible, or even possible. And, even if none of this amounts to proof, it is equally true that repeated or deeply ingrained falsehoods cannot be accepted for want of evidence to the contrary.

The following picture emerges. Ceraunus appears to have left Alexandria in the company of his mother Eurydice and his sister Ptolemais when they sailed to Miletos to celebrate the latter's marriage to Demetrius Poliorcetes. It is possible, however, that he went directly to Antioch to ask Seleucus for aid in recovering what he considered his rightful throne. This occurred in the spring of 285. If Ceraunus went first to Miletos, he may then have gone directly from there to Antioch or, if there is any truth to Memnon's claim that he was an αἰχμάλωτος (prisoner-of-war), he may have accompanied Demetrius on his expedition into Asia Minor only to be captured when the Besieger was forced to surrender to Seleucid forces. The same passage of Memnon, describing events out of chronological context, suggests that Ptolemy (not yet disparaged as Ceraunus) was at the Seleucid court before his father's death. Seleucus, far from treating him as a pris-

---

[58] Bevan (1902) 72–73.
[59] Grainger (1990) 193.
[60] For the ancient sources see Longega (1968) 44–67. For Duris and Phylarchus, Müller (2009) 83. Duris is regularly adduced as a source of sensational elements; see in general Kebric (1977). On Phylarchus, see Bengtson (1975) 116: "ein Stück typisch hellenistischer Geschichtsschreibung nach der Art des Phylarchos, der sich bekanntlich in der Schilderung von Schrekkensszenen nicht genugtun konnte." ("a piece typical of Hellenistic historiography in the style of Phylarchus, who, as is well known, could not get enough in his depiction of shocking scenes.") This may be so but, on the basis of the surviving fragments, we have no indication of the substance or tone of his account of Ceraunus.

oner, welcomed him as the unfortunate son of an old friend: for Ptolemy Soter had supported Seleucus when he was driven from Babylon by Antigonus in 315 and helped him recover his satrapy in 312. It should be noted that, during this period, he may have met his benefactor's son, at that time a mere boy, at the court in Alexandria.[61]

In the meantime, Arsinoë had asserted herself at the court in Lysimachea, persuading her husband that Agathocles was plotting against him and bringing about his death at the hands of her own son Ptolemy. This young man was confused by the sources with his namesake, the later Ceraunus, and this gave rise to the myth that he had gone to Lysimachea and there, paradoxically, conspired against his brother-in-law (the man who might have been able to help him recover his kingdom) with Arsinoë, the full sister of the very man (Philadelphus) who had supplanted him as Soter's heir. If he had worked in concert with Arsinoë, what had he hoped to gain? And what need was there for him to flee to Lysimachus' enemy Seleucus? Indeed, we are told that it was precisely because Lysimachus took no action against the perpetrators of Agathocles' murder that Lysandra fled (along with her children and followers) to the safety of Seleucus' court (Paus. 1.10.4: ὡς γὰρ δὴ τότε ὁ Λυσίμαχος ἀνελεῖν τὸν Ἀγαθοκλέα Ἀρσινόῃ παρῆκε, Λυσάνδρα παρὰ Σέλευκον ἐκδιδράσκει...). Why she would trust her brother after his alleged role in her husband's murder is not explained. Nor does it make sense that Seleucus would, on the one hand, pose has Agathocles' avenger and, on the other, harbor his murderer in his household. Finally, what was the reason for Arsinoë's later distrust of Ceraunus, if he had been the agent through whom she had enhanced her own power?

Encouraged by Seleucus' favorable treatment of Ceraunus, Lysandra and her followers, as well as Alexander son of Lysimachus, sought refuge with him after Agathocles' death. But Seleucus, victorious at Corupedium and the realizing that Macedonia was within his grasp, reconsidered his own position and abandoned his support of both Lysandra and Ceraunus. For this reason, the pro-Agathocles party conspired with Ceraunus to murder the man they viewed as a usurper. It is undeniable that there was a certain madness to Ceraunus' method, but for the most part he was able to seize political advantage when it presented itself and his decisive opportunism should not be dismissed as irrationality. Since there was still a faction that supported Arsinoë's son Ptolemy, the Agathocles party regarded Ceraunus as their protector. Lysandra, it appears, had no male offspring and Alexander, the son of an Odrysian wife, was not considered a serious can-

---

[61] Demetrius of Phaleron was later supposed to have incurred the wrath of Philadelphus by recommending to Soter that he leave his kingdom to Ceraunus (Diog. Laert. 5.78).

didate.⁶² Lysimachus' daughter Eurydice, who had once been married to Antipater son of Cassander and whom her father had imprisoned in 287, must have died (possibly even of natural causes). She was a sister of Agathocles and might have been the perfect royal wife for Ceraunus.⁶³ Finally, when it became clear that a portion (at least) of Macedonia was holding out against the new king, proclaimed in Lysimachea, Ceraunus devised the plan to secure his position by marrying Arsinoë and placing her children under his control. How the pro-Agathocles party reacted to this move, we do not know. But, once securely on the throne, Ceraunus sensed that there was little threat from a faction that had not been able to produce a viable alternative. Arsinoë, for her part, was transformed by the sources from the shrew who plotted Agathocles' death into the victim of Ceraunus' cold-blooded ambition. This distorted picture is reinforced by further sensationalism and factual error in modern scholarship. Typically, E. R. Bevan writes:⁶⁴ "She [sc. Arsinoë] was *little more than a girl* [emphasis added], but she was also, as we have seen, a Macedonian princess, with not a little of the tigress. Yet Ceraunus could outmatch her in cunning and ferocity."⁶⁵

As it turned out, Ceraunus was the first and most dynamic of a series of ephemeral kings. But, although he had approached his most difficult political dealings with cold calculation, he literally lost his head when he unwisely chose war over negotiation with the Gauls. Deprived of his birthright by his brother Philadelphus, apparently through the machinations of the latter's moth-

---

62 Although Polyaenus (6.12) makes him the son of Amastris, Pausanias (1.10.4) claims that his mother was an Odrysian. I do not see on what basis Droysen (1836) 635 and Niese (1893) I 402 conclude that this Odrysian woman was also the mother of Agathocles. Beloch (1927) IV² 2.130: "Agathokles war also ohne Zweifel von Nikaea geboren." A marriage of Ceraunus and Lysandra seems to have been out of the question. Although Arsinoë married her full brother, Philadelphus, it appears that such a practice was not acceptable in Macedonia.
63 For Eurydice see Heckel (2021) no. 455; Carney (2000) 159–160. Imprisoned by her father: Just. 16.2.4. It is hard to imagine that she could have been alive in 281 and not have been a factor. As the widow of Antipater (Heckel (2021) no. 128; he was killed by his father-in-law in 287), she would have offered a new husband a legitimate claim to the Macedonian throne. But the same was true of Lysandra, the widow of Alexnder V, who will not have been pleased to see Eurydice agitating on her husband's behalf at the court in Lysimachea. In short, it would have been to the benefit of both Agathocles and Lysimachus himself to remove her from contention. Ceraunus, now approaching forty, must have had at least one wife (legitimate or otherwise). Justin, two separate occasions, mentions that he offered a daughter in marriage to Pyrrhus (17.2.15; 24.1.8). The objections of Hammond (1988) are not convincing.
64 Bevan (1927) 57.
65 Arsinoë was in her mid-to-late thirties when she married Ceraunus. Interestingly, Justin (24.4.11) dismisses Ceraunus (who was now almost forty) as "a callow youth" (*inmaturi iuvenis*) who foolishly went to war with the Gauls.

er, Berenice, and the acquiescence of Soter, he sought reinstatement with the help of Seleucus. In the process, he aborted the last serious attempt to unify Alexander's Asian and Macedonian realms, destroying the kingdom of Thrace and seriously weakening Macedonia as well. Though he was not solely responsible for the chaos, his name will be forever associated with the death knells of Alexander's empire. In his unbridled quest for personal power, he drove the final nails in its coffin. As Heinen notes: "nachdem er einmal von der Herrschaft in Ägypten verdrängt worden war, sah sich Keraunos gezwungen, überall mit störender Hand einzugreifen, wenn er sich einen Thron erobern wollte."[66]

Bibliography

Ager (2018): Sheila Ager, "Building a Dynasty: the Families of Ptolemy I Soter", in: Tim Howe (ed.), *Ptolemy I Soter. A Self-Made Man*, Philadelphia, 36–59.
Beloch (1927): Karl Julius Beloch, *Griechische Geschichte*, Berlin and Leipzig.
Bengtson (1975): H. Bengtson, *Herrschergestalten des Hellenismus*. Munich.
Bevan (1902): Edwyn Robert Bevan, *The House of Seleucus*, Vol. 1, London.
Bevan (1927): Edwyn Robert Bevan, *A History of Egypt under the Ptolemaic Dynasty*, London.
Bouché-Leclercq (1903): Auguste Bouché-Leclercq, *Histoire des Lagides*, Vol. 1, Paris.
Carney (2000): Elizabeth D. Carney, *Women and Monarchy in Macedonia*, Norman.
Carney (2013): Elizabeth D. Carney, *Arsinoë of Egypt and Macedon. A Royal Life*, Oxford.
Cohen (1973): Getzel M. Cohen, "The Marriage of Lysimachus and Nicaea", in: *Historia* 22, 354–356.
Collins (1997): Nina L. Collins, "The Various Fathers of Ptolemy I", in: *Mnemosyne* 50, 436–476.
Droysen (1836): Johann Gustav Droysen, *Geschichte der Nachfolger Alexanders*, Hamburg.
Ellis (1994): Walter M. Ellis, *Ptolemy of Egypt*, London.
Grainger (1990): J. D. Grainger, *Seleukos Nikator. Constructing a Hellenistic Kingdom*, London.
Grainger (2019): J. D. Grainger, *Antipater's Dynasty. Alexander the Great's Regent and his Successors*. Barnsley and Philadelphia.
Gow, A. F. S. (1950). *Theocritus*. Edited with a translation and commentary. 2 Volumes. Cambridge.
Hammond (1988): N. G. L. Hammond, "Which Ptolemy gave Troops and Stood as the Protector of Pyrrhus' Kingdom?" *Historia* 37: 405–413.
Heckel (1985): Waldemar Heckel, "The 'Boyhood Friends' of Alexander the Great", in: *Emerita* 53: 285–289.
Heckel (1986): Waldemar Heckel, "Factions and Macedonian Politics in the Reign of Alexander the Great", in: *AM* 4, 293–305.

---

[66] Heinen (1972) 93: "after he had finally been ousted from the rule of Egypt, Ceraunus felt compelled to insert himself everywhere as a disruptive force, if he hoped to win a throne for himself."

Heckel (1989): Waldemar Heckel, "The Granddaughters of Iolaus", in: *Classicum* 15, 32–39.
Heckel (2002): Waldemar Heckel, "The Politics of Distrust: Alexander and his Successors", in: D. Ogden (ed.), *The Hellenistic World: New Perspectives*. London: 83–95.
Heckel (2016): Waldemar Heckel, *Alexander's Marshals. A Study of the Makedonian Aristocracy and the Politics of Military Command*, London.
Heckel (2021): Waldemar Heckel, *Who's Who in the Age of Alexander and his Successors. From Chaironeia to Ipsos (338–301 BC)*, London.
Heinen (1972): Heinz Heinen, *Untersuchungen zur hellenistischen Geschichte des 3. Jahrhunderts v. Chr.* Historia Einzelschriften, Heft 20, Wiesbaden.
Kebric (1977): R. B. Kebric, *In the Shadow of Macedon. Duris of Samos*, Historia Einzelschriften 29, Wiesbaden.
Landucci (1992): Franca Landucci Gattinoni, *Lisimaco di Tracia*, Milan.
Landucci (2003): Franca Landucci Gattinoni, *L'ate del potere. Vita e opere di Cassandro di Macedonia*. Historia Einzelschriften 171. Stuttgart.
Lehmann-Haupt (1905): Carl Friedrich Lehmann-Haupt, "Hellenistische Forschungen: 2. Seleukos, König der Makedonen", in: *Klio* 5, 244–254.
Lehmann-Haupt (1907): Carl Friedrich Lehmann-Haupt, "Seleukos Nikators makedonisches Königtum", in: *Klio* 7, 449–453.
Lehmann-Haupt 1909: Carl Friedrich Lehmann-Haupt, "Nochmals Seleukos Nikators makedonisches Königtum", in: *Klio* 9, 248–251.
Longega (1968): Gabriella Longega, *Arsinoe II*, Rome.
Lund (1992): Helen S. Lund, *Lysimachus. A Study in Early Hellenistic Kingship*, London.
Kahn and Tammuz (2008): D. Kahn and O. Tammuz, "Egypt is difficult to enter: Invading Egypt—A Game Plan (seventh–fourth centuries BCE)", *JSSEA* 35: 37–66.
Müller (2009): Sabine Müller, *Das hellenistische Königspaar in der medialen Repräsentation*, Berlin.
Müller (2012): Sabine Müller, "Ptolemaios und die Erinnerung an Hephaistion", in: *Anabasis* 3, 75–91.
Niese (1893): Jürgen Anton Benedikt Niese, *Geschichte der griechischen und makedonischen Staaten seit der Schlacht bei Chaeronea*, Vol. 1, Gotha.
Ogden (1999): Daniel Ogden, *Polygamy, Prostitutes and Death. The Hellenistic Dynasties*, London.
Ogden (2017): Daniel Ogden, *The Legend of Seleucus. Kingship, Narrative and Mythmaking in the Ancient World*, Cambridge.
Reuss (1907): Friedrich Reuss, "Hellenistische Beiträge: 2. Seleukos und Ptolemaios Keraunos", in: *RhM* 62, 595–600.
Reuss (1909): Friedrich Reuss, "Das makedonische Königtum des Seleukos Nikator", in: *Klio* 9, 76–79.
Seibert (1967): Jakob Seibert, *Historische Beiträge zu den dynastischen Verbindungen in hellenistischer Zeit*, Wiesbaden.
Tarn (1913): William Woodthorpe Tarn, *Antigonos Gonatas*, Oxford.
Tarn (1928): William Woodthorpe Tarn, "Macedonia and Greece", *CAH* VII: 197–223.
Walbank (1988): Frank William Walbank and Nicholas G. L. Hammond, *A History of Macedonia*, Vol. 3, Oxford.
Welles (1970): C. Bradford Welles, *Alexander and the Hellenistic World*, Toronto.

Wheatley and Dunn (2020): Pat Wheatley and Charlotte Dunn, *Demetrius the Besieger,* Oxford.
Will (1984): Éduard Will, "The Succession to Alexander", *CAH* VII.1²: 23–61.
Worthington (2016): Ian Worthington, *Ptolemy I. King and Pharaoh of Egypt,* Oxford.
Yardley (1994). J.C. Yardley tr., *Justin. Epitome of the* Philippic History *of Pompeius Trogus.* With introduction and explanatory notes by R. Develin. Atlanta.

II The Courts of Philip and Alexander in the Eyes of Contemporary Greeks

Jeremy Trevett
Diplomatic Activity at the Court of Philip II

Introduction

The reception of foreign envoys was an important function of the court of Philip II, during whose reign Macedonia acquired a dominant position in the Aegean world and, in consequence, had for the first time frequent and extensive diplomatic dealings, bilateral and multilateral, with numerous other states, Greek and non-Greek.[1] The kingdom of Macedonia changed rapidly under Philip, and the development of his court as the primary *locus* of diplomatic interaction with the Greek city-states and others was part of this process. It is also an aspect of Philip's court about which we are particularly well informed through the contemporary evidence of a number of lawcourt speeches delivered by two rival Athenian politicians, Demosthenes and Aeschines, who both served as envoys to the Macedonian court in 346 BC.

Although Philip's reign marks a clear watershed, earlier Macedonian kings had certainly engaged in diplomacy with, and received ambassadorial visits from, various states and kingdoms, both Greek and non-Greek. There were, for example, extensive dealings between Macedonia and Athens in the fifth and earlier fourth centuries, including the making of several alliances as well as the establishment of ties of friendship between the king and individual leading Athenians.[2] But our knowledge of the reception of envoys at court before the mid-fourth century is limited to Herodotus' lurid and, as it stands, unbelievable account of the murder of Persian ambassadors at the court of Amyntas I in the late 6th century (5.17–21).[3] Of the very many diplomatic visits that must have

---

1 On the reception of ambassadors as an important function of the Hellenistic court see Strootman (2014) 195–198.
2 For example: a fragmentary late-5th-cent. inscription records an alliance between Athens and Perdiccas (*IG* i^3 89); Andocides describes himself as an ancestral guest-friend (*xenos*) of Archelaus (Andoc. 2.11); an alliance was made between Athens and Amyntas III in 370s (*IG* ii^2 102 = Tod 129); the Athenian general Timotheus received a gift of timber from Amyntas ([Dem.] 49.26); the Athenian general Iphicrates was adopted by Amyntas and took care of his orphaned children (Aeschin. 2.26–29; Theopomp. *BNJ* 115 F 289).
3 This story, involving young Macedonian men of the court disguising themselves as women in order to catch the lecherous Persian ambassadors off guard, is clearly not credible as an account of what happened, although it is of considerable interest in the context of later Macedonian at-

been made to the Macedonian court during Philip's reign, the vast majority are not directly attested in the sources. Numerous Greek cities are known to have had dealings with him, all of which will have involved the despatch of envoys.[4] On occasion, multiple Greek embassies were in Macedonia at the same time.[5] There were also diplomatic visits from non-Greeks. For example, Plutarch gives an account, possibly apocryphal, of the courtesy with which Philip's son Alexander received Persian envoys during his father's absence on campaign (*Alex.* 5.1). To these we can add the reception of envoys from the various neighbouring kingdoms with which Philip had dealings throughout his reign, as well as the series of royal weddings which Philip used to cement diplomatic settlements.[6]

But our evidence skews heavily towards Greece in general and Athens in particular. Such knowledge as we have about embassies from other places comes mostly from Athenian sources, and it is about the experience of Athenian envoys at the Macedonian court that we are much the best informed. Of fundamental importance are the two opposing speeches delivered in 343 by rival Athenian politicians, Demosthenes and Aeschines, in the course of the former's prosecution of the latter for misconduct as an envoy to Philip in 346 (Dem. 19 and Aeschin. 2).[7] These two long texts deal with a pair of Athenian embassies to Philip. Of these, the first was sent to negotiate the terms of a peace (the peace of Philocrates) to bring an end to the state of war between Philip and Athens, the second to administer to Philip the oaths that would ratify the peace. These events are revisited in the two opposing speeches from Aeschines' prosecution of Demosthenes' supporter Ctesiphon in 330 (Aeschin. 3 and Dem. 18), but the specificity and detail of the earlier speeches are largely absent. The two speeches of 343 together constitute the single most substantial piece of literary evidence for any aspect of Philip's court. They are concerned with the conduct of diplomatic visits to Macedonia, were written by participants, and were composed and delivered within three years of the events they describe. They must, however, be treated

---

tempts to conceal their subjection to the Persians. See most recently Harrison (2019), suggesting that it represents a distorted recounting of a genuine diplomatic marriage.

4 For Philip's diplomatic dealings with the Greeks see Ryder (1994).

5 See e.g. Aeschin. 2.108, referring to the occasion of the second Athenian embassy of 346: "when the embassies came together at Pella."

6 On Philip's multiple marriages see Satyrus fr. 21 quoted at Ath. 13.557b–e, with Tronson (1984). The one wedding about which we hear in any detail is that of his daughter Cleopatra to Alexander of Epirus in 336, since this was the occasion of his own death: see Diod. 16.91.4–93.2. On royal weddings as important events at Hellenistic courts see Strootman (2014) 198–199.

7 For detailed commentaries see Paulsen (1999) (both speeches) and MacDowell (2000) (Demosthenes' speech).

with considerable caution as sources. Lawcourt speeches were written to achieve conviction or acquittal rather than to provide a truthful or comprehensive record of events. Each speaker aimed to convince the jurors that he had acted correctly and that his opponent had behaved disreputably or illegally. For most matters we have only one man's account; where they both discuss the same occasion, there is often disagreement about what happened.[8] Whilst there were limits to the amount of outright invention that would have been possible, everything was presented in such a way as to support the speaker's case, and it is impossible to assume that either man is ever telling the whole truth. Moreover, the actual conduct of the embassies takes up only part of the speeches, and the time spent at Philip's court only a relatively small part of that. Neither speech contains a continuous narrative (Aeschin. 2.22–38 on the first embassy comes closest) and the two men are largely silent about many aspects of their visits to the Macedonian court because they are not relevant to their argument. In addition, by 343 the peace was unpopular at Athens, and each man is keen to shift the blame for it onto the other. Finally, it would be wrong to suppose that either man's depiction of Philip and his court is neutral, since each portrays him in a way that was consistent with his broader oratorical purpose.[9]

The process by which the Peace of Philocrates was negotiated is fraught with a number of historical problems, not least because of the disagreements between Aeschines and Demosthenes about what happened when.[10] Many of these are not directly relevant to our subject. It is, however, important to keep in mind the broad context of the Athenian embassies of 346, since this helps illuminate the reception that they received. After the fall of Olynthus in 348, Philip controlled northern Greece and held the upper hand over Athens. There was scant support elsewhere in Greece for joining Athens in continued military opposition, and in addition Philip held as prisoners a number of Athenian soldiers who had been captured at Olynthus (Aeschin. 2.15). He was keen to consolidate his military successes by making peace from a position of strength and had an interest in securing Athenian, and more broadly Greek, loyalty and support.[11] Ap-

---

8 See Adcock and Mosley (1975) 127: "Tantalizingly the speeches, though concerned with similar events, coincide in almost no detail."
9 On the differing portrayal of Philip in the speeches of Demosthenes and Aeschines see Guth (2011), esp. 185–186.
10 On the Peace of Philocrates see (e.g.) Hammond and Griffith (1979) 329–347; Harris (1995) 50–106.
11 His desire to end hostility with Athens was clearly sincere, whether or not he was already planning a campaign against the Persian Empire, which would require (1) a state of peace in

preciation of this context is important because, both on this occasion and more generally when he received envoys at court, Philip wished not just to negotiate, but also to present himself in a particular way that was consonant with his broader political aims *at the time*. An important corollary is that diplomatic interactions at the Macedonian court will have taken very different forms depending on where the envoys came from, at what point in his reign the visit took place, and its circumstances and purpose. In other words, we cannot easily generalize about diplomacy at the court of Philip from Athens' embassies of 346.

Meeting Philip

Aeschines offers a vivid account of the meeting of the members of the first embassy with Philip and takes malicious pleasure in recounting Demosthenes' embarrassment at it (2.22–38). After talking about the selection of the ten Athenian envoys and their journey north (2.18–21), he proceeds to relate how their audience with Philip unfolded. Although the venue for the audience is nowhere stated, it is a reasonable presumption that it was the royal palace at Pella. What the palace was like at this point of Philip's reign is unclear. Earlier Macedonian palaces had, it seems, been modest structures resembling large fortified farmhouses, and Philip was certainly responsible for the construction of spectacularly large and impressive new palaces at Pella and at Aegae, with multiple reception rooms, extensive dining facilities, and nearby or attached theatre.[12] If the new palace at Pella was in use by 346, which is by no means certain, and if it was comparable in scale and design to that at Aegae, with its great antechamber or waiting room fitted with stone benches, it would indeed have been an intimidating place, especially for those among the envoys who had never previously visited Macedonia.[13] The ten Athenians were, Aeschines says, called in to the presence of the king (2.22). Each of them, as they had arranged beforehand, spoke in order of age from oldest to youngest. Aeschines does not say who besides Philip was present on the Macedonian side, but it is likely that his senior advisers were in attendance, as well as guards. He starts by summarizing his own speech, which dealt with relations between Athens and Macedonia earlier in the

---

Greece; (2) some measure of Athenian naval support; (3) from the point of propaganda, a situation which enabled him to present himself as a champion of Greece.

[12] The development of the Argead royal palaces is discussed in brief by Strootman (2014) 60–65.

[13] On the palace at Aegae see Kottaridi (2011a) esp. 301–304 for its date, 317–318 for the waiting room.

fourth century and with Athens' claim to the city of Amphipolis, at considerable length (2.25–33).¹⁴ After the other nine envoys had spoken, Demosthenes, who was the youngest, rose to speak. In his nervousness, however, he dried up and was unable to deliver the speech that he had prepared. Philip encouraged him to relax and try again, but he broke down a second time (2.35).¹⁵ An awkward silence followed—this was to have been the final speech—and a herald instructed the envoys to withdraw (2.36). They then spent time in a waiting room, bickering with each other, until Philip's servants summoned them back in (2.37). Philip had been considering what he had heard and presumably discussing it with his advisers. The envoys re-entered and sat down, whereupon Philip responded in person to their individual speeches (2.38). It was a display of argumentative virtuosity, one man replying to ten. The content of Philip's remarks is not mentioned, but Aeschines on the journey home said to his fellow envoys that he had shown excellent memory in his replies to what was said (2.42), and later spoke to the Athenian assembly about Philip's retentive memory and skill at speaking (2.48). His Greek, moreover, was excellent: Demosthenes later claimed that Aeschines had described Philip as "the most Greek of men, a very formidable speaker" (Ἑλληνικώτατον ἄνθρωπον, δεινότατον λέγειν) (19.308).¹⁶ Demosthenes himself, according to Aeschines, said that Philip was the most formidable (the same word) man under the sun (2.41).¹⁷ Even before the envoys met Philip one of them, Cimon, had feared that his presentation of his case would overwhelm them (2.21). Demosthenes does not offer his own account of this episode, perhaps an implicit admission that his speech was not a success.¹⁸ Philip emerg-

---

14 This is not the only occasion on which Aeschines spoke at length to Philip: Demosthenes (19.20) reports that in a meeting of the Assembly after the return of the second embassy he "recounted a long speech, including a summary of the high points, that he said he delivered to Philip …"
15 This episode is well analysed in terms of Demosthenes' unmanliness by Roisman (2010), esp. 395.
16 "Most Greek" must relate to his generally civilized manner as much as his command of the language. On the one hand, this stands against the politically motivated denigration of the Macedonians as non-Greek *barbaroi* (see e.g. Dem. 9.31). On the other, would anyone ever describe in such terms a man whose Greekness was not in some doubt? On the Macedonians as *barbaroi* see succinctly Pownall (2020).
17 The Greek adjective here translated as formidable, *deinos*, has connotations of skill but could also mean strange or terrible. See LSJ s.v. δεινός.
18 Demosthenes might, for example, not have accepted Aeschines' version of what happened as true, but nevertheless have judged it better to direct his attack elsewhere rather than seek to defend himself.

es from Aeschines' narrative as courteous, impressive, and wholly in control of the situation.

At this audience, and more generally during the envoys' time at court, Philip is described as having conducted himself towards the Athenian ambassadors in an open and accessible manner.[19] He engaged directly with them, collectively and individually, and made himself available for discussion, though it can safely be assumed that he was attended at all times by an entourage of bodyguards and others.[20] Demosthenes says, for example, that Aeschines and others of the ambassadors never stopped talking to Philip in private (19.175, 278). He even claims that on the second embassy Aeschines secretly visited Philip in his tent at night in order to help him draft a diplomatic letter to the Athenians, and that he remained behind for a full day and night when the other envoys set off home (19.175).[21] Aeschines ridicules the story of a secret trip—that he sneaked out of his tent without waking his mess-mates and paddled down the river to Philip's tent—but does not dispute that private meetings took place (2.124–125).[22] There is no trace of any distancing royal ceremonial or of attempts on Philip's part to intimidate the ambassadors. This is unsurprising, since his court was, by comparison with those of his son Alexander and the Successors, markedly informal. Demosthenes' claim that on a slightly later occasion Aeschines, when he attended Philip's celebration of the ending of the Third Sacred War, abased himself (προὐκυλινδεῖτο), using the same word that Isocrates used to describe the ritual form of deference (*proskynesis*) practised at the Persian court (19.338; cf. Isoc. 4.151), is surely metaphorical, though the choice of word is loaded. Nor is Philip in these speeches ever referred to as king. As he styled himself on his coins, in inscribed treaties, and in his correspondence, so here he is just Philip.[23]

---

[19] That such informality was normal in the time of Philip emerges from the strong Macedonian opposition to his son Alexander's attempt to introduce a more elaborate court ceremonial.
[20] On royal bodyguards see Hammond (1991); Heckel (2016) 245–259. Philip's dispensing with his guards in the theatre at Aegae on the day of his death (Diod. 16.93.1) implies that he was routinely accompanied by them. At the same time, as Diodorus says, his decision to stand them down served to demonstrate to those present that he felt safe and at ease.
[21] Spawforth (2007) 94–97 and 112–120 discusses the state tent that Alexander used on campaign and suggests, without reference to this passage, that it "may well have been a legacy from Philip, who perhaps acquired it during his years of intensive campaigning in Thrace" (96).
[22] Secret in a different way are the negotiations reported to have been conducted between Philip and the Athenian envoys Antiphon and Charidemus in 357 (Theopompus *BNJ* 115 F 30).
[23] Inscriptions: see for example Rhodes-Osborne, *GHI* no. 50 (alliance with Chalcidians, 357/6); Letter: [Dem.] 12.1 "Philip to the Athenians [sends] greetings." On Macedonian royal style see Errington (1974), who accepts the view that kings before Alexander did not style themselves as King of the Macedonians. Cf., however, Lane Fox (2011) 359–360, though there is an impor-

The king's Companions and advisers are mentioned only occasionally. Aeschines claims maliciously that Philip and his Companions had been led to expect a barnstorming speech from Demosthenes (2.34), and that some of the Companions had predicted to the Athenian envoys, incorrectly as it turned out, that Philip would restore the Boeotian cities whose independence had been crushed by his ally Thebes (Aeschin. 2.137). In a similar vein, he asserts that Demosthenes heard from all Philip's friends (ἀκούων δὲ τῶν ἐκείνου φίλων ἁπάντων) that he would free the rest of the Athenian prisoners in the event of peace (2.100).[24] In these cases we get a glimpse of a diplomatic role that senior Companions might play: to direct—or misdirect—envoys' thoughts in a particular direction.[25] But they are represented as clearly subordinate to Philip: Antipater and Parmenion, senior generals who served as ambassadors to Athens, are pointedly described by Demosthenes (19.69), in contradistinction to Athens' envoys who are answerable to the people, as "men serving a master" (δεσπότῃ διακονοῦντες). Philip debates with the envoys and makes decisions on his own.

Philip's manner towards the ambassadors was notably affable. We have already seen his sympathetic response to Demosthenes' breakdown. An Athenian who had been sent as envoy to Philip in the previous year, Ctesiphon, was open in his praise of him, speaking of his kindness (φιλανθρωπίαν) (Aeschin. 2.13). Ctesiphon was also a member of the first embassy of 346 and is described as confessing to his fellow ambassadors on their way home that in all his life "he had never yet seen such a pleasant and delightful man" (οὐ πώποθ' οὕτως ἡδὺν οὐδ' ἐπαφρόδιτον ἄνθρωπον ἑωρακὼς εἴη) (Aeschin. 2.42). He later reported to the Athenian assembly about Philip's conversation, his appearance, and his "dexterity" at drinking (περί τε τῆς ἐντεύξεως τῆς Φιλίππου καὶ τῆς ἰδέας αὐτοῦ καὶ τῆς ἐν τοῖς πότοις ἐπιδεξιότητος) (Aeschin. 2.47).[26] This favourable impression is one that Philip was clearly keen to foster,[27] given his desire to reach an agreement

---

tant distinction between what Philip *was* (i.e., king) and how he represented himself to the Greeks.

24 Probably the term "friends" basically means *hetairoi*. On "friend" replacing "companion" as the regular term for courtiers in the Hellenistic period see Herman (1980/1981).

25 Carey (2000) notes *ad loc.* (140): "Whether the *hetairoi* in question were simply thinking aloud or were actively pursuing Philip's policy of keeping everyone guessing is unclear." Given Philip's propensity for artful misdirection the latter seems more likely. Demosthenes claims (19.68) that Philip was hesitant to lie on his own behalf.

26 The Greek word *epidexiotes* (cf. English "dexterity") implies a combination of tact, wit, good manners, and moderation. The symposium was characterized by a series of unwritten rules of appropriate conduct.

27 Comparable language is used by Diodorus to describe Philip's manner in 336 at the time of the wedding of his daughter Cleopatra: "he was agreeable (φιλοφρονούμενος) to all [the Greeks]

with Athens, and not all embassies will have found him so easy to deal with (see below). Moreover, his manner may have been congenial, but this did not make him any the more minded to make concessions to the Athenians, as they soon found out to their cost.

The first embassy was received in Macedonia, but Philip's court moved with him, and diplomatic activity could also take place on the road or on campaign. On the second embassy Demosthenes was in a hurry to get the king to swear his oaths as soon as possible and authored a motion to the Athenian assembly that the general Proxenus find out where in Thrace Philip was and convey the envoys directly to him (19.154). He claims that they would have reached Philip much earlier if they had gone to the Hellespont (i.e. to the region where he was campaigning) rather than to Macedonia (19.162). While Philip was away, the envoys had to wait for his return, "sitting there idly in Pella" (19.166). There is a hint here that Pella was something of a gilded cage for the ambassadors in Demosthenes' claim that when he grew suspicious of the delay and wanted to sail immediately back to Athens, and indeed had rented a boat for that purpose, he was not permitted to sail (19.323). Even when Philip got back to Pella, he did not swear the oaths immediately but continued to keep the envoys waiting as he made his preparations to march south. When he set out with his army into central Greece, the oaths still unsworn, all the envoys, Athenians and others, accompanied him. The requisite oaths were finally sworn and witnessed at an inn near the Temple of the Dioscuri at Pherae in Thessaly (19.158).[28]

Hospitality: wining and dining

In Greek inter-*polis* diplomacy, visiting envoys were largely left to fend for themselves,[29] or were looked after by their city's *proxenos* (see below), but at Macedonia they were guests of the king and consequently treated with lavish hospitality. There are frequent references in the speeches to feasts and drinking-parties, which we know from other sources to have been regular and important features of the Macedonian court.[30] Again, Demosthenes and Aeschines mention these events not for their intrinsic interest or significance but as opportunities to dis-

---

both in private and in public" (16.89.2) and "he was determined to make himself agreeable (ἐφιλοτιμεῖτο φιλοφρονεῖσθαι) to the Greeks" (16.91.6).
28 On this episode see Müller (2020).
29 So Adcock and Mosley (1975) 163–164.
30 On Macedonian royal dining and drinking see Carney (2007/2015); Pownall (2010); Kottaridi (2011b).

credit each other. Thus when Aeschines describes their being summoned to a dinner at which Demosthenes behaved disagreeably, it is his opponent's bad manners rather than the meal itself that is important (2.39). Demosthenes for his part complains repeatedly about those Athenian ambassadors who had been seduced by Philip's hospitality: "I saw them crowing about how the Macedonians are so sumptuous and splendid (εὐδαίμονας καὶ λαμπρούς) in bestowing hospitality" (19.235). Macedonia was agriculturally rich, meat was plentiful, and the king could afford, indeed was expected, to offer the most lavish of spreads. No wonder the envoys were impressed. Royal banquets could also be very large, particularly on special occasions or when envoys from multiple cities were present at the same time. For example, Aeschines refers to a dinner for two hundred guests hosted by Philip at Phocis to celebrate the end of the Sacred War (2.162), and for the wedding of his daughter Cleopatra "out of all Greece he summoned his personal guest-friends and ordered the members of his court to bring along as many as they could of their acquaintances from abroad" (Diod. 16.91.2). The archaeological evidence for extensive banqueting facilities in the palace at Aegae clearly supports the picture painted by literary sources.[31]

Philip himself often presided at these events, and leading Macedonian and Greek members of court were presumably invited to help host the envoys. In attendance at one banquet was Philip's ten-year-old son, the young Alexander, who entertained the company as they were drinking by playing the *cithara* and reciting poetry (Aeschin. 1.168). As for drinking, it is notable, in light of Theopompus' denunciation of the debauchery of Philip's court and of Plutarch's account of the drunken quarrel between Alexander and Philip over the latter's decision to marry Attalus' niece,[32] that the only inebriation alleged in these speeches is on the part of some of the Athenian envoys who took part in a symposium hosted by an exiled fellow-citizen. As Demosthenes tells it, the participants, with Aeschines to the fore, abused and finally ordered the flogging of a female Olynthian captive who had been brought to the party. There is a strong emphasis on their loss of self-control, and Demosthenes concludes that the "drunken misconduct of this scum was terrible" (καὶ γὰρ ἡ παροινία τοῦ καθάρματος τουτουὶ δεινή) (19.198). As we have seen, one of the qualities for which Ctesiphon praised Philip was his good manners when drinking. If heavy drinking was typically Macedonian, Philip seems to have been, in this respect, on his best

---

[31] See Kottaridi (2011) 323–327 (extensive dining facilities included places for a total of 230 couches).

[32] Debauchery: Theopompus *BNJ* 115 F 62, 224, 225a–b, 236 etc., with Flower (1994) 104–111. In support of his claim that Philip was a heavy drinker (φιλοπότης) Athenaeus collects a number of passages, primarily from Theopompus: 10.435a–d. Quarrel: Plut. *Alex.* 9.6–11.

Greek behaviour. A fragment of Theopompus throws an interesting sidelight on this. At Chaeronea (i.e. after his defeat of the Greek army in 338) Philip invited the Greek envoys who had come to him to dinner. This must have been a sombre occasion, given the circumstances, but as soon as the envoys left Philip and his Companions began a riotous all-night drinking party to celebrate their victory (*BNJ* 115 F 236).[33]

Diplomatic gifts

A much more awkward aspect of Philip's hospitality, as far as the envoys were concerned, were the gifts that he offered them. Royal largesse was a fundamental aspect of the Macedonian court: the king routinely distributed gifts of various kinds, including titles, appointments, estates, objects of value, to those he wished to reward and whose loyalty he sought to secure.[34] Gift-giving was a structural element of the Macedonian monarchy: the king's generosity demonstrated his wealth and power, and served as an index of his royal status and thus his effective performance as king.[35] It was also a regular element of Macedonian diplomacy. For example, at the very start of his reign, Philip reached settlements with the Paeonians and Thracians by giving them gifts (Diod. 16.3.4). Macedonia was by no means unusual in this regard: a culture of gift-giving characterized the monarchies of the region—the evidence for Thrace is particularly strong—as well as Persia.[36] It was, however, emphatically not a part of Greek inter-*polis* diplomacy, and the offering of gifts to Greek ambassadors proved a source of considerable embarrassment, to them if not to Philip.

Banquets and symposia are frequently mentioned as the occasions on which Philip offered gifts. A significant text is Diodorus' vivid description of the festiv-

---

[33] The order is inverted at Plut. *Mor.* 715c: Philip got extremely drunk after the battle, but immediately sobered up when the Greek envoys came to discuss terms.

[34] On gift-giving in antiquity see the collection of papers in Carlà and Gori (2014). On gift-giving by Argead kings see Mitchell (1997) 148–166 (Philip) and 167–169 (Alexander). On Philip's grants of land in conquered territory to his supporters see Diod. 16.34.5; *Syll.*³ 332; cf. Plut. *Alex.* 15.3–6 (Alexander's grants of land before starting for Asia).

[35] See Strootman (2014) 152: "giving lavish gifts was a means to attain or confirm superior status." Plutarch's collection of anecdotes about Alexander's gift-giving (*Alex.* 39) arguably misses the point in seeing this as a reflection of his very generous nature (φύσει δὲ ὢν μεγαλοδωρότατος).

[36] See Mitchell (1997) 111–133 (Persia) and 134–147 (Thrace).

ities that Philip organized to celebrate his capture of Olynthus in 348 (16.55.1–2):[37]

> After the capture of Olynthus, he celebrated the Olympian festival to the gods in commemoration of his victory and offered magnificent sacrifices; and he organized a great festive assembly at which he held splendid competitions and thereafter invited many of the visiting strangers to his banquets. In the course of the carousals he joined in numerous conversations, presenting to many guests drinking cups as he proposed the toasts, awarding gifts to a considerable number, and graciously making such handsome promises to them all that he won over a large number to crave friendship with him. (tr. Sherman)

> μετὰ δὲ τὴν ἅλωσιν τῆς Ὀλύνθου Ὀλύμπια ποιήσας τοῖς θεοῖς ἐπινίκια μεγαλοπρεπεῖς θυσίας συνετέλεσεν· πανήγυριν δὲ μεγάλην συστησάμενος καὶ λαμπροὺς ἀγῶνας ποιήσας πολλοὺς τῶν ἐπιδημούντων ξένων ἐπὶ τὰς ἑστιάσεις παρελάμβανε. παρὰ δὲ τοὺς πότους πολλαῖς ὁμιλίαις χρώμενος καὶ πολλοῖς μὲν ποτήρια διδοὺς κατὰ τὰς προπόσεις, οὐκ ὀλίγοις δὲ δωρεὰς ἀπονέμων, πᾶσι δὲ μεγάλας ἀπαγγελίας εὐχαρίστως ποιούμενος πολλοὺς ἔσχεν ἐπιθυμητὰς τῆς πρὸς αὐτὸν φιλίας.

Turning to the contemporary evidence of the speeches, Demosthenes praises the Theban envoys for declining a series of gifts that Philip offered to them at a banquet (19.139–140):

> Ambassadors came to him from Thebes, at the same time as we were sent there by you. He wanted to give them money—indeed, a large amount, they said. This was declined and not accepted by the Theban ambassadors. Afterwards at a sacrifice and dinner Philip was drinking and treating them kindly (φιλανθρωπευόμενος πρὸς αὐτούς), and among much else, such as war-spoils and that sort of thing, he finally tried to present (προύπινεν) silver and gold cups to them. All these they rejected, and in no way compromised themselves. In the end Philon, one of the ambassadors, made a comment which deserved to have been made not on the Thebans' behalf but on yours, men of Athens. He said he was pleased and delighted to see Philip treating them generously and kindly. They themselves were his friends and guests even without these gifts; but with regard to the business of the city, which was his present concern, they requested him to exercise this kindness by some act worthy both of himself and of the Thebans, and in that way they agreed that the whole city as well as themselves would be on his side. (tr. MacDowell)

The Greek verb translated here as "tried to present" (προύπινεν) merits consideration. Its primary meaning, as its etymology makes clear, is to "drink to (the health of) another."[38] It can also mean "make a present of the cup to the person pledged" and, more generally and without any particular reference to drinking,

---

[37] Diodorus' source is unclear: for a succinct discussion of the likely sources of Diod. 16 see McQueen (1995) 8–14.
[38] The verb can also mean to drink before (*LSJ* s.v., sense I).

"give freely, make a present of." In this passage, the sense of drinking to someone is certainly present: Philip drank to the health of the Theban envoys and at the same time offered them valuable gifts.[39] Toasts were routinely made on these occasions: In *On the False Embassy* Demosthenes says of Aeschines that at the celebrations to mark of the end of the Sacred War "he wore a garland and sang the paean with Philip and drank his health" (καὶ συνεστεφανοῦτο καὶ συνεπαιώνιζεν Φιλίππῳ καί φιλοτησίας προύπινεν) (19.128), and in *On the Crown* (18.296) he associates drinking to Philip and banqueting with him with treason: Aeschines and those like him "have pledged freedom first to Philip and now to Alexander, measuring happiness by their stomach and by the most shameful practices" (τὴν ἐλευθερίαν προπεπωκότες πρότερον μὲν Φιλίππῳ, νῦν δ'Ἀλεξάνδρῳ, τῇ γαστρὶ μετροῦντες καὶ τοῖς αἰσχίστοις τὴν εὐδαιμονίαν).

The connection between gift-giving and hospitality is also present in a slightly different form in Demosthenes' account of Philip's offer of gifts, first individually and then collectively, to the Athenian envoys (19.166–168):

> So what was this offer of money by Philip to us collectively? To explain that to you too, Philip was testing us all. In what way? By sending to each of us individually and offering a quite large amount of money, men of Athens. When he failed with any one man (I ought not to mention myself, but the facts and the results will be enough to make it clear), he supposed that everyone would ingenuously accept what was given collectively, and thus the men who had sold themselves individually would be safe, if we all participated to even a small extent in receiving it collectively. So that's why it was being offered, under the name of hospitality (ξένια δὴ πρόφασιν). When I put a stop to it, these men made another distribution among themselves. When I asked Philip to spend the money on the prisoners, he couldn't very well give these men away and say "But So-and-so and So-and-so have it', nor avoid the expense. So he agreed to my request … (tr. MacDowell)

Philip's diplomatic gifts to Greek ambassadors took various forms. In addition to the money, miscellaneous items of booty, and gold and silver cups that were allegedly offered to the Theban and Athenian envoys, Demosthenes claims that Aeschines, before he was supposedly corrupted by Philip, had been appalled to encounter on the road one Atrestidas of Arcadia who was accompanied by a crowd of thirty women and children. These, it emerged, were Olynthian prisoners, i.e. slaves, whom he had received as a gift (δωρεὰν) from Philip.[40] Demosthenes also claims that Philocrates and Aeschines earn income from property in the territory of Athens' defeated allies (19.145), and that Philocrates sold

---

[39] On Hellenistic kings' gifts of cups and plates to those dining with them see Strootman (2014) 156 and n. 57.
[40] Dem. 19.305–306. On the enslavement of the Olynthians after the capture of their city see Diod. 16.53.3.

wheat, built houses, imported timber, and exchanged gold—these last two distinctively Macedonian exports and hence, he claims, evidence of bribery (19.114).⁴¹ Later in the speech Demosthenes further alleges that Philocrates had brought free Olynthian women to Athens, his insinuation being that the relationship was in some way exploitative or improper (19.309).⁴² In addition to material gifts, banquets also provided Philip the opportunity to be seen to grant favours, as for example when he agreed to the comic actor Satyrus's request—solicited over drinks—to free the Athenians who had been captured in the fall of Olynthus.⁴³

Given that our focus is on the working of the Macedonian court, there is no occasion to explore in detail how the king's gifts were interpreted by the Greeks. As is well known, the same Greek word, δῶρον, could mean either gift or bribe according to context and point of view.⁴⁴ For Demosthenes, even if they were wrapped in the language of hospitality, they were tantamount to bribes, and the correct course was to turn them down, or else seek to divert them to some communal benefit. He insists that his fellow envoys Aeschines and Philocrates, the latter of whom had by the time of the speech already fled into exile rather than stand trial, had been bribed by Philip at Pella to betray Athens' interests. One of the things that he sets out to prove is that Aeschines and Philocrates "took gifts and payments" (19.8). The same claim is repeated in various forms dozens of time in the speech: Aeschines took gifts; he sold himself; he was bribed; he acted for money; he is a traitor. Aeschines, on trial for his life, naturally denies receiving anything.⁴⁵ But the matter was complicated, since ambassadors had not only to act appropriately, but also to avoid giving offence to the powerful

---

41 Timber and gold (i.e. gold coins of Philip—but only later in his reign, according to Le Rider [1977] from the mid- 340s) were distinctively Macedonian exports; on timber see n. 2 above and Borza (1987).
42 The circumstances are unclear. The implication is that this was discreditable, and we have seen references to the fate of Olynthian women and children enslaved by Philip. But MacDowell (2000) 340 – 341 suggests that, since the Olynthians are described as free, this may in fact have been an act of charity on Philocrates' part towards refugees.
43 Aeschin. 2.156; Dem. 19.193 – 195.
44 On this ambiguity see Harvey (1985); Herman (1987) 75 – 81. The latter observes (7) that "when seen from the perspective of the community, gift-exchange with an outsider—the essential characteristic of guest-friendship—could appear as bribery." On attitudes to bribery at Athens see Taylor (2001a) and (2001b). On bribery of envoys see Perlman (1976). Accepting a bribe was an offence at Athens: [Ar.] *Ath. Pol.* 54.2.
45 See e.g. Aeschin. 2.3, 23, 93. On Demosthenes' insistence that there was widespread (pro-Macedonian) treachery on the part of Greek political leaders see Cargill (1985).

man with whom they were negotiating by too brusque a refusal of his proffered gifts.

Philip's diplomatic gifts were, we may be sure, not given for nothing. As Moses Finley wrote in *The World of Odysseus*, "The word 'gift' is not to be misconstrued. It may be stated as a flat rule of both primitive and archaic society that no one ever gave anything, whether goods or services or honors, without proper recompense, real or wishful, immediate or years away, to himself or to his kin."[46] The envoys who received gifts were not expected to give counter-gifts, but there was still the expectation of a return.[47] For Philip, such gifts were part of the regular currency of diplomacy: they cost him little and served effectively to create or strengthen ties with the recipient and to influence him in his favour, which is what he hoped to achieve. Over the appropriateness of giving and receiving diplomatic gifts, there was clearly a clash between two different cultures. As Lynette Mitchell has shown, Greeks, and the Athenians in particular, had difficulty in understanding how gift-cultures worked, to their disadvantage.[48] But it would be wrong to suppose that there was any cultural misunderstanding on Philip's part. He was familiar with the Greek city-states and with attitudes at democracies such as Athens. Any awkwardness that the giving of gifts might cause was their problem, not his. Indeed, in view of the number of political trials that these embassies gave rise to at Athens, one might suspect an element of deliberate mischief-making in his generosity.

Varieties of friendship: *philia* and *xenia*

The provision of generous hospitality, the offering of gifts, and the granting of favours all served one overarching purpose: to create or reinforce personal ties between Philip and their recipients. Aeschines' relationship with Philip is a central preoccupation of Demosthenes, who refers to it repeatedly. The terms that he generally uses to describe it are *philos/philia* (the general Greek words for "friend" and "friendship"), and *xenos/xenia* ("guest-friend" and "guest-friendship"), often paired together. Thus, for example, he claims that Aeschines holds Philip's *xenia* and *philia* far above his own city (19.248) and is one of his *xenoi* and *philoi* (19.314). Earlier in the speech he refers to the sudden, and

---

[46] Finley (2002) 60–61.
[47] See Herman (1987) 38–39 on unequal "friendships" where the goods (i.e. gifts) of the higher-status party are repayable by the lower-status party in the form of services.
[48] Mitchell (1997) chaps. 6–8.

therefore suspicious, appearance of trust and friendship (πίστιν καὶ φιλίαν) between Philip and Aeschines (19.27). And so on repeatedly.

Friendship (*philia*) was the more general term. Between states, it was a routine part of the language of diplomacy: it appears for example in Philip's alliance with the Chalcidic League of the 350s, where the inscribed text records the advice of the Delphic oracle that the two parties become friends and allies.⁴⁹ In such texts alliance meant something concrete, and imposed obligations on the contracting parties, whereas friendship did not. Similarly, Philip's friendship with visiting envoys was a usefully nebulous concept: it was not an official designation, was not marked by any public ceremony, and cost him nothing to grant.⁵⁰ *Xenia* in principle meant something more specific: a formalized friendship between individual members of two different communities. In his fundamental study of the concept, Gabriel Herman argues that it was an overwhelmingly upper-class institution with its roots in the Archaic period, which imposed obligations on each party to support the other, and was entered into by means of a series of rituals and ceremonies (hence his tranlation of the term as "ritualized friendship"). Whilst in its ideal form it involved two parties of approximately equal status, this was not always the case, and *xenos*-relationships could be unequal. Indeed, the terms *philia* and *xenia* both cloaked the marked *inequality* between Philip and the Athenian envoys and the creation of what look more like patron-client relationships.⁵¹ Whether Aeschines did in fact have a formal relationship of *xenia* with Philip, and if so by what means this relationship was established, are different matters, and hard to assess on the evidence we have.⁵²

As with gift-giving, so with the creation of personal ties there was a clash between two markedly different political cultures. In Macedonia, everything was personal. Diplomacy was the sole responsibility of the king, who not only entered into formal agreements in his own name but also operated informally using various mechanisms of influence to create personal ties with those envoys

---

49 On friendship in Greek diplomatic texts see Adcock and Mosley (1975) 206–209. Philip and the Chalcidic league: Rhodes-Osborne, *GHI* no. 50 line 12.
50 On the use of *philos* as a quasi-title for Hellenistic courtiers see Herman (1980/1); Konstan (1997) 95–98.
51 Herman (1987), esp. 34–40 on social status.
52 Aischines does not address the charge, and Demosthenes provides no direct evidence. As for what ritual would have been involved, the most relevant (indirect) evidence would seem to come from Aisch. 3.224, where Aischines accuses Demosthenes of being a *xenos*-killer for his role in the execution of the alleged Macedonian spy Anaxinus of Oreus, a man whose "right hand Demosthenes clasped, making him a *philos* and *xenos*." McQueen (1995) 125–126 (note *ad* Diod. 16.54.4) usefully lists those, Athenians and others, whom Demosthenes accused of being *xenoi* and/or *philoi* of Philip.

and foreign leaders with whom he dealt. In Athens, on the other hand, envoys served collectively, were appointed for a single embassy, and were held strictly accountable for their actions and for any financial transactions in which they engaged. Personal relationships between individual Athenian envoys and foreign rulers could easily be construed as being at best a conflict of interest and at worst treasonable. And yet, in this period such a traditional approach was becoming harder to sustain: Athens was obliged to deal with the Macedonian king and could not choose the terms on which it did so. There was, indeed, a long history of prominent Athenians, especially generals on campaign in the region, having ties with the Macedonian court and receiving gifts from the king.[53] Such ties had in the past usually been unproblematic, since they served to increase Athenian influence in a region in which the city had a long-standing strategic interest.[54] What had changed by 346 was, quite simply, the balance of power. Now, Philip was the dominant party. In this period, personal relationships between leading citizens and Macedonian kings increasingly came to be essential for any city-state that wished to advance its interests effectively. And *vice versa:* Philip benefitted from dealing directly with political leaders of the Greek *poleis* whom he knew to be well-disposed towards him. Demosthenes' claim that "these men" (i.e. Aeschines and Philocrates) advised Philip to "have a few friends in Athens to do business and manage affairs among you" (19.138) was little more than a statement of the obvious, so far as advancing his interests was concerned.[55] At the same time, Greek cities, Athens included, increasingly benefited from the access to the king that such well-connected "friends" provided. For example, in 335 the Athenian politician Demades, who had links with the Macedonian court, successfully intervened with Alexander and persuaded him to back down from his demand that the city hand over a number of leading politicians after the failed revolt of Thebes (Diod. 17.15.3). A little later still, an inscription commemorates the influence that Gorgus of Iasos wielded at Alexander's court on behalf of the people of his home city and of Samos.[56] And in the Hellenistic period, having friends at court was vital to the getting the king's attention and securing his favour.

---

[53] See n. 1.

[54] Usually, but not always: in the 460s the general Cimon was charged with accepting bribes from the Macedonian king Alexander I (Plut. *Cim.* 14.2–4).

[55] The speaker of [Dem.] 7.33–34, generally accepted to be Demosthenes' ally Hegesippus, claims that Philip has promised in his recent letter to confer benefits on the Athenians if they would trust "his friends and those who speak on his behalf" (τοις μὲν αὐτοῦ φίλοις καὶ ὑπὲρ αὐτοῦ λέγουσι).

[56] Rhodes-Osborne, *GHI* no. 90.

The diplomatic uses of Greeks at court

Philip also made use of Greek members of his court to facilitate the conduct of diplomacy with the city-states of Greece. During his reign a number of prominent Greeks were resident in Macedonia and were associated with the court. Theopompus writes very pejoratively of those who flocked to his court, from Macedonia, Thessaly and the rest of Greece, as flatterers and chancers (*BNJ* 115 F 224). One does not have to accept his characterization of them to accept that he is referring to a real phenomenon. Diodorus, in his description of Philip's celebration of the capture of Olynthus in 348 (quoted above), writes that he invited many of the resident foreigners to participate in the festivities (16.55). This is a category of people who would merit systematic examination with a view to delimiting the extent of Philip's outer court.[57] For example, Demaratus of Corinth, a leading pro-Macedonian in his own city (Dem. 18.295), is described as a guest-friend of Philip, played an important role at court and later accompanied Alexander on campaign.[58] Some Greeks were exiles from their own city, others—artists, architects, writers, and the like—were invited or made their way to Pella because they had a particular skill to offer. Some made private visits and stayed for longer or shorter times: Demosthenes claims that his fellow-Athenian Phrynon sent his teenage son to Philip (19.230), refers to another Athenian, Pythocles, visiting him (19.225), and describes how the actor Neoptolemus liquidated his assets in Athens and decamped to Philip's court (5.8). Aeschines claims that Callias of Chalcis "went off to Macedonia and went around with Philip and was termed one of his Companions (*hetairoi*)" (3.89). There were, in short, plenty of variously talented Greeks at hand whose services Philip could call on.

One role that members of this group might perform was the providing of hospitality, especially to envoys from their home city. Diplomatic visits could be lengthy. The members of Athens' second embassy of 346 hung around in Pella "for three whole months", according to Demosthenes, waiting for Philip to return from Thrace (Dem. 19.155; 18.30), although this delay was clearly exceptional.[59] Even if he was physically present, Philip was presumably not available or will not have wished to host visiting ambassadors every day. Twice we hear of Athe-

---

[57] On the concept of the inner and outer courts see Strootman (2014) 32. The outer court consisted of those who were not permanent members of it. On the frequent Hellenistic formula "spending his time with the king" (*diatribon para toi basilei*) see Herman (1980/1981) 106–107.
[58] Heckel (2006) 107 s.v. 'Demaratus [1].'
[59] For a monarch to keep envoys waiting was a common way to show them that he was more important than they: as Strootman (2014) 196 put it, "Waiting is an instrument of power."

nian envoys being entertained by fellow-citizens who lived in Macedonia. First, Demosthenes relates a shameful episode when members of the first Athenian embassy were invited one evening to a drinking-party (*symposion*) hosted by 'Xenophron, son of Phaedimus who had been one of the Thirty', i.e. one of the oligarchs who had ruled Athens in 404–3 (19.196–198).⁶⁰ Demosthenes says that he himself refused to attend the event but that his fellow-ambassadors all went.⁶¹ The reason he mentions this invitation is that it led to the abuse by some of the envoys of a female Olynthian captive (see above). Aeschines gives a different account of the evening and names the host as Xenodicus, whom he describes as one of the companions of Philip (2.157).⁶² And later in the same speech, Demosthenes says that Philip has recently banished the Athenian poet Xenoclides from his court on the ground that he had entertained (ὑπεδέξατο) an Athenian embassy led by Hegesippus, an intransigent and outspoken opponent of Macedon (and ally of Demosthenes). This latter embassy, sent to request a renegotiation of the Peace of Philocrates at a time of rising tension between Philip and Athens, clearly met a frostier reception than those of 346, and Xenoclides was apparently punished for his involvement with it (19.331).⁶³ In offering hospitality to their visiting compatriots, such men played the role that in a city-state would have been played by the Athenian *proxenos* (i.e. the citizen appointed by the Athenians to represent their interests there), one of whose duties was to host envoys from the city that he represented.⁶⁴

---

60 The list of the names of the Thirty Tyrants at Xen. *Hell.* 2.3.2 contains a Phaedrias but no Phaedimus. That these are the same man would seem likely, but is unprovable.
61 Demosthenes' statement that he decided not to attend is clearly intended to distance himself from the discreditable events that took place at the party, as is the detail that the host's father had been a member of the hated Thirty. Whether, as a habitual drinker of water (Dem. 6.30; 19.46), he was in fact teetotal and avoided the party for that reason as well is unclear.
62 Xenodicus (if Aeschines is correct about the name) could conceivably have been an Athenian, honoured by the king with the title of *hetairos*. The name is attested at Athens, in a casualty list of the late 5th century (*IG* I³ 1191.368).
63 The use of the deictic pronoun ('this man here') indicates that he was in Athens, if not in the courtroom, at the time of the speech. He may be the same as the Athenian Xenoclides "the poet" who was later stripped of his citizen rights (see [Dem.] 59.26–28).
64 See Mack (2015) 70–71 on "the provision of hospitality to individuals sent by the granting *polis*" as a service that *proxenoi* regularly performed. So far as is known, there were in this period no Athenian *proxenoi* in Macedonia. More than a century earlier, in a speech in Herodotus, it is claimed (8.143.3) that Alexander I had been *proxenos* of the Athenians at the time of the Persian invasion of Greece. And an Athenian decree of 407/6 (*IG* i³ 117) seems to record the appointment of the Macedonian king Archelaus and his sons as *proxenoi* and benefactors of Athens, although of the restored word προχσένος (l. 36) only the last letter is preserved.

Second, Philip made use of Greek orators and writers. His court included various Greek men of letters—philosophers, rhetoricians, historians, actors, doctors—who competed for his patronage and favour.[65] Through their writings and in other ways these men could play an important role in shaping Greek opinion in favour of Philip and his policies. For example, in an apparently genuine letter of the 340s, Speusippus, head of the Academy in Athens, writes to Philip attacking Isocrates for showing insufficient zeal in advancing the king's interests.[66] Such men could also be employed in diplomatic dealings with their fellow Greeks. An important figure in this regard is Python of Byzantium, a pupil of the Athenian rhetorician Isocrates and member of Philip's court. An ancient biography of Isocrates describes Python simply as "Philip's *rhetor*."[67] How he came to Pella we do not know: he may have been a pro-Macedonian exile from his home city, or perhaps he was recommended by his teacher. Clearly a skilled speaker, he was despatched to Athens in 343 to discuss revision of the terms of the Peace of Philocrates; there he delivered a letter from Philip to the Athenians and made a speech to the assembly.[68] In 338 he served as the most distinguished of Philip's ambassadors to the Boeotian League, and is described by Diodorus as famous for his eloquence (Diod. 16.85.3). He is mentioned by Aeschines in his attempt to refute Demosthenes' allegation (discussed above) that he had secretly gone to Philip's tent during the night and written for him the letter that he sent to the Athenians (2.124): one of Aeschines' arguments against this claim is that Philip had no need of his services, since he could equally well have either written the letter himself or employed Python or Leosthenes to do so for him.[69] Leosthenes was another Athenian, a general who had fled to Macedonia after being condemned to death for treason (Diod. 15.95; Aeschin. 2.21). Whether either of these men did help Philip with his diplomatic correspondence is unknowable, but Aeschines regarded it as plausible that the drafting or editing of royal letters could be entrusted to educated Greeks.[70]

---

65 On literati at Philip's court see Pownall (2017).
66 On this text see Markle (1976); Natoli (2004).
67 Westermann (1845) 257, which is also the source for the information that he was a pupil of Isocrates.
68 See [Dem.] 7.18–23; Dem. 18.136; Dem. *Ep.* 2.10.
69 This passage clearly bears on the authorship of the later *Letter of Philip* preserved in the Demosthenic corpus ([Dem.] 12). Hammond and Griffith (1979) 714–716 ("Afterthoughts on the *Letter of Philip*") see Python or Eumenes as possible authors.
70 Philip later employed the Greek Eumenes of Cardia as his secretary: see Anson (2015) 43–53.

Conclusion

During the reign of Philip, Macedonia, which had been far from isolated previously, began to have an increasing number of diplomatic dealings with a variety of other states, Greek and non-Greek. As Philip's power grew, and Macedonian foreign policy entanglements became more numerous, it is no surprise that the reception of ambassadors became a significant part of the life of the court. The contemporary evidence of two Athenian envoys to Philip, tendentious as it is, gives us a precious insight into how diplomacy was transacted at court. It is clearly impossible to generalize from this case, which relates to Philip's dealings with just one, albeit very important, Greek city at a particular point of his reign. It is likely, for example, that visits to Pella from Illyrian or Thacian kings, or Persian envoys, or Thessalian aristocrats, which certainly took place but about which we have little if any direct evidence, would have proceeded differently. In the case of Philip's dealings with the Athenians, we see a tension between his ways and theirs. Whilst he was keen to emphasize his mastery of Greek culture, he conducted diplomacy in traditional Macedonian style. The more the balance of power swung towards him, the more he could dictate the rules of the game. Of central importance was his use of the court as the venue for extending lavish hospitality, giving gifts, and creating personal ties with individual envoys, with the intention of making them well disposed if not indeed indebted to him. His dealings with those at court—Companions, guest-friends and foreign envoys —were all of a kind, and served to create a web of personal connections radiating from Pella that allowed him to impose his will in Macedonia and throughout Greece. In short, the Macedonian court was not just the place where diplomacy happened but also the mechanism by which it was conducted. Much of what was typical about the reception of envoys in the courts of the Hellenistic period—the importance of royal hospitality and generosity, the use of courtiers as intermediaries, the need for the monarch to show himself as affable—can already be clearly seen at Philip's court.

Bibliography

Adcock and Mosley (1975): Frank Adcock and Derek J. Mosley, *Diplomacy in Ancient Greece*, London and New York.

Anson (2015): Edward M. Anson, *Eumenes of Cardia: A Greek Among Macedonians*, 2nd ed., Boston and Leiden.

Borza (1987): Eugene N. Borza, "Timber and Politics in the Ancient World: Macedon and the Greeks", in: *Proceedings of the American Philosophical Society* 131, 32–52.

Carey (2000): Christopher Carey, *Aeschines*, Austin.
Cargill (1985): Jack Cargill, "Demosthenes, Aeschines, and the crop of traitors", in: *Ancient World* 11 (1985) 75–85.
Carlà and Gori (2014): Filippo Carlà and Maja Gori (eds.), *Gift Giving and the 'Embedded' Economy in the Ancient World*, Heidelberg.
Carney (2007/2015): Elizabeth D. Carney, "Symposia and the Macedonian elite: the unmixed life", *Syllecta Classica* 18 (2007) 129–180, reprinted with afterword in *King and Court in Ancient Macedonia: Rivalry, Treason and Conspiracy*, Swansea, 2015, 225–264.
Errington (1974): R. Malcolm Errington, "Macedonian 'royal style' and its historical significance", in: *JHS* 94 (1974) 20–37.
Finley (2002): Moses I. Finley, *The World of Odysseus*, New York.
Flower (1994): Michael A. Flower, *Theopompus of Chios: History and Rhetoric in the Fourth Century BC*, Oxford.
Guth (2011): Dina Guth, *Character and rhetorical strategy: Philip II of Macedonia in fourth century Athens*, diss. U. of Michigan.
Hammond (1991): Nicholas G. L. Hammond, "The Various guards of Philip II and Alexander III", in: *Historia* 40 (1991) 396–418.
Hammond and Griffith (1979): Nicholas G. L. Hammond and Guy T. Griffith, *A History of Macedonia Volume II: 550–336 B.C.*, Oxford.
Harris (1995): Edward M. Harris, *Aeschines and Athenian Politics*, New York and Oxford.
Harrison (2019): Thomas Harrison, "A Persian marriage feast in Macedon? (Herodotus 5.17–21)", in: *CQ* 69.2 (2019) 507–514.
Harvey (1985): F. David Harvey, "*Dona ferentes:* some aspects of bribery in Greek politics", in: *History of Political Thought* 6.1–2 (1985) 76–117
Heckel (2006): Waldemar Heckel, *Who's Who in the Age of Alexander the Great*, Malden and Oxford.
Heckel (2016): Waldemar Heckel, *Alexander's Marshals: A Study of the Makedonian Aristocracy and the Politics of Military Leadership*, 2nd ed., Abingdon and New York.
Herman (1980/1981): Gabriel Herman, "The 'Friends' of the early Hellenistic rulers: servants or officials?", in: *Talanta* 12/13 (1980/1981) 103–149.
Herman (1987): Gabriel Herman, *Ritualised Friendship and the Greek City*, Cambridge.
Konstan (1997): David Konstan, *Friendship in the Classical World*, Cambridge.
Kottaridi (2011a): Angeliki Kottaridi, "The Palace of Aegae", in: Robin Lane Fox (ed.), *Brill's Companion to Ancient Macedon*, Boston and Leiden, 297–323.
Kottaridi (2011b): Angeliki Kottaridi, "The Royal banquet: a capital institution", in: *Heracles to Alexander the Great*, Oxford, 167–180.
Lane Fox (2011): Robin Lane Fox, "Philip of Macedon: Accession, ambitions, and self-presentation", in: Robin Lane Fox (ed.), *Brill's Companion to Ancient Macedon*, Boston and Leiden, 335–366.
Le Rider (1977): Georges Le Rider, *Le monnayage d'argent et d'or de Philippe II, frappé en Macédoine de 359 à 294*, Paris.
MacDowell (2000): Douglas M. MacDowell, *Demosthenes: On the False Embassy (Oration 19)*, Oxford.
Mack (2015): William Mack, *Proxeny and Polis: Institutional Networks in the Ancient Greek World*, Oxford.

Markle (1976): Minor M. Markle, "Support of Athenian intellectuals for Philip", in: *JHS* 96, 80–99.
McQueen (1995): Earl I. McQueen, *Diodorus Siculus: The Reign of Philip II: The Greek and Macedonian Narrative from Book XVI*, London.
Mitchell (1997): Lynette G. Mitchell, *Greeks Bearing Gifts: The Public Use of Private Relationships in the Greek World, 435–323 BC*, Cambridge.
Müller (2020): Sabine Müller, 'Pherai, inn' in: W. Heckel *et al.* (eds.), *Lexicon of Argead Makedonia*, Berlin, 414–415.
Natoli (2004): Anthony F. Natoli, *The Letter of Speusippus to Philip II*, Stuttgart.
Paulsen (1999): Thomas Paulsen, *Die Parapresbeia-Reden des Demosthenes und des Aischines*, Trier.
Perlman (1976): Shalom Perlman, "On bribing Athenian ambassadors", in: *GRBS* 17, 223–233.
Pownall (2010): Frances Pownall, "The Symposia of Philip II and Alexander III: the view from Greece", in: Elizabeth D. Carney and Daniel Ogden (eds.), *Philip II and Alexander the Great*, Oxford, 55–65.
Pownall (2017): Frances Pownall, "The Role of Greek literature at the Argead court", in Sabine Müller *et al.* (eds.), *The History of the Argeads: New Perspectives*, Wiesbaden, 215–229.
Pownall (2020): Frances Pownall, "Barbaroi" in: W. Heckel *et al.* (eds.), *Lexicon of Argead Makedonia*, Berlin, 134–135.
Roisman (2010): Joseph Roisman, "Rhetoric, manliness and contest", in: I. Worthington (ed.), *A Companion to Greek Rhetoric*, Oxford, 393–410.
Ryder (1994): Timothy T. B. Ryder, "The Diplomatic skills of Philip II", in: I. Worthington (ed.), *Ventures into Greek History*, Oxford, 228–257.
Spawforth (2007): Anthony Spawforth, "The Court of Alexander the Great between Europe and Asia," in A. J. S. Spawforth (ed.), *The Court and Court Society in Ancient Monarchies*, Cambridge, 82–120.
Strootman (2014): Rolf Strootman, *Courts and Elites in the Hellenistic Empires*, Edinburgh.
Taylor (2001a): Claire Taylor, "Bribery in Athenian politics Part I: accusations, allegations, and slander", in: *Greece and Rome* 48, 53–66.
Taylor (2001b): Claire Taylor, "Bribery in Athenian politics Part II: ancient reaction and perceptions", in: *Greece and Rome* 48, 154–172.
Tronson (1984): Adrian Tronson, "Satyrus the Peripatetic and the marriages of Philip II", in: *JHS* 104, 116–126.
Westermann (1845): Anton Westermann, *Biographoi: Vitarum Scriptores Graeci Minores*, Braunschweig.

Craig Cooper
Kairos, Mistrust of Tyranny and the Rhetoric of Court in Demosthenes' *Olynthiacs*

In 349/8 Philip II attacked the Chalcidian League headed by Olynthus. Earlier in 352 Olynthus had concluded peace with Athens, even at that time discussing the possibility of an alliance, actions that contravened their alliance with Philip (Dem. 3.7, 23.109; Lib. *Hypoth.* 1.2).[1] At some point in 351, Philip made some sort of military demonstration to signal his displeasure with Olynthus (Dem. 4.17; 1.12–13), though it seems he did not force the Olynthians to break off their peace treaty with Athens.[2] But now faced with outright Macedonian aggression, Olynthus sent envoys to Athens seeking that alliance, along with military aid. Philochorus (*BNJ* 328 F49–51) mentions three expeditions despatched to Olynthus by the Athenians over the course of the year, each time in response to an Olynthian request for help. The *Olynthiacs* were delivered by Demosthenes over a series of meetings of the Assembly to rally the Athenians to the Olynthian cause.[3] Even in antiquity, questions were raised about the order in which they were delivered. Dionysius of Halicarnassus (*Ad Amm.* 1.4) had arranged them as 2–3–1, whereas his contemporary Caecilius Caleacte (fr. 136 Ofenloch: *schol.* Dem. 2.1) argued against him, considering the *First Olynthiac* as the first one delivered in the series and accepting the traditional manuscript order. Mod-

---

[1] For Philip's alliance with Olynthus of 357/6 see Rhodes and Osborne no. 50; Diod. 16.8.3 with the discussion of Hammond and Griffith (1979) 243–246; Sealey (1993) 111, 137–8; Worthington (2008) 42–43; on the peace treaty of 352 between Athens and Olynthus see Hammond and Griffith (1979) 297–298; Worthington (2008) 68.
[2] Hammond and Griffith (1979) 296–299; Worthington (2008) 68–69. Dem. 1.13 suggests that Philip's demonstration of force against Olynthus in 352 followed soon after his Thracian campaign against Heraion Teichos, after he recovered from his illness: Sealey (1955) 82. The reference in Dem. 4.17 to Philip's "sudden campaigns against Thermopylae, Chersonese and Olynthus" date the *First Philippic to 351:* Sealey (1955) 82–83; Hammond and Griffith (1979) 298 n. 3; Pearson (1981) 120 with n. 3; Trevett (2011) 68–69, 75 n. 17. Cawkwell (1962a) 125–127 associates the *First Philippic* with the commissioning of Charidemus' expedition (Dem. 4.43; 3.4), which was dispatched in the fall of 351. Ellis (1966) dates the *First Philippic* to 350; cf. MacDowell (2009) 211–213.
[3] For details of Philip's campaign against Olynthus in 349/8, see Cawkwell (1962a); Carter (1971); Ellis (1976) 93–99; Cawkwell (1978) 82–90; Hammond and Griffith (1979) 315–328; Worthington (2008) 74–83 and Worthington (2013) 132–144.

https://doi.org/10.1515/9783110622942-006

ern scholars have differed both on the order and the timing of their delivery, though it is generally accepted that the *Third Olynthiac* was the last in the series, based on the dire tone of the speech and Demosthenes' explicit call to reform the Theoric Fund (Dem. 3.11), something which he mentions only obliquely in the *First Olynthiac* (1.19) and completely ignores in the *Second*.[4] It seems *Olynthiacs* 1 and 2 were delivered in the context of the first appeal for help from the Olynthians,[5] perhaps in one meeting of the Assembly or in successive meetings, as Athenians debated the question of an alliance and the implications of sending aid, and the *Third Olynthiac* in a subsequent meeting of the Assembly, after the situation in the Chalcidice had started to deteriorate, perhaps a few months after Demosthenes had delivered his first speech on the matter.[6] In any case, it may be best to follow Tuplin, and see the three *Olynthiacs* as exactly contemporaneous to one other, each one addressing the same situation in three different

---

[4] McQueen (1986) 52; Trevett (2011) 30; contrast Tuplin (1998) 276–278, who summarizes and points out the deficiencies in the arguments for the consensus that the *Third Olynthiac* is the last of the speeches.

[5] Cawkwell (1962a); Ellis (1967): references in *Olynthiacs* 1 and 2 (1.2, 10; 2.2, 11) point to a date before the alliance was concluded and military aid dispatched to Olynthus. Ellis (1967) has argued that *Second Olynthiac* was delivered first, based on Demosthenes' treatment of Thessaly, with Dem. 1.22 suggesting a worsening of the situation between Philip and the Thessalians over the question of Pagasae and Magnesia. Dem. 2.11 simply refers to entering negotiations with Philip on Magnesia, whereas Dem. 1.22 calls for fortifying Magnesia and withholding market and port dues; contrast Erbse (1956) 371 and Eucken (1984), as well as Tuplin (1998), 278–279. Sealey (1955) 92–96 accepts the traditional order, on the basis that Dem. 1.17 refers to an attack by Philip not on Olynthus itself but only its dependent cities and by accepting the scholia's inference that the general alluded to in Dem. 2.25 as on trial was Chares, who commanded the first and third expeditionary force. Sealey (1955) 93 and Sealey (1993) 138–139 place the *Second Olynthiac* after the despatch of the first expeditionary force. Cf. also Fox (1997) 195–199.

[6] Ryder (2000) 49. Trevett (2011) 53 suggests at the time of the delivery of the *Third Olynthiac* Athens' first relief force had not yet been sent, as Demosthenes makes no mention of it. Dem 3.16 seems to indicate that the alliance with Olynthus had been concluded and support promised: Sealey (1955) 94. Cawkwell (1962a) 134 also argues, on the basis of Dem. 3.6–7, for a close association between the third speech and speeches 1 and 2, suggesting that the appropriate context is the early stages of the war, whereas others have argued that it was delivered after Olynthus' final appeal to Athens in 348: Worthington (2008) 77 and (2013) 139. At Dem. 3.6, with the words εἰ γὰρ μὴ βοηθήσετε παντὶ σθένει κατὰ τὸ δυνατόν, "if you do not send aid 'with all your strength to the best of your ability'", Demosthenes seems to be quoting from the recently signed alliance: Sandys (1924) 191–192; McQueen (1986) 167; Trevett (2011) 58 n. 18, and the speech may be a response to foot-dragging on the part of the Athenians in despatching the first expeditionary force. See also Ellis and Milns (1970) 36, Cawkwell (1978) 86–87 and Hammond (1994) 60.

rhetorical ways.⁷ There is even the possibility, as MacDowell has suggested, that one or more of the speeches were never actually delivered.⁸ Even if all three speeches were delivered, they did not have the desired effect. The Athenian response was limited at best.⁹

Despite the limited success of the *Olynthiacs*, they do mark an important step in Demosthenes' development as a public speaker. Demosthenes presents himself as a self-assured statesman,¹⁰ showing greater confidence in his rhetorical powers;¹¹ the speeches reveal a rhetorical intensity, for which he became famous in antiquity.¹² The arguments are more focused with Demosthenes adapting his demegoric speeches to the style of his successful forensic speeches: the apologetic manner in which he introduces himself and the importance of narrative to create a compelling argument to act;¹³ there is both a force and clarity not evident in Demosthenes' earlier deliberative speeches,¹⁴ a combination of fullness and brevity or as some ancient critics explained, rapidity and abundance, where a single idea is expanded and repeated, restated and reworked in a series of short clauses.¹⁵ The speeches themselves are rich in metaphor and similes.¹⁶

---

7 Tuplin (1998) 280; cf. Erbse (1956) who argues that they were delivered at the same meeting of the Assembly and Pearson (1981) 123 at short intervals between them.
8 MacDowell (2009) 238.
9 In the end, the first expeditionary force under the command of Chares consisted of 2000 Thracian peltasts and 30 triremes already with Chares, deployed in the north Aegean, and an additional 8 triremes (Philochorus *BNJ* 328 F49). See Cawkwell (1962a) 130–134 on the anemic response by Athens and possible strategic reasons for providing such limited aid; cf. Carter (1971) 418–419, and especially Burke (1984) and Burke (2002) for economic considerations behind the Athenian response. Contrast Hammond (1994) 51–52, 60, who considers the Athenian response robust.
10 Yunis (1996) 259.
11 Pearson (1964) 96.
12 Kennedy (1994) 74; see Yunis (1993) 260–261; Milns (2000) 210; Cooper (2000) 229–230 and Cooper (2004) 155–156. This intensity was created by emotional rhetoric achieved through figures of speech and thought: Wooten (2010) 14–17, but the emotional intensity of *Philippic 1*, as Wooten (2010) 17–18 points out, is lacking in the *Olynthiacs 1 & 2*, the tone of which appears earnest and calm, but found in *Olynthiac 3*, which could be explained by the context, if the speech was delivered after repeated delays by Athens in despatching its initial relief force.
13 Pearson (1964) 101–102, 104–106; Pearson (1981) 122–123; cf. Milns (2000) 211 and Wooten (2008) 11–14. This new style is first evident in the *First Philippic*.
14 Pearson (1964) 96; Cooper (2004) 153.
15 Hermogenes *On Types of Style* 68 (Wooten (1987) = Rabe 318); see Wooten (1989) 582–584 for his analysis of Hermogenes with reference to *Third Philippic* 36–37 to illustrate this combination of rapidity and abundance. Cf. Cooper (2004) 153–154. On fewer and more focused arguments with more circular presentation of ideas (ring composition) see Wooten (2008) 11–12 and Wooten (2010) 6–9 particularly at 9–13 for an analysis of the *Olynthiacs*.

One important theme, explored in these speeches, is that of *kairos*, and many of Demosthenes' arguments and vivid descriptions turn on that theme.

In this paper, I would like to explore how images and descriptions of the Macedonian court, as they are presented by Demosthenes across the *Olynthiacs* and *Philippics*, but more particularly in the first two *Olynthiacs*, are exploited by Demosthenes and connect to his broader rhetorical strategy and his argument about *kairos*. As we shall see, various rhetorical strategies are used by Demosthenes throughout the speeches, in an attempt to persuade the Athenians to act. In the *First Olynthiac* (Dem. 1) Demosthenes contrasts Philip's speed with Athens' indolence. Philip, we are told, has an immense advantage over the Athenians in terms of the speed and opportunity of war (*kairos*): he is Master of Policy, general, treasurer and is always at the head of an army (Dem. 1.4). But tyranny like this is mistrusted by constitutional forms of government (*politeiai*), including that of Olynthus. In that context, Demosthenes argues, the Athenians must not let the opportunity (*kairos*) slip, as so often happened in the past (Dem. 1.8). Their reluctance to act has raised Philip to his present prosperity well beyond that of any Macedonian before him. But now an opportunity has come from Olynthus, unsolicited, better than any other opportunity before (1.9). In public matters a city, which fails to use the opportunity that presents itself, is like a man who fails to protect his possessions (1.11). Restless activity is ingrained in Philip to the point that he cannot keep still. If Philip assumes the stance that he must always increase his holdings, whereas the Athenians refuse to face difficulties, then the only expectation is for the war to be transferred to Athens (1.14). By their indolence the Athenians will be acting like a man who has borrowed at high interest for a temporary benefit, only to forfeit his estates in the end. The rhetorical strategy is to argue that an unexpected opportunity has presented itself to the Athenians, which they must seize upon to preserve their interests. At the heart of the speech is a comparison between Philip's relentless activity and Athens' continual hesitation.

In the *Second Olynthiac* Demosthenes adopts a different rhetorical strategy that aims to show that Philip's strength is illusory. At the centre of the argument is a description of a Macedonian court full of corruption and debauchery (2.17–20). There was some hint of this in the *First Olynthiac*, when Demosthenes stated that tyranny is mistrusted by *politeiai*, constitutional forms of government. But here he expands on the theme more fully. Philip has gained power through rapacity and crime, but underneath there is no solid substructure based on truth and justice, which are essential for affairs of state as found in constitutional

---

16 Tuplin (1998) 282–285.

forms of government. Any slip by Philip will undo him (2.10). By itself, we are told, Macedonia is weak and full of defects (2.14). And the biggest weakness is the court itself. Anyone experienced in war and battle, out of jealously, Philip keeps in the background as he wants all the credit for himself, insatiable ambition being one of his many faults. Any prudent and just man, who is unable to tolerate the daily licentiousness of his life, his drunkenness and lewd dancing, is pushed aside and considered of no account. Those about him are robbers and flatters, capable of getting drunk and preforming lewd dances, the likes of whom have been expelled from Athens but welcomed into his court. As Demosthenes notes, these provide great proof of Philip's *kakodaimonia*; though his present success overshadows it, any slip on his part will fully expose it (2.18–20). The Macedonian court has thus become Athens' *kairos*.

First Olynthiac

In the *First Olynthiac* a key word or theme is *kairos*, as indeed it is across all three speeches.[17] The Athenians are repeatedly told that they must seize "the opportunity," the *kairos* that is before their eyes.[18] At 1.8 Demosthenes urges them not to let the opportunity that has fallen into their lap to slip by, as has often happened in the past, when they had returned from the Euboean expedition (357) and the Amphipolitans Hierax and Stratocles were present on the *bema*, urging them to sail and take possession of Amphipolis. If the Athenians had shown the same concern about their own interests as they had for Euboeans, Amphipolis would have been theirs. In this case *kairos* had presented itself in the voice of the envoys from Amphipolis making their pleas from the speaker's platform. This image of *kairos*, as it were speaking out in the Athenian Assembly, is picked up in a startling metaphor at the beginning of the speech, where at 1.2 *kairos* is personified: "The present *kairos* (the attack on Olynthus by Philip), men of Athens, all but speaks uttering a voice that you must take hold of those matters, if you are concerned for their safety."[19] At 1.1 Demosthenes has just urged the Athe-

---

[17] Tuplin (1998) 279 and 314 n. 42; Usher (2004) 58. See Dem. 1.2, 3, 8, 9, 11, 20, 24; 2.2, 8, 30; 3.3, 5, 6, 7, 16, 35. Cf. Pearson (1981) 130; Jaeger (1938) 129–133, who argues that the *First Olynthiac* is "built up on the motif of *Kairos*."
[18] For detailed studies of the meaning of *kairos* in Greek literature of the 5th and 4th centuries see Wilson (1980) and Wilson (1981).
[19] Dem. 1.2: ὁ μὲν οὖν παρὼν καιρός, ὦ ἄνδρες Ἀθηναῖοι, μόνον οὐχὶ λέγει φωνὴν ἀφιεὶς ὅτι τῶν πραγμάτων ὑμῖν ἐκείνων αὐτοῖς ἀντιληπτέον ἐστίν, εἴπερ ὑπὲρ σωτηρίας αὐτῶν

nians to listen attentively to those who wish to give advice, both those with well-considered plans (like Demosthenes himself), but also those who might offer advice "on the spur of the moment" (ἐκ τοῦ παραχρῆμ'). And *Kairos*, who has just showed up, can be imagined as mounting the bema and speaking on the spur of the moment, like other speakers in the Assembly.[20] At 1.9, after Demosthenes had cited the examples of Amphipolis and the sieges of Pydna, Potidaea, Methone and Pagasae, all which had been captured by Philip, he comments "now a certain *Kairos* has come to the city, this one of the Olynthians, unsolicited, one no less important than those ones before."[21] The way the Greek is structured would suggest that Demosthenes is still thinking metaphorically of *kairos* as an envoy, like the ones who came from Amphipolis and spoke from the bema, and like the one who is imagined at the beginning of his speech as all but speaking out with a voice. There is a sustained image here.

The personification of *Kairos* is fascinating; we can imagine that Demosthenes has in mind some sort of image, like Lysippus' statue of the deified *Kairos*, who appears for a fleeting moment, only to race by, if not immediately grabbed by his fore-locks.[22] More than one modern scholar has connected, at least implicitly if not explicitly, Demosthenes' personification of *Kairos* with the Lysippean statue, even if the latter simply "imbued with life" what Demos-

---

φροντίζετε. Tuplin (1998) 283 notes that the image is ambiguous, somewhere between metaphor and simile.
20 Tuplin (1998) 283 notes that *kairos* is being assimilated into the Assembly speakers noted in Dem. 1.1, especially those who will speak ἐκ τοῦ παραχρῆμ'. Later (299), however, Tuplin suggests that at 1.1. Demosthenes attempts to assimilate himself with those who have ideas on the spur of the moment rather than those arriving with well-considered ideas, but according to tradition Demosthenes rarely spoke ἐπὶ καιροῦ, "at the moment": Plut. *Dem*. 8.2 with the discussion of Cooper (2000) 228–229. Theophrastus wrote a work περὶ καιρῶν, which was a work of rhetoric, in which this discussion of Demosthenes likely figured: Cooper (2000) 242 n. 14. For modern discussion of the place of *kairos* in 5th and 4th century Greek rhetoric see Carter (1988).
21 Dem. 1.9: νυνὶ δὴ καιρὸς ἥκει τις, οὗτος ὁ τῶν Ὀλυνθίων, αὐτόματος τῇ πόλει, ὃς οὐδενός ἐστιν ἐλάττων τῶν προτέρων ἐκείνων.
22 Lysippus's statue either stood before his workshop in Sicyon or in Olympia, where a base in the form of an astragal has been found, near the altar to Kairos, which stood at the stadium entrance (Paus. 5.14.9). See Pollitt (1986) 53–54; Johnson (1927), 163–165 and Appendix 1 nos. 33–39, 67 for ancient references and descriptions, and Prauscello (2006) 514–515. Posidippus (Austin & Bastianini no. 142) provides a near-contemporary description of the statue, which was set up by the artist, we are told "as a lesson," whether as an "allegorical elaboration" on the fleeting and ephemeral nature of opportunities (Pollitt (1986) 54), or as a didactic statement about his art (Stewart 1978). For translations of Posidippus' epigram see Pollitt (1990) 103, Austin and Bastianini (2002) 181 and Prauscello (2006) 513.

thenes was only thinking and expressing metaphorically.²³ Certainly later rhetoricians, like Alexander Numenius, were struck by the vividness of the image that Demosthenes presents here.²⁴ In his work *On Figures of thought and style* (Περὶ τῶν τῆς διανοίας καὶ τῆς λέξεως σχημάτων) under the heading *Dramatization or Personification* (Περὶ προσωποποιΐας), which he defines as "the shaping of a person who from the beginning never existed or once existed but is no longer" (ἡ προσωποιΐα δὲ ἐστι προσώπου διάπλασις ἤτοι τὴν ἀρχὴν μὴ γενομένου πώποτε μεν, ἢ γενομένου μέν, οὐκ ἔτι δὲ ὄντος), Alexander (Spengel 3.19.15–30) cites two examples, "the present *kairos*" of *Olynthiac* 1.2 and Aeschines 3.257, the latter passage representing an example of "someone who once existed but is no longer." In that passage Aeschines invites the jurors to imagine they see on the *bema*, where Aeschines now stands, Solon (and other benefactors of the city), urging them with restraint as is fitting for him (σωφρόνως, ὡς προσῆκον αὐτῷ, δεόμενον), not to heed Demosthenes' arguments. We cannot be sure, but Aeschines' language suggests that he is visualizing the statue of Solon on Salamis, which he expressly asks the jurors of the Timarchus case (Aeschin. 1.25) to recall, as a reminder of the posture Solon held, with hand in robe, when he addressed the Assembly, in sharp contrast to the antics of Timarchus. Demosthenes (19.251) indicates clearly that Aeschines had enacted the pose, when he made his criticism of Timarchus. Nor was Demosthenes himself above making dramatic gestures. Aeschines (3.167) ridicules Demosthenes for whirling around in circle on the bema, as if he was maneuvering against Alexander. As Aeschines insinuates, Demosthenes orchestrated this gesture to fit his claim of organizing the Laconian uprising and causing the Thessalians and Perrhaebians to revolt. Demosthenes' response (18.232) confirms that he did just that, as he complains that Aeschines mimicked his words and gestures but deflects Aeschines' criticism by suggesting the fate of Greece did not depend on whether he spoke this or that word or moved his hand this or that way.²⁵ In the present context, we can well imagine Demosthenes making a gesture to emphasize how fleeting the present *kairos* was. It may be too fanciful to suggest that Demosthenes had a specific statue or image in mind when he spoke his words,

---

23 Stafford (1998) 55 n. 14; Usher (1999) 221 n. 177; Usher (2004) 58.
24 Later descriptions of the statue by Callistratus (*Statuaram Descriptiones* 6) and Himerius (*Eclogae* 14.1) seem largely rhetorical exercises. On this point, see Johnson (1927) 164.
25 See Cooper (2004) 157–160 for a discussion of these passages from Aeschines and Demosthenes in the context of the importance that Demosthenes placed on declamation for rhetorical persuasion.

but the personification was certainly memorable enough to be noted by ancient rhetoricians.[26]

Returning to the opening sections of the speech, what is also envisioned is a spirited debate in the Assembly. On the one side is the present *Kairos* speaking out and urging the Athenians to act on behalf of Olynthus, the envoy from Olynthus, as it were. On the other side is Philip, who at 1.3 is characterized by Demosthenes as one might a speaker's opponent as "villainous and clever" (πανοῦργος καὶ δεινός), yielding some points, when it suits him, at other times making threats that might appear reasonable and credible; at other times slandering. This sustained imagery of a debate within the Assembly has an important rhetorical point, as debate and freedom of expression (*isêgoria*) characterizes constitutional forms of government like Athens, another important theme within the *Olynthiacs*.

At 1.20 after proposing a relief force to Olynthus and a naval expedition to raid Philip's territory, Demosthenes turns to the question of funding the expedition.[27] The soldiers must be provided for, i.e. there must be a military fund and a single system for receiving pay and for performing one's duties, whereas the Athenians think they should appropriate the money for festivals without any trouble.[28] If that is the case the only option left is to introduce an *eisphora* as the circumstances demand. Others have proposed other measures for raising money. The Athenians, Demosthenes urges, should choose one proposal that they think is advantageous, "and while there is still an opportunity, a *kairos*, take hold of the matters." *Kairos* has now been assimilated into the very propos-

---

[26] Much depends on when Lysippus was active as a sculptor. He may have been active as early as the 370s, which could mean that the statue was created before 349, though some scholars place the Kairos statue in second half of the fourth century. On an early date for start of his career see Pollitt (1986) 47; for arguments for either an earlier or later date to the start of his career see Johnson (1927) 58–73, who concludes that Lysippus was born in 375 at the earliest as there is no indication of any work before 350.

[27] Demosthenes' strategy (1.17) of despatching two forces, a relief force consisting of citizen soldiers, and a raiding force of triremes and soldiers, is essentially what he recommends in the *First Philippic*, delivered in 351: Cawkwell (1978) 87; Sealey (1993) 138; Ryder (2000) 54; Worthington (2008) 74; MacDowell (2009) 232; Worthington (2013) 133.

[28] This is a veiled reference to the Theoric Fund. Libanius in his *Hypothesis* to the speech (Dem. 1 *Hyp.* 10 Foerster) speaks of a law introduced forbidding anyone on the pain of death from proposing the transfer of Theoric money to the Stratiotic Fund. For a discussion on Demosthenes and the Theoric Fund see Harris (2006) 121–139, Harris (2018a) 166–167 n. 218 and Harris (2019) 375. Cf. Cawkwell (1962b), Cawkwell (1963) 53–56, Hansen (1976) and Mader (2005) 14–20. If indeed the law existed (see the arguments against it by Harris), it has been attributed to Eubulus on basis of the scholia to Dem. 1.1 (Dindorf 33.11): Hansen (1976) 239 and Hansen (1991) 263.

al adopted by the Assembly to raise money to fund the expedition. At 1.24 Demosthenes urges the Athenians to consider Philip's *akairia*, his lack of *kairos*, as their own *kairos* and readily undertake the matter.[29] In this context, the difficulty facing Philip that denies him *kairos* and in turn becomes Athens' *kairos* is the attitude of the various *ethnoi* that he has conquered, the Paeonians or Illyrians, who would prefer to be autonomous and free than to be slaves, unaccustomed to being subservient to anyone and in particular to a person who is hubristic. Hubris defines the tyrant.[30] And a similar point is made earlier in the speech about Olynthus, which, as we have seen, has now become Athens' *Kairos*, speaking out in the Assembly. At 1.5 Demosthenes notes that the Olynthians are not fighting for glory or some piece of land but to prevent the overthrow and enslavement of their country, fully aware of how Philip treated the Amphipolitans and the Pydnaeans. Almost as a gnomic truism, Demosthenes then states "tyranny, I think, is wholly distrusted by constitutional forms of government, especially when they share a border."[31] The argument is meant to anticipate and address any objections to Demosthenes' earlier point at 1.4, where he argues that Philip's immense advantage over the Athenians in terms of the speed and *kairos* of war, as general, ruler and treasurer wrapped into one man, cannot effect any kind of reconciliation with the Olynthians, given their distrust of the tyrant. Consequently, Olynthus' distrust of Philip, the tyrant, has become Athens' *kairos*, and as we have seen metaphorically speaks out in the Assembly, the very symbol of constitutional and democratic governments.[32]

Distrust of the tyrant is a common rhetorical theme in Athenian oratory. For instance, in his opening remarks against Timarchus (1.4) Aeschines, when he de-

---

29 Dem. 1.24: δεῖ τοίνυν ὑμᾶς, ὦ ἄνδρες Ἀθηναῖοι, τὴν ἀκαιρίαν τὴν ἐκείνου καιρὸν ὑμέτερον νομίσαντας ἑτοίμως συνάρασθαι τὰ πράγματα. Demosthenes uses the word *kairos* two further times in 1.24: first, the Athenians are to reflect on how readily Philip would march on them if he should have such a *kairos* as they currently have, with a war on their borders; and secondly, would they not be ashamed, if they did not dare, when they had the *kairos*, to do to Philip the very things he would do, if he was able.
30 Rosivach (1988) 53–54; for this linkage between hubris and tyranny in oratory see Lys. 33.22, Isoc. 4.80, Dem. 17.3, 82, with Hendren's (2015) discussion of Meidias' tyrannical traits in Dem 21.
31 Dem. 1.5: καὶ ὅλως ἄπιστον, οἶμαι, ταῖς πολιτείαις ἡ τυραννίς, ἄλλως τε κἂν ὅμορον χώραν ἔχωσι. Cf. Leopold (1981) 235–236 for a discussion of this passage, which is patterned on the arguments in the Demosthenes' *For the Freedom of the Rhodians* (Dem. 15.17–18).
32 See Harris (2018b) for a discussion of Demosthenes' use of the stereotype of the tyrant in his characterization of Philip throughout his political speeches. Leopold (1981) focuses on the theme of distrust as a basic principle of the foreign policy advocated by Demosthenes across his deliberate speeches. My goal here is to understand this theme within the broader context of Demosthenes' rhetorical strategy in the *Olynthiacs*. Cf. Harris (2019) 374.

lineates the differences between tyranny, oligarchy and democracy, notes that tyranny and oligarchy are governed by temperaments of those in power, whereas democracies are governed by the rule of law.[33] In a democracy, the person of the citizen and the constitution are protected by the laws, whereas tyrants and oligarchs are protected by distrust and armed forces.[34] Distrust characterizes the rule of tyrants, both the tyrant towards others, and others toward the tyrant.[35] And that is Demosthenes' point in the *First Olynthiac*.[36]

Likewise, in the *Second Philippic* (6.24–25) Demosthenes argues that the one common bulwark, something innate in men of good sense, which is good and a source of salvation for everyone involved, but especially for democracies against tyrants, is mistrust. For every king and tyrant, he states, is an enemy of freedom and the law. As we have seen, in Athenian rhetoric the rule of law and its corollary freedom characterize democracies as opposed to tyranny.[37] In the *Third Philippic* (9.38) Demosthenes comes close to equating *kairos* with distrust of tyranny, something he has made explicit in the *First Olynthiac* in connection with Olynthus:

> And so, the *kairos* of each situation, which fortune often equips even the careless against the attentive, could not be bought from politicians or generals, nor our concord with one another, nor our mistrust of tyrants and barbarians, nor any such thing, but now all things are exported as if from a market.[38]

---

[33] Aeschines makes essentially the same statement at 3.6, with a couple of variations: though he equates democracies with the rule of law, particularly as it is administered through the courts, he does not mention distrust as the tyrant's protection, but instead speaks of the juror's vote as an essential guarantee of their freedom of speech, another important aspect of democracy. On this point, see Cooper (2011) 204. Cf. Dem. 24.75–76.

[34] As Harris (2018b) 167 notes, in Athenian political discourse the tyrant was the antithesis of the rule of law and democracy. Cf. Leopold (1981) 228–229, who notes that this antithesis goes back to Herodotus (3.80.2–6; 7.104.1–5), and Rosivach (1988) 47, 53, 55–56, who notes that tyranny represents the opposite of *isonomia*, *isêgoria* and *isokratia*, features of democracy. For rhetorical examples, see Aeschin. 1.4–5, 3.6, 220–221; Dem. 15.17–20, 22.52–53, 23.124–126, 24.75–76. Cf. Miller (2002) 413.

[35] Cf. Harris (2018b) 169.

[36] In Dem. 23.108, Demosthenes argues that Olynthian distrust began with Philip's growing power: Leopold (1981) 231.

[37] On freedom as a defining feature of democracy see Arist. *Pol.* 1317a40–1317b2 with the discussions of Farrar (2007) 179–80 and Cooper (2011) 199–200.

[38] Dem. 9.38: τὸν οὖν καιρὸν ἑκάστου τῶν πραγμάτων, ὃν ἡ τύχη καὶ τοῖς ἀμελοῦσιν κατὰ τῶν προσεχόντων πολλάκις παρασκευάζει, οὐκ ἦν πρίασθαι παρὰ τῶν λεγόντων οὐδὲ τῶν στρατηγούντων, οὐδὲ τὴν πρὸς ἀλλήλους ὁμόνοιαν, οὐδὲ τὴν πρὸς τοὺς τυράννους καὶ τοὺς βαρβάρους ἀπιστίαν, οὐδ' ὅλως τοιοῦτον οὐδέν. [39] νῦν δ' ἅπανθ' ὥσπερ ἐξ ἀγορᾶς ἐκπέπραται ταῦτα. Sim-

The context of this statement is a comparison between the Greeks of Demosthenes' day, who allow Philip's hubris of Greece to go unavenged (9.34), with the Greeks of old (9.36) who were as eager for freedom as the Greeks of today are for slavery: "There was something at that time, men of Athens, in the dispositions of the many, which does not exist now, which even overcame the wealth of Persia and led Greece to freedom."[39] The Persian King was both a barbarian and a tyrant, and at 9.38 the two are equated in the distrust of tyrants and barbarians that Demosthenes tells us could not be bought in past, but now can, as it were, be purchased on the open market from politicians and generals.[40] Philip himself has earlier in the speech (9.31) been described in scathing language by Demosthenes as the worst kind of barbarian, "who is not only not a Greek and not related to the Greeks, but not even a barbarian from a place which is honorable to mention but from wretched Macedonia from whence it was formerly impossible to buy a decent slave."[41] Perhaps one could speak with some admiration of Persia and the Great King, but certainly not of Macedonia or Philip, who at the same time as being made out to be a barbarian, is presented as a barbarian of the worst kind and presumably of the worst kind of tyrant. Indeed, Demosthenes provides his audience in the Third *Philippic* with a litany of wrongs (9.26–35) committed by Philip against the Greeks: the destruction of Olynthus, Methone and Apollonia, along with 32 cities in Thrace, and the destruction of Phocis. He has robbed the Thessalians of their *politeiai* and in their place set up tetrarchies to enslave them. In Euboea he has installed tyrannies, and the list goes on. To crown his hubris, he is now organizing the Pythian Games, a festival common to the Greeks. What we find in these early demegoric speeches of Demosthenes is a constellation of ideas, around *kairos*, distrust of tyranny, freedom and *politeiai*. The *Kairos*, which we see in the *First Olynthiac*, speaking freely from the bema of the Assembly, the very symbol of constitutional forms of government, appears in the form of the mistrust that the Olynthians and members of other *politeiai* have toward tyranny.

---

ilar rhetorical arguments from past actions of the Greeks are found in Lys. 33.6–9; Dem. 15. 23–24; Hyp. 6 (*Epit.*) 20–21.
39 Dem. 9.36: ἦν τι τότ', ἦν, ὦ ἄνδρες Ἀθηναῖοι, ἐν ταῖς τῶν πολλῶν διανοίαις, ὃ νῦν οὐκ ἔστιν, ὃ καὶ τοῦ Περσῶν ἐκράτησε πλούτου καὶ ἐλευθέραν ἦγε τὴν Ἑλλάδα.
40 See Dem. 14.6–7 and Dem. 15.8, where the orator characterizes the Persian King in similar terms as he does Philip in the *Olynthiacs* and *Philippics*. At Dem. 14.6 the Persian King is called *barbaros*; at Dem. 3:16 Philip is so labelled.
41 Dem 9.31: οὐ μόνον οὐχ Ἕλληνος ὄντος οὐδὲ προσήκοντος οὐδὲν τοῖς Ἕλλησιν, ἀλλ' οὐδὲ βαρβάρου ἐντεῦθεν ὅθεν καλὸν εἰπεῖν, ἀλλ' ὀλέθρου Μακεδόνος, ὅθεν οὐδ' ἀνδράποδον σπουδαῖον οὐδὲν ἦν πρότερον πρίασθαι.

Second Olynthiac

Demosthenes' argument in the *First Olynthiac*, that Olynthian distrust of Philip has proven to be Athens' opportunity to act is anticipated or echoed, depending on which speech was delivered first, in the *Second Olynthiac*. At 2.8, after describing how Philip had in turn hoodwinked first Athens with promises of handing over Amphipolis, then Olynthus with promises of Potidaea and finally the Thessalians with promises of Magnesia, Demosthenes states "Philip's affairs have reached this point of *kairos* ... that those who have once been deceived will not trust him further."[42] The distrust that Philip's perfidy has engendered is now proven to be a *kairos*, an opportunity to act upon, and to persuade the Athenians not to hesitate but to act quickly; Demosthenes attempts to show that Philip's power as tyrant is in fact illusory and can be quickly undone, as it is not based on anything permanent or lasting. Demosthenes needs to make this additional point to counter any possible objection or thought on the part of his audience, who may accept Demosthenes' argument that once deceived neighbouring states will no longer trust Philip, but still think he will retain power by force because he controls the harbours and towns. As Demosthenes argues at 2.9–10, "whenever someone gains power, as Philip has, from greed and villainy, the first pretext and a small slip can overturn and destroy everything. For it is, it is, men of Athens, impossible for an unjust perjurer and liar to gain permanent power, but such things last for moment and short time."[43] And here Demosthenes uses a simile to underscore his point and conclude this part of the speech: "just as the strongest parts of a house, I think, or of a ship or any such structures must be the substructures, so too the principles and bases of all actions must be truth and justice." But there is none of this, Demosthenes concludes, in Philip's accomplishments.[44]

---

[42] Dem. 2.8: καιροῦ μὲν δή, ὦ ἄνδρες Ἀθηναῖοι, πρὸς τοῦτο πάρεστι Φιλίππῳ τὰ πράγματα: ἢ παρελθών τις ἐμοί, μᾶλλον δ' ὑμῖν δειξάτω, ἢ ὡς οὐκ ἀληθῆ ταῦτ' ἐγὼ λέγω, ἢ ὡς οἱ τὰ πρῶτ' ἐξηπατημένοι τὰ λοιπὰ πιστεύσουσιν, ἢ ὡς οἱ παρὰ τὴν αὐτῶν ἀξίαν δεδουλωμένοι Θετταλοὶ νῦν οὐκ ἂν ἐλεύθεροι γένοιντ' ἄσμενοι.

[43] Dem. 2.9–10: ὅταν δ' ἐκ πλεονεξίας καὶ πονηρίας τις ὥσπερ οὗτος ἰσχύσῃ, ἡ πρώτη πρόφασις καὶ μικρὸν πταῖσμα ἅπαντ' ἀνεχαίτισε καὶ διέλυσεν. οὐ γάρ ἔστιν, οὐκ ἔστιν, ὦ ἄνδρες Ἀθηναῖοι, ἀδικοῦντα κἀπιορκοῦντα καὶ ψευδόμενον δύναμιν βεβαίαν κτήσασθαι, ἀλλὰ τὰ τοιαῦτ' εἰς μὲν ἅπαξ καὶ βραχὺν χρόνον ἀντέχει.

[44] Dem. 2.10: ὥσπερ γὰρ οἰκίας, οἶμαι, καὶ πλοίου καὶ τῶν ἄλλων τῶν τοιούτων τὰ κάτωθεν ἰσχυρότατ' εἶναι δεῖ, οὕτω καὶ τῶν πράξεων τὰς ἀρχὰς καὶ τὰς ὑποθέσεις ἀληθεῖς καὶ δικαίας εἶναι προσήκει. τοῦτο δ' οὐκ ἔνι νῦν ἐν τοῖς πεπραγμένοις Φιλίππῳ.

To underscore further that Philip's position is not based on a solid foundation, Demosthenes turns to a description of Philip's court at 2.17–20. As Aeschines noted in the opening of *Against Timarchus*, tyranny and oligarchy are protected by distrust, and such distrust is at the centre of Philip's court. Demosthenes notes four weaknesses, and his account, we are told, is based on a report from a man who has been in Macedonia and is completely incapable of lying (ὡς δ' ἐγὼ τῶν ἐν αὐτῇ τῇ χώρᾳ γεγενημένων τινὸς ἤκουον, ἀνδρὸς οὐδαμῶς οἵου τε ψεύδεσθαι), unlike Philip who has been characterized earlier by Demosthenes as a perjurer and liar, whose success based on injustice lacks the substructure of a lasting foundation. There is a lovely symmetry between the earlier passage and our court description, each ending in a simile to make Demosthenes' rhetorical point: at 2.10 the simile of a building lacking a solid substructure and here a patient with an underlying disease.[45]

Demosthenes points to four weaknesses in Philip's court.[46] First Philip's mercenaries and foot companions are no better than any other troops; secondly, anyone experienced in war and battle are removed by Philip out of jealousy, which is unsurpassed, the obvious distrust of the tyrant towards others. Thirdly, anyone who is prudent and just, who cannot stomach the licentiousness of Philip's lifestyle, the drunkenness and lewd dancing, is pushed aside and regarded of no account. Finally, the remainder who surround Philip are robbers and flatters, men capable of getting drunk and performing such lewd dances, which Demosthenes hesitates to mention. This report, Demosthenes tells us, is so obviously true as Philip includes in his company the notorious public slave Callias and other such men, mimes and poets of shameful songs that are intended to raise a laugh.[47] The notoriety of Philip's court and its drinking parties is mentioned by Diodorus (16.55, 87) and Theopompus (*BNJ* 115 FF 27, 162, 224–225, 282). In particular, in book 49 of his *Philippica*, in F 225 a–b, Theopompus seems to echo Demosthenes' description: there we are told that Philip would reject all those who were orderly in their behavior and took care of their private property, but he honored and promoted men who were extravagant and lived

---

[45] See Turpin (1998) 284–285. There may be a further symmetry if, as Wooten (1979) 160 argues, "the first pretext" (ἡ πρώτη πρόφασις) in 2.9 is used in a medical sense.

[46] As Harris (2018b) notes, these are stereotypical weaknesses attributed to tyrants that do not necessarily apply to Philip.

[47] Dem. 2.19: Καλλίαν ἐκεῖνον τὸν δημόσιον καὶ τοιούτους ἀνθρώπους, μίμους γελοίων καὶ ποιητὰς αἰσχρῶν ᾀσμάτων, ὧν εἰς τοὺς συνόντας ποιοῦσιν εἵνεκα τοῦ γελασθῆναι, τούτους ἀγαπᾷ καὶ περὶ αὐτὸν ἔχει.

for drink and dice.⁴⁸ If we accept that this passage in the *Second Olynthiac* was not revised, based on Demosthenes' familiarity with Philip's court from his time on the embassy surrounding the negotiation over the Peace of Philocrates (in 346),⁴⁹ it may well be that at the time of the actual delivery of the *Second Olynthiac* stories of the excesses of Philip's court had begun to reach Athens, or better yet were simply conjured up here by Demosthenes' mention of the notorious Callias, whose behaviour was obviously familiar to Athenians. We know nothing of him, but we do know of another public slave from Aeschines, Pittalacus, who was well off (Aeschin. 1.54), ran a gambling business and had his own house; he liked to frequent a gaming house that specialized in gaming tables, cockfighting and dice. Whether such behaviour characterized all public slaves, it certainly characterized Pittalacus (if we can believe Aeschines), and the way Demosthenes speaks of Callias, he seems to be a public slave of a similar ilk. In any case, it is rhetorically effective, as the audience's familiarity with the likes of Callias and other public slaves substantiates the veracity of the claims of his anonymous source, and contrast with Philip's dishonestly, highlighted earlier in the speech.

Demosthenes concludes his description of Philip's court with another simile, but before he does, he comments on what he has just described about Philip's court and the company it keeps: "And yet these things, even if one thinks they are small, men of Athens, are for men of good sense, great proof of that man's mind and *kakodaimonia*."⁵⁰ As he further notes, Philip's current success only masks his underlying condition, but "if he stumbles in any way, at that moment these vices of his will be fully exposed."⁵¹ The comment here alludes to what Demosthenes had said earlier at 2.9, where he noted "a small stumble

---

48 See Flower (1994) 105–111, who in comparing Dem. 2.17–19 with FF 162, 224, 225a–b, 236, notes that "their agreement indicates that this picture of court life was fairly widespread and could not have been a literary or rhetorical invention by Theopompus." But was it a rhetorical invention by Demosthenes? Perhaps. Pownall (2005) 267–271, though pointing out the striking similarities between Demosthenes and Theopmpus, notes the uncertainty of determining who served as the source of the other. But see Shrimpton (1991) 165–171, who tentatively suggests that Theopompus was Demosthenes' informant.
49 Cf. Dem. 19.196–198.
50 *Kakodaimonia* is obviously a loaded word here; its extended meaning can carry the idea of delusion or perversion: MacGregor (1950) 61; McQueen (1986) 147. In Ar. *Plut.* 510 it is coupled with *mania*. In *EN* 1097b2–4 (cf. *Pol.* 1325b14–15) Aristotle argues that people should pursue virtue, like honour, not only for its intrinsic value but also to promote *eudaimonia*, which is the opposite of *kakodaimonia*, the latter being thus cultivated by the deliberate pursuit of vices: Heinaman (1993) 48, 52, 55–56
51 Dem. 2.20: ἀλλ', οἶμαι, νῦν μὲν ἐπισκοτεῖ τούτοις τὸ κατορθοῦν· αἱ γὰρ εὐπραξίαι δειναὶ συγκρύψαι τὰ τοιαῦτ' ὀνείδη· εἰ δέ τι πταίσει, τότ' ἀκριβῶς αὐτοῦ ταῦτ' ἐξετασθήσεται. Cf. 2.9: ἡ πρώτη πρόφασις καὶ μικρὸν πταῖσμα ἅπαντ' ἀνεχαίτισε καὶ διέλυσεν.

will overthrow and destroy everything." And to hit home this point, just as he had in the earlier passage, Demosthenes concludes with a simile:

> for as in bodies, so long as someone is healthy, nothing is noticed, but when some infirmity happens, everything is disturbed, whether a fracture, sprain, or any other underlying problem, so it is the case with cities and tyrannies, while they conduct foreign wars, their evils are undetected by many, but when war along their borders entangle them, it makes everything clear.[52]

The infirmities of Philip's tyranny are to be found in his court, which dismisses the competent and surrounds itself with a group of flattering reprobates, some of whom were familiar, so Demosthenes intimates, to the Athenians. These vices reveal his underlying *kakodaimonia*, which in turn presents another *kairos* that should encourage the Athenians not to hesitate in committing to a campaign. Philip's current successes only mask this innate or underlying weakness, which once exposed, like a pre-existing disease, will lead to his downfall. His power was gained through greed and deception, and was not based on truth and justice, which should be the guiding principles of any political action, creating goodwill that binds allies together, particularly among *politeiai*, constitutional forms of government. Philip's perfidy has thus engendered mistrust, and Olynthus with its growing distrust of Philip, so Demosthenes argues, has presented the Athenians with the opportunity they need to act and expose further the weakness of Philip's tyranny, namely the distrust, which not only neighbouring *politeiai* feel toward Philip, but also his own distrust of those in his court.

Bibliography

Austin and Bastianini (2002): Colin Austin and Guido Bastianini (eds.), *Posidippi Pellaei quae supersunt omnia*. Milan.
Burke (1984): Edmund M. Burke, "Eubulus, Olynthus, and Euboea", in: *TAPA* 114, 111–120.
Burke (2002): Edmund M. Burke, "The Early Speeches of Demosthenes: Elite Bias in the Response to Economic Crisis", in: *Classical Antiquity* 21.2, 165–193.
Carter (1971): John M. Carter, "Athens, Euboea, and Olynthus", in: *Historia* 20.4, 418–429.
Carter (1988): Michael Carter, "*Stasis and Kairos*: Principles of Social Construction in Classical Rhetoric", in *Rhetoric Review* 7.1, 97–112.

---

52 Dem. 2.21: ὥσπερ γὰρ ἐν τοῖς σώμασιν, τέως μὲν ἂν ἐρρωμένος ᾖ τις, οὐδὲν ἐπαισθάνεται, ἐπὰν δ' ἀρρώστημά τι συμβῇ, πάντα κινεῖται, κἂν ῥῆγμα κἂν στρέμμα κἂν ἄλλο τι τῶν ὑπαρχόντων σαθρὸν ᾖ, οὕτω καὶ τῶν πόλεων καὶ τῶν τυράννων, ἕως μὲν ἂν ἔξω πολεμῶσιν, ἀφανῆ τὰ κακὰ τοῖς πολλοῖς ἐστιν, ἐπειδὰν δ' ὅμορος πόλεμος συμπλακῇ, πάντ' ἐποίησεν ἔκδηλα.

Cawkwell (1962a): George L. Cawkwell, "The Defence of Olynthus", in: *CQ* 12.1, 122–140.
Cawkwell (1962b): George L. Cawkwell, "Demosthenes and the Stratiotic Fund", in: *Mnemosyne* 15, 377–383.
Cawkwell (1963): George L. Cawkwell, "Eubulus", in: *JHS* 83, 47–67.
Cawkwell (1978): George L. Cawkwell, *Philip of Macedon*, London and Boston.
Cooper (2000): Craig Cooper, "Philosophers, Politics, Academics: Demosthenes' rhetorical reputation in antiquity", in: Ian Worthington (ed.), *Demosthenes: Statesman and Orator*, London and New York, 224–245.
Cooper (2004): Craig Cooper, "Demosthenes: actor on the political and forensic stage", in: C.J. Mackie (ed.), *Oral Performance and its Context*, Leiden and Boston, 145–161.
Cooper (2011): Craig Cooper, "Oligarchy and the Rule of Law", in: David Edward Tabachnick and Toivo Koivukoski (eds.), *On Oligarchy: Ancient Lessons for Global Politics*, Toronto, Buffalo and London, 196–216.
Ellis (1966): John R. Ellis, "The Date of Demosthenes' First Philippic", in: *Revue de Études Grecques* 79, 636–639.
Ellis (1967): John R. Ellis, "The Order of the *Olynthiacs*", in: *Historia* 16.1, 108–111.
Ellis (1976): John R. Ellis, *Philip II and Macedonian Imperialism*, Princeton.
Ellis and Milns (1970): John R. Ellis and Robert D Milns, *The Spectre of Philip*, Marrickville.
Farrar (2007): Cynthia Farrar, "Power to the People", in: Kurt A. Raaflaub *et al.* (eds.), *Origins of Democracy in Ancient Greece*, Berkley, Los Angeles and London, 170–195.
Flower (1994): Michael Attyah Flower, *Theopompus of Chios: History and Rhetoric in the Fourth Century BC*, Oxford.
Foerster (1915): Richard Foerster (ed.), *Libanii Opera* Volume 8, Leipzig.
Fox (1997): Robin Lane Fox, "Demosthenes, Dionysius and the Dating of Six Early Speeches", in: *Classical et Mediaevalia* 48, 167–203.
Hammond (1994): Nicholas G.L. Hammond, *Philip of Macedon*, London.
Hammond and Griffith (1979): Nicholas G.L. Hammond and Guy T. Griffith, *History of Macedonia II 550–336 B.C*, Oxford.
Hansen (1976): Mogens Herman Hansen, "The Theoric Find and the *graphe paranomon* against Apollodorus", in: *GRBS* 17, 235–246.
Hansen (1991): Mogens Herman Hansen, *The Athenian Democracy in the Age of Demosthenes: Structure, Principles and Ideology*, Oxford.
Harris (2006): Edward M. Harris, *Democracy and the Rule of Law in Classical Athens: Essays on Law, Society, and Politics*, Cambridge.
Harris (2018a): Edward M. Harris, *Demosthenes, Speeches 23–26: The Oratory of Classical Greece*, Austin.
Harris (2018b): Edward M. Harris, "The Stereotypes of Tyranny and the Tyranny of Stereotypes: Demosthenes on Philip II of Macedon", in: Myrina Kalaitzi *et al.* (eds.) *Βορειοελλαδικά: Tales from the lands of the ethne. Essays in honour of Miltiades B. Hatzopoulos*, Athens, 167–178.
Harris (2019): Edward M. Harris, "Speeches to the Assembly and in Public Prosecutions (Dem. 1–24), in: Gunther Martin (ed.), *The Oxford Handbook of Demosthenes*, Oxford, 365–388.
Heinaman (1993): Robert Heinaman, "Rationality, Eudaimonia and Kakodaimonia in Aristotle", in: *Phronesis*, 38.1, 31–56.

Hendren (2015): T. George Hendren, "Meidias Tyrannos; Meidias' Tyrannical Attributes in Demosthenes 21", in: *Illinois Classical Studies* 40.1, 21–43.
Jaeger (1938): Werner Jaeger, *Demosthenes*, Berkeley and London.
Johnson (1927): Franklin P. Johnson, *Lysippos: a study of the work of Lysippos, and an attempt to identify in existing sculpture copies of his original works*, Durham.
Leopold (1981): John W. Leopold, "Demosthenes on Distrust of Tyrants", in: *GRBS* 22:3, 227–246.
MacDowell (2009): Douglas M. MacDowell, *Demosthenes the Orator*, Oxford and New York.
Mader (2005): Gottfried Mader, "*Pax Duello Mixta:* Demosthenes and the Rhetoric of War and Peace", in: *Classical Journal* 101.1, 11–35.
MacGregor (1950): John M. MacGregor, *The Olynthiac Speeches of Demosthenes*, Cambridge.
McQueen (1986): Earl I. McQueen, *Demosthenes Olynthiacs*, London.
Miller (2002): Jeff Miller, "Warning the 'Dêmos': Political Communication with a Democratic Audience in Demosthenes", in: *History of Political Thought* 23.3, 401–417.
Milns (2000): Robert D. Milns, "The public speeches of Demosthenes", in: Ian Worthington (ed.), *Demosthenes: Stateman and Orator*, London and New York, 205–223.
Pearson (1964): Lionel Pearson, "The Development of Demosthenes as a Political Orator", in: *Phoenix* 18.2, 95–109.
Pearson (1981): Lionel Pearson, *The Art of Demosthenes*, Ann Arbor.
Pollitt (1986): Jerome J. Pollitt, *Art in Hellenistic Age*, Cambridge.
Pollitt (1990): Jerome J. Pollitt, *The Art of Greece: Sources and Documents*, Cambridge.
Pownall (2005): Frances Pownall, "The Rhetoric of Theopompus", in: *Cahiers des Etudes Anciennes* 42, 255–278.
Prauscello (2006): Lucia Prauscello, "Sculpted Meanings, Talking Statues: Some Observations on Posidippus 142.12 A–B (= XIX G–P) ΚΑΙ ΕΝ ΠΡΟΘΥΡΟΙΣ ΞΗΚΕ ΔΙΔΑΣΚΑΛΙΗΝ", in: *AJP* 127.4, 511–523.
Rosivach (1988): Vincent J. Rosivach, "The Tyrant in Athenian Democracy", *QUCC* 30.3, 43–57.
Ryder (2000): Timothy T.B Ryder, "Demosthenes and Philip II", in: Ian Worthington (ed.), *Demosthenes: Stateman and Orator*, London and New York, 45–89.
Sandys (1924): John Edwin Sandys, *The First Philippic and the Olynthiacs of Demosthenes*, London.
Sealey (1955): Raphaël Sealey, "Dionysius of Halicarnassus and Some Demosthenic Dates", in: *Revue de Études Grecques* 68, 77–120.
Sealey (1993): Raphaël Sealey, *Demosthenes and His Time*, New York and Oxford.
Shrimpton (1991): Gordon S. Shrimpton, *Theopompus the Historian*, Montreal and Kingston.
Spengel (1856): Leonhard von Spengel, *Rhetores Graeci* Volume 3. Lipsiae.
Stafford (1998): Emma J. Stafford, "Masculine values, feminine forms: on the gender of personifies abstractions", in: Lin Foxhall and John Slamon (eds.), *Thinking Men: Masculinity and its Self-representation in the Classical Tradition*, 43–56.
Stewart (1978): Andrew F. Stewart, "Lysippan Studies 1: The Only Creator of Beauty", in: *AJA* 82.2, 163–171.
Trevett (2011): Jeremy Trevett, *Demosthenes, Speeches 1–17: The Oratory of Classical Greece*, Austin.
Tuplin (1998): Christopher Tuplin, "Demosthenes' 'Olynthiacs' and the Character of the Demegoric Corpus", in: *Historia* 47.3, 276–320.

Usher (2004): Stephen Usher, "*Kairos* in Fourth-Century Greek Oratory", in Michael Edwards and Christopher Reid (eds.), *Oratory in Action*, Manchester and New York, 52–61.
Usher (1999): Stephen Usher, *Greek Oratory: Tradition and Originality*, Oxford.
Wilson (1980): John R. Wilson, "Kairos as 'Due Measure'", in: *Glotta* 58, 177204.
Wilson (1981): John R. Wilson, "Kairos as 'Profit'", in: *Classical Quarterly* 31.2, 418–420.
Wooten (1979): Cecil W. Wooten, "Unnoticed Medical Language in Demosthenes", in: *Hermes* 107.2, 157–160.
Wooten (1987): Cecil W. Wooten, *Hermogenes'* On Types of Style, Chapel Hill and London.
Wooten (1989): Cecil W. Wooten, "Dionysius of Halicarnassus on the Style of Demosthenes", in: *AJP* 110, 576–588.
Wooten (2008): Cecil W. Wooten, *A Commentary on Demosthenes*' Philippic 1: *With Rhetorical Analysis of* Philippics II and II, Oxford.
Wooten (2010): Cecil W. Wooten, "On the Road to *Philippic III:* The Management of Argument and the Modulation of Emotion in the Deliberative Speeches of Demosthenes", in: *Rhetorica* 28.1, 1–22.
Worthington (2013): Ian Worthington, *Demosthenes of Athens and the Fall of Classical Greece*, Oxford and New York.
Worthington (2008): Ian Worthington, *Philip II of Macedonia*, New Haven and London.
Yunis (1996): Harvey Yunis, *Taming Democracy: Models of Political Rhetoric in Classical Athens*, Ithaca and London.

Thomas C. Rose
The Exile of Demochares of Leuconoe Revisited

The career of Demochares of Leuconoe provides a useful case study in the vicissitudes of Athens in the early Hellenistic period, as the Athenians sought to reconcile their desire for freedom and autonomy with the political, economic, and strategic imperatives of Philip, Alexander, and the Successors. As a young man, Demochares was a fiery and uncompromising critic of the Macedonians, every inch the epigone of his uncle, the famous orator Demosthenes. He later worked in concert with Demetrius Poliorcetes, but was exiled after his relationship with either Poliorcetes or the king's Athenian partisans soured. Demochares returned from exile in 286,[1] after an Athenian rebellion had driven Demetrius' garrison from the *asty*. He then led or organized embassies to the courts of a number of rulers, including Lysimachus and Ptolemy, and he may have sought an entente with Demetrius' son Antigonus through the mediation of the philosopher Zenon.[2] Evidently this strident opponent of royal interference in Athenian internal affairs eventually came to terms with the absolute necessity of maintaining close connections with the various royal courts.[3]

Demochares has received a good deal of attention in recent years,[4] but the length of his exile and the circumstances that prompted it have been almost entirely absent from the scholarly discourse. This has not always been the case. In the 19th and early 20th centuries the date of Demochares' exile was a matter of controversy, with some scholars, including Droysen, De Sanctis, and Beloch arguing that Demochares was exiled in the late 290s, in large part because they adhered to an erroneous date for the so-called Four Years' War or anachronistic

---

I owe special thanks to the conference organizer and editor Frances Pownall. Shane Wallace read a draft of this paper and offered many helpful comments.

1 All dates are BCE.
2 [Plut.] *Mor.* 851e; Diog. Laert. 7.14.
3 The most useful account of Demochares' interactions with the Hellenistic kings is Paschidis (2008) 153–159; cf. Marasco (1984) 69–74.
4 E.g. Habicht (1993); Tracy (2000); Paschidis (2008) esp. 153–159; Cooper (2009); O'Sullivan (2009) esp. 133–137, 205–220; Bayliss (2011) esp. 172–176; Dmitriev in *BNJ* 75; Roisman and Worthington (2015) 271–275.

ideas about the nature of Athenian "party politics,"[5] and others, notably Ferguson and Tarn, advocating for a date some ten years earlier, based on Plutarch's narrative in his *Life of Demetrius*.[6] In an important article published in 1962, Leonard Smith aimed to demolish the arguments of the down-daters and prove beyond any doubt that Ferguson and the proponents of the high chronology that dated Demochares' exile to the late 4th century were correct.

Smith's arguments are elegant in their simplicity and entirely plausible. He notes that there are only two sources for the episode: Plutarch, in his *Life of Demetrius*, and the posthumous request for honors (*aitēsis*) that was submitted to the Athenians on Demochares' behalf by his son Laches.[7] Since Plutarch mentions the exile of Demochares in his narrative of Demetrius' scandalous activities in Athens during the winter of 304/3, and since the *aitēsis*, while chronologically vague, links his exile with events that can plausibly be dated to the same time, Smith concluded that the exile of Demochares should be fixed in 303 and any further attempt to downdate it would be "gratuitous and unnecessary.[8]" Smith's chronology has held the field ever since.[9] In this chapter, I suggest that we entertain the notion that those scholars who sought to date the exile of Demochares in the 290s may have been correct, even if the bases for their chronological schemes were not. But before we proceed any further, a brief survey of the career of Demochares prior to his exile is in order.

---

5 E.g. Droysen (1836), who places the Four Years' War in c. 297–294 and argues that Demochares was exiled on two separate occasions; De Sanctis (1893) places the Four Year' War in the period 294–288; Beloch (1925) 227 with n. 1 and (1927) 445–451 dates the exile of Demochares to some point after the recall of the partisans of Demetrius of Phalerum in 292/1 and has him return in 288; Manni (1951) 89–91 dates the exile of Demochares to 294. For a lucid assessment of political alliances in early Hellenistic Athens and the dangers of applying anachronistic party terminology to them, see esp. Luraghi (2014) 200–204.
6 Ferguson (1911) 122; Tarn (1913) 42 with n. 10; Marasco (1984) 54 n. 64 with additional bibliography.
7 The request was subsequently approved by the Assembly ([Plut.] *Mor.* 847d–e). For a translation and commentary, see Roisman and Worthington (2015) 271–275.
8 Smith (1962) 118.
9 E.g. Marasco (1984) 52–59; Habicht (1997) 72; Kralli (2000) 154; Paschidis (2008) 154; Bayliss (2011) 172; Osborne (2012) 22; Luraghi (2014) 199; Roisman and Worthington (2015) 273 n. 13.

I Demochares, Plutarch's *Life of Demetrius*, and early Hellenistic Athens

Like Demosthenes, Demochares of Leuconoe was an accomplished orator and a passionate defender of Athenian democracy. The *aitēsis* presented by his son Laches is preserved in the pseudo-Plutarchan *Lives of the Ten Orators* ([Plut.] *Mor.* 851d–f) and represents the most detailed account of his career, despite the fact that it conspicuously omits any mention of events before 307. The little we can discern about his early career confirms that Demochares adopted the fervently anti-Macedonian posture of his famous uncle. Seneca rather dubiously relates that, as a member of an Athenian delegation to Philip of Macedon, Demochares suggested to the king that he go and hang himself.[10] After the Lamian War, he urged the Athenians to resist Antipater's demand that they surrender their anti-Macedonian orators, among them Demosthenes.[11] The tradition that Demochares voiced this opposition clad in a himation and wearing a sword may be a later embroidery, but there is no reason to doubt that Demochares had already emerged as a prominent figure before the death of Antipater in 319.[12] Indeed, Demochares was prominent enough to be attacked by the comic poet Archedicus, an associate of Antipater who played an active role in the oligarchy installed in Athens in 322.[13] Demochares' work of contemporary history is almost entirely lost, but the few surviving fragments indicate that the work was in part an extended exercise in apology for the policies of Demosthenes,[14] and included polemical attacks on Antipater, his friends, and the peripatetic philosopher Demetrius of Phalerum, the leader of a regime that came to power in Athens in 317 with the backing of Antipater's son Cassander and a Macedonian garrison in Piraeus.[15]

In 307 Demetrius Poliorcetes seized Piraeus by a brilliant naval stratagem and ejected Cassander's garrison. He then entered Athens to a rapturous reception, allowed Demetrius of Phalerum and his associates to withdraw in safety to

---

10 *De Ira* 23.2–3. It seems unlikely that Demochares would have been senior enough to participate in any Athenian embassy to Macedon during the reign of Philip II. If there is any truth to Seneca's narrative, the Philip in question must be either Philip III (Alexander's half-brother) or Philip IV (the son of Cassander).
11 [Plut.] *Mor.* 847d.
12 Habicht (1993) 255–256; *pace* Marasco (1984) 56–57.
13 On Archedicus, see Polyb. 12.13.1–6; *Suda* α 4083 s.v. Ἀρχέδικος; Habicht (1993).
14 Cooper (2009) 318; Dmitriev in *BNJ* 75.
15 Demochares *BNJ* 75 F2, 5, 7; Marasco (1984) 95.

Thebes, and announced the restoration of the *patrios politeia*.¹⁶ The return of democratic government prompted a flurry of legislative and diplomatic activity in the city. The Athenians hailed Demetrius and his father Antigonus as *Sōtēres*, showered them with an unprecedented array of divine honors, and established two new tribes with the Saviors as eponyms.¹⁷ Euchares of Conthyle was tasked with recording the laws that re-instituted democratic procedures and placing them on display for all to see at the monument of the Eponymous Heroes, which was now expanded to accommodate images of Antigonus and Demetrius.¹⁸ Demochares soon emerged as a leading figure in the restored democracy and a champion of retributive policies against those who were tainted by association with the preceding regime. A number of prominent oligarchs, including the orator Deinarchus, were driven out of the city,¹⁹ and Demochares was probably the driving force behind a decree that brought the philosophical schools under the aegis of the Council and Assembly and resulted in the temporary exile of Theophrastus and other philosophers connected to Demetrius of Phalerum.²⁰ When Poliorcetes departed in early 306 to campaign against Ptolemy in Cyprus, Egypt, and Rhodes, the Athenians were forced to defend their freshly won freedom against Cassander in a struggle known as the Four Years' War.²¹ Demochares took a leading role in the defense of the city. According to the *aitēsis*, "he had repaired the walls, prepared arms and missiles and siege machinery, and fortified the city in the time of The Four Years' War" ([Plut.] *Mor.* 851d).²² In supervising the overhaul of the Athenian fortifications, Demochares followed in the footsteps of Demosthenes, who had taken the lead in refortifying the city

---

16 Philochorus *BNJ* 328 F 66; Diod. Sic. 20.45; Plut. *Demetr.* 8–9.
17 On the divine honors for the Antigonids, see esp. Mikalson (1998) 75–104; Habicht (2017) 30–59.
18 Euchares served on the board of *nomothetai* responsible for presenting bills that reformed the constitution to the Assembly; he was honored for his work at the end of the archon year 304/3 (*IG* II² 487). For the nature of Euchares' project as *anagrapheus tōn nomōn*, see esp. Canevaro (2011) 74–76. On the monument of the Eponymous Heroes and its modification, see Shear (1970).
19 Philochorus *BNJ* 328 F 66; Plut. *Demetr.*9; [Plut.] *Mor.* 850d.
20 Ath. 3.610e–f; Habicht (1988) 7–10; O'Sullivan (2009) 205–206; Canevaro (2011) 72–78.
21 This conflict is almost entirely ignored by Diodorus and Plutarch and is known to us primarily through contemporary inscriptions and several chronologically confused passages in Pausanias. For various reconstructions of the conflict, see Ferguson (1911) 112–118; Beloch (1925) 158–160; Smith (1962) 116–117; Gullath (1982) 176–179; Habicht (1997) 74–76; Landucci-Gattinoni (2003) 75–78; Oliver (2007) 116–119.
22 All translations are the author's.

after the defeat at Chaeronea in 338.²³ By 304, however, Cassander had seized Salamis and the Attic border forts, staged attacks on Eleusis, and laid siege to Athens.²⁴ The fall of the city seemed imminent. The Athenians were delivered from these fears when King Demetrius, who had claimed the royal title after his naval victory over Ptolemy in 306, abandoned the siege of Rhodes and landed at Aulis in Boeotia in the summer of 304. He drove Cassander out of Attica, pursued him beyond Thermopylae, and routed him near Heraclea.²⁵ He then returned to Athens where he was greeted with another round of divine honors²⁶ and granted the right to take the *opisthodomos* of the Parthenon for his quarters. We are told that Demetrius passed the winter of 304/3 in proverbially dissolute fashion. According to Plutarch, whose sources for Demetrius' stays in Athens are manifestly hostile to the king,²⁷ he held court on the Acropolis and spent his days cavorting with whores, cuckolding citizens, and stalking a comely young boy.²⁸ Plutarch crowns this shameful litany with a brief description of the events that culminated in the exile of Demochares. When a certain Cleaenetus attempted to have his father's debts cancelled by obtaining a letter of support from Demetrius, the Athenians assented but voted that henceforth no citizen should bring a letter from Poliorcetes before the Assembly. Plutarch reports that Demetrius was enraged and Stratocles of Diomeia, a strident supporter of the king and the most prolific legislator in Athenian history, moved quickly and decisively to placate him:²⁹

> In response, the frightened Athenians quickly rescinded the decree. Some of those that had introduced or supported the decree were killed, while others were sent into exile. The Assembly approved a further decree stating that any order issued by King Demetrius should

---

23 On Demosthenes' role as τειχῶν ἐπιμελητής, see Dem. 18.118; Aeschin. 3.17; [Plut.] *Mor.* 845f–846a; Tracy (2000) 228. In his request for honors for Demosthenes ([Plut.] *Mor.* 851a), Demochares praises his uncle's contribution to this fortification project.
24 Polyaenus 4.11.1; Paus. 1.35.2; *IG* II² 467, 469, 470, 505, 1954.
25 Diod. Sic. 20.100.5–6; Plut. *Demetr.* 23.1–4.
26 According to Plutarch (*Demetr.* 10.6), the spot where Demetrius first stepped down from his chariot was consecrated and covered with an altar, which they styled the altar of Demetrius *Kataibatēs*, "the Descender" an epithet usually reserved for Zeus. On the date of this honor, see Habicht (2017) 35.
27 On Plutarch's sources for the *Demetrius*, see Sweet (1951); Manni (1953) vii–xxiii; Flacelière and Chambry (1977) 10–13; Hornblower (1981) 67–70; Marasco (1981) 35–70; Andrei (1989) 42–49; Santi Amantini *et al.* (1995) xxi–xxiv; Chaniotis (2013) 68–69; Rose (2015) 40–56.
28 Plut. *Demetr.* 24.2–5.
29 Plut. *Demetr.* 24.7–9. On the career of Stratocles, who proposed at least twenty-eight extant decrees, many of them honoring Demetrius or his supporters, see esp. Tracy (2000); Paschidis (2008) 78–106; Bayliss (2011) 152–186; Luraghi (2014).

be deemed righteous towards the gods and just towards men. When some aristocrat declared that Stratocles was mad to propose such measures, Demochares of Leuconoe responded, "he would certainly be mad not to be mad" (μαίνοιτο μεντἄν…εἰ μὴ μαίνοιτο). For Stratocles profited from his flattery, but Demochares was discredited for this joke and sent into exile. (Plut. *Demetr.* 24.9 – 12)

Before we consider the context of these events, it is worth pointing out that Demochares' pithy assessment of Stratocles, an old enemy of Demosthenes,[30] directly echoes one of Demosthenes' most famous speeches. In *On the False Embassy*, Demosthenes claims that Philip of Macedon had learned from his time in Thebes that "democracy is the most unstable and erratic thing in the world;"[31] the king was thus fully alive to the fact that he could pursue his own interests in Athens most efficiently by securing the loyalty of two or three influential citizens who would do his bidding, and not by courting the goodwill of the *demos*. Indeed, Philip "would certainly be mad" (μαίνοιτο μεντἄν) to pursue the latter course of action.[32] This grouping of Thebes, a Macedonian king, and the specter of royal interference in Athenian affairs makes the quotation especially apt in an early third century context, as we will see.[33]

Setting aside for the moment the implausibility of Demochares being sent into exile merely for remarking that Stratocles was crazy like a fox, the chronology merits special attention. In Plutarch's narrative, Demochares' exile appears between two events that we can date with certainty: after Demetrius took up residence in the Parthenon in late 304, and before the account of the king's Peloponnesian campaign of 303.[34] For Smith, who praises the "exceptionally accurate and lucid chronological framework" of the *Demetrius*, Plutarch's notice allows us to confidently assign the exile of Demochares to 303 where he remained, by this reckoning, for seventeen years.[35]

---

30 Stratocles had spoken for the prosecution when Demosthenes was charged with accepting bribes from Harpalus in 324/3 (Din. 1.1; Photius 447a).
31 Dem. 19.136.
32 Dem. 19.138. Luraghi (2014) 199 n. 23 notes the similarity of Demochares' quip to a witticism attributed to Themistocles when the latter was in exile (Plut. *Them.* 29.7).
33 That Demochares was alluding to his uncle's speech seems all but certain: in the extant Greek corpus the phrase μαίνοιτο μεντἄν appears in only these two instances.
34 The date of Demetrius' Peloponnesian campaign is confirmed by Diodorus (20.103) and contemporary Athenian inscriptions. The primary objectives of the campaign seem to have been realized by the spring of 303 (Paschidis 2008, 93), when Demetrius returned to Athens to be initiated into the Eleusinian Mysteries.
35 Smith (1962) 115. The generally accepted notion that Demochares spent his exile at the court of Lysimachus is plausible, but not certain (Gabbert 1997, 18; Kralli 2000, 154).

Plutarch's readers who are familiar with his habitual disregard for chronological precision may take a skeptical view of Smith's affirmation, and for good reason—the *Demetrius* is replete with chronological errors. Important historical episodes are omitted, and the radical compression or displacement of events can create illusions of proximity and causation.[36] Further complicating matters is the unique position of the *Demetrius/Antony* pair in Plutarch's biographical project: in contrast to his usual practice, Plutarch offers these *Lives* as explicitly negative examples meant to discourage imitation.[37] This revision of his ethical and didactic goals led Plutarch to deviate from his usual historiographical approach. With the exception of two excerpts from a comedy by Philippides that are offered as representative of historical reality,[38] Plutarch does not acknowledge a single source for his historical narrative,[39] and, in those rare instances when we can identify his probable source for a given episode, he does not seem to have subjected his material to the degree of scrutiny he applies in other *Lives* with different aims.[40] Indeed, Plutarch mentions the exile of Demochares immediately after a breathless account of the *aretē* and *sōphrosynē* of "Democles the Beautiful," who commits suicide by hurling himself into a cauldron of boiling water rather than submit to the lecherous advances of Demetrius.[41] The story of the heroic resistance of Democles, whose name means "glory of the *dēmos*," has real allegorical force, but it is almost certainly a fiction.[42]

All of this may give the reader pause, but it is Plutarch's tendency to depart without warning from his generally diachronic narrative and present his material thematically that poses the greatest challenge to reconstructing early Hellenistic chronology with the *Demetrius*. This is most readily evident in his treatment—the most comprehensive of any ancient source—of the divine honors granted Deme-

---

36 On the compositional devices Plutarch deploys in abridging and adapting his source material, see esp. Pelling (2002) 91–96; see Rose (2015) 10 and *passim* for chronological problems in the *Demetrius*.
37 Plut. *Demetr.* 1.
38 Plut. *Demetr.* 12.7, 26.5. The events described in the second fragment are corroborated by other sources, but some or all of the material in the first are comic exaggerations or inventions.
39 He mentions Lynceus' account of a dinner party arranged by Lamia (*Demetr.* 27.4), but does not quote from it or give any indication that he has seen it. A comparison with the *Alexander*, in which Plutarch cites some two dozen historical authorities, is instructive.
40 Rose (2015) 54–55.
41 Plut. *Demetr.* 24.4–5.
42 The story, which appears only in the *Demetrius*, may ultimately derive from a comedy. On Democles, see Rose (2015) 219–220; Wheatley and Dunn (2020) 209.

trius by the Athenians.⁴³ There is no need to rehearse them all here, but several may bear on the date of Demochares' exile and will warrant our attention in due course: the renaming of the City Dionysia, the Attic month Mounichion, and the final day of each month, traditionally known as "the Old and the New," as the Demetria, Demetrion, and Demetrias, respectively.⁴⁴ Plutarch relates all of the honors in the context of Demetrius' first stay in Athens in 307, but we now know, thanks to the continual expansion of the contemporary epigraphic assemblage and the work of a number of scholars, most notably Christian Habicht, that the Athenians granted them intermittently over a period of at least fifteen years.⁴⁵ In the absence of parallel accounts against which Plutarch's narrative of events can be checked, we are well advised to treat his chronology with caution, especially when he presents a thematically arranged collection of events. And this is precisely what Plutarch seems to be doing in *Demetrius* 24–27, where he sets the *Life's* most elaborate treatment of Demetrius' personal excesses and divine pretensions against the backdrop of Athens. The exile of Demochares is one of several unattributed anecdotes illustrating intermittent acts of democratic resistance to the king's interventions in the city and a pervasive atmosphere of discontent with the king's behavior.⁴⁶ By the end of Chapter 27, Plutarch has wrapped up his survey of the political and religious turmoil aroused in Athens by the presence of the divine Demetrius and his court: he has nothing more to say about Demochares, Stratocles, divine honors, or Athenian politics. The sense that we are dealing with a collection of material bought together to illustrate Demetrius' *hybris* and not a particular moment in Athenian history is only heightened when Plutarch resumes his historical narrative with an account of the catastrophic Antigonid defeat at Ipsus.⁴⁷

---

43 Plut. *Demetr.* 10–13.
44 Plut. *Demetr.* 12.2.
45 On the chronology of the Athenian honors for Demetrius, see esp. Mikalson (1998) 75–103; Habicht (2017) 31–39.
46 Others episodes include the suicide of Democles (24.2–5), Stratocles' ingenious manipulation of the calendar to allow Demetrius' unusual initiation into the Mysteries (26), a toast mocking Demetrius' royal rivals (25.7), Demetrius levying a crushing tax on the Athenians (or perhaps the Thessalians) so that his *hetairai* could purchase cosmetics (27.1–2), and a lengthy excursus on Demetrius' paramour Lamia (27.3–14). With the exception of Demetrius' Eleusinian initiation, all of these anecdotes are dateless or apocryphal.
47 Demetrius' behavior on the Acropolis is explicitly described as *hybris* (24.1). On the striking juxtaposition of Demetrius' outrages in Athens and his defeat at Ipsus, see Pelling (1988) 25.

II The *Aitēsis* of Laches

Diodorus provides the primary check for events before the Battle of Ipsus in 301, when his detailed narrative abruptly breaks off, but he never mentions Demochares or democratic resistance to Demetrius in Athens, nor do any of the surviving fragments of Demochares' own work address his exile. What we do have is Laches' request for the highest honors for his father, which gives a very different account of the actions that prompted Demochares' exile:

> He had repaired the walls, prepared arms, missiles, and machinery, and fortified the city at the time of The Four Years' War. He had made peace, truce, and a military alliance with the Boeotians, for which he was exiled by those who overthrew the democracy (ἀνθ' ὧν ἐξέπεσεν ὑπὸ τῶν καταλυσάντων τὸν δῆμον). ([Plut.] *Mor.* 851d–e)

There is no mention of Demochares' opposition to Demetrius' policies or the honors voted him in Athens. Indeed, Demetrius is never named in the *aitēsis*, despite the fact that Laches issued his request in 270, a time of intense anti-Macedonian sentiment in the city as the Athenians prepared to take up arms against Demetrius' son Antigonus Gonatas.[48] Instead, Laches cites an Athenian alliance with the Boeotians as the proximate cause for his father's exile. This alliance is generally placed in the context of the Four Years' War, and Demetrius certainly did force the Boeotians to renounce their allegiance to Cassander and enter the Antigonid system of alliances after he returned to central Greece in 304.[49] But the question of why Demochares would be exiled for arranging an Athenian alliance with Boeotia has never been addressed. And if his actions during the Four Years' War are also cited as prompting his exile—since there is no strong break between the two statements, both could conceivably be antecedents of ἀνθ' ὧν ἐξέπεσεν ("for which he was exiled")—why would he be exiled for his heroic defense of the city? There is absolutely no reason why any of this would arouse the anger of Demetrius or his partisans in Athens in 304/3, a time when the defense of Athens and the establishment of an alliance of Greek states under Antigonid leadership were prime strategic and political imperatives for Demetrius and his father.

---

[48] In the so-called Chremonidean War which began in 269 (*IG* II³ 912). Luraghi (2018) demonstrates that Athenian honorary decrees tend to avoid any mention of foreign political domination of the city, although Demochares, in the *aitēsis* he submitted for Demosthenes (see below), did not hesitate to name Antipater as the agent of his uncle's demise ([Plut.] *Mor.* 851c; cf. Luraghi (2018) 219.

[49] Diod. Sic. 20.100.5–6; Plut. *Demetr.* 23.3.

Demetrius had set about securing the defenses of Athens immediately after he entered the city in 307. Early in the archon year 307/6 one of the most ambitious fortification projects in Athenian history was begun. An inscription (*IG* II² 463) preserves a decree and *syngraphai* (commissioned reports) for the comprehensive overhaul of the Athenian defenses, including the fortification circuits of Athens and Piraeus and the Long Walls that connected them. On the strength of the notice in the *aitēsis* that Demochares was responsible for refortifying the city, his name is plausibly restored as the proposer of the decree. The work began when Demetrius and his fleet were based in Attica[50] and cannot have been undertaken without his approval or his financial backing.[51] Demetrius left behind troops when he departed for Cyprus in 306[52] and appointed a key subordinate to coordinate the defense of Attica.[53] He may also have provided them with torsion catapults, which appear in Athenian inventories for the first time in 306/5.[54] In preparing the defenses of Athens, Demochares was working hand in glove with Poliorcetes; if the Athenian alliance with Boeotia mentioned in the *aitēsis* does belong to 304 or 303, then Demochares was serving the interests of Demetrius by arranging it.[55]

And what are we to make of the agents of Demochares' exile—"those who overthrew the democracy" (τῶν καταλυσάντων τὸν δῆμον)? The phrase *katalusai ton dēmon* and its variants are formulaic for a threat, real or perceived, to democratic government. In the 4th and early 3rd centuries it is a charge that is frequently leveled at oligarchs or those suspected of oligarchic sympathies.[56] Diodorus remarks that Demetrius restored freedom to the Athenians fifteen years after "the democracy was overthrown" (δῆμος…καταλυθείς) by Antipater;[57]

---

[50] The division of the work into ten tribal segments indicates that the administrative reorganization required by the expansion to twelve tribes had not yet been completed, so the decree and *syngraphai* must date to early in the archon year 307/6.
[51] Rose (2019) 178–180. Demetrius had arrived in Attica with a war chest of 5,000 talents (Plut. *Demetr.* 8.4).
[52] *IG* II² 469 and 1492b; Billows (1990) 151 and cf. 389, 430–431, 443.
[53] Adeimantus of Lampsacus was probably appointed as στρατηγὸς ἐπὶ τὴν χώραν in 306/5 and 305/4 (Petrakos 1999, 32–33, 430; Oliver 2007, 117–118; Wallace 2013, 144–147), but the suggestion that he held this post in 294/3 and 293/2, a time when Demetrius' interventions in Athenian affairs are well-documented, is also plausible (Habicht 2006, 427 n. 38). In either case, the Athenians were hardly "left to fend for themselves against Cassander" (so Bayliss 2011, 169).
[54] *IG* II² 1487, ll.84–90; Campbell (2011) 681; cf. Marsden (1969) 70–71. Additional aid from the Antigonids was forthcoming: Demetrius sent 1,200 panoplies to Athens in 306 (Plut. *Demetr.* 17.1), and Antigonus sent an additional donation of grain and money in 305 (*IG* II² 1492).
[55] Smith (1962) 118 concedes that an Athenian alliance at this time was "almost a necessity."
[56] E.g. Lysias 30.10; Dem. 19.294; *IG* II³ 911 l. 84; [Plut.] *Mor.* 851c; cf. Xen. *Hell.* 2.3.28.
[57] Diod. Sic. 20.46.3.

according to Philochorus, Deinarchus and the oligarchic supporters of Demetrius of Phalerum were sent into exile in 307 on the charge of overthrowing the democracy (τῶν καταλυσάντων τὸν δῆμον);[58] the comic poet Philippides, in a fragment that cannot be dated with any precision, suggested that the honors Stratocles orchestrated for Demetrius were tantamount to the destruction of the democracy (ταῦτα καταλύει δῆμον);[59] when Demochares returned from exile in 286/5 after the fall of an oligarchic regime that had been established in Athens by Poliorcetes (see below), he characterized the preceding regime as *oligarchia* and *katalusis ton dēmon*.[60] But the regime in place in Athens from the restoration of 307 until some point after the battle of Ipsos in 301 was furiously democratic if the work of Euchares of Conthyle and the extraordinary number of extant decrees of the Assembly are any indication,[61] and Demetrius was at pains to present himself as a liberator and champion of Athenian democracy and Greek freedom more broadly. Indeed, the Greek campaigns Demetrius carried out from 304 to 302 marked the culmination of an Antigonid policy of support for the "Freedom of the Greeks" dating back more than a decade.[62]

Antigonus recognized the necessity of securing the goodwill of the Greek *poleis* and exploited the propaganda value of posing as the champion of Greek freedom. In 315, he decreed that all the Greek cities be free, autonomous, and ungarrisoned, and promptly dispatched messengers to spread the word far and wide.[63] Whether Antigonus' commitment to Greek freedom was motivated by anything more than a cynical calculation of political expediency is debata-

---

58 Philochorus *BNJ* 328 F 66.
59 "These destroy the democray" (Plut. *Demetr.* 12.7). Plutarch cites another fragment of Philippides, in which the poet mocks Stratocles for his role in Demetrius' unusual initiation into the Eleusinian Mysteries, later in the *Demetrius* (26.5). That the two fragments belong to the same play, and are in fact contiguous (although presented by Plutarch in reverse order), was first posited by August Meineke, and has been broadly accepted (O'Sullivan 2009b, 64). Some commentators have placed the *didaskalia* of Philippides' play in the years immediately after the battle of Ipsus in 301 (e. g. Mastrocinque (1979), 265–267), but the poet was already established as a courtier in the court of Lysimachus by the time of the battle (*IG* II³ 877 ll. 16–18), and there is no indication that he ever returned to Athens before his *agonothesia* in 284/3 (*IG* II³ 877).
60 [Plut.] *Mor.* 851d; *IG* II³ 911 l. 81; Osborne (2012) 43.
61 Tracy (2000) 229 notes that we have a total of 2 inscriptions from the entire ten-year reign of Demetrius of Phalerum; there are at least 16 from 307/6 alone. On activity in the Assembly in these years, which exceeds that of any comparable period in the history of the Athenian democracy, see Dinsmoor (1931) 13–15; Tracy (2000); Thonemann (2005) 64; Osborne (2012) 21–22.
62 Wallace (2014) esp. 236–237; Rose (2018) 263–265; cf. Gruen (1984) 134–138; Billows (1990) esp. 197–205.
63 Diod. Sic. 19.61.3–4.

ble,⁶⁴ but it was a propaganda masterstroke that generated tremendous enthusiasm for the Antigonid cause in the Greek *poleis*, even as it undermined the position of Cassander, who maintained garrisons in many cities in central and southern Greece.

In 312 the Antigonid general Polemaeus arrived in Boeotia with orders to free the Greeks.⁶⁵ He drove Cassander's garrisons from Phocis and freed Eretria, Oropus, and Thebes. His success fired the hopes of many Athenians, and Demetrius of Phalerum was forced to make a truce with Polemaeus and open negotiations with Antigonus about an alliance.⁶⁶ Demetrius Poliorcetes signaled his own commitment to Greek freedom by twice freeing Athens, and, early in 303, he embarked on a campaign aimed at liberating the Peloponnesian cities from the garrisons of his rivals and garnering support for an alliance of Greek states under Antigonid leadership.⁶⁷ Contingents of Athenian volunteers participated in the campaign, which proved an extraordinary success, as Macedonian garrisons were forced from cities in the Argolid, the Corinthia, and Arcadia. Contemporary inscriptions demonstrate the euphoric reaction in Athens. In Elaphebolion 304/3 (March/April 303) a decree of the Assembly vowed annual sacrifices to Athena Nike, Agathe Tyche, and the Antigonid Saviors as a commemoration (*hypomnēma*) of the safe return of the Athenian soldiers serving with Demetrius and the restoration of freedom and autonomy to the Greek cities.⁶⁸ The Antigonid *philos* Medon arrived in Athens later that spring to announce the return to Athenian control of several strategically vital sites on the Attic frontier. In return, the Athenians honored Medon for his contributions to "the salvation of the *dēmos* and the freedom of the other Greeks,"⁶⁹ and approved, on the motion of Stratocles, a remarkable alteration of the calendar: the current month, Mounichion (April/May 303), was regarded as Anthesterion and Boedromion in turn so that

---

64 On the varying approaches adopted by the Successors with regard to the "Freedom of the Greeks," see Simpson (1959); Wehrli (1968) 103–129; Gruen (1984) 132–157; Billows (1990) 190–205; Dixon (2007); Dixon (2014) 50–67; Wallace (2011) 157–160; Dmitriev (2011) 112–134, 139–141; Poddighe (2013) 236–238; Meeus (2014) 284–286.
65 Diod. Sic. 19.77.
66 Diod. Sic. 19.78. Subsequent events in the Peloponnese drew Polemaeus away from central Greece, relieving the internal pressure on Demetrius of Phalerum. He would control Athens for another five years.
67 Diod. Sic. 20.100, 102–103; Plut. *Demetr.* 25.1–4.
68 *Agora* 16.114; Woodhead (1981).
69 *SEG* 36.165 + *SEG* 39.101 ll. 16–18: ὑπὲρ τῆς τοῦ δήμου σωτηρίας καὶ τῆς τῶν ἄλλων Ἑλλήνων ἐλευθερίας. On the date of the decree and its relation to the highly unusual initiation of Demetrius, see esp. Woodhead (1989); Paschidis (2008) 92–95.

Demetrius could be initiated into the Eleusinian Mysteries in record time.[70] A laudatory inscription set up in 303 by Athenian volunteers serving in the Peloponnese hails "Demetrius the Great" for the liberation of Athens and many other Greek cities, and calls for the erection of a temenos and altars for annual sacrifices to the divine king, as well as an equestrian statue to be set up in the Agora next to the personified image of democracy.[71]

Antigonid propaganda coupled with Demetrius' campaigns of liberation paid rich dividends. At the Isthmian Games in the spring 302, the Hellenic League was formally constituted with Antigonus and Demetrius as dual *hēgemones*.[72] A copy of the League charter found at Epidaurus reveals that the immediate aim of the alliance was the continued prosecution of the "common war" against Cassander.[73] Although the League, and the loyalty of most Greek cities to Demetrius, would not survive his defeat at Ipsus in 301, in the summer of 302 he moved north to carry on the war with Cassander at the head of a massive army that included no less than 25,000 allied Greek hoplites, many of them Athenian.[74]

If Plutarch's *Demetrius* is not the reliable chronological guide that some would have it be, if the circumstances surrounding the exile of Demochares described in the *aitēsis* are difficult to reconcile with the documented political landscape of 304/3, and if the heavy-handed program of exile and execution described by Plutarch is hardly consonant with contemporary Athenian inscrip-

---

[70] Plut. *Demetr.* 26.3–4. Full initiation was normally a three-stage process extending over a period of more than a year and a half. The preliminary Lesser Mysteries took place in the Attic month Anthesterion, the Greater Mysteries in Boedromion. Those who had undergone these first two stages were then eligible for full initiation, the Epopteia, at the celebration of the Greater Mysteries the next year. On the stages of initiation, see esp. Clinton (2004); Parker (2005) 342–360.

[71] *ISE* no. 7 = *SEG* 25.149. In addition, three fragmentary decrees authorizing naturalization of Antigonid *philoi* were approved on the penultimate day of 304/3 (June/July 303: *IG* II² 486 + *SEG* 36.163; *SEG* 36.164; *SEG* 16.58). Since citizenship seems to have been extended to these men on the recommendation of Poliorcetes, the decrees have been interpreted as epigraphic evidence of just the sort of intervention Plutarch describes in the Cleaenetus affair (so Paschidis 2008, 99–101; Luraghi 2014, 197–198). But Demetrius' *philoi* were honored for their actions on behalf of Athenian freedom and democracy (*SEG* 36.164 ll. 10–15), and the decrees hardly amount to rule by epistolary fiat. Rather, they are further evidence of Demetrius' attempts to position himself as the champion and guarantor of democracy in Athens and freedom in the Greek *poleis*.

[72] Plut. *Demetr.* 25.

[73] *IG* IV² 1. 68 ll. 71–72.

[74] Diod. Sic. 20.110.4; *IG* II³ 877 ll. 16–25.

tions and Antigonid policy and propaganda,[75] then it hardly seems "gratuitous and unnecessary" to seek a more appropriate chronological context for the subversion of the democracy, a controversial alliance with the Boeotians, and Demochares' subsequent exile.

III Revolt in Boeotia, Oligarchy in Athens

We find just such a context in the chaotic environment of central Greece in the second half of the 290s. After the disaster at Ipsus in 301, the Hellenic League evaporated and the Athenians informed their erstwhile Savior that he was no longer welcome in the city.[76] Stratocles, a ubiquitous presence in Athenian documents from the period 307–301, abruptly falls out of the epigraphic record. If he was in exile, one wonders why Demochares did not return now that Demetrius and his partisans had fallen from favor. Demetrius himself had lost his father and much of the Antigonid Empire; he was left with his fleet, his considerable talents, and control of a string of fortified harbor cities in Phoenicia, Cyprus, and Cilicia. By 296 he had recovered enough strength to hazard a return to mainland Greece. In Demetrius' absence, Athens had fallen under the sway of Lachares, a mysterious figure who had managed to seize power, perhaps with the support of Cassander.[77] Demetrius laid siege to the city and starved the Athenians into submission. He entered the city at the time of the Dionysia in 295 and dramatically proclaimed the return of democracy in the theatre of Dionysus.[78] The democratic restoration was commemorated with a radical reform of the civic calendar, but the new regime was undermined from its inception by the garrisons Demetrius installed in Piraeus and on the Hill of the Muses before he departed to campaign in the Peloponnese.[79] Demetrius inflicted two defeats on the

---

[75] The shrewd Beloch (1925, 227 n. 1) thought Plutarch's chronological placement of Demochares' exile was "completely absurd" given the state of Athenian relations with Poliorcetes before the Battle of Ipsus.
[76] Plut. *Demetr.* 30.
[77] *P.Oxy.* 17.2082 = *FGrH* 257a; Plut. *Demetr.* 33.1; Paus. 1.25.7. The ancient sources, universally hostile, label him a tyrant, but there is precious little evidence for the identity and career of Lachares or the nature of his ascendancy. Cf. Ferguson (1929) 12–14; Habicht (1997) 83; Dreyer (1999) 17–76; Paschidis (2008) esp. 125–129; Osborne (2012) 25–36.
[78] Plut. *Demetr.* 34.4–5; Thonemann (2005), with important corrections in Osborne (2006) 70–76.
[79] Plut. *Demetr.*34.6. A contemporary inscription (*IG* II^3,1 851) reveals that a miniature prytany year was instituted in which each of the twelve tribes was in prytany for approximately nine days

Spartans, but he was soon lured away from Laconia by developments in the North.[80] In 294 he exploited the chaos stemming from a bloody dispute between Cassander's sons and seized the throne of Macedon.[81] He was acclaimed king sometime that autumn.[82] Soon thereafter he solidified his hold on Thessaly and concluded "friendly agreements" with the Boeotians, probably in early 293.[83]

Demetrius' eminence in Greece now rivalled that of Philip II after Chaeronea, but his ascendancy led to an alliance of Greek states that aimed to liberate central and southern Greece from Antigonid control. More than forty years earlier, Alexander had advanced from Illyria to Boeotia by a series of forced marches because he feared a rebellious Thebes supported by Athens, Sparta, and Aetolia;[84] at least three of these states were now coalescing against Demetrius. A Boeotian alliance with the Aetolian *koinon* at this time is epigraphically attested,[85] and this union of the two most significant powers in central Greece was bolstered by the arrival in Thebes of an army led by the Spartan adventurer Cleonymus.[86] The Boeotians rose in open revolt against Demetrius with Thebes as the epicenter of the uprising.[87]

What was the Athenian response to this nascent anti-Antigonid alliance and the revolt in Boeotia in spring 293? Plutarch is no help; Athens virtually disappears from his narrative from the Dionysia of 295 until the Athenian revolt in 287.[88] In the absence of his testimony we have only the epigraphic record to illuminate events in the city. Almost exactly one year after Demetrius' appearance in the Theater of Dionysus, the Athenians commemorated the democratic restora-

---

over the course of the final months of 296/5. On the calendar of 296/5, see esp. Osborne (2006) 71–72.
80 Plut. *Demetr.* 35; Polyaenus, *Strat.* 4.7.9.
81 Plut. *Demetr.* 36–37.
82 Cassander died at Pella in the spring of 297 (Eusebius/Porphyry *FGrH* 260 F3; *POxy* 2082), and his sons reigned for a combined three and a half years (Eusebius/Porphyry *FGrH* 260 F3.5–6). Thus, Demetrius was crowned king in Macedon late in 294.
83 Plut. *Demetr.* 39.1: συμβάσεις μέτριαι περὶ φιλίας.
84 Arr. *Anab.* 1.7.4.
85 *StVA* III, 463a; Gullath (1982) 195–196; Scholten (2000) 19–20; Mackil (2013) 96–97.
86 Plut. *Demetr.* 39.2. Cleonymus had departed Sparta for Italy in 303 after being passed over for the Agiad throne and had been operating independent of the Spartan authorities for nearly a decade (Diod. Sic. 20.104–105; Livy 10.2). Whether he was recalled to act as regent and was leading an official mission of the Spartan army (so Bradford 1977, 246; Marasco 1980, 51–55; Cartledge and Spawforth 2002, 28), or he led this force into Boeotia on his own initiative (so Lévêque 1957, 136; Paschidis 2008, 313 n.1), is not clear.
87 Plut. *Demetr.* 39–40; Diod. Sic. 21.14.
88 The one exception is a brief mention of the Pythian Games of 290, which Demetrius staged in Athens (*Demetr.* 40.7).

tion of 295 with a decree granting honors to the Antigonid officer Herodorus for his efforts to ensure that the *dēmos* "might continue to have democracy."[89] There are no preserved documents from 294/3, but three fragmentary decrees proposed on the same day in late 293/2 testify to some startling developments in the city. All three decrees demonstrate that the secretary of the Council had been replaced by an *anagrapheus*, an office linked to the oligarchic regime of 321/0 – 319/8,[90] and one reveals that Olympiodorus, a decorated general and a hero of the Four Years' War, served two consecutive terms as eponymous archon beginning in 294/3.[91] It is unlikely that such a prominent figure could attain the office by lot even once; the second term confirms that he was appointed in some way. Not only had the practice of filling the office by sortition been abandoned, but Olympiodorus seems to have exercised enhanced powers,[92] and there is little doubt that he was Demetrius' hand-picked commissar in the city.[93] Demetrius' decision to jettison even the pretense of democratic procedures should probably be linked to his need to exercise influence in Athens indirectly after his departure for Macedon in 294.[94] Like Cassander before him, he opted to do so through a local luminary. This pivot to oligarchy in Athens was cemented in 292/1 when Theophrastus convinced Poliorcetes to permit the repatriation of those partisans of Demetrius of Phalerum who had been exiled in 307 on charges of "overthrowing the democracy" (τῶν καταλυσάντων τὸν δῆμον).[95] The last of the decrees of 293/2 reveals that Stratocles, charged with the same offense (ταῦτα καταλύει δῆμον) in a comedy of Philippides,[96] had emerged from nearly a decade of obscurity to propose the highest honors for a well-known oligarch.[97] The decree stipulates that these honors be announced at the City Dionysia, a festival that

---

[89] *IG* II³ 853 ll. 23 – 24. The decree shows that the traditional procedure for grants of citizenship under democratic government was still in effect (Osborne 2012, 33 – 34).
[90] *IG* II³ 857, 858, 859; *SEG* 45.101; *Agora* 16.167; Dow (1963).
[91] *IG* II³ 858 certifies 293/2 as the second archontal year of Olympiodorus (ἐπὶ Ὀλυμπιοδώρου ἄρχοντος δεύτερον ἔτος), demonstrating that he was also the eponymous magistrate in 294/3
[92] Diogenes Laertius (6.23) refers to Olympiodorus as ὁ Ἀθηναίων προστατήσας.
[93] Dinsmoor (1931) 13; Marasco (1984) 68; Tracy (2003) 12; Osborne (2012) 34. The archonship had not been held more than once since the extended term of Damasias in the years 582/1– 580/79 ([Arist.] *Ath. Pol.* 13.2). On Olympiodorus, see Paus. 1.26.1 – 3, 10.18.7, 10.34.3; Shear (1978); Habicht (1985) 90 – 92; Kralli (2000) 137 – 138; Paschidis (2008) 133 – 139; Luraghi (2018) 211 – 215.
[94] Buraselis (1982) 88; Habicht (1997) 90 – 91; Luraghi (2014) 219.
[95] Philochorus *BNJ* 328 F67; [Plut.] *Mor.* 850d.
[96] Kock *CAF* III F 25 = Plut. *Demetr.* 12.7.
[97] *IG* II³ 857. Philippides of Paeania, not to be confused with the comic poet, Philippides of Cephale.

had been referred to by its traditional name in the Herodorus decree, but is now dubbed the Dionysia and Demetrieia.[98]

The absence of evidence from the crucial year 294/3 frustrates attempts to date these constitutional and ritual changes with any precision. We can say for certain only that they were instituted at some point after Herodorus was honored in the spring of 294 and before the re-emergence of Stratocles in the spring of 292. If Olympiodorus was not chosen by lot for his first turn as archon in 294/3, then Demetrius intervened to appoint him before the archon year began in July 294. But the timing of the decrees of 293/2 may have more to tell us about ritual innovations for Demetrius. All were proposed on the final day of the Attic month Mounichion—the very day and month whose names were purportedly changed to Demetrias and Demetrion. That this was not just a fabulous coincidence is confirmed by the fact these decrees were proposed at a principal meeting of the Assembly (*kyria ekklēsia*) held on the first day of the prytany of the tribe Pandionis.[99] Five days' notice was required to convene a meeting of the Assembly and, for logistical reasons, meetings were generally not held until the first eight days of a prytany had passed. A *kyria ekklēsia* held on the first day of a prytany is without parallel.[100] Clearly, extraordinary measures were taken to ensure that this meeting fell on the day most intimately associated with Demetrius in Athens. Since the date is given in traditional terms and not explicitly dubbed the Demetrias of Demetrion it may have been chosen as a commemoration (*hypomnēma*) of the day that was so designated. Both Mounichion and "the Old and the New" are well-attested in Athenian documents after 307, the year in which Plutarch seems to situate the honors, but the onomastic changes are corroborated by other sources[101] and probably represent one-time honors awarded in a year not represented in the epigraphic assemblage.[102] The previous Mounichion—that of 294/3—is surely the strongest candidate for the re-named month and day. If the honors do belong to the spring of 293, it is striking that the Athe-

---

98 *IG* II³ 857 l. 42. The decree demonstrates that Demetrius did not simply replace Dionysus as the festival's honorand, as Plutarch suggests. On this appended festival, a neat complement to Demetrius' Dionysiac self-fashioning, see esp. Buraselis (2012). After Demetrius lost control of Athens the festival returned to its traditional name (*IG* II³ 870).
99 I addressed the timing of this meeting in an earlier paper (Rose 2018, 279–280 with n. 156), but overlooked the significance of the prytany date and suggested some alternative explanations for the renaming of the month Mounichion.
100 Osborne (2012) 57 n. 10. *Agora* 16 124 (1) records a meeting on the first day of the seventh prytany in 302/1, but this was certainly an *ekklēsia synklētos* (an emergency meeting summoned at short notice) and not a *kyria ekklēsia*: Hansen (1979) 153–154; Woodhead (1997) 198.
101 Plut. *Demetr.* 12.2; Philochorus *BNJ* F 166; Polemon F 7 (Preller) = Harp. s.v. Ἕνα καὶ νέα.
102 Habicht (2017) 37; Rose (2018) 180.

nians honored Demetrius precisely ten years after Stratocles twice altered the calendar to allow for Demetrius' Eleusinian initiation in Mounichion of 304/3, and that they felt compelled to do so during the revolt in Boeotia.

IV Dating the Exile of Demochares

According to Laches, Demochares was exiled by "those who overthrew the democracy" after he brokered an Athenian alliance with the Boeotians. Since these events map comfortably onto the geo-political landscape of central Greece in the late 290s, a time of oligarchy in Athens and rebellion in Boeotia, and since the chronological reliability of Plutarch's account is suspect, we should consider downdating Demochares' exile by fully a decade.

An alternative scenario runs as follows. Demochares, who had been biding his time in Athens, just as he had during the ten-year reign of Demetrius of Phalerum, saw his Demosthenes moment in the spring of 293 and seized it. He convinced the Athenians to ally with the Boeotians and lend some degree of support to the nascent anti-Antigonid coalition, despite the Macedonian garrisons that occupied Athens and Piraeus. If so, the Athenian alliance with the Boeotians mentioned in the *aitēsis* was not an agreement between two states drawn into Demetrius' orbit at the conclusion of the Four Year' War, but evidence of a shared aspiration to throw off the power of the Macedonian king ten years later and a revival of the alliance that was brokered by Demosthenes and broken on the field at Chaeronea in 338.[103] A coalition of Boeotia, Athens, Sparta, and Aetolia posed a real threat to Macedonian hegemony in central Greece, but Demetrius' swift response ensured that this alliance never got off the ground. Polyaneus tells us that Demetrius sent a herald with a declaration of war to the Boeotarchs assembled at Orchomenus. On the very next day the king himself appeared with his army in Boeotia. He did not advance immediately on Thebes, but took up a position in a potent *lieu de mémoire*, Chaeronea.[104] Cleonymus beat a hasty retreat, no aid materialized from Aetolia or elsewhere, and Demetrius laid siege to Thebes.[105] If the Athenians did express support for the Boeotian revolt, they will have been desperate to propitiate Demetrius. The conferral of extraordinary honors and the punishment of those responsible for the alliance would have been a good place to start. Demochares was exiled and the Athenians altered

---

[103] On Demosthenes' leading role in forging this alliance, see Dem. 18.214; Plut. *Dem.* 18.1–2; [Plut.] *Mor.* 851b.
[104] Polyaenus 4.7.11.
[105] Plut. *Demetr.* 39.3; Diod. Sic. 21.14.1–2.

their calendar to honor Demetrius. Mounichion became Demetrion, the "Old and the New" became Demetrias. Perhaps this was also the context for Stratocles' proposal that Demetrius' every command "should be deemed righteous towards the gods and just towards men."[106] All of this was taking place as the archontal year of Olympiodorus was nearing its end. Evidently, he was not among those who urged support for the Boeotians since Demetrius opted to extend his term for a second year, just as he appointed Peisis as polemarch in Thespiae and installed the historian Hieronymus of Cardia as his *epimelētēs* in Boeotia after the surrender of Thebes.[107] Perhaps it was in his second term that Olympiodorus acquired the enhanced powers recorded in the sources.

There are at least two historical parallels for just such an abortive alliance between Athens and Thebes. In 379, the Athenians had allied themselves to Thebes and supported the Theban exiles who engineered the liberation of the city from a Spartan garrison. Diodorus claims that the Athenians sent the general Demophon with a substantial force to assist in the siege of the Spartan garrison on the Cadmeia,[108] while Xenophon's account limits Athenian aid to a private initiative undertaken by two unnamed generals.[109] Xenophon and Plutarch agree that panic spread through Athens when a large Spartan army marched past Attica into Boeotia. The Athenians renounced any support for the rebellion in Thebes and exiled or executed those citizens who had urged it.[110]

Events in Boeotia some four decades later provide an even more robust analogue. In 335 rumors reached central Greece that Alexander had been killed in Illyria. The Thebans voted for rebellion and attacked the Macedonian garrison on the Cadmeia.[111] Troops were dispatched from Aetolia and the Peloponnese in

---

[106] Plut. *Demetr.* 24.10. The language of the decree (ὅ τι ἂν ὁ βασιλεὺς Δημήτριος κελεύσῃ) is quite similar to another decree declaring that Demetrius' response to an Athenian embassy should be regarded as an oracular utterance (ὅ τι δ' ἂν χρήσῃ, ταῦτα πράττειν τὸν δῆμον). Plutarch (*Demetr.* 13.2) places the latter decree in his narrative of events in 307, but it almost certainly belongs to the late 290s (Mikalson 1998, 97).
[107] Plut. *Demetr.* 39.4–5. Habicht (1997) 91 notes that Hieronymus and Olympiodorus held different offices but "their functions must have been quite similar." Demetrius' appointments did not have the desired effect. Thebes soon revolted again (Plut. *Demetr.* 39.6), and Olympiodorus was a key figure in the Athenian revolt of 287 (Paus. 1.26.1–2)
[108] Diod. Sic. 15.26–27. Deinarchus' brief reference to these events (1.39) supports the account of Diodorus.
[109] On these conflicting accounts, see esp. Steinbock (2012) 260–267.
[110] Xen *Hell.* 5.4.19; Plut. *Pelop.* 14. Xenophon's account has only the two generals prosecuted while Plutarch describes a broader effort to punish supporters of the revolt in Boeotia.
[111] Arr. *Anab.* 1.7.1–2; Plut. *Dem.* 23.1–3; Justin 11.2.

support of Thebes,¹¹² and Demosthenes personally sent arms to the rebels.¹¹³ There was also some degree of official support for the Thebans in Athens, but, again, the exact nature and extent of Athenian aid is unclear. Plutarch claims that the Athenians allied themselves to the Thebans and were preparing to fight alongside them,¹¹⁴ while Diodorus relates that the Athenian Assembly voted to support Thebes and mobilized the full citizen levy, but awaited further developments before sending them across the Attic border.¹¹⁵ In any case, Alexander's lightning advance into Boeotia in 335 choked off the nascent coalition of Greek states. Thebes was destroyed, the Arcadians condemned to death those who had encouraged the revolt, and Alexander demanded the surrender of a number of Athenian orators, Demosthenes included, who had urged support for the revolt.¹¹⁶ The sources give variant lists of the orators targeted by Alexander; in the end only Charidemus was exiled.¹¹⁷

Plutarch's seemingly contradictory account is surely the principal objection to the speculative scenario outlined above, even if the low chronology is not at all incompatible with his description of Demochares' exile at a time of when Stratocles was influential with the *dēmos* and Demetrius was openly interfering in the internal affairs of the city. We might explain his placement of Demochares' exile in a survey of the tumultuous relationship between Demetrius and the Athenians as an act of temporal dislocation akin to his anachronistic treatment of some of the divine honors for the king, but if Demochares was exiled for convincing the Athenians to ally with the Boeotians in 293, why doesn't Plutarch say so? I can offer no definitive answer for Plutarch's silence, but note that Plutarch did not set out to write a historical account of Demetrius' career, and the loss of every other narrative history dealing with contemporary events has left the *Demetrius* to shoulder a historical burden it was never designed to bear. In addition, Plutarch was clearly not well-informed about the career of Demochares or events in Athens in the early third century. In his only other reference to Demochares, Plutarch refers to him simply as a "relative" (*oikeios*) of Demosthenes, and there is nothing to indicate that he ever read Demochares' work of contem-

---

112 Din. 1.18–19; Diod. Sic. 17.8.6.
113 Diod. Sic. 17.8.5; Plut. *Dem* 23.1.
114 Plut. *Dem.* 23.1–2; Aeschin. 3.238–239 seems to confirm an alliance.
115 Diod. Sic. 17.8.4–6. Habicht (1997) 14–15 accepts Diodorus' account. For a more skeptical view, see Sealey (1993) 203.
116 For the Arcadian response, see Arr. *Anab.* 1.10.1. For Alexander's demands, see Arr. *Anab.* 1.10.1–6; Diod. Sic. 17.15.1–5; Plut. *Dem.* 23.4–6.
117 Diod. Sic. 17.115; Arr. *Anab.* 1.10.4–6; Plut. *Dem.* 23.4; Bosworth (1980) 92–96.

porary history.[118] He has nothing to say about the oligarchic regime in power in Athens in the late 290s, the return of Stratocles, or the repatriation of the exiled partisans of Demetrius of Phalerum. Olympiodorus, probably the most prominent Athenian of his generation, is nowhere in Plutarch. The one event in Athens from this period that Plutarch does treat in any depth, the Athenian rebellion of 287 and Demetrius' consequent siege of the city, is contradicted in many details by the honorary decrees for the Athenian brothers Phaedrus and Callias of Sphettus, both principal figures in the revolt.[119]

Despite all of this, the alternative version of events proposed here cannot be proven, though one can hope that a new find will vindicate or refute it. In the meantime, downdating the exile of Demochares has a number of virtues in addition to those already discussed. If Demochares was exiled in 293 for his role in forging an ill-fated alliance with the Boeotians, we no longer have to consign him to oblivion for seventeen years—the low chronology would have him absent for only seven. We no longer have to wonder why he did not return from exile to Athens after Ipsus—he had not yet left. If Demochares was in Athens during the tyranny of Lachares and the oligarchic regime that took power in 294/3, just as he was for the ten-year reign of Demetrius of Phalerum, we can better understand the rather strained insistence in the *aitēsis* that Demochares was the only prominent Athenian of his time that never took part in any political regime other than democracy:

> he was exiled on behalf of democracy, and he never took part in oligarchy or held any office at a time when the democracy had been overthrown (καταλελυκότος τοῦ δήμου); he was the only Athenian politician of his time who never sought to change his country's constitution to something other than democracy; he executed his civic duty in such a way that all the judgements, laws, courts, and common property of the Athenians were preserved in safety; and he never said or did anything contrary to democracy. ([Plut.] *Mor.* 851f)

The neat division of the Athenian polity into two opposing camps—democrats and destroyers of the democracy—occludes a reality that was far messier and more complex.[120] Every Athenian of the era was forced to reckon with Deme-

---

118 Plutarch does cite Demochares in a litany of divergent accounts of the death of Demosthenes (Demochares *BNJ* 75 F 6 = Plut. *Dem.* 30.4), but he probably did not obtain this information directly from Demochares' History (Marasco 1984, 180).
119 Plut. *Demetr.* 46.2–3. *IG* II³ 911; *IG* II³ 985. Osborne (2012, 16), characterizes Plutarch's account of the revolt and siege as "pitifully brief, uninformative, and occasionally palpably incorrect."
120 For an exploration of the commemorative strategies utilized by Demochares and his contemporaries as they sought to present themselves as uncompromising democrats and implacable

trius—with his intermittent presence in the city and with his determination to project power and influence in the Greek *poleis* and to exploit their resources and strategic potential.[121] The king's ability to confer benefits and protection on the Athenians was manifest, but his interventions undermined Athenian freedom and autonomy, especially after 295. Was resistance or collaboration the proper course for a patriot? Despite the testimony of Laches, it is clear that Demochares, like many of his influential contemporaries, opted for a little of both. He worked closely with Demetrius in the years after 307 and remained in Athens during the ascendancy of a number of un-democratic regimes before brokering an anti-Demetrian alliance with the Boeotians. Olympiodorus acted as Demetrius' commissar in the city, but led the assault that expelled the king's garrison from the Hill of the Muses in the spring of 287.[122] While Olympiodorus attacked the garrison, Phaedrus of Sphettus, an influential figure under the oligarchy installed in 294/3, led the crucial effort to secure the grain harvest.[123] Phaedrus' brother Callias and the poet Philippides took a different line: both opted to pursue Athenian interests, and their own, from inside the courts of Demetrius' bitter rivals, and Callias led a contingent of Ptolemaic troops in support of the Athenian rebellion.[124]

The portrait of Demochares as an uncompromising democratic purist that emerges from Laches' request faithfully reflects Demochares' own efforts to rehabilitate Demosthenes and position himself as the heir to his uncle's legacy. He undertook this project in earnest after his recall from exile; we can glimpse the results in the surviving fragments of his History and in the request for honors for Demosthenes.[125] In the latter, he praised Demosthenes for his work in

---

opponents of the Macedonians, see Shear (2012); Shear (2020) esp. 272–275. Luraghi (2018, 220–224) offers insightful commentary on the Athenian struggle to articulate in their decrees the intervention of foreign powers in Athenian affairs. His brief analysis (220–221) of the *aitēsis* for Demochares is informed by, and depends on, a late-fourth century date for his exile.

121 On the crucial importance of the Greek *poleis* for the Hellenistic dynasts, see esp. Ma (1999) 152–74; Paschidis (2008) 19–24 and *passim*.

122 Paus. 1.26.1–2; cf. Plut. *Demetr.* 46.1–3.

123 Phaedrus held a series of generalships during the 290s and 280s. On his career and the extant Athenian decree in his honor (*IG* II^3 985), see esp. Paschidis (2008) 140–145; Shear (2020).

124 Callias was a *philos* of Ptolemy, just as Philippides was a *philos* of Lysimachus (*IG* II^3 877; Plut. *Demetr.* 12.8). Both had returned to the courts of their royal patrons when they were honored with "career decrees" in Athens, and there is no indication that either ever resettled in Athens. On Callias and the decree in his honor (*IG* II^3 911) see esp. Shear (1978); Shear (2010); Luraghi (2018).

125 Like the request of Laches, the *aitēsis* of Demochares is preserved at the end of the *Lives of the Ten Orators* ([Plut.] *Mor.* 850f–851c). For a translation and commentary, see Roisman and

strengthening the fortifications of Athens and forging an alliance with the Thebans,[126] and lamented that his uncle, who had "achieved more for freedom and democracy than any statesman of his time," was "exiled under an oligarchy after the democracy had been overthrown."[127] If Demochares was exiled for supporting an anti-Macedonian alliance with the Boeotians, we can more fully appreciate the degree to which his career was an exercise in *imitatio Demosthenis*, and we can savor the exquisite symmetry of the anti-Macedonian policies of Demosthenes and his nephew. Like Demosthenes, Demochares forged an alliance with the Boeotians to resist a Macedonian king; like Demosthenes, his dreams were dashed at Chaeronea. Fortunately for Demochares, the analogue with his uncle extends no further. In his History, Demochares offers a fanciful account of his uncle's death. Contrary to the reports of other sources, he claims that Demosthenes did not sip from a poison pen as the bounty hunters closed in. Instead, the gods intervened and granted the fallen champion of Athenian democracy a painless death in the Sanctuary of Poseidon at Calauria.[128] No one needed to concoct such a fantasy ending for Demochares. After the successful Athenian revolt of 287, he returned home to play a leading role in a regime styled "the democracy of all Athenians."[129] He took control of finances in the cash-strapped city, proposed a fund-raising mission to the court of Ptolemy, and personally led two Athenian embassies to the court of Lysimachus, returning home each time with substantial gifts from the king.[130] This final stage of Demochares' career, like the careers of his contemporaries Callias and Philippides, demonstrates that hunting patronage at the courts of the Successors was viewed as patriotic

---

Worthington (2015) 269–271; Shear (2017). The *aitēsis* was submitted in 281/0; the latest dateable fragment from Demochares' History (*BNJ* 75 F 10) records the death of Agathocles in 289.
126 [Plut.] *Mor.* 851a–b.
127 [Plut.] *Mor.* 851c: πεπολιτευμένῳ τῶν καθ' ἑαυτὸν πρὸς ἐλευθερίαν καὶ δημοκρατίαν ἄριστα· φυγόντι δὲ δι' ὀλιγαρχίαν, καταλυθέντος τοῦ δήμου. The language here anticipates that of Laches' request: φυγόντι μὲν ὑπὲρ δημοκρατίας, μετεσχηκότι δὲ οὐδεμιᾶς ὀλιγαρχίας οὐδὲ ἀρχὴν οὐδεμίαν ἠρχότι καταλελυκότος τοῦ δήμου· (he was exiled on behalf of democracy, and he never took part in oligarchy or held any office at a time when the democracy had been overthrown) [Plut.] *Mor.* 851f.
128 Demochares *BNJ* 75 F 6 = Plut. *Dem.* 30.4. Plutarch himself prefers the story of the poison pen (*kalamos*), but preserves a number of alternate accounts, most of which culminate with Demosthenes' suicide by poison secreted somewhere on his person (*Dem.* 29.1–30.3)
129 ἡ δημοκρατία ἡ ἐξ ἁπάντων Ἀθηναίων, *IG* II³ 911 ll. 82–83; Osborne (2012) 43–50.
130 [Plut.] *Mor.* 851e. Demochares is also credited with leading a delegation to the court of a certain Antipater. The identity of this dynast remains a vexed question; for a discussion, see Roisman and Worthington (2015) 274 n. 17.

behavior under the "democracy of all Athenians." As his last public act, Demochares submitted an *aitēsis* for the suite of highest honors—for Demosthenes.[131]

Bibliography

Andrei (1989): Osvaldo Andrei, *Plutarco: Demetrio*, Milan.
Bayliss (2011): Andrew Bayliss, *After Demosthenes: The Politics of Early Hellenistic Athens*, London.
Beloch (1925): K.J. Beloch, *Griechische Geschichte*, 2nd ed. vol. 4.1, Berlin.
Beloch (1927): K.J. Beloch, *Griechische Geschichte*, 2nd ed. vol. 4.2, Berlin.
Billows (1990): Richard Billows, *Antigonus the One-Eyed and the Creation of the Hellenistic State*, Berkeley.
Bosworth (1980): A.B. Bosworth, *A Historical Commentary on Arrian's* History of Alexander, vol.1, Oxford.
Bradford (1977): A.S. Bradford, *A Prosopography of Lacedaemonians from the Death of Alexander the Great, 323 B.C., to the Sack of Sparta by Alaric, A.D. 396*, Munich.
Buraselis (1982): Kostas Buraselis, *Das hellenistische Makedonien un die Ägäis*, Munich.
Buraselis (2012): Kostas Buraselis, "Appended Festivals: The Coordination and Combination of Traditional Civic and Ruler Cult Festivals in the Hellenistic and Roman East," in: J. Rasmus Brandt and Jan W. Iddenq (eds.) *Greek and Roman Festivals: Content, Meaning, and Practice*, Oxford, 247–265.
Campbell (2011): Duncan Campbell, "Ancient Catapults: Some Hypotheses Revisited," in: *Hesperia* 80.4, 677–700.
Canevaro, M. (2011): Mirko Canevaro, "The Twilight of Nomothesia: Legislation in Early Hellenistic Athens (322–301)," in: *Dike* 14, 55–85.
Cartledge and Spawforth (2002): Paul Cartledge and Anthony Spawforth, *Hellenistic and Roman Sparta*, 2nd ed., New York.
Chaniotis (2013): Angelos Chaniotis, "Empathy, Emotional Display, Theatricality and Illusion in Hellenistic Historiography," in: Angelos Chaniotis and Pierre Ducrey (eds.) *Emotions in Greece and Rome: Texts, Images, Material Culture*, Stuttgart, 53–84.
Clinton (2004): Kevin Clinton, "Stages of Initiation in the Eleusinian and Samothracian Mysteries," in: Michael B. Cosmopoulos (ed.) *Mysteria: The Archaeology of Ancient Greek Secret Cults*, London, 50–78.
Cooper (2009): Craig Cooper, "(Re)making Demosthenes: Demochares and Demetrius of Phalerum on Demosthenes," in: Pat Wheatley and Robert Hannah (eds.) *Alexander and his Successors: Essays from the Antipodes*, Claremont, California, 310–322.
De Sanctis (1893): Gaetano De Sanctis, "Contributi alla Storia Atheniese della Guerra Lamiaca alla Guerra Cremonidea," in: G. Beloch (ed.) *Studi di Storia Antica* II, Rome, 3–62.
Dinsmoor (1931) W.B. Dinsmoor, *The Archons of Athens in the Hellenistic Age*, Cambridge.

---

[131] For the date, see [Plut.] *Mor.* 847d.

Dixon (2007): Michael Dixon, "Corinth, Greek freedom, and the Diadochoi, 323–301," in: Waldemar Heckel, Lawrence Tritle, and Pat Wheatley (eds), *Alexander's Empire: Formulation to Decay*, Claremont, California, 151–178.
Dixon (2014): Michael Dixon, *Late Classical and Early Hellenistic Corinth*, London.
Dmitriev (2011): Sviatoslav Dmitriev, *The Greek Slogan of Freedom and Early Roman Politics in Greece*, Oxford.
Dow (1963): Sterling Dow, "The Athenian Anagrapheis," in: *HSCP* 67, 37–54.
Dreyer (1999): Boris Dreyer, *Untersuchungen zur Geschichte des spätklassichen Athen* (322–ca. 230 v. Chr.), Stuttgart.
Droysen (1836): J.G. Droysen, "Der vierjährige Krieg," in: *Zeitschrift für die Altertumswissenschaft* III, nos. 20, 21, 161–170.
Ferguson (1911): William Ferguson, *Hellenistic Athens: An Historical Essay*, London.
Ferguson (1929): William Ferguson, "Lachares and Demetrius Poliorcetes," in: *CP* 24, 1–31.
Flacelière and Chambry (1977): Robert Flacelière and Émile Chambry, *Plutarque. Vies. Tome XIII: Démétrios-Antoine*, Paris.
Gabbert (1997): Janice Gabbert, *Antigonus II Gonatas: A Political Biography*, London.
Gruen (1984): Erich Gruen, *The Hellenistic World and the Coming of Rome*, v.1, Berkeley.
Gullath (1982): Brigitte Gullath, *Untersuchungen zur Geschichte Boiotiens in der Zeit Alexanders und der Diadochen*, Frankfurt.
Habicht (1985): Christian Habicht, *Pausanias' Guide to Ancient Greece*, Berkeley.
Habicht (1988): Christian Habicht, *Hellenistic Athens and her Philosophers*, Princeton.
Habicht (1993): Christian Habicht, "The Comic Poet Archedikos," in: *Hesperia* 63, 253–356.
Habicht (1997): Christian Habicht, *Athens from Alexander to Antony*, Cambridge.
Habicht (2006): Christian Habicht, *Athènes hellénistique: Histoire de la cité d'Alexandre le Grand à Marc Antoine*, 2nd ed., Paris.
Habicht (2017): Christian Habicht, *Divine Honors for Mortal Men in Greek Cities: The Early Cases*, Ann Arbor, Michigan.
Hansen, M. (1979): Mogens Hansen, "Ἐκκλησία Σύγκλητος in Hellenistic Athens," in: *GRBS* 20, 149–156.
Hornblower (1981): Jane Hornblower, *Hieronymus of Cardia*, Oxford.
Kralli (2000): Ioanna Kralli, "Athens and her leading citizens in the early Hellenistic period (338 B.C.–261 B.C.): The evidence of the decrees awarding the highest honours," in: *Archaiognosia* 10, 132–163.
Landucci-Gattinoni (2003): Franca Landucci-Gattinoni, *L'arte del potere: Vita e opera di Cassandro di Macedonia*, Stuttgart.
Lévêque (1957): Pierre Lévêque, *Pyrrhos*, Paris.
Luraghi (2014): Nino Luraghi, "Stratokles of Diomeia and Party Politics in Early Hellenistic Athens," in: *C&M* 14, 191–226.
Luraghi (2018): Nino Luraghi, "Documentary Evidence and Political Ideology in Early Hellenistic Athens," in: H. Börm and N. Luraghi (eds.) *The Polis in the Hellenistic World*, Stuttgart, 209–228.
Ma (1999): John Ma, *Antiochus III and the Cities of Western Asia Minor*, Oxford.
Mackil (2013) Emily Mackil, *Creating a Common Polity: Religion, Economy, and Politics in the Making of the Greek Koinon*, Berkeley.
Manni (1951): Eugenio Manni, *Demetrio Poliorcete*, Rome.
Manni (1953): Eugenio Manni, *Plutarchi: Vita Demetri Poliorcetis*, Florence.

Marasco (1980): Gabriele Marasco, *Sparta agli inizi Dell' età Ellenistica: Il Regno Di Areo I (309/8–265/4 a. C.)*, Florence.

Marasco (1981): Gabriele Marasco, "Introduzione alla biografia plutarchea di Demetrio," in: *Sileno* 7, 35–70.

Marasco (1984): Gabriele Marasco, *Democare di Leuconoe: Politica e Cultura in Atene fra IV e III Sec. A.C.*, Florence.

Marsden (1969): *Greek and Roman Artillery*, Oxford.

Mastrocinque (1979): Attilio Mastrocinque, "Demetrios tragodoumenos: propaganda e letteratura al tempo di Demetrio Poliorcete," in: *Athenaeum* 57, 260–276.

Meeus (2014): Alexander Meeus, "The Territorial Ambitions of Ptolemy I," in: Hans Hauben and Alexander Meeus (eds.), *The Age of the Successors and the Creation of the Hellenistic Kingdoms (323–276 B.C.)*, Leuven, 263–306.

Mikalson (1998): Jon Mikalson, *Religion in Hellenistic Athens*, Berkeley.

Oliver (2007): Graham Oliver, *War, Food, and Politics in Early Hellenistic Athens*, Oxford.

Osborne (2006): Michael Osborne, "The Eponymous Archons of Athens from 300/299 to 286/85," in: *Ancient Society* 36, 69–80.

Osborne (2012): Michael Osborne, *Athens in the Third Century B.C.*, Athens.

O'Sullivan (2009): Lara O'Sullivan, *The Regime of Demetrius of Phalerum in Athens, 317–307 BCE*, Leiden.

O'Sullivan (2009b): Lara O'Sullivan, "History from Comic Hypotheses: Stratocles, Lachares, and P.Oxy. 1235," in: *GRBS* 49, 53–79.

Parker, R. (2005) Robert Parker, *Polytheism and Society at Athens*, Oxford.

Paschidis (2008): Paschalis Paschidis, *Between City and King: Prosopographical Studies on the Intermediaries between the Cities of the Greek Mainland and the Royal Courts in the Hellenistic Period, 322–190 BC*, Athens.

Pelling (1988): Christopher Pelling, *Plutarch: Life of Antony*, Cambridge.

Pelling (2002): Christopher Pelling, *Plutarch and History*, Swansea.

Petrakos (1999): Basileios Petrakos, *Ὁ Δῆμος τοῦ Ραμνοῦντος II: Οἱ ἐπιγραφές*.

Poddighe (2013): Elizabeth Poddighe, "Propaganda Strategies and Political Documents: Philip III's Diagramma and the Greeks in 319 BC," in: Victor Alonso Troncoso and Edward M. Anson (eds.) *After Alexander: The Time of the Diadochi (323–281 BC)*, Oxford, 225–240.

Roisman and Worthington (2015): Joseph Roisman and Ian Worthington, *Lives of the Attic Orators: Texts from Pseudo-Plutarch, Photius and the Suda*, Oxford.

Rose (2015): Thomas Rose, "A Historical Commentary on Plutarch's *Life of Demetrius*," Phd. Diss. Iowa.

Rose (2018): Thomas Rose, "Demetrius Poliorcetes, *Kairos*, and the Sacred and Civil Calendars of Athens," in: *Historia* 67, 258–287.

Rose (2019): Thomas Rose, "Demetrius the Besieger (and Fortifier) of Cities," in: Jeremy Armstrong and Matthew Trundle (eds.) *Brill's Companion to Sieges in the Ancient Mediterranean*, Leiden, 169–190.

Santi Amantini et al. (1995): Luigi Santi Amantini et al., *Plutarco: Le Vite di Demetrio e di Antonio*, Milan.

Scholten (2000): Joseph Scholten, *The Politics of Plunder: Aitolians and their Koinon in the Early Hellenistic Era, 279–217 B.C.*, Berkeley.

Sealey (1993): Raphael Sealey, *Demosthenes and His Time: A Study in Defeat*, Oxford.

Shear (1970): T.L. Shear, Jr., "The Monument of the Eponymous Heroes in the Athenian Agora," in: *Hesperia* 39, 171–176.
Shear (1978): T.L. Shear, Jr., *Kallias of Sphettos and the Revolt of Athens in 286*, Princeton.
Shear (2010): Julia Shear, "Demetrios Poliorketes, Kallias of Sphettos, and the Panathenaia," in: Gary Reger, F.X. Ryan, and Timothy F. Winters (eds.), *Studies in Greek Epigraphy and History in Honor of Stephen V. Tracy*, Paris, 135–153.
Shear (2012): Julia Shear, "The Politics of the Past: Remembering Revolution at Athens," in: John Marincola, Lloyd Llewellyn-Jones, and Calum Maciver (eds.), *Greek Notions of the Past in the Archaic and Classical Eras: History without Historians*, Edinburgh, 276–300.
Shear (2017): Julia Shear, "Writing Past and Present in Hellenistic Athens: The Honours for Demosthenes," in: Irene Berti, Katharina Bolle, Fanny Opdenhoff, and Fabian Stroth (eds.) *Writing Matters: Presenting and Perceiving Monumental Inscriptions in Antiquity and the Middle Ages*, Berlin, 161–190.
Shear (2020): Julia Shear, "An Inconvenient Past in Hellenistic Athens: The Case of Phaidros of Sphettos," in: *Histos* Supplement 11, 269–301.
Simpson (1959): R.H. Simpson, "Antigonus the One-Eyed and the Greeks," in: *Historia* 8, 385–409.
Smith (1962): Leonard Smith, "Demochares of Leuconoe and the Dates of his Exile," in: *Historia* 11, 114–118.
Steinbock (2012): Bernd Steinbock, *Social Memory in Athenian Public Discourse*, Ann Arbor.
Sweet (1951): Waldo Sweet, "Sources for Plutarch's *Demetrius*," in: *CW* 44, 177–181.
Tarn (1913): W.W. Tarn, *Antigonus Gonatas*. Oxford.
Thonemann (2005): Peter Thonemann, "The Tragic King: Demetrios Poliorketes and the City of Athens," in: Olivier Hekster and Richard Fowler (eds.), *Imaginary Kings: Royal Images in the Ancient Near East, Greece and Rome*, Stuttgart, 63–86.
Tracy (2000): Stephen Tracy, "Athenian Politicians and Inscriptions of the Years 307–302," in: *Hesperia* 69, 227–233.
Tracy (2003): Stephen Tracy, *Athens and Macedon: Attic Letter-Cutters of 300 to 220 B.C.*, Berkeley.
Wallace (2011): Shane Wallace, "The Freedom of the Greeks in the Early Hellenistic Period (337–262 BC). A Study in Ruler-City Relations," Ph. D. Diss., Edinburgh.
Wallace (2013): Shane Wallace, "Adeimantus of Lampsacus and the Development of the Early Hellenistic Philos," in: Victor Alonso Troncoso and Edward M. Anson (eds.) *After Alexander: The Time of the Diadochi*, Oxford, 142–158.
Wallace (2014): Shane Wallace, "Defending the Freedom of the Greeks: Antigonos, Telesphoros, and the Olympic Games of 312 B.C," in: *Phoenix* 68, 235–246.
Wehrli (1968): Claude Wehrli, *Antigone et Demetrios*, Geneva.
Wheatley and Dunn (2020): Pat Wheatley and Charlotte Dunn, *Demetrius the Besieger*, Oxford.
Woodhead (1981): A.G. Woodhead, "Athens and Demetrios Poliorketes at the End of the Fourth Century B.C.," in: H.J. Dell and Eugene N. Borza (eds.) *Ancient Macedonian Studies in Honor of Charles F. Edson*, Thessaloniki, 357–367.
Woodhead (1989): A.G. Woodhead, "The Calendar of the Year 304/03 BC in Athens," in: *Hesperia* 58, 297–301.
Woodhead (1997): A.G. Woodhead, *The Athenian Agora* XVI. *Inscriptions: The Decrees*, Princeton.

Sabine Müller
Philip II, Alexander III, and Members of Their Court in Greek Comedy

The appearances of Macedonians on the Greek comic stage shed light on their contemporary perception by a wider and heterogeneous Greek public: not only the civic body, citizens reflecting the wide range of social hierarchies, but also metics, foreign guests, and other non-citizens (often watching from unofficial sites) formed part of the audience.[1] In order to secure applause and laughter, the jokes had to refer to elements of the public discourse, common knowledge, or at least rumors and gossip.[2] Often, the images of the Macedonians in Greek comedy include features that can also be found in their depictions by Attic orators and Greek historiographers.[3] While only few references to Macedonians are known, even in the age of Philip II and Alexander III, the following observations might perhaps sharpen the view regarding clichés and exaggeration within the Greek depiction of Macedonians.[4]

Macedonians first became objects of ridicule on the Greek comic stage when their degree of prominence in the Greek public made them interesting enough. The first extant reference is a joke by Hermippus about Perdiccas II.[5] A major part of the latter's reign was overshadowed by Athens' policies in northern Greece. In order to preserve his realm's autonomy and prevent it from becoming

---

All comic fragments are cited from the edition of Kassel and Austin. All dates are BC if not indicated otherwise. The translations of the passages from Athenaeus are those of S.D. Olson if not indicated otherwise.
Acknowledgements: I am grateful to Frances Pownall for inviting me to her conference and this volume and to Sulo Asirvatham and Anneli Purchase.

1 Roselli (2011) 81; Roselli (2013) 27. The constitution of the audience changed from Old Comedy to New Comedy, cf. Roselli (2013) 30–31. According to Asper (2005) 5–6, in the 5th century, the rich Athenians dominated.
2 On other concepts of comedy and publicity see Halliwell (1993).
3 Cf. Davidson (1993) 65; Hubbard (2010); Lape (2004) 206–212; Baron (2017) 216.
4 Müller (2016) 57–60; Müller (2020). For the role of political puns in Middle Comedy see Webster (1970) 23–49; Carrière (1979) 149–150; Nesselrath (1997); Olson (2007) 220–226; Arnott (2010) 301–305; Henderson (2014); Sorrentino (2014) 976; Mastellari (2016). On Greek perceptions of the Macedonians see Asirvatham (2008); Asirvatham (2010) 100–104.
5 On Perdiccas II see Borza (1990) 132–160; Roisman (2010) 146–154; Psoma (2014); Müller (2017).

https://doi.org/10.1515/9783110622942-008

a plaything in the Peloponnesian War, Perdiccas strategically employed the art of diplomacy.

F 63 K-A, presumably from Hermippus' *Phormophoroi* and dating to the 420s,[6] lists typical regional articles of trade imported to Athens such as *silphion* from Cyrene, papyrus from Egypt, mercenaries from Arcadia, or salt fish from the Hellespont.[7] Inserting political puns aimed at two Athenian allies in the northern Greek theatre of war who were perceived as troublesome, Hermippus includes mange from the Odrysian ruler Sitalces for the Spartans and many ships full of lies from Perdiccas.[8] The destination of the Argead "specialty" is controversial: Sparta, Athens, or both? Hermippus may have invited his audience to laugh either about the miserable Spartans receiving Sitalces' mange *and* Perdiccas' shiploads of lies (wishful thinking) or about Athens' own frustrated expectations in her dealings with him.[9] In the latter case Hermippus joked about the delivery of lies instead of timber for the fleet of the Athenians who were the main customers of Macedonia's ship-building timber, traditionally controlled by the Argead ruler.[10]

Hermippus' contemporary Aristophanes seems to have reinforced this image of Perdiccas as an out-and-out liar in his *Birds*, performed first in 414, shortly before Perdiccas' death, when the situation had forced him to ally with Athens again.[11] Aristophanes mentions a traitor and the theme of "escaping like a partridge" (the Greek word *perdix* is reminiscent of Perdiccas' name) in the sense that a *perdix* fools the hunter under false pretences:

> εἰ δ' ὁ Πεισίου προδοῦναι τοῖς ἀτίμοις τὰς πύλας
> βούλεται, πέρδιξ γενέσθω, τοῦ πατρὸς νεοττίον·
> ὡς παρ' ἡμῖν οὐδὲν αἰσχρόν ἐστιν ἐκπερδικίσαι.
>
> Does the son of Peisias want to betray the gates of the city
> to the foe? Let him become a partridge, the fitting offspring of his father;
> among us there is no shame in escaping as cleverly as a partridge.[12]

---

6 Gilula (2000) 82; Gkaras (2008) 141.
7 Gkaras (2008) 126–148.
8 Ath. 1.27e–28a. Cf. Gkaras (2008) 127, 136–138; Müller (2017) 201–207; Müller (2020) 404.
9 Gilula (2000) 80; Gkaras (2008) 137–138. It is generally assumed that the play predates Sitalces' death in 424. Cf. Pellegrino (2000) 197; Gkaras (2008) 123; Storey (2014) 106. Perdiccas formed an alliance with Sparta in 424 (Thuc. 4.79.2) but had contacted Sparta already on the eve of the Peloponnesian War (Thuc. 1.57.4).
10 Borza (1987); Bissa (2009), 107–109, 111–143, 149–151; Psoma (2015); Müller (2017) 56–57, 192–194, 204.
11 Thuc. 7.9.1.
12 Ar. *Av.* 766–768. Trans. E. O'Neill.

Since Aristophanes often introduced a neologism in order to make a pun,[13] ἐκπερδικίζειν, only attested in this verse, is mostly seen as a joke about Perdiccas as an unreliable ally.[14] Supposedly, the actor will have pronounced the word as if it was written with two *kappa*, ἐκπερδικ-κίσαι, to make sure that the pun secured applause.[15] The term can likely be paralleled to politically and ideologically colored words such as μηδίζειν, λακωνίζειν, μακεδονίζειν or φιλιππίζειν.[16] Thus, ἐκπερδικ(κ)ίζειν, literally "doing the Perdiccas," could mean to sympathize or collaborate with him, be his partisan or agent. The notions of lies, deception, and duplicity are implicit.

The Athenocentric view that turned Perdiccas' efforts to save his realm into the crookeries of a nightmarish ally is also prevalent in Thucydides, the main literary source for Perdiccas' reign. The historiographer portrays him as the personification of unreliability who betrayed *all* of his allies and broke treaties in record time.[17] This biased portrayal has much in common with Hermippus' reference to Perdiccas as a merchant of lies and Aristophanes' pun on the deceiving *perdix*. Apparently, they all reflect and at the same time cement distinctive features of Perdiccas' public image in Athens.

In the late 5th or early 4th century, the comic poet Strattis wrote a lost play that Athenaeus variously calls *Macedonians*, *Pausanias*, or *Macedonians or Pausanias*.[18] It is mostly assumed that its title was *Macedonians* while Pausanias was a character in the play.[19] Scholars identify Strattis' protagonist either with the Argead ruler Pausanias who reigned in 394/3, the Thessalian lover of the courtesan Lais (since she is mentioned in F 27 K-A), or Pausanias of Cerameis, the life partner of the famous Athenian tragic poet Agathon.[20] While the uncertainty remains, the Argead ruler Pausanias seems an unlikely person to be of interest to a Greek audience. In his short reign he was constantly occupied with civil war in Macedonia and there is no record of any interactions with Greek *poleis*.[21] Pausanias of Cerameis, on the contrary, was a person of a certain prominence in Athens: mentioned by Plato and the love of an Athenian celebrity, Agathon, who

---

13 Schreiber (1974) 97.
14 Moreno (2007) xxiii. Cf. Schreiber (1974) 97–98; Müller (2017) 216–224.
15 Hose (1940) 88. ἐκ emphasizes the meaning of the term.
16 On the meaning of φιλιππίζειν see Cooper (2007).
17 Cf. Thuc. 1.56.2–57.5, 62.2; 2.95.2, 101.5; 4.124.1–125.1; 5.83.4; cf. Badian (1993) 151–185, 239–244; Asirvatham (2008) 243–245; Müller (2017a) 33–38.
18 Storey (2011) III, 247. *Suda*, Strattis σ 1178 lists them separately. Cf. Storey (2011) III, 247. On the date see Carrière (1979) 271; Miles (2009) 321; Orth (2009) 17–19.
19 Orth (2009) 144; Storey (2011) III, 247.
20 Orth (2009) 146, 156–157.
21 Cf. March (1995) 279; Roisman (2010) 158; Müller (2016) 199.

himself had been ridiculed on the comic stage.²² In addition, Pausanias had a connection with Macedonia: when Agathon was invited by Archelaus to his court and spent his last years there, Pausanias accompanied him.²³ If he was Strattis' protagonist, the comic effects could have been created by an Athenian's experiences in Macedonia, mockingly described as a cultural clash.²⁴ However, given the scarcity of evidence, this remains hypothetical; Pausanias may also have been the lover of Lais. The same is true for the interpretation of F 29 K-A as a pun on the uncouth, strange dialect of the Macedonians.²⁵ The subject is a non-Athenian term for a fish:

> ἡ σφύραινα δ' ἐστὶ τίς;
> φησὶν ὁ ἕτερος· κέστραν μὲν ὕμμες ὠττικοὶ κικλήσκετε.
>
> *sphyraina?* What do you mean?
> And the other replies: "Wha' ye Attics ca' a hammer-fush, ma freen."²⁶

Although it is tempting and not difficult to imagine that the non-Athenian speaker was a Macedonian and that Strattis made fun of the Macedonians as hillbillies and lowbrows speaking a dialect foreign to Athenian ears,²⁷ it is uncertain. Aristophanes usually has his Persians and other foreigners speaking bad, barely comprehensible Greek. Strange dialects were a common device in Old Comedy and Strattis also ridiculed the Thebans because of their linguistic differences.²⁸

Macedonians may have been mentioned by Ephippus of Athens, active from ca. 370 to ca. 340.²⁹ If, as is likely, the term "Mygdonians" refers to Macedonians,³⁰ they appear in the verses of a fantastic monologue in his *Geryones* (F 5

---

22 Pl. *Prot.* 315d–e; *Symp.* 176a; 177e, 193b–c; Ar. *Thesm.* 138–192.
23 Ael. *VH* 2.21. Cf. Miles (2009) 231 with n. 419.
24 Orth (2009) 145–148. Papachrysostomou (2008) 220, n. 43 believes at least that the setting was Macedonia.
25 Orth (2009) 17–19.
26 Ath. 7.323b. Trans J. M. Edmonds. Cf. Wilkins (2000) 282; Miles (2009) 195.
27 Edmonds (1959) 205; Orth (2009) 147–148. For example, later on, Demosthenes (9.31) called Macedonia a place where it was not even possible to buy a decent slave. Cf. Lape (2004) 207; Asirvatham (2008) 245–249.
28 F 49 K-A. Cf. Miles (2009) 195. Willi (2010) 509 believes him to be a Boiotian and the Macedonians to be mute figures. F 32 K-A of Strattis' *Macedonians* does not provide any further insight: it is about a piece of a tunny fish. Cf. Miles (2009) 138.
29 Suda, ε 3979. Cf. Arnott (2010) 287.
30 Webster (1970) 41; Carrière (1979) 308; Dušanić (1980-81) 10; Freeman (1996) 22, n. 42; Konstantakos (2011) 244. The term was perhaps used because of the Argead estates located in Central Macedonian Mygdonia (Thuc. 1.58.2). The suggestion of Dušanić (1980-81) 16 that Mygdonia was an independent realm of the pretender Pausanias in 366–359 contradicts all extant evidence. In

K-A), reused in his *Peltastes* (F 19 K-A).[31] The subject of the recital is the preparation of a huge fish in an immense cooking pot, apparently the Aegean, for the giant Geryones, one of Heracles' adversaries.[32] Mythological parodies were popular in the first half of the 4th century, in particular stories about Heracles.[33] Ephippus imagines Geryones as a mighty king whose meal the neighboring peoples helped to prepare:[34]

τούτῳ δ' ὁπόταν ναέται χώρας
ἰχθὺν τιν' ἕλωσ' οὐχ ἡμέριον,
τῆς περικλύστου δ' ἁλίας Κρήτης
μείζω μεγέθει, λοπὰς ἔστ' αὐτῷ
δυνατὴ τούτους χωρεῖν ἑκατόν.

καὶ περιοίκους εἶναι ταύτῃ
Σινδούς, Λυκίους, Μυγδονιώτας,
Κραναούς, Παφίους. τούτους δ' ὕλην
κόπτειν, ὁπόταν βασιλεὺς ἕψῃ
τὸν μέγαν ἰχθὺν καὶ προσάγοντας
καθ' ὅσον πόλεως ἔστηκεν ὄρος,
τοὺς δ' ὑποκαίειν. λίμνην δ' ἐπάγειν
ὕδατος μεστὴν εἰς τὴν ἅλμην,
τοὺς δ' ἅλας αὐτῷ ζεύγη προσάγειν
μηνῶν ὀκτὼ συνεχῶς ἑκατόν.

περιπλεῖν δ' ἐπὶ τοῖς ἄμβωσιν ἄνω
πέντε κέλητας πεντασκάλμους,
περιαγγέλλειν τ': 'οὐχ ὑποκαίεις,
Λυκίων πρύτανι; ψυχρὸν τουτί·
παύου φυσῶν, Μακεδὼν ἄρχων
σβέννυ, Κέλθ', ὡς μὴ προσκαύσῃς.'

368, Eurydice hired the mercenary general Iphicrates who expelled him (Aeschin. 2.27–29; Nep. 11.3.2). It is uncertain if the pretender Pausanias who appeared in 360/59 was identical with him (Diod. 16.2.6). Cf. Worthington (2008) 20; Müller (2016) 238. The question remains why Ephippus speaks of the ruler of Macedon but not of the Macedonians.
31 Ath. 8.347b–c.
32 Ath. 8.346f. Cf. Edmonds (1959) 147, 157–159; Webster (1970) 40–43; Nesselrath (1990) 218–220; Nesselrath (1997) 273–274; Konstantakos (2011). Some scholars believe that the cooking-pot symbolizes the Mediterranean, cf. Webster (1970) 40–42; Carrière (1979) 308; Freeman (1996) 23 (a parody of it as a pond in Pl. *Phaid.* 109b).
33 Arnott (2010) 294–295; Konstantakos (2011) 223–224; Konstantakos (2014), 160–180.
34 Konstantakos (2011) 244; Orth (2014) 1011.

> Whenever the inhabitants of the country catch
> An exceptional fish for him,
> One larger in size than Crete, which rests
> in the middle of the sea, he has a casserole-dish
> capable of holding 100 of these.
>
> The people who live on its edge
> Are Sindians, Lycians, Mygdonians,
> Cranaï, and Paphians. They chop
> wood when the king is cooking
> his big fish, and bring as
> much as the city's walls can hold
> and set fire to it. They also bring a lake
> full of water for the stewing-brine;
> 100 teams of oxen work continuously for eight
> months to transport the salt for it.
>
> Five fast little boats
> Sail about on top of the rim
> And carry his orders around: "Light the fire,
> Lycian commander! This part's cold!"
> "Stop blowing on it, ruler of Macedon!"
> "Quench that flame, Celt—watch you don't burn it!"[35]

According to Athenaeus, in the *Peltastes* the speech is the nonsense dinner-talk of some boastful person,[36] mostly interpreted as a *miles gloriosus* priding himself with his mighty employer.[37] The latter is sometimes identified with the Persian Great King whose luxurious banquets were a common element of the Greek imagery of the Achaemenid court.[38] As for Ephippus' *Geryones*, some scholars have interpreted the fragment (or the whole lost play) as an allegory alluding to contemporary policies. Geryones was identified with the Athenian *strategos* Timotheus operating in the Aegean to restore the Athenian hegemony, or the Persian king (without any personalization).[39] Alternatively, the ruler of Macedonia has

---

35 Ath. 8.346f–347b. Trans. S. D. Olson.
36 Ath. 8.347c.
37 Nesselrath (1990) 276; Sorrentino (2014) 987.
38 Tuplin (1996) 151.
39 The Persian King: Davidson (1993) 61. Timotheus and an allegory of Athens' foreign policy in the 360s: Webster (1970) 40–41; Dušanić (1980-81) 10–24; Wallace (1995) 208. The hypothesis of Dušanić (1980-81) 21 that Geryones symbolized Athens and Heracles Thebes is not very convincing. Cf. Nesselrath (1990) 219, n. 119: an Athenian audience would not have been amused given the fact that Geryones was killed by Heracles.

been thought to represent Alexander III.[40] However, given our limited knowledge about the play, the warnings against reading it as a full-scale political satire seem justified.[41] Ephippus may have been "dropping a few satirical hints at the hot political affairs of the day"[42] but it is far from certain that these references were more than occasional. However, as for the "Mygdonians," Ephippus may have referred to images of the Macedonian "barbarians" from the hinterland which already permeated Athenian public discourse, perhaps since "Mygdonians" may have sounded more outlandish than "Macedonians".[43] Interestingly, while the Cranaï, identified by most scholars with the Athenians,[44] did not get any instruction on how to handle the fish, the non-Greek Lycians, Celts, and Mygdonians nearly burnt the dish and needed to be instructed.

Similarly enigmatic is F 5 K-A by the Middle comedy poet Heniochus. It is debated to which decade of the 4th century the fragment dates. It is about the gathering of the Greek cities in Olympia where they want to offer sacrifices for their liberation from *phoroi* (the term of the tribute that the members of Athens' Delian League had to pay and that became one of their major grievances in the 5th century). But the cities were plagued by *Aboulia* (lack of counsel) and infatuated by the ladies *Democratia* and *Aristocratia*.[45] In scholarship, the fragment is variously linked with the foundation of the Second Athenian League in 378/77 (because of the change of nomenclature for the tributes: *syntaxeis* instead of *phoroi*), Athens' loss of the Social War in 355, or the establishment of the Corinthian League in 337.[46] Scholars advocating the latter credit Heniochus with a pro-Macedonian attitude and depiction of the Argead monarchy as some higher force superseding democracy and aristocracy and ending the internal wars in Greece.[47] However, given the tense atmosphere prevalent in Athens in the 330s, Revermann's doubts about a comedy along these lines for an Athenian audience are

---

40 Edmonds (1959) 159.
41 Nesselrath (1990) 218–219; Nesselrath (1997) 273–274; Konstantakos (2011) 246.
42 Konstantakos (2011) 246. Cf. Nesselrath (1990) 219–220.
43 Strab. 7.3.2. identifies them as Thracians. However, Mygdonia belonged to the Argead estates located in Central Macedonia (Thuc. 1.58.2).
44 Based on Hdt. 8.44.2; Ar. *Ach.* 75. Cf. Edmonds (1959) 159; Webster (1970) 41; Carrière (1979) 308; Dušanić (1980-81) 10; Freeman (1996) 22, n. 43; Konstantakos (2011) 244. I am grateful to Frances Pownall's suggestion that the term may have been chosen by Ephippus to show that all these people were "barbarians."
45 Cf. Webster (1970) 44; Nesselrath (1997) 274–275; Revermann (1999) 25–27; Nightingale (2004) 62–63; Sommerstein (2014) 300; Mastellari (2016) 431–432.
46 For an overview, see Revermann (1999) 26–27.
47 Webster (1970) 44; Mastellari (2016) 432.

plausible.⁴⁸ Making Athenian recipients laugh in the aftermath of Chaeronea by praising the Macedonian supremacy as a heavenly sent benefaction seems unfortunate, even as irony or satire.

One of Philip's generals mentioned in Greek comedy was Adaeus, a commander of his *misthophoroi* (professional soldiers).⁴⁹ He became subject of Athenian ridicule because he was defeated by the Athenian *strategos* Chares.⁵⁰ It was one of the rare occasions when Chares did not come off worse against the Macedonians. The comic poet Heraclides uses Adaeus' nickname "the Rooster" (Ἀλεκτρυών) in order to mockingly allude to a cock fight between him and Chares (F 1 K-A):⁵¹

> ἀλεκτρυόνα τὸν τοῦ Φιλίππου παραλαβών·
> ἀωρὶ κοκκύζοντα καὶ πλανώμενον
> κατέκοψεν οὐ γὰρ εἶχεν οὐδέπω λόφον.
> ἕνα κατακόψας μάλα συχνοὺς ἐδείπνισεν
> Χάρης Ἀθηναίων τόθ' ὡς γενναῖος ἦν.

> Chares one night caught Philip's cock astray
> And crowing loud before the dawn was gray,
> And cut his throat—it seems he had no crest –
> And on one fowl fed nearly all the rest
> Of Athens.

And another speaker adds:

> I say he's one of the best.

Heraclides refers to the double meaning of λόφος for a rooster's comb, helmet-crest, or crest of a hill in an military context.⁵² He portrays Adaeus as celebrating his victory prematurely, crowing too soon.⁵³ Chares caught him off guard and Adaeus had not even time to get his helmet on. Thus, the comic effect was pro-

---

48 Revermann (1999) 27, n. 8.
49 Parke (1933) 162.
50 Pritchett (1974) 77. On Chares see Parker (1986); Moysey (1985); Landucci Gattinoni (1994) 52–58; Bianco (2002).
51 Ath. 12.532d-f = Theopomp., *BNJ* 115 F 249; Duris, *BNJ* 74 F 35; Antiphanes F 296 K-A. Trans. S. D. Olson. Landucci Gattinoni (1997) 76, 83, 93–94 thinks that Duris inserted the citation of Heraclides. Cf. Baron (2017) 230; Pownall (2020b).
52 Borthwick (1966) 4 pointing at Aristoph. *Av.* 279–293. Cf. Pownall (2020b).
53 Borthwick (1966) 5; Parker (1986) 37. Immoderate boastfulness is a topical element of Greek depictions of the "other."

duced by the image of an exultant Macedonian rooster who was unable to put his comb up and perished against a well-bred Athenian cock. While it is unclear where Adaeus got his nickname from, Heraclides created the impression that it derived from his boastfulness.[54] Portraying Chares as the superior general, he drops the term γενναῖος, technically used of the highest class of cock or hen and also for the aristocratic elite.[55]

An Athenian audience might have remembered Adaeus' defeat because it was connected with a benefaction to the *demos*. According to Theopompus' *On the money stolen from Delphi*, Chares celebrated his victory by organizing a public sacrificial dinner in the Athenian agora, financed by 60 talents from the Delphic treasury.[56] The depiction that Chares wasted all of the money on a dinner party corresponds with the rumors about his extravagance; the lion's share will have been paid to his soldiers.[57] Since Theopompus connects the victory with the Third Sacred War, it it is roughly dated between the winter of 354/3 and the death of the Phocian general Onomarchus in 352.[58] The battle is assumed to have taken place at Thracian Cypsela because in his *The Self-Mourner*, Damoxenus locates Adaeus there having a drink (F 1 K-A).[59]

The protagonist of Mnesimachus' contemporary play *Philippos* is identified by most scholars with Philip II.[60] It is possible but not provable that the play treated the Athenian envoys negotiating the Peace of Philocrates (346) at Philip's court in Pella.[61] Since Philip had the upper hand politically and the Peace quickly became unpopular with the Athenians, the subject provided rich material for mockery. In F 7 K-A (from Athenaeus), at a symposium that preceded hostilities, a boastful speaker presents himself and his companions as so warlike that they literally eat weapons:

---

[54] Parke (1933) 145. Pownall (2020b) may be right connecting it with the crest of Adaeus' helmet.
[55] Borthwick (1966) 5 referring to Aristoph. *Av.* 285.
[56] Theopomp., *BNJ* 115 F 249. Cf. Salmond (1996) 49; Baron (2017) 228–230; Pownall (2020b). On Theopompus' work on the money from Delphi see Pownall (2004) 155.
[57] Pritchett (1974) 80, n. 122, 81; Salmond (1996) 49; Bianco (2002) 15. On Chares' bad reputation see Moysey (1985) 222.
[58] Parker (1986) 36; Landucci Gattinoni (1997) 94; Pownall (2020b). On the function of a public sacrificial dinner in Athens see Garnsey (1999) 133–134. On the Third Sacred War see Pownall (2020a).
[59] Cf. Ath. 11.468f. See Edmonds (1961) 210–211. Cf. Wirth (1985) 51; Landucci Gattinoni (1997) 94–95; Pownall (2020b).
[60] Edmonds (1959) 367; Carrière (1979) 165, 280; Nesselrath (1990) 327; Papachrysostomou (2008) 210; Arnott (2010) 301; Sorrentino (2014) 976; Orth (2014) 1023; Mastellari (2016) 430.
[61] Cf. Carrière (1979) 165, 280; Arnott (2010) 301; Papachrysostomou (2008) 210, 214.

> ἆρ' οἶσθ' ὁτιὴ πρὸς ἄνδρας ἐστί σοι μάχη,
> οἳ τὰ ξίφη δειπνοῦμεν ἠκονημένα,
> ὄψον δὲ δᾷδας ἡμμένας καταπίνομεν;
> ἐντεῦθεν εὐθὺς ἐπιφέρει τραγήματα
> ἡμῖν ὁ παῖς μετὰ δεῖπνον ἀκίδας Κρητικάς,
> ὥσπερ ἐρεβίνθους, δορατίων τε λείψανα
> κατεαγότ', ἀσπίδας δὲ προσκεφάλαια καὶ
> θώρακας ἔχομεν, πρὸς ποδῶν δὲ σφενδόνας
> καὶ τόξα, καταπέλταισι δ' ἐστεφανώμεθα.

> So do you realize that you'll be fighting men
> Who eat sharpened swords for dinner
> And gobble down flaming torches as a side-dish?
> Then right after the slave brings us
> Cretan arrowheads as an after-dinner snack,
> like chickpeas, plus some shattered fragments
> of javelins; and we use shields and breastplates
> as pillows, and put slings and bows
> by our feet, and wear catapults as garlands.[62]

This weapon fanatic is mostly believed to be a Macedonian trying to intimidate a potential opponent. Often, he is identified with Philip himself, a caricature of the tough, bellicose ruler.[63] However, as he does not speak any (Macedonian) dialect, other scholars think that it is Demosthenes addressing the Macedonians. It is argued that Mnesimachus made fun of his rhetorical style reputed to be often bombastic.[64] Thus, in his *Heroes* (F 12 K-A), the contemporary comic poet Timocles, known for his sharp political puns, ridiculed Demosthenes' efforts to rally the Athenians against Philip by joking that the orator ate catapults and spears while his eyes flashed war.[65] Given the record of Athenian failures and Macedonian successes from the 350s to the early 340s, such a tirade about Athens' military superiority would have been funny indeed, however more in a tragicomic way. The boastful monologue, if it was spoken by Demosthenes, would also

---

[62] Ath. 10.421c. Trans. S. D. Olson.
[63] Webster (1970) 64; Papachrysostomou (2008) 210–212; Konstantakos (2011) 168, n. 43; Orth (2014) 1023; Moloney (2014) 85; Mastellari (2016) 4390. Cf. Nesselrath (1990) 327, n. 124. Arnott (2010) 301 thinks that the subject is the efficiency of Philip's army. Wilkins (2000) 282 calls it a parody of a militaristic form of dining.
[64] Papachrysostomou (2008) 212–213. On criticism of Demosthenes' style: Aeschin. 3.72, 166–167; Demetrius of Phalerum, *BNJ* 228 F 16, 18b. Cf. Arnott (2010) 304.
[65] Ath. 6.224a–b. Cf. Wallace (1995) 208; Mastellari (2016) 425; Arnott (2010) 290. On Timocles' political overtones see Arnott (2010) 290, 304–305; Sorrentino (2014) 976; Orth (2014) 1045; Mastellari (2016) 425–429.

have produced laughter if the audience had Aeschines' claim in mind that Demosthenes promised fountains of oratory in Pella to make Philip restore Amphipolis to Athens but in the actual situation lost heart and collapsed.[66] However, the catapults may as well allude to Philip's innovation in siege engines. The extreme warlikeness with its touch of uncouthness seems to reflect stereotypical Greek images of the Macedonians.[67] In addition, the Cretan arrowheads as a dessert may hint at the established *topos* of the Macedonian untrustworthiness. Since Cretans were reputed to be untrustworthy and corrupt liars,[68] swallowing Cretan arrowheads may imply that bellicose uncouthness was accompanied by dishonesty.

F 8 K-A of Mnesimachus' *Philippos* contains a telling pun on contemporary policies providing a clue for the play's dating. Two servants, table attendants, or dinner-guests discuss the absence of the Pharsalians:

(A) τῶν Φαρσαλίων
ἥκει τις, ἵνα ⟨καὶ⟩ τὰς τραπέζας καταφάγῃ;
(B) οὐδεὶς πάρεστιν. (A.) εὖ γε δρῶντες. ἆρά
που ὀπτὴν κατεσθίουσι πόλιν Ἀχαιϊκήν;

(A) Did any of the Pharsalians come in order to eat the tables?
(B) None of them is there. (A) Good for them. Maybe
they are gobbling down a roasted Achaean city?[69]

The roasted city, a warlike metaphor of destruction,[70] alludes to Thessalian Halus.[71] The Athenians sympathized with Halus in its dispute with the Pharsalians who were supported by Philip. As he was actively at war against Halus during the negotiations of the Peace, he successfully insisted on its exclusion from the treaty. Still in 346, he conquered Halus and gave it to his Pharsalian allies who enslaved the population.[72] Accordingly, F 8 shows the Pharsalians as ruthless, greedy gluttons who literally swallow everything. This depiction is in accordance with the Greek *topos* of Thessalian decadence and the rumor that Phi-

---

66 Aeschin. 2.21, 34–35.
67 Pownall (2010).
68 Plat. *Nom.* 636c–d; Callim. *Hymn to Zeus* 7–8. Cf. Atkinson (1980) 184.
69 Ath. 10.418b–c. Cf. Papachrysostomou (2008) 216–219.
70 Cf. Dušanić (1980–81) 24; Wilkins (2000) 282; Papachrysostomou (2008) 218–219 (pointing at Aristophanes' *Peace* 242–252).
71 Edmonds (1959) 369; Webster (1970) 43; Mastellari (2016) 429–430.
72 Dem. 19.36, 159, 163, 174. Cf. Wirth (1985) 77, 81–82, 86, 91, 106; Worthington (2008) 87–88, 91, 98–99, 102–103.

lip welcomed them at his court because he shared their dissoluteness.⁷³ In the case that the speaker of F 7 was Philip, the characterization of the city-eating Pharsalians corresponded with this image: Philip's allies were as rude and merciless as the Macedonian ruler himself; they had "philippized."

The subject of Mnesimachus' short fragment F 9 K-A is the (non-existent) delicacy of bird's milk symbolizing abundance.⁷⁴ It may hint at the theme of the luxury of Macedonian dinner-parties and link this fragment with Mnesimachos' F 10 K-A treating gluttony and decadence at the Argead court.

F 10 K-A is about another glutton: Philip's courtier Dorion, a flute player, reputed to have been a devoted fish eater.⁷⁵ Since at Athens, the eating of fish was considered an expensive activity of the upper classes, *opsophagia* was associated with extravagance, depravity, corruption, and unlimited greed, in a political interpretation linked with imperialism and tyranny.⁷⁶ The negative notions are reflected in Demosthenes' accusation of Aeschines that he spent the bribes from Philip on prostitutes and fish.⁷⁷

In F 10, somebody, perhaps one of the party guests or servants hoping for the remains of the meal, complains that even at night, Dorion stays inside with them. He is termed a "shell-blower" or "dish-blower," λοπαδοφυσητής.⁷⁸ According to Edmonds, this wordplay implies that Dorion "blew on the dishes so as to be able to handle the food sooner."⁷⁹ Papachrysostomou points out that, given that λοπάς can mean a shallow casserole for stewing and a shellfish, Dorion used the shellfish as an *aulos* in order to keep on eating even when he did his job as a musician.⁸⁰ However, there might be a little more to it: an indecent pun associating fish-eating, *aulos* playing, and sexual activities that *aulos* players, due to the proverbial bad reputation of their profession through its frequent occupation by slaves and also the *aulos*' association with radical or even ochlocratic democratic resonances,⁸¹ were frequently associated with.⁸² Additionally,

---

73 Theopomp., *BNJ* 115 F 49, F 162. Cf. Pownall (2009) 244–246.
74 Ath. 9.387b. Cf. Papachrysostomou (2008) 219. It may have been a dinner table prepared for Philip and his Athenian guests.
75 Theopomp., *BNJ* 115 F 236; Ath. 8.337b–338b.
76 Davidson (1993) 54–57. Cf. Gilula (1995) 391–394; Marchiori (2000) 327, 329–330.
77 Dem. 19.229. Cf. Davidson (1993) 53; MacDowell (2000) 298.
78 Ath. 8.338b. Cf. Papachrysostomou (2008) 217, 220.
79 Edmonds (1959) 369. Olson in the LCL edition of Athenaeus translates: casserole-dish-player.
80 Papachrysostomou (2008) 220.
81 The *aulos* was seen as a poster child for the democratizing effects of the New Music "revolution" in Athens at the end of the fifth century, with hedonistic and dissolute implications as opposed to the stringed lyre associated with the more restrained banquets of the aristocratic

as women are sometimes likened to fishes and the love of fish could metaphorically hint at sexual desire,[83] the passage may refer to Philip's alleged dissolute symposia:[84] Dorion may in fact have taken part in an orgy. If this was the case, he was depicted as a mirror image of the ruler himself, imagined to be the supreme master of vice and gluttony surrounded by scoundrels and dancers (according to Demosthenes).[85]

Decadence was also a central theme of the depiction of Alexander's Macedonian treasurer Harpalus on the comic stage. Since his appearance in Greek comedy is widely studied,[86] there will be only some short remarks. A Greek audience was interested in Harpalus because of his Athenian connections, Athenian citizenship, and role in triggering a big corruption scandal when seeking refuge in Athens in 324.[87] Subjects of comic references to Harpalus were his extravagant *dolce vita* with his Greek *hetaerae* Pythionice and Glycera at Babylon and Tarsus[88] and the money he brought to Athens. In *Delos*, Timocles joked about the potential recipients of Harpalus' bribes (F 4 K-A):

Δημοσθένης τάλαντα πεντήκοντ' ἔχει,
μακάριος, εἴπερ μεταδίδωσι μηδενί (...)
ὅ τ' ἐν λόγοισι δεινὸς Ὑπερείδης ἔχει

---

elite. See e. g. West (1992) 356–372; Csapo (2004) 207–248; Franklin (2013) 213–236. I am grateful to Frances Pownall for this information.
82 Theopomp., *BNJ* 115 F 213 (= Ath. 12.532b–d); Apul. *Met.* 8.26.4–5; Plut. *Per.* 1.5. See also Richlin (2016) 86, n. 29.
83 Davidson (1997) 2–22, 26–35, 144–147; Henry (2000) 504; Marchiori (2000) 326; Richlin (2016) 83.
84 On Macedonian symposia in Greek eyes see Pownall (2010) 55–65.
85 Dem. 2.18–19. Cf. Theopomp., *BNJ* 115 F 224, F 225a, F 236. Cf. Pownall (2004) 149–152.
86 Kotlinska (2005); Müller (2006) 76–83; Shaw (2014) 125–128; LeGuen (2014) 261–263; Kotlinska-Toma (2015) 115; Pownall (2017) 223.
87 Hyp. 5; Plut. *Demosth.* 25; Ath. 6.245f–246a; Just. 13.5.9–10; Diod. 17.108.7–8. Cf. Heckel (2006) 130.
88 Ath. 13.586c, 595c–e. For example, Philemon ridiculed Harpalus' royal pretensions in *The Man of Babylon* (F 15 K-A = Ath. 13.595c). Cf. Edmonds (1961) 12–13. In the contemporary satyr-play *Agen* attributed to Python of Catana or Python of Byzantium or even to Alexander III—which is highly incredible, *contra* Kotlinska (2005)—Harpalus is persuaded by some *magoi* to make them invoke Pythionice's ghost at her tomb (Ath. 13.595f–596a). Cf. Shaw (2014) 123–128. Ironically, the scene refers to Aeschylus' *Persae* 619–681 in which the ghost of the wise Darius I appears to comfort his widow Atossa. In *Agen*, the grain Harpalus gave to the Athenians during a famine and therefore was granted citizenship is characterized as Glycera's grain and death-warrant for the Athenians who took the grain. The production date of the play is controversial. Cf. LeGuen (2014) 261–263; Shaw (2014) 125–128.

τοὺς ἰχθυοπώλας οὗτος ἡμῶν πλουτιεῖ·
ὀψοφάγος γάρ, ὥστε τοὺς λάρους εἶναι Σύρους.

Demosthenes has 50 talents.
He's a lucky guy—provided he's not offering anyone else a share (...)
And Hyperides the clever speechwriter got a bit.
He'll make our fish-sellers rich;
because he is enough of †a gluttont to make the seagulls look like Syrians![89]

In fact, Demosthenes was charged and found guilty of taking 20 talents from Harpalus,[90] and Hyperides was not one of the suspects but one of the ten prosecutors of Demosthenes. The pun on the seagulls refers to the Greek idea that Syrians did not eat any fish.[91] Summing up the picture emerging from the comic references to Harpalus, the seducer of the Athenian politicians, he appears as a typical Macedonian libertine in Greek literature: fond of luxury, immoderate, exploiting buyable Greek women and bribable Athenian politicians. Under Macedonian control, obviously, ridiculing representatives of its regime and their alleged Athenian agents and partisans as counter-images of the "good" Athenian citizen was one way to react to the lost autonomy, find an outlet for resentments, and create comic effects with a comforting value.[92]

Another comic subject that could be associated with the Macedonians was men without beards. While it is generally assumed that the fashion of shaving the beard was introduced by Alexander,[93] Theopompus—however polemically—attests to it already at Philip's court.[94] Personal hygiene was culturally coded: the "good" male Greek citizen was expected to get the balance right between filthiness and effeminacy.[95] Since up to the later part of the 4th century, most Athenian men were bearded, the new trend that also arrived in Athens

---

[89] Ath. 8.341f–342a. Trans. S. D. Olson. Cf. Edmonds (1959) 614–615; Olson (2007) 222–224; Arnott (2010) 304; Henderson (2014) 185, 187; Mastellari (2016) 425–426.
[90] Hyp. 5.6–7, 10; Din. 1.3–8, 96. The fine he did not pay may have been 50 talents.
[91] Ath. 8.346c–d. Cf. Marchiori (2000) 335–337. In his *Icarians* or *Icarian Satyrs*, Timocles had Hyperides transformed into a river rich of fish, blustering with boasts and watering the plains of anyone who hires him (F 17 K-A = Ath. 8.341e–342a). Cf. Mastellari (2016) 427.
[92] Such a comforting effect is also proposed by Lape (2010) 284 in reference to the re-evaluation of Athenian identity in Menander's comedies.
[93] Cf. Arnott (1996) 744; Lape (2004) 228, n. 70; Alonso Troncoso (2010) 13 on the base of Ath. 13.565a. Alonso Troncoso (2010) 20 argues that Alexander wanted to create a new image different from the Greeks, Ionians, and Persians. Hölscher (2009) 12–54 sees it as an imitation of the youthful images of Achilles and Heracles.
[94] Theopomp., *BNJ* 115 F 225a–b. For a critical analysis see Pownall (2005) 258–261; Müller (2016) 72, 178–179.
[95] Frass (2002) 467–476.

was apparently viewed with suspicion and ridiculed as a visible sign of loss of morals and unmanliness.⁹⁶ In a play with an uncertain title by Alexis, active from the 350s up perhaps to the 270s,⁹⁷ a speaker, according to Arnott an old-school *senex* or *paedagogus*, is upset about the new fashion of beardless men (F 266 K-A). In his view, they are examples of depravity denying their virility:⁹⁸

τί γὰρ αἱ τρίχες λυποῦσιν ἡμᾶς, πρὸς θεῶν;
δι' ἃς ἀνὴρ ἕκαστος ἡμῶν φαίνεται,
εἰ μή τι ταύταις ἀντιπράττεσθ' ὑπονοεῖς.

Because, what trouble does hair cause us, by the gods,
When it's what makes apparent that we're all men –
Unless you are planning to do something that suggests the contrary?

There is a sexual suspicion implicit; the speaker hints that shaving the chin creates effeminacy and may lead to the sexual submission to another man in the passive (perceived as "unmanly") sexual role.⁹⁹

In Alexis' *Lebes* (a cauldron for boiling water and meat), a cook appears who uses elaborately scientific language explaining why his treatment of burnt fish or meat will be successful.¹⁰⁰ His cure is praised by another person who exclaims that he sounds like a doctor and calls him Glaucias (F 129 K-A). Arguing against the suggestion that Glaucias was the cook's real name, Arnott states that he was dignified with the name of a famous contemporary physician: Glaucias who worked at the Macedonian court and failed to cure the sick Hephaestion.¹⁰¹ While it has been suggested that the play dates to the years preceding Hephaestion's death in 324,¹⁰² an Athenian audience suffering from Macedonian dominion may have been more amused if it dated *after* his death. A bitter complaint by Hyperides in his gloomy *Epitaphios* seems to indicate that Hephaestion's posthu-

---

96 Arnott (1996) 744.
97 Arnott (2010) 283.
98 Ath. 13.565b. Trans. S. D. Olson. Cf. Arnott (1996) 745–747; Webster (1970) 121–122. In Menander's *Sikyonioi* 264, who in his *Kolax* jokes about Alexander's reputation as the greatest drunkard in history every toady tries to emulate (F 2 K-A = Ath. 10.434b-c; cf. Plut. *Mor.* 57a; Pernestorfer (2009) 66–67, 112–113), Moschion is rendered a *lastauros*, a term Theopompus uses for Philip's *hetairoi* (*BNJ* 115 F 224, F 225a), and made fun of his smooth-shaven effeminate appearance. Cf. Lape (2004) 228.
99 Arnott (1996) 746.
100 Ath. 9.383c–e. Cf. Edmonds (1959) 430–433; Arnott (1996) 362–393; Orth (2014) 1031. On the boastful cook in Middle Comedy see Nesselrath (1990) 307–309; Arnott (2010) 319–322; Wilkins (2000); Sorrentino (2014) 986.
101 Plut. *Alex.* 72.1–2. Cf. Edmonds (1959) 433; Arnott (1996) 364.
102 Arnott (1996) 365.

mous heroic cult was also installed in Athens: Hyperides polemicizes that the poor Athenians were forced to honor the house slaves (*oiketai*; putting it into plural as a rhetorical means of exaggeration) of "these people" (the Macedonians).[103] Against this background, Alexis' pun may have been more comforting if the Athenians were reminded of a physician who did *not* save the life of one of the Macedonian oppressors.

A major example of the parody of political catchwords in Greek comedy is the vivid echo of the infamous quibbling in the matter of Halonnesus. In 343, trying to appease the disgruntled Athenians, Philip proposed to amend the Peace of Philocrates and offered them the small island of Halonnesus as a gesture of goodwill. Demosthenes and his supporters thundered that Philip could not give (*didomi*) Halonnesus to them, but only give it back (*apodidomi*), as it was Athens' rightful possession.[104] This quibble was echoed in alien contexts for a comic effect by several comic poets of the time.[105] For example, in his *Stratiotes*, Alexis uses the catchphrase for a baby nobody wants (F 212 K-A):

ἐγὼ δέδωκα γάρ τι ταύταις; εἰπέ μοι.
οὐκ, ἀλλ' ἀπέδωκας ἐνέχυρον δήπου λαβών.

Why, have I given these ladies anything?
No, given back something under bond.[106]

These puns on the Halonnesus affair may perhaps be another implication that the Athenians overestimated their political situation and possibilities and underestimated Macedonia's military strength and political strategies. Jokes were made about the policy of giving Philip the cold shoulder while this policy paved the way to Chaeronea.[107] The picture that emerges is consistent: the Attic orators kept on evoking Athens' glorious past and feeding the illusionary

---

103 Hyp. 6.21.
104 Aeschin. 3.83; [Dem.] 7.2; [Dem.] 12.12–14. Worthington (2008) 114, 117–118, 125.
105 Ath. 6.223d–224b. Cf. Edmonds (1959) 245; Arnott (1996) 70, 605–608; Arnott (2010) 302–303. Also Antiphanes made fun of it (F 167 K-A). Cf. Nesselrath (1990) 190–191; Willi (2002) 177; Arnott (2010) 286; Erbì (2011) 173–177; Orth (2014) 1012–1022, 1040; Mastellari (2016) 423–424. Edmonds (1959) 219, 223, 345, 239, 263 argues that Antiphanes' play *The Cyclops* (Ath. 7.295f) alludes to Philip after he had lost his eye in 354, that *The Rogue-Hater* (Ath. 6.226d) alludes to Demosthenes who always depicted Philip as a rogue and that Anaxilas' The *Goldsmith* (Ath. 10.416d) was about Philip issuing his first cold coinage. However, in Middle Comedy, titles often identified a character by his or her profession, cf. Arnott (2010) 311–312.
106 Trans. S. D. Olson.
107 On this policy see Wirth (1985) 87–133; Worthington (2008) 105–135.

hope for a restoration of Athenian supremacy;[108] the comic poets ridiculed political catchwords associated with problems caused by Macedonia's unstoppable rise that were in fact no laughing matter at all. Summing up the portrayal of the Macedonians on the Greek comic stage, the Argead rulers appear as reckless, untrustworthy, deceptive liars, boastful and warlike. They and their fellow Macedonians are depicted as uncouth brutes. The Argead court appears to be crowded with gluttons, fish-eaters, and effeminates who are parasites keen on participating in lavish banquets. Before Chaeronea, these portrayals of the Macedonians made fun of a politically troublesome occasional ally or opponent and underlined that the Athenians felt culturally and politically superior. After Chaeronea, the comic portrayals may reflect that while having lost their political autonomy to the Macedonians, the Athenians still felt culturally and morally superior.

Abbreviations

K-A = Rudolf Kassel and Colin Austin, *Poetae Comici Graeci*, I-VIII, Berlin and New York 1983–2001.

Bibliography

Alonso Troncoso (2010): Victor Alonso Troncoso, "The Bearded King and the Beardless Hero: From Philip II to Alexander the Great", in: Elizabeth D. Carney and Daniel Ogden (eds.), *Philip II and Alexander the Great: Father and Son, Lives and Afterlives*, Oxford, 13–24.
Arnott (1996): W. Geoffrey Arnott, *Alexis: The Fragments. A Commentary*, Cambridge.
Arnott (2010): W. Geoffrey Arnott, "Middle Comedy", in: Gregory Dobrov (ed.), *Brill's Companion to the Study of Greek Comedy*, Leiden and Boston, 279–331.
Asirvatham (2008): Sulochana R. Asirvatham, "The Roots of Macedonian Ambiguity in Classical Athenian Literature", in: Timothy Howe and Jeanne Reames (eds.), *Macedonian Legacies*, Claremont, 235–255.
Asirvatham (2010): Sulochana R. Asirvatham, "Perspectives on the Macedonians from Greece, Rome and Beyond", in: Joseph Roisman and Ian Worthington (eds.), *Blackwell's Companion to Ancient Macedonia*, Oxford and Malden, MA, 99–124.
Asper (2005): Markus Asper, "Group Laughter and Comic Affirmation: Aristophanes' Birds and the Political Function of Old Comedy", in: *Hyperborus* 11, 5–29.
Atkinson (1980): John E. Atkinson, *A Commentary on Q. Curtius Rufus' Historiae Alexandri Magni, Books 3 and 4*, Amsterdam and Uithoorn.

---

[108] Cf. Dem. 3.24; 15.35; Aeschin. 1.6–7, 25–26; 2.75–78, 164–165. Cf. Lape (2004) 207 on Demosthenes' "ultraconservative model of Athenian identity."

Badian (1993): Ernst Badian, *From Plataea to Potidaea. Studies in the History and Historiography of the Pentecontaetia*, Baltimore.
Baron (2017): Christopher Baron, "Comedy and History, Theory and Evidence in Duris of Samos", in: *Histos Suppl.* 6, 211–239.
Bianco (2002): Elisabetta Bianco, "Carete, cane del popolo?", in: *Ancient Society* 32, 1–28.
Bissa (2009): Errietta M. A. Bissa, *Governmental Intervention in Foreign Trade in Archaic and Classical Greece*, Leiden.
Borthwick (1966): E. K. Borthwick, "Death of a Fighting Cock", in: *The Classical Review* 16, 4–5.
Borza (1987): Eugene N. Borza, "Timber and Politics in the Ancient World: Macedon and the Greeks", in: *PAPS* 131, 32–52.
Borza (1990): Eugene N. Borza, *In the Shadow of Olympus. The Emergence of Macedon*, New Jersey.
Carrière (1979): Jean-Claude Carrière, *La carnaval et la politique. Une introduction à la comédie grecque suivie d'un choix de fragments*, Paris.
Cooper (2007): Craig Cooper, "The Rhetoric of Philippizing", in: Waldemar Heckel et al. (eds.), *Alexander's Empire. Formulation to Decay*, Claremont, 1–12.
Csapo (2004): Eric Csapo, "The Politics of the New Music", in: Penelope Murray and Peter Wilson (eds.), *Music and the Muses: The Culture of 'Mousike' in the Classical Athenian City*, Oxford, 207–248.
Davidson (1993): James Davidson, "Fish, Sex and Revolution in Athens", in: *CQ* 43, 53–66.
Davidson (1997): James Davidson, *Courtesans and Fishcakes: The Consuming Passion of Classical Athens*, London.
Dušanić (1980–1981): Slobodan Dušanić, "Athens, Crete and the Aegean after 366/5 BC", in: *Talanta* 12–13, 7–29.
Edmonds (1959; 1961): John M. Edmonds, *The Fragments of Attic Comedy*, Vol. II, Vol. IIIa, Leiden.
Erbì (2011): Margherita Erbì, "Demostene nella commedia di mezzo", in: Mauro Tulli (ed.), *L'autore pensoso: un seminario per Graziano Arrighetti sulla coscienza letteraria dei Greci*, Pisa, 173–177.
Freeman (1996): Philip M. Freeman, "The Earliest Greek Sources on the Celts", in: *Études Celtiques* 32, 11–48.
Franklin (2013): John C. Franklin, "'Songbenders of Circular Choruses': Dithyramb and the 'Demise of Music'", in: Peter Wilson and Barbara Kowalzig (eds.), *Dithyramb in Context*, Oxford and New York, 213–236.
Frass (2002): Monika Frass, "Körperpflege als Ausdrucksmittel für Geschlechterrollen", in: Christoph Ulf and Robert Rollinger (eds.), *Geschlechter—Frauen—Fremde Ethnien in antiker Ethnographie, Theorie und Realität*, Innsbruck, 467–484.
Garnsey (1999): Peter Garnsey, *Food and Society in Classical Antiquity*, Cambridge.
Gilula (1995): Dwora Gilula, "Comic Food and Food for Comedy", in: John Wilkins et al. (eds.), *Food in Antiquity*, Exeter, 386–399.
Gilula (2000): Dwora Gilula, "Hermippus and his Catalogue of Goods (fr. 63)", in: David Harvey and John Wilkins (eds.), *The Rivals of Aristophanes. Studies in Athenian Old Comedy*, London, 75–90.
Gkaras (2008): Christophoros Gkaras, *Hermippos: Die Fragmente. Ein Kommentar*, PhD Thesis Freiburg (https://www.freidok.uni-freiburg.de/data/6517).

Halliwell (1993): Stephen Halliwell, "Comedy and Publicity in the Society of the *polis*", in: Alan H. Sommerstein et al. (eds.), *Tragedy, Comedy and the Polis*, Bari, 321–340.
Hose (1940): H. F. Hose, "Personalities in Aristophanes", in: *G&R* 9, 88–95.
Heckel (2006): Waldemar Heckel, *Who's Who in the Age of Alexander the Great*, Oxford and Malden, MA.
Henderson (2014): Jeffrey Henderson, "Comedy in the Fourth Century II: Politics and Domesticity", in: Michael Fontaine and Adele S. Scarfuro (eds.), *The Oxford Handbook of Greek and Roman Comedy*, Oxford, 181–198.
Henry (2000): Madeleine Henry, "Athenaeus the Ur-Pornographer", in: David Braund and John Wilkins (eds.), *Athenaeus and His World*, Exeter, 503–510.
Hölscher (2009): Tonio Hölscher, *Herrschaft und Lebensalter: Alexander der Große*, Basel.
Hubbard (2010): Thomas R. Hubbard, "Attic Comedy and the Development of Theoretical Rhetoric", in: Ian Worthington (ed.), *Blackwell's Companion to Greek Rhetoric*, Oxford and Malden, MA, 490–508.
Konstantakos (2011): Ioannis M. Konstantanakos, "Ephippos' *Geryones:* A Comedy between Myth and Folktale", in: *AAntHung.* 51, 223–246.
Konstantakos (2014): Ioannis M. Konstantakos, "Comedy in the Fourth Century I: Mythological Burlesque", in: Michael Fontaine and Adele S. Scarfuro (eds.), *The Oxford Handbook of Greek and Roman Comedy*, Oxford, 160–180.
Kotlinska (2005): Agnieszka Kotlinska, "Comment Alexandre et Python créaient le dramé, c'est-à-dire ce que le literature grecque doit à Harpale", in: *Eos* 92, 44–55.
Kotlinska-Toma (2015): Agnieszka Kotlinska-Toma, *Hellenistic Tragedy: Texts, Translations and a Critical Survey*, London.
Landucci Gattinoni (1994): Franca Landucci Gattinoni, "I mercenari nella politica ateniese dell'età di Alessandro: Parte I Soldati e ufficiali mercenari ateniese al servizio della Persia", in: *AncSoc* 25, 33–61.
Landucci Gattinoni (1997): Franca Landucci Gattinoni, *Duride de Samo*, Rome.
Lape (2004): Susan Lape, *Reproducing Athens. Menander's Comedy, Democratic Culture, and the Hellenistic City*, Princeton.
Lape (2010): Susan Lape, "Menander's Comedy", in: James J. Clauss and Martine Cuypers (eds.), *Blackwell's Companion to Hellenistic Literature*, Oxford and Malden, MA, 282–296.
LeGuen (2014): Brigitte LeGuen, "Theatre, Religion and Politics at Alexander's Travelling Court", in: Eric Csapo et al. (eds.), *Greek Theatre in the Fourth Century BC*, Berlin, 249–274.
MacDowell (2000): Malcolm MacDowell, *Demosthenes. On the False Embassy*, Oxford.
March (1995): Duane A. March, "The Kings of Macedon: 399–369", in: *Historia* 54, 257–282.
Marchiori (2000): Antonia Marchiori, "Between Ichthyophagists and Syrians. Features of Fish-Eating in Athenaeus' Books Seven and Eight", in: David Braund and John Wilkins (eds.), *Athenaeus and his World. Reading Greek Culture in the Roman Empire*, Exeter, 327–338.
Mastellari (2016): Virginia Mastellari, "Middle Comedy: Not only Mythology and Food. The Political and Contemporary Dimension", in: *AAntHung* 46, 421–433.
Miles (2009): Sarah N. Miles, *Strattis, Tragedy, and Comedy*, PhD Thesis University of Notthingham.

Moloney (2014): Eoghan Moloney, "*Philippus in acie tutior quam in theatro fuit* (Curt. 9.6.25). The Macedonian Kings and Greek Theatre", in: Eric Csapo et al. (eds.), *Greek Theatre in the Fourth Century BC*, Berlin, 231–248.

Moreno (2007): Alfonso Moreno, *Feeding the Democracy: The Athenian Grain Supply in the Fifth and Fourth Centuries BC*, Oxford.

Moysey (1985): Robert A. Moysey, "Chares and Athenian Foreign Policy", in: *CJ* 80, 221–227.

Müller (2006): Sabine Müller, "Alexander, Harpalos, Pythionike und Glykera," in: Vasile Lica (ed.), *Philia. Festschrift für Gerhard Wirth*, Galatzi, 71–106.

Müller (2016): Sabine Müller, *Die Argeaden. Geschichte Makedoniens bis zum Zeitalter Alexanders des Großen*, Paderborn.

Müller (2017): Sabine Müller, *Perdikkas II.—Retter Makedoniens*, Berlin.

Müller (2020): Sabine Müller, "Comedy, Greek", in: Waldemar Heckel et al. (eds.), *Lexicon of Argead Makedonia*, Berlin, 176–179.

Nesselrath (1990): Heinz-Günther Nesselrath, *Die attische Mittlere Komödie*. Berlin and New York.

Nesselrath (1997): Heinz-Günther Nesselrath, "The Politics of Athens in Middle Comedy", in: Gregory W. Dobrov (ed.), *The City as Comedy. Society and Representation in Athenian Drama*, Chapel Hill and London, 271–288.

Nightingale (2004): Andrea Wilson Nightingale, *Spectacles of Theatre in Greek Philosophy: Theoria in its Cultural Context*, Cambridge.

Olson (2007): Stuart Douglas Olson, *Broken Laughter. Select Fragments of Greek Comedy*, Oxford.

Orth (2009): Christian Orth, *Strattis: Die Fragmente. Ein Kommentar*, Berlin.

Orth (2014): Christian Orth, "Die Mittlere Komödie", in: Bernhard Zimmermann and Angelos Rengakos (eds.), *Die Literatur der klassischen und hellenistischen Zeit*, Munich, 995–1051.

Papachrysostomou (2008): Athina Papachrysostomou, *Six Comic Poets. A Commentary on Selected Fragments of Middle Comedy*, Tübingen.

Parke (1933): Herbert W. Parke, *Greek Mercenary Soldiers*. Oxford.

Parker (1986): Richard Wayne Parker, *ΧΑΡΗΣ ΑΓΓΕΛΗΘΕΝ. Biography of a Fourth-Century Athenian strategos*, PhD Thesis University of British Columbia.

Pellegrino (2000): Matteo Pellegrino, *Utopie e immagini gastronomiche nei frammenti dell'Archaia*, Bologna.

Pernestorfer (2009): Matthias Johannes Pernestorfer, *Menanders Kolax: Ein Beitrag zu Rekonstruktion und Interpretation der Komödie*, Berlin and New York.

Pownall (2004): Frances Pownall, *Lessons from the Past: The Moral Use of History in Fourth Century Prose*, Ann Arbor.

Pownall (2005): Frances Pownall, "The Rhetoric of Theopompus", in: *Cahiers des Études Anciennes* 42, 255–278.

Pownall (2009): Frances Pownall, "The Decadence of the Thessalians", in: Pat Wheatley and Robert Hannah (eds.), *Alexander and his Successors. Essays from the Antipodes*, 237–260.

Pownall (2010): Frances Pownall, "The Symposia of Philip II and Alexander III of Macedon", in: Elizabeth D. Carney and Daniel Ogden (eds.), *Philip II and Alexander the Great: Father and Son, Lives and Afterlives*, Oxford, 55–65.

Pownall (2017): Frances Pownall, "The Role of Greek Literature in Intellectual Macedonian Circles", in: Sabine Müller et al. (eds.), *The History of the Argeads—New Perspectives*, Wiesbaden, 215–229.

Pownall (2020a): Frances Pownall, "Third Sacred War", in: Waldemar Heckel et al. (eds.), *Lexicon of Argead Makedonia*, Berlin, 495–498.

Pownall (2020b): Frances Pownall, "Duris of Samos 76", *BNJ online*, second edition (forthcoming).

Pritchett (1974): W. Kendrick Pritchett, *The Greek State at War*, Vol. II, Berkeley and L.A.

Psoma (2014): Selene Psoma, "Athens and the Macedonian Kingdom from Perdikkas II to Philip II", *REA* 116, 133–144.

Psoma (2015): Selene Psoma, Athenian Owls and the Royal Macedonian Monopoly on Timber", in: *MHR* 30, 1–18.

Revermann (1999): Martin Revermann, "The Shape of the Athenian Orchestra in the Fifth Century: Forgotten Evidence", in: *ZPE* 128, 25–28.

Roisman (2010): Joseph Roisman, "Classical Macedonia to Perdiccas III", in: Joseph Roisman and Ian Worthington (eds.), *Blackwell's Companion to Ancient Macedonia*, Oxford and Malden, MA, 145–165.

Roselli (2011): David Kawalko Roselli, *Theater of the People, Spectators and Society in Ancient Athens*, Austin.

Roselli (2013): David Kawalko Roselli, "Politics and Audiences in Ancient Greece", in: Richard Butsch and Sonia Livingstone (eds.), *Meanings of Audiences. Comparative Discourses*, London and New York,

Salmond (1996): Paul D. Salmond, "Sympathy for the Devil: Chares and Athenian Politics", in: *G&R* 43, 43–53.

Schreiber (1974): Fred Schreiber, "A Double-Barreled Joke: Aristophanes, Birds 38", in: *AJPh* 95, 95–99.

Shaw (2014): Carl A. Shaw, *Satyric Play: The Evolution of Greek Comedy and Satyr Drama*. Oxford.

Sommerstein (2014): Alan H. Sommerstein, "The Politics of Greek Comedy", in: Martin Revermann (ed.), *The Cambridge Companion to Greek Comedy*, Cambridge, 291–305.

Sorrentino (2014): Giada Sorrentino, "Gattungsmerkmale der Mittleren und Neueren Komödie", in: Bernhard Zimmermann and Angelos Rengakos (eds.), *Die Literatur der klassischen und hellenistischen Zeit*, Munich, 967–995.

Storey (2011): Ian Storey, *Fragments of Old Comedy*, Vol. 1–3, London and Cambridge, Mass. 2011

Storey (2014): Ian Storey, "The First Poets of Old Comedy", in: Michael Fontaine and Adele S. Scarfuro (eds.), *The Oxford Handbook of Greek and Roman Comedy*, Oxford, 25–112.

Tuplin (1996): Christopher Tuplin, *Achaemenid Studies*, Stuttgart.

Wallace (1995): Robert W. Wallace, "Speech, Song and Text, Public and Private", in: Walter Eder (ed.), *Die athenische Demokratie im 4. Jahrhundert v. Chr. Vollendung oder Verfall einer Verfassungsform?*, Stuttgart, 199–217.

Webster (1970): Thomas B. Lonsdale Webster, *Studies in Later Greek Comedy*, Manchester[2].

West (1992): Martin L. West, *Ancient Greek Music,* Oxford.

Wilkins (2000): John Wilkins, *The Boastful Chief. The Discourse of Food in Ancient Greek Comedy*, Oxford.

Willi (2002): Andreas Willi, *The Language of Greek Comedy*, Oxford.

Willi (2010): Andreas Willi, "The Language of Old Comedy", in: Gregory Dobrov (ed.), *Brill's Companion to the Study of Greek Comedy*, Leiden and Boston, 471–510.
Wirth (1985): Gerhard Wirth, *Philipp II. Geschichte Makedoniens 1*, Stuttgart.
Worthington (2008): Ian Worthington, *Philip II of Macedon*, Oxford.

III The Influence of Persia and the Ancient Near East on Alexander's Court

Elizabeth Baynham
Bosworth on Alexander and the Iranians Revisited: Alexander's Marriages to Persian Brides at Susa: A Study of Arrian, *Anabasis* 7.4.4 – 8

I should start with some background explanation of this chapter. Forty years ago, in the Centenary Issue of the *Journal of Hellenic Studies* (1980), my partner, the late A.B. Bosworth, published an article entitled "Alexander and the Iranians" in which he argued that the ancient evidence did not sustain the modern, highly influential, if now outdated, hypothesis of social ideology in relation to Alexander's treatment of Persians—namely, the so-called "Policy of Fusion" — which had been suggested in the nineteenth century by Johann Gustav Droysen, taking his cue from Plutarch.[1] In one of his last unpublished (and un-annotated) papers that Bosworth was working on before Parkinson's Disease stopped his capacity to write in 2010/11, he revised his 1980 views in a piece named, aptly enough, "Alexander and the Iranians Revisited." He did not substantially change his overall thesis at all; in fact, in a typical Bosworthian pithy *bon mot* he concluded: "I remain convinced that it is misleading to think in terms of fusion. Fission is more appropriate."[2]

There has been a lot more scholarship added to the subject over the last decade including the fine work of Pierre Briant, Maria Brosius, Branko F. Van Oppen de Ruiter, Sabine Müller, Waldemar Heckel, and Marek Olbrycht. It is important that more attention has been given to archaeological, numismatic, and Persian and Babylonian evidence; however, scholarly opinion remains divided on issues such as what Alexander's aims were (or if he even had a "policy" at all), the

---

[1] For earlier bibliography, see Bosworth (1980a) 1, with n. 2.; cf. Hamilton (1987) 467–486. The "Policy of Fusion" (or *Verschmelzungspolitik*) was a term used in modern scholarship to describe Alexander's systematic integration of Macedonians and Persians through actions like the king's adoption of aspects of Persian dress and customs, his appointment of Persian satraps, as well as Persian nobles like Darius' brother to his guard, his use of Persian troops, and intermarriage; on the latter, cf. Plut. *Mor.* 329 f: "nor by lifeless and unfeeling bonds, but by the ties of lawful love and chaste nuptials and mutual joy in children that they join the nations together" (trans. F.C. Babbitt). See also Bosworth (1983) 131–150; most recently re-published in Karanos (2019).
[2] Bosworth (2010).

king's understanding of Achaemenid culture and court structure, and the extent of Persian integration, as well as resistance, and Persian factional rivalry.³

Yet marriage is critical to any court society as it not only offers potential alliances with powerful families or even countries, but underpins the court's future through the provision of heirs. One area of alleged integration between Macedonians and Persians where Bosworth *did* modify his earlier interpretation, was the episode of the mass marriages between Macedonians and Persians.

In his 1980 article Bosworth was dismissive, merely reiterating Franz Hampl's view that the marriages were one sided, because at the Susa ceremony, no Persian noble received a Greek or Macedonian wife—even though it would have been "relatively easy" (Bosworth's words) for Alexander to have brought Greek women out to Persia. Instead, Hampl (and Bosworth) argued that taking the women of a defeated people–or indeed, Indigenous women (as in the Americas and Colonial Australia) —is indicative of the power of the conqueror.⁴

In his revised version, Bosworth was more circumspect. The main source for the Susa marriages is Arrian, *Anabasis* 7.4.4 – 8. This has bearing for Pat Wheatley and myself, as we are undertaking to finish the third volume of Bosworth's Commentary on Arrian. He left too much of it to abandon, and it was his life's work. Most of Brian's draft manuscript for Book Seven was completed at the time of his death, although the Susa marriages chapter is one of the few gaps that he left. Thanks to Bosworth (2010) Wheatley and I have a good idea of the direction of his thought; however, inevitably, it is the task of those completing unfinished work to not only update it, but perhaps add something of one's own. So what I have to offer in this contribution, with respect to Brian's *manes*, is a kind of blend, and I hope it will be a harmonious one. I did ask Brian a few years before he died why he had done so much of Arrian's *Anabasis* Book Seven at the expense of Book Six, and he just shrugged and said: "It sort of smoothed out that way." Ask a silly question.

In Bosworth (2010) Bosworth argues that Alexander, at least in terms of his own propaganda (or the construction of our sources) presented himself as a descendant of Perseus, whose precedent he followed in journeying to the oracle at Siwah in 331 (cf. Arr. *Anab.* 3.2.2), and as the rightful Successor to the Persian throne. In Greek mythology, the Argive hero Perseus was the father of Perses,

---

3 In general, see Briant (2002); (2012); (2015); Brosius (2003) 169–196; Van Oppen de Ruiter (2014), 25–41; Heckel (2020); Müller (2013) 199–214; (2014); Marek Olbrycht, in a series of compelling articles, has argued for extensive "Iranization" of Alexander's administration and army; see Olbrycht (2011) 231–252; (2013) 159–182; (2014) 37–62; (2015) 196–212; (2016) 61–72; (2017) 194–211.
4 Hampl (1954), 115–123, at 119; cf. Bosworth (1980a), 10–12 with n. 94.

the eponymous founder of the Persian Empire (so Hdt 7.61; cf. 7.150.2),[5] and indeed after his victory over Darius III at Issus, and prior to final victory over Darius at Gaugamela, Alexander (in his response to Darius' first peace offer), portrays Darius as a usurper (cf. Arr. *Anab.* 2.14.5–6). In other ancient sources, Bagoas the Vizier murdered the previous Great King, Arses, and then placed Darius on the throne supposedly as his puppet; in Arrian's text Alexander accuses Darius of the regicide with the help of Bagoas.[6]

In his *Commentary* on Arrian (1980), Bosworth also suggests that Alexander may be hinting (cf. Arr. *Anab.* 2. 14. 5) that Darius was not of royal blood when he seized the throne "contrary to Persian law." In fact, in the wake of the extensive dynastic murder at the accession of the previous Great Kings, Artaxerxes Ochus and Arses, Darius, a great nephew of Artaxerxes II, was probably one of the few senior surviving males of the Achaemenid house.[7] However, Alexander treated Sisygambis, the Persian Queen Mother, and the other members of Darius' family whom he had captured at Issus, like they were his kinsfolk, even refusing to ransom them.[8] He was not coming as an alien invader, intent on seizing territory to which he had no claim, but a legitimate ruler who was taking what was his own —as well as reuniting with his Persian "family."

Bosworth (2010) may also be right to suggest that under the guidance of Persian priests, Alexander could well have undergone Persian royal investiture ceremony at the old capital, Pasargardae, eating fig cake, chewing turpentine wood, and drinking sour milk while wearing the traditional dress of Cyrus, founder of

---

[5] Hesiod (*Theog.* 371) mentions a Titan by the name of Perses; the tradition attesting Perses as the son of Perseus appears at least by the Classical period, and after; cf. Hellanicus *BNJ* 687a F 1a; 687a F 1b; Plat. *Alc.* I, 120e; cf. Ps. Apollod. *Bibl.* 2.48–49. See Munson (2009), 457–70, especially 458, n. 7; on Hellanicus of Lesbos, see D. Lenfant (2007), 201–202; Frances Pownall's commentary on Hellanicus, *BNJ* 687a F. See also below, n. 13.
[6] Bagoas' assassination of Arses: Diod. 5.4–5; Plut. *De Alex. fort.* 340b b; Ox. Chron. *BNJ* 255 F 5; Strab. 15.3.24 [736]. On Alexander's letter of response to Darius' first peace offer, see Bosworth (1980b) 227–233; the content of the letter is almost certainly contrived, most likely by Alexander's court historian, Callisthenes, and designed to depict Alexander as the rightful king of Asia.
[7] Bosworth (1980b) 232; cf. Arr. *Anab.* 3.19.4 who mentions a certain Bisthanes as a son of Artaxerxes Ochus, with Diod. 17.5.4–5 l; cf. Bosworth (1980b) 335; Berve (1926), 2.109 no. 215; Heckel (2006) 72.
[8] On Darius' offer to ransom his family after their capture at Issus, see Arr. *Anab.* 2.14.1; 2.25.1 (10,000 talents, the offer of all territory west of the Euphrates, his daughter's hand in marriage, and alliance); cf. Plut. *Alex.* 29.7–8; Diod. 17.54.1–5; Curt. 4.11.1–22; Just. 11.12.3–15; Val. Max. 6.4 ext. 3; see Bosworth (1980b) 256–257. Alexander consistently refused to accept money for the Persian royal family's safe return; cf. Arr. *Anab.* 2.14.8; Curt. 4.11.15.

the Persian Empire.⁹ We have no evidence that he did, but the silence of our sources (which in general omit so much important information) does not necessarily prove that he did not. He had certainly visited the tomb of Cyrus (cf. Arr.*Anab.* 6.29.9: Strabo 15.3.7) and ordered Aristobulus to supervise its restoration when he found out that it had been plundered (Arr. *Anab.* 6.29.10 – 11).¹⁰ Given that Onesicritus quotes inscriptions from the tomb of Darius I at Naqš-i Rustam (*BNJ* 134 F 35 = Strabo 15.3.8), it is highly likely that Alexander and his staff visited these sites.¹¹ Had he lived longer, Alexander could have even gone so far as to imitate Darius I at Behistun, and proclaimed his own version of how he had liberated the Persians, especially if the great relief panels from the Shrine of the Bark at Luxor which show Alexander as Pharaoh honouring Egyptian gods (along with other iconography) may be taken as a parallel.¹² The Luxor panels were carved under the direction of Egyptian priests (although presumably with the authorization—and probable funding—of Cleomenes, Alexander's governor of Egypt), in order to establish continuity, and acceptance of Alexander as the new Pharaoh. In view of Egyptian religious laws, the panels had to have been produced while the king was still alive.¹³

The fact that Alexander encountered stiff resistance at the Persian Gates, or that he looted the lower city of Persepolis and destroyed the palace (accidental or otherwise) in 331¹⁴ did not contradict the Panhellenic spin of a war of vengeance because of the Persian invasions of Greece over a century before.¹⁵ Punishment of the Persians could still be inflicted by a descendant of Perseus, who was claiming ancestral lands.

However, as soon as Darius III was assassinated by his own nobles in 331 BC presenting Alexander with a formidable rival in Bessus, who was the leader of the coup against the former Great King, it suited the Macedonian king to change tack, and offer himself as Darius' rightful avenger.

---

9 Bosworth (2010); on the Persian enthronement ceremony, cf. Plut. *Art.* 3.1–2, with Briant (2002) 523–524.
10 On Alexander's visits to Cyrus' tomb, see Brunt's note on his emendation of Arrian's text; (1983) 195, n. 5.; on Cyrus' tomb, see Bosworth's analysis of Arrian's and Strabo's treatment of Aristobulus' tradition; (1988) 46–55; see also Pownall, Aristoboulos of Kassandreia *BNJ* 139 F 51a.
11 See Müller (2014) 58–65; also (2012) 45–66; and (2021).
12 On the Shrine of the Bark, see Abd el-Raziq (1984).
13 On Cleomenes' likely role in funding the carvings on the Luxor temple see Baynham (2015) 131, with nn. 27–30. See also Schäfer (2007) 54–74.
14 All dates are BC unless otherwise stated.
15 On Panhellenism in general see Flower (2000); Mitchell (2007).

As we saw earlier, Arrian noted Alexander's descent from Perseus; according to Greek mythology, Argive Perseus married Andromeda, the daughter of Cepheus,[16] and fathered Perses, ancestor of the Persians. According to Herodotus (7.150), Xerxes' envoys to Argos in 481 BC supposedly tried to ensure Argive neutrality by appealing to their common ancestry. While there may have been some historical substance in Persian attempts to obtain Argive co-operation (as Argos appears to have been neutral) the story of some kind of cultural connection between the two peoples appears to have been generated by the Greeks alone.[17] However, for the Susa marriages our Alexander sources (at least to my knowledge) seem to have overlooked the mythological paradigm of an earlier union between Greeks and Persians.

The Susa marriages were held in 324 BC. Yet these weddings were preceded by an immediate context of Persian unrest and satrapal insubordination, if not outright rebellion. In Media, Baryaxes had pretended to the throne, while in the satrapy of Persis, Orsines, a descendant of Cyrus himself had established himself as governor without authorization.[18] In Hyrcania another would-be usurper, Autophradates, had been arrested by Phrataphernes, a Persian loyal to Alexander, while Craterus, en route from India, who joined up with Alexander in Carmania, brought in Ordanes, another rebel.[19]

By 324 BC only three Iranian satraps were still in power, but nevertheless controlling strategic areas of the Persian empire, including Phrataphernes, Atropates—who had arrested Baryaxes—and, in Sogdiana, Oxyartes, who was Alexander's father-in-law from his marriage to Roxane in 327 BC. Phrataphernes

---

16 Cepheus is described as the king of Ethiopia in the surviving fragments of Euripides' lost play *Andromeda*, a tradition which is also reflected in Ps.-Apollod. *Bibl.* 2.4849, and Ov. *Met.* 4. 669–672, but the location is uncertain; cf. Roscher (1884–1937) 2.1109–13; Collard and Cropp (2008) 124–155.

17 See How and Wells (1912) 189; cf. Dewald's note, in Waterfield and Dewald (1998) 700. Argos' neutrality; cf. Hdt 7.148–152 although he also states (7.151) that after the Persian Wars, King Artaxerxes looked favourably upon the Argives. Argos does not appear to have sent forces to Thermopylae (cf. Hdt 7.202.1; 204.1) nor to the battle of Plataea. (cf. Hdt. 9.28.4; 9.31; Paus. 5.23.2). See also Piérart (2004) 603, 612; Tomlinson (1972) 33.

18 Baryaxes: Arr. *Anab.* 6.29.3; on his assumption of the royal title, cf. Briant (2002) 740–741; Orsines (Orxines): Arr. *Anab.* 6.29.2, 30.1; cf. Curt. 10.1.22–38; Strabo 15.3.7 (730); Berve (1926) 2.294 no. 592, Heckel (2006) 186; cf. Atkinson (2009) 93–99.

19 Autophradates, a "delinquent satrap" (so Bosworth, [1995], 122) had ignored several orders from Alexander to come to court (Arr. *Anab.* 4.18.2; cf. Curt. 8.3.17). He was possibly arrested as early as 329/28 BC and replaced by Phrataphernes (see Heckel [2006] 65) although Bosworth suggests that he may have held out against capture and eventual execution until late 325 BC. Ordanes had stirred up rebellion in Drangiana or Arachosia; Arr. *Anab.* 6.27.3; Curt. 9.10.19; 10.1.9; Berve, 2.293–294 no. 590; Heckel (2006) 185.

and Atropates had originally stayed loyal to Darius, but had sided with Alexander against Darius' assassin Bessus, whom they regarded as a usurper and regicide.[20] Their positions—along with that of Oxyartes—were to be confirmed shortly after Alexander's death in the Babylon settlement of 323 BC.[21]

Artabazus, the former satrap of Hellespontine Phrygia, is another interesting Persian ally, who had previously remained loyal to Darius. He was of royal descent on his mother's side, as his grandfather was Artaxerxes II. Moreover, his daughter, Barsine, was one of Alexander's lovers and gave him his first born child, a son, Heracles, in 327 BC Artabazus helped Alexander put down rebellion in Areia and Sogdiana in the north eastern part of the Persian Empire in 329 and was made satrap of Bactria. He was discharged from the office in 327 under what seem to have been amicable circumstances.[22]

On his return from India, Alexander not only eliminated Persian satraps whom he considered insubordinate. He executed Macedonian officers as well in the so-called purge of 325; as Curtius pointedly remarked (9.10.29), the *carnifex* (butcher) followed Alexander's triumphant (if inebriated) procession through Carmania. But when the King reached Susa in the winter of 324 BC, he ordered the famous mass marriage in which ninety or so of the Macedonian *hetairoi* took Persian or Median brides, while at the same time Alexander gave generous donations to over 10,000 soldiers who had previously married native women (Arr. *Anab.* 7.4.8).[23]

The phenomenon of collective marriage is not unknown in history, and even occurs today with such ceremonies being performed in many countries around

---

20 Atropates was appointed to govern Media in 328/7 BC (Arr. *Anab.* 4.18.3) and seems to have retained Alexander's good will throughout his remaining reign; see Berve (1926) 2.91–2 no. 180, Heckel (2006) 61–62. On the positions and influence of Atropates and Phratapherens, also see Olbrycht (2013) 160–162.

21 For Atropates' confirmation at Babylon in 323 BC, see Diod. 18.3.3; Just. 13.4.13; cf. Yardley, Wheatley and Heckel (2011) 95–96.

22 On Artabazus, see Berve (1926), 2.82–84 no 152; Heckel (2006) 55. On his appointment to Bactria see Arr. *Anab.* 3.29.1; Artabazus asked to retire from office about a year later on account of his age; cf. Arr. *Anab.* 4.17.3; cf. Curt. 8.1.19; Bosworth (1995) 118 is skeptical of the excuse given that Artabazus was probably under 60 (he is dismissive of Curtius' statement [6. 5. 3] that the satrap was in his nineties); more recently, Heckel (2018) 93–109; cf. (2020) 167–70, has suggested that Artabazus fell out of Alexander's favour, and was marginalized.

23 Cf. Plut. (*Alex.* 70. 2) who states that Alexander gave a gold cup to 9,000 guests; he also conflates Alexander's payment of soldiers' debts with this episode; cf. Just. 12.10.9–11.4; Curt. 10.2.8; Diod. 17.109.2

the globe, including the United States, throughout Asia, and the Middle East.[24] However, Alexander's action was unprecedented in the ancient world.

Perhaps Romanists may protest at this point, citing the example of Romulus, founder of Rome, and the so-called "Rape" of the Sabine Women. But with respect, the Sabine "mass marriages"—if they can even be called that—were not quite the same as Alexander's Susa unions. The seizure of the Sabine women is a story associated with Rome's legendary origins; its extant sources are comparatively late. Although Plutarch could well have been influenced by earlier Alexander histories on the Susa marriages (in addition to Roman narratives like Livy) the tale itself appears to be strongly associated with the motif of bride-snatching in Indo-European mythology.[25] According to Livy (1.9), the fledgling city, facing a shortage of women—and hence the prospect of extinction within a generation—had invited its neighbours, including the Sabines, to a festival with games and horse racing in honour of Equestrian Neptune.[26] At a pre-arranged signal, the daughters of the Sabines were then carried off by force, amid mass fear, outrage, and confusion. Conciliation and formal marriage only appear to have occurred at a later point; moreover the Sabines not only attempted recovery of their offspring, but reprisal. While it could be argued that Alexander and his army as the victors were also ultimately taking Persian women by force, the Susa marriages were presented as an intended—and "joyful"—celebration—which is not the case in any version of the Sabine women's story. However, the symbolism of such synoecism on the long term is a different matter: a great city arose.

The Susa marriages were truly extraordinary. Arrian and Plutarch describe the wedding ceremony, which was conducted according to Persian ritual—whereas Alexander's earlier marriage to the Bactrian princess, Roxane, had been formalized in Macedonian custom (so Curt. 8.4.27–28). The Persian ceremony seems to have been irritating to the Macedonians, as Arrian lists the ritual as one of the soldiers' grievances in the lead up to the Opis mutiny (*Anab.* 7.6.2).

---

24 The Unification Church of South Korea, founded by the late Reverend Sun Myung Moon, is probably the best known advocate of mass marriage in popular culture; see https://www.bbc.com/news/av/world-asia-21489927. Collective marriage could also be used for economic reasons; for example, weddings involving up to 18 couples at a time were commonly held by impecunious Polish immigrants in American cities like New York or Chicago in the early part of the 20th century; see McBee (2000) 224.
25 Cf. Livy 1.9–13 with Ogilvie (1965) 64–66; see Cic. *Rep.* 2.12; Dion. Hal. 2.30.1; Plut. *Rom.* 14–20; cf. Ov. *Ars Am.* 1.4. See also Mallory (1991) 139.
26 See Stem (2007) 435–471.

As several scholars have noted, not all ancient Alexander historiography is favourable to the unions, and modern opinion almost universally sees the marriages from the Macedonian perspective as forced, and thereby resented.²⁷

Diodorus (17.107.6) seems to have been more interested in the self-immolation of the Brahmin sage, Caranus, which he describes immediately before the Susa weddings. Curtius' narrative of the episode has probably been lost, as Book 10 is extensively undermined by *lacunae*. Presumably he included one, since he has Alexander explain his motives to his foreign soldiers within the context of the Macedonians' mutiny at Opis (Curt. 10.3.11). Justin (12.11.9) depicts Alexander's decision to include his Macedonian officers so as to prevent any reproach (*crimen*) against him.

Nevertheless, the Susa mass marriages were exemplary and festive.²⁸ Alexander had an innate talent for exhibitionism, and it is clear that the ceremonies were intended as a grand show. Chairs were placed in order of rank, toasts were drunk, hymns were sung, and the brides—most likely dressed in all their splendid finery—were brought in, and joined by the hand to their designated bridegrooms. Alexander had also provided dowries for all the Persian noble women (Arr. *Anab.* 7. 4. 8), and we can well imagine Plutarch's gold canopied pavilion (*Mor.* 329–330d–e; cf. *Alex.* 70.2), flowers, garlands, cheering, an abundance of wine and food, and a party atmosphere. Indeed, Plutarch himself claims (*Mor.* 329d–e) it was one wedding where he would have liked to been a guest.

Likewise Aelian (*VH* 8.7) and Athenaeus (12.538b–539a = *BNJ* 125 F 4), whose tradition probably derives from the same eyewitness (namely Alexander's court chamberlain, Chares of Mytilene) also describe a lavish tent built over about half a mile, golden couches, supporting pillars inlaid with precious gems and metals, costly fabrics including curtains embroidered with animals hung on golden rods, and thick carpets. The festivities lasted over five days, and featured the best entertainment of the day—famous musicians, vocalists, actors, and acrobats. Allegedly the entire army took part in the feasting and celebrations. While there is probably a degree of exaggeration in all these accounts, we need not doubt that the extravagance was immense, and the spectacle fantastic.²⁹

---

27 Cf. Hamilton (1999) 194–195; Yardley and Heckel (1997) 272. Grainger's description of the Susa marriages as "one of Alexander's most bizarre performances" is not untypical; see Grainger (1990) 11.
28 On the importance of the display of wealth at Argead marriages see Carney (2017) 139–150.
29 For discussion of Chares' description, see S. Müller's Commentary in *BNJ* 125 F 4; Chares could well have been involved in the organization of the festivities; so Weber (2009) 95. On

Arrian also provides a list of the bridal couples starting with Alexander. Here the Persian Great King Darius I in the late sixth century BC (ca. 521/20) offers an interesting parallel. Persian kings were polygamous, and in Darius' case, marriage to women of certain bloodlines and families offered him particular advantages. Darius' own accession was shaky before he was able to consolidate his power and become one of the most successful kings the Persian Empire had known. One of his problems was that he was not immediately related to Cyrus, the founder of the Persian Empire. He had to enforce his claim, which he did by more or less contriving his own genealogy, and by marrying into Cyrus' family—two daughters of Cyrus, a daughter of Cambyses' brother, Smerdis (Bardiya), and a daughter of his fellow conspirator, Otanes (cf. Hdt. 3.88).[30] While it is true that Darius' genealogical claims cannot at least been any worse than those of his fellow conspirators, he needed to ensure the loyalty of Otanes' powerful faction, as well as his own dynastic line; henceforth, his children would have the blood of Cyrus.

At the Susa weddings, Alexander, like Darius I, married more than one wife, and he too, took care to consolidate royal blood lines. He may have been advised of Darius' earlier precedent by Persian consultants;[31] we have no specific evidence for this, but we do hear of prestigious Persians like Oxyathres (brother of Darius III) enrolled among Alexander's Companions (Plut. *Alex.* 43.7; Curt. 6.2.11), and appointed to the king's guards (Diod. 17.77.4; Curt. 7.5.40; *Metz Epit.* 2).

Also if Cleitus' outburst at the fatal banquet in Maracanda in 328 BC had any substance, there were Persian *rhabdouchoi* (officials or guards) who may have dealt physical punishment to those who breached royal protocols (cf. Plut. *Alex.* 51.1). We know of other areas where Alexander adopted aspects of Persian culture, such as a form of blended dress;[32] moreover the king's demonstrable respect for, if not imitation of Cyrus suggests that he was well aware of Persian history. Even if his view of the founder was predominantly Hellenocentric, and shaped by Herodotus and Xenophon, Alexander would have been almost certainly receptive to Persian input.

Alexander's use of Achaemenid pavilions, see Alonso Troncoso and Álvarez Rico (2017) 113–124; Collins (2017) 71–76.
30 On Darius' marriage alliances, see Brosius (1996) 47–64; on Darius' genealogical claims and accession, see Briant (2002) 110–114.
31 I am grateful to Professor Sabine Müller for this suggestion.
32 Curt. 6. 6. 2–12; Just. 12.3.8–4.11; Diod. 17.77.4–6; Plut. *Alex.* 45.1–2, *Mor.* 330a; Arr. *Anab.* 4.7.4, Val. Max. 9.5 ext 1; *Metz Epit.* 1–2; see Yardley and Heckel (1997) 203–205; Bosworth (1995) 30; Olbrycht (2014) 37–62, especially 47–52. See also Collins (2012) 371–402.

At the Susa ceremonies, Alexander married a daughter of Darius III and a daughter of a previous Great King, Artaxerxes Ochus. Hephaestion, Alexander's Chiliarch at the time, also married a daughter of Darius and full sister to Alexander's bride (I will come back to this aspect). Craterus, another of Alexander's leading generals, was wed to Amastris, the daughter of Oxyathres. Perdiccas was given the daughter of Atropates, satrap of Media. Nearchus' bride, Barsine, was the daughter of the elder Barsine, daughter of Artabazus, as well as Alexander's lover, and mother of his son, Heracles.

Alexander was thus rewarding Persian loyalty; as we have seen, leaving aside the Achaemenid female line, several of the Persian fathers whom Arrian names had sided with Alexander. Heckel has argued recently that Artabazus was out of favour and had been sidelined by 324, but if this were the case we may well wonder why his family were so honoured at Susa.[33] Two of his daughters, Artacama (or Apama; so Plut. *Eum.* 1.7) and Artonis, were given away in prestigious marriages to men who were both very close to the king; the former to Ptolemy, Alexander's bodyguard, and the latter to Eumenes, his secretary.[34]

Although Arrian names Aristobulus as his source at 7.4.4, Bosworth thought that Arrian could also have been drawing on Nearchus for the information on Artabazus, as the latter wanted to stress the connections of his own bride. Bosworth may well be right, but leaving aside Nearchus'—and indeed Alexander's—personal relationship with Barsine, Artabazus and his family had a long history of guest friendship with the Macedonian royal house. The satrap himself had even taken refuge at Philip's court when he had been forced to flee his satrapy in about 352. He stayed in Macedonia for several years (Diod. 16.52.3–4; cf. Curt. 5.9.1; 6.5.2), so he would have known Alexander as a child.

One name stands out among the Macedonian bridegrooms. Seleucus is an important exception for several reasons. As a commander of Alexander's elite troops, the hypaspists, he was not an insignificant figure, but he was not as highly placed as the other marshals in Arrian's list, or indeed, as we shall see, some of Alexander's other commanders whom he does *not* include.

---

33 See above, n. 22.
34 On Artacama, see Heckel (2006) 55–56, with n. 136; Berve (1926) 2.52 no. 97. Like the Argead and Achaemenid kings and several of the Diadochoi, Ptolemy was polygamous. We do not know what happened to Artacama; most scholars claim that Ptolemy repudiated or neglected her after Alexander's death; Müller (2013) 204, argues that a Persian wife would have been a "liability" for Ptolemy in Egypt; however, Ogden (1999) 69, while recognizing the consensus view, also admits that Artacama could well have lived out her life at Ptolemy's court. On Artomis, see Heckel (2006) 56; Berve (1926) 2.84–85 no. 155.

Seleucus married Apame (whom Arrian does not name),[35] daughter of the rebel Bactrian satrap Spitamenes, from the large and more densely populated north eastern region of the Persian Empire. Bosworth saw this union as an echo of Alexander's earlier marriage to Roxane which was also intended to reconcile the bride's father to the new regime, as well as creating an alliance.[36]

Seleucus' marriage would also help to ensure the loyalty of Spitamenes' family in the powerful eastern satrapy of Bactria—and like Roxane herself, or indeed some of the non-Macedonian brides of Philip II,[37] Apame would be to some extent a hostage. And as Heckel notes, there were may well have been other brides who were brought over from this region.[38]

However, I think we can add something else to the inclusion of Seleucus and his marriage to Apame. It is important to note that Arrian's list is highly selective. It contains something like less than 10% of the names of the officers and their brides, as Arrian states (*Anab.* 7.4.6) that about 80 other Macedonian *hetairoi* were also given the "noblest" daughters of the Persians and Medes.

Arrian names two of Alexander's personal *somatophylakes* (bodyguards), Perdiccas and Ptolemy and their brides, but the king's other bodyguards, Lysimachus, Peithon and Leonnatus must have surely been given well-connected women. Another notable omission is Peucestas—who had saved Alexander's life at the Malloi fortress in India—and who later became celebrated (or notorious) for adapting Persian customs and language.[39] Yet these men are not mentioned within the context of the Susa marriages—so why is Seleucus—who was a field officer at the time—highlighted? Arrian had the benefit of hindsight, and so do we—Seleucus is obviously singled out because of his glittering success story that was to come.[40]

It is worth noting that Arrian gives Seleucus a favourable press elsewhere. In Book 7.22.3–6, Arrian relates a *logos* (story) about Alexander losing his *kausia* (cap) with the royal diadem while sailing around marsh lands of the Euphrates

---

35 Bosworth (2010). Apame's marriage to Seleucus; cf. Plut. *Demetr.* 31.5; App. *Syr.* 57 [295–6]; Strabo 12.8.15 [578]; cf. 16.2.4 [750]; Plin. *HN* 6.13
36 Roxane; cf. Arr. *Anab.* 4.19.5–6; Curt. 8.4.19–30; Plut. *Alex.* 47.7–8; *Mor.* 332e; *Metz Epit.* 29–31; Diod. 17 *Contents;* see also Bosworth (1995) 130–133.
37 On the seven brides of Philip II, only two were native Macedonian, cf. Athen. 13.557b–e with Tronson (1984) 116–216; Carney (2000) 52–81; on captive women and their role as hostages, see Müller (2020) 81–96; especially her conclusions, 92–93.
38 Heckel (2006) 246.
39 On Peucestas, see Heckel (2006) 203–205; Berve (1926) 2.318–19 no. 634. On Peucestas' adoption of Persian customs as well as becoming the first Macedonian to learn fluent Persian; cf. Arr. *Anab.* 6.30.2–3; cf. Diod. 19.14.5.
40 On the myth making surrounding Seleucus, see Ogden (2017).

in 323 BC not long before his death. There were several variants as to how the diadem was retrieved as well as what it presaged. One of the versions that Arrian cites claims that the man who brought Alexander's diadem back was Seleucus and that the episode portended his future reign over Babylon (7.22.5). In the manuscript of *Arrian III*, Bosworth rightly notes that the tradition for this story is not from his regular authorities, and indeed Arrian gives Aristobulus' version (7.22.4); namely, one of the sailors brought the diadem back and was given a talent as a reward, but also a flogging because he had fastened the diadem around his own head to keep it dry. Arrian also notes that in most versions the sailor was beheaded for wearing the diadem in order to neutralize the evil omen associated with another head wearing the diadem which was not the king's.[41]

Bosworth suggests Aristus of Salamis as a possible source for the version which names Seleucus as the helpful swimmer.[42] Aristus was at the court of Seleucus II, and he would have had an interest in promoting the divine legitimacy of the dynasty's right to rule. Aristus was also the source for the story (about which Arrian expresses some skepticism) that the Romans sent envoys to Alexander in 324 BC, again not long before his death (*Anab.* 7.15.5). However, after noting Seleucus' role in one version of the diadem story Arrian adds an encomium of the future ruler—which, although perhaps inspired by propagandist sources, was also probably his own composition: "For in my opinion it is beyond dispute that Seleucus became the greatest king among those who inherited the empire after Alexander: he was the most royal in temperament and had the greatest sway after Alexander himself."[43]

Bosworth—who became progressively fascinated with Arrian's capacity for intertextuality the longer he engaged with the historian's work—also points out a prominent literary echo. Xenophon in the *Anabasis* begins his encomium of Cyrus the Younger with a statement that it was universally agreed that he was the most royal and the most worthy to rule after the elder Cyrus (Xen. *An.* 1.9.1). The vocabulary of the two passages is more or less identical, with an emphasis on royalty. Alexander and the elder Cyrus are paired as empire builders, while Seleucus and the younger Cyrus epitomise the qualities of kingship. But unlike Cyrus the Younger—who died fighting against his brother at the disastrous Battle of Cunaxa—Seleucus fulfilled his promise. It is also interesting that Arrian (*Anab.* 7.22.5) expresses such a high opinion of Seleucus' career, describing him as the "greatest king" with the most royal *gnomon* (mind) and by implication ranking

---

[41] See Pownall's commentary *BNJ* 139 F 55 and F 58 on the "substitute king" ritual.
[42] Bosworth (2010).
[43] Bosworth's translation (2010).

him above Ptolemy, whose *History* Arrian had chosen as his most important eyewitness source, and who became a King himself as Arrian notes in the Preface to his own work.

So given Arrian's view of Seleucus, singling him out at the Susa marriages is not out of place. But we can take this even further.

As we saw earlier, Seleucus married Apame, a daughter of Spitamenes. It is evident that the Persian women conferred substance and power. Amastris, a Persian princess, royal cousin of Darius' daughter Stateira, and the wife of Craterus, brought him considerable prestige, before becoming a queen in her own right. Now it is true that Craterus gave her away in marriage to someone else, namely Dionysius, the ruler of Heraclea Pontica, after he had married Antipater's daughter Phila during the First Diadoch War in 321, but the arrangement appears to have been amicable (cf. Memnon *BNJ* 434 F 1.4). Twenty years later she was in sole control of the city and was so attractive in terms of the resources she possessed, that Lysimachus, ruler of Thrace, and another of Alexander's Successors, offered her marriage in order that she could maintain his army prior to the battle of Ipsus.[44]

Likewise Nearchus promoted his own wife's connections, particularly the claims of Heracles, his wife's brother and son of his mother-in-law, Barsine, during the succession debate at Babylon in the aftermath of Alexander's death, although it is also important to note that there was strong opposition from Alexander's marshals to any of Alexander's sons of mixed cultures becoming king.[45]

Eumenes is another example of someone who seems to have benefited from the Susa unions.[46] Plutarch (*Eum.* 1.6–7) notes that marriage to Barsine's sister brought him considerable advantage. When Eumenes had to fight Craterus in 321 he appointed his brother-in-law, Pharnabazus as one of the two cavalry commanders (*Eum.* 7.1). So as Bosworth noted, the evidence does not suggest that Alexander's officers were dragged (in his words), "kicking and screaming to the altar."

---

44 Amastris: see Memnon *BNJ* 434 F 1.4; cf. Strabo 12.3.10 [544]; Steph Byz. s.v. "Amastris," see Heckel (2006) 21; Berve (1926) 2.24 no. 50; Burstein (1974) 75–86; cf. Lund (1992) 75 with n. 73, who notes marriage to Amastris brought reinforcement to Lysimachus' own claims to territory Alexander had "inherited" from the Achaemenids; see also Ogden (1999) 58; Müller (2013) 209–210 and most recently, Van Oppen de Ruiter (2020) 17–37.
45 Nearchus' promotion of Heracles; see Curt.10.6.12; cf. Just. 13.2.6, who states Heracles' claims were favoured by Meleager; for discussion of Heracles in the Succession debate at Babylon, see Bosworth (2002) 38–40; Yardley, Wheatley and Heckel (2011) 66–70, Atkinson (2009) 181–184.
46 See Anson (2004) 46, with n. 60; on Pharnabazus' connections, Schäfer (2002) 87, n. 154.

We do not know a lot about what happened to the other Persian brides: apparently Stateira and her sister, Drypetis, Hephaestion's widow were killed by Roxane and Perdiccas shortly after Alexander's death (so Plut. *Alex*. 77.6), and probably Parysatis, the daughter of Artaxerxes Ochus, was murdered at the same time. However, the fate of Perdiccas' own Persian wife, the unnamed daughter of Atropates is lost to us. Perdiccas was certainly active in trying to arrange other marriage alliances—with Nicaea, Antipater's daughter, as well as Cleopatra, Alexander's sister—after the king's death. Atropates' daughter could well have remained in Perdiccas' entourage until his assassination on the Nile in 321/20 BC but the Persian satrap himself proved a remarkable survivor, and she may have re-joined her father's house when Perdiccas was killed.[47]

We often tend to forget that Alexander's early death meant that any long term arrangements he had in mind were not given the chance to come to fruition—literally so, in the case of the Susa marriages. Arrian emphasizes that Alexander was looking ahead to the next generation. Was there a shortage of noble Persians to marry Persian brides? Achaemenid kings, like Macedonian kings, were polygamous, and the Persian elite classes possibly were as well (cf. Hdt. 1.135), although this is uncertain and problematic.[48]

It is hard to know how much Alexander's conquests had decimated the Persian male aristocracy, as casualty figures in ancient sources are notoriously unreliable.[49] For example, after the battle of Issus (333 BC) Arrian (*Anab*. 2.11.8) gives the names of five Persian nobles who had been killed including two satraps, and also claims that some 100,000 had died among the rank and file, although presumably this figure would also include local recruits from provinces. Arrian also states (*Anab*. 3.1.2) that Mazaces who had been appointed satrap of Egypt surrendered the province to Alexander as he did not have sufficient Persian forces to defend it; likewise, the Persian governors of the powerful and rich cities of Susa and Babylon also opened their gates to Alexander in 331 and were re-appointed by him.[50]

---

[47] On Perdiccas' marriage alliances: Arr. *Succ*. 1.21; cf. Diod. 18.23.1–3; Just. 13.6.5–6. See Yardley, Wheatley and Heckel (2011) 140–142. On the career of Atropates, see Heckel (2006) 61–62, Berve (1926) 2.91–92 no. 180.

[48] On Herodotus and Persian marriage practices; see Asheri (2007) 170; on the distinctions between Persian wives, concubines, and domestics, see Briant (2002) 277–286; cf. Brosius (1996) 31–41.

[49] See Brunt (1976) 163, with n. 6.

[50] Abulites surrendered Susa to Alexander; see Arr. *Anab*. 3.16.6–9; Curt. 5.2.16; Diod. 17.65.5; Mazaeus opened Babylon; cf. Arr. *Anab*. 3.16.3–4; Curt. 5.1.17–19, 44; Diod. 17.64.4–6.

But to answer Hampl's claim which we noted earlier—namely, that the marriages were one sided and the mark of the conqueror—there was simply no need to bring Greek or Macedonian women out to Persia. The Persian noble women brought with them money, land, resources, and family alliances.[51] Nor was it a matter of the invaders simply taking what they had "won by the spear." As the experience of the events of 329/28 BC had shown, it was better to work with a population than to try to subdue it.

Bosworth notes that Alexander also extended his generosity to more than 10,000 soldiers who had married native women.[52] Even allowing for exaggeration, it is a large figure, and it is likely that the king himself had encouraged the relationships. Justin (12.4.2–11) refers to the children born *in castris* (in the camp): Alexander intended to keep these boys with him, so that he would a have a ready supply of troops. In Arrian's text, Alexander reminds his mutinous army at Opis that he had made the same mixed cultural marriage as they had (*Anab.* 7.10.3). However, he also emphasizes (*Anab.* 7. 12.1–3) during his discharge of the Macedonian veterans following his reconciliation with the army, that he would keep their locally born sons with him, claiming that he would repatriate them himself when he returned to Europe. Arrian describes these promises as "vague and uncertain" (*Anab.* 7.12.3); possibly in his view, Alexander had no intention of ever letting these children go. Their world would be the camp, and their loyalty would be to the king.[53]

Did Alexander envisage a similar destiny for the future children of the nobility—a kind of blended aristocracy of the court parallel to the children of the camp?

A new generation of commanders and governors who would strengthen his own sovereignty? Bosworth thought that he did, but I am not so sure—or rather, as happens with human relationships, I suspect the story was more complicated.

It may not have been easy or even desirable to keep mixed noble offspring away from their Persian ancestral homes, as Bosworth suggested Alexander would have had to do. Some of these women came forcefully into their own. Of the nine attested Persian brides who were wed at Susa; two, if not three, were murdered after Alexander's death, and we do know what happened to four of the others. But two of the Susa wives became queens.[54]

---

51 Brosius (1996) 77–80.
52 Bosworth (2010).
53 On this relationship, see Anson (2020) 238–239.
54 See Meeus (2009) 236 with n. 7 and Van Oppen de Ruiter (2014) 25–38 who forcefully challenge the modern view that Alexander's marshals repudiated their Persian wives when Alexander died.

Achaemenid women like Atossa, Amestris, Parysatis and even Darius III's mother Sisygambis were formidable figures. An investigation of the power of Persian royal women is not within the parameters of this chapter;[55] moreover, Western sources often depict Persian royal women as a literary stereotype of ruthless, barbarian schemers.[56]

However, the female members of the Achaemenid family –particularly the mothers of kings—like court mothers in other cultures and in other periods in history—could, and did exercise real influence. Alexander restored Sisygambis, mother of the previous Great King, Darius III, to her former status and dignity, treated her with great respect, visited her several times, and even recognized her as another "mother", conferring the title upon her (Curt. 5.2.21–22; cf. Just. 13.1.5).[57] Sisygambis also successfully interceded with Alexander over the life of her one of her relatives (Curt. 5.3.13–15), thereby exercising a prerogative which seems to have been associated with Persian royal women, especially the king's mother. She committed suicide after Alexander's death.[58]

Arrian's text is emphatic that Alexander had a genuine desire for mixed offspring who were connecting him through kinship ties with his own men; not only to the rank and file as we have seen, but also to the man who was dearer to him than anyone else—namely Hephaestion. Arrian states (*Anab.* 7.4.5) that the reason why Hephaestion was given Drypetis, full sister to Alexander's wife, Stateira, was precisely because Alexander wanted his children to be cousins to Hephaestion's.[59] As Brunt and Heckel have noted, the Susa marriages are indicative of the primacy of Hephaestion's power, and significantly too, Hephaestion had been a supporter of Alexander's pro Iranian policy.[60] But Alexander's desire

---

[55] In general, see Brosius (1996) 69, 105–122; on Parysatis and Ctesis, especially 110–112.
[56] For example, Atossa, wife of Darius I supposedly suggested that Darius should invade Greece (Hdt. 3.134), Amestris, Xerxes' wife, apparently incited her brother in law to revolt by murdering his wife (Hdt. 9.110–113), while Parysatis, the wife of Darius II and mother of Artaxerxes II, allegedly contrived the death of the powerful satrap of Lydia, Tissaphernes, whom she held responsible for the death of one of her sons, Cyrus the Younger (Diod. 14.80.6–8; cf. Xen. *Hell.* 3.4.25–26).
[57] Sisygambis, see Heckel (2006) 251; Berve (1926) 2.356–57 no. 711; Briant (2002) 772–773; Brosius (1996) 21, 67–68; Carney (1996) 563–583.
[58] Curt. 10.5.24; Diod. 17.118.3; Just. 13.1.5; on the privilege of Persian royal women to intercede on behalf of others, see Brosius (1996) 116–122.
[59] Van Oppen de Ruiter (2014) 28 also points out that by marrying Drypetis to Hephaestion Alexander was avoiding future rivalry, should she bear a son to someone else.
[60] Brunt (1983) 511–512; cf. Heckel (1992) 86, who calls Hephaestion's part in the Susa marriages "no less than a symbolic share in the empire"; on Hephaestion's support for Alexander's "Orientalizing"; Heckel (2006) 136.

for a blood connection with his beloved Hephaestion via their children was not to be. Within six months, Hephaestion would be dead at Ecbatana.[61]

Forty years ago Bosworth was right to strip away much of the Western idelology associated with understanding Alexander's so called "Orientalizing" and return the debate to interpreting the ancient evidence.[62] Ten years ago he revised his earlier work, but this time with a greater emphasis on the Susa marriages and their meaning for Alexander's court—and the future of that court.[63] Bosworth—like Arrian before him—rightly highlighted Seleucus. Alexander's plans did not quite come to be realized, at least for himself and Hephaestion. However, in one very real way the aim of the Susa marriages *was* fulfilled—by someone else.

For Seleucus and Apame, history is unequivocal. They became the parents of a great dynasty, that of the Seleucids in Asia, commanding by far the biggest part of the former Persian Empire, including much of the old Persian heartland.[64]

Bibliography

Abd el-Raziq (1984): Mahmud Abd el-Raziq, *Die Darstellungen und Texte des Sanktuars Alexanders des Großen im Tempel von Luxor*, Mainz.
Alonso Troncoso and Álvarez Rico (2017): Victor Alsonso Troncoso and M. Álvarez Rico, "Alexander's Tents and Camp Life", in: Sabine Müller *et al.* (eds.), *The History of the Argeads: New Perspectives*, Wiesbaden, 113–124.
Anson (2004): Edward M. Anson, *Eumenes of Cardia: A Greek Among Macedonians*, Leiden.
Anson (2020): Edward M. Anson, "The Father of the Army: Alexander and the Epigoni", in: M. D'Agostini *et al.* (eds.), *Affective Relations and Personal Bonds in Hellenistic Antquity*, Oxford, 227–242.
Asheri (2007): David Asheri *et al.*, *A Commentary on Herodotus Books I-IV*, Oxford.

---

[61] Hephaestion's death; Arr. *Anab.* 7.14; Plut. *Alex.* 72; Diod. 17.110.8; Just. 12.12.11; Polyaenus *Strat.* 4.3.31; Ephippus of Olynthus *BNJ* 126; see Heckel (2006) 136–137, Berve (1926) 2.167 no. 347.
[62] Bosworth (1980a).
[63] Bosworth (2010).
[64] This chapter was first given as a conference paper in Edmonton, May, 2018; I would like to thank Professor Frances Pownall and her colleagues for the invitation to attend a wonderful meeting and for their splendid hospitality; I am also grateful for Professors Sulochana Asirvatham, Waldemar Heckel, Daniel Ogden, Sabine Müller, Hugh Bowman, Christian Djurslev, Timothy Howe, Fred Naiden, Philip Bosman, Jeanne Reames, Giustina Monti, Stanley Burstein, and William Greenwalt for their comments; to Professor Ben Garstad and his family for looking after me; to Dr. Reuben Ramsey for research assistance, to Dr. Diana Newport-Peace for her careful reading and criticism of this chapter, to Professor Cathy Coleborne for research support. Finally I appreciate the help of the editors of this volume: their insightful comments, corrections, and additional references have very much strengthened this contribution.

Atkinson (2009): John E. Atkinson and John C. Yardley, *Curtius Rufus, Histories of Alexander the Great Book 10*, Oxford.
Baynham (2015): Elizabeth J. Baynham, "Cleomenes of Naucratis, Villain or Victim", in: Timothy Howe et al., (eds.), *Greece, Macedon and Persia, Studies in Social, Political and Military History in Honour of Waldemar Heckel*, Oxford, 127–134.
Berve (1926): Helmut Berve, *Das Alexanderreich auf prosopographischer Grundlage*, 2 vols. Munich.
Bosworth (1980a): A. Brian Bosworth, "Alexander and the Iranians", in: *Journal of Hellenic Studies* 100, 1–21.
Bosworth (1980b): A. Brian Bosworth, *A Historical Commentary on Arrian's History of Alexander*, Vol. I, Oxford.
Bosworth (1988): A. Brian Bosworth, *From Arrian to Alexander*, Oxford.
Bosworth (1983): A.B. Bosworth, "The Impossible Dream; W.W. Tarn's Alexander in Retrospect", in: *Ancient Society. Resources For Teachers* 13.3, 131–150; reprinted in *Karanos*, Bulletin of Ancient Macedonian Studies 2 (2019) 77–95.
Bosworth (1995): A. Brian Bosworth, *A Historical Commentary on Arrian's History of Alexander*, Vol. II, Oxford.
Bosworth (2002): A. Brian Bosworth, *The Legacy of Alexander*, Oxford.
Bosworth (2010): A. Brian Bosworth, "Alexander and the Iranians Revisited," unpublished paper.
Briant (2002): Pierre Briant, *From Cyrus to Alexander*, Indiana.
Briant (2012): Pierre Briant, *Alexander the Great and His Empire*, New Jersey.
Briant (2015): Pierre Briant, *Darius in the Shadow of Alexander*, Cambridge, Mass.
Brosius (1996): Maria Brosius, *Women in Ancient Persia*, Oxford.
Brosius (2003): Maria Brosius, "Alexander and the Persians", in: J. Roisman (ed.), *Brill's Companion to Alexander the Great*, Leiden, 169–196.
Brunt (1976): Peter A. Brunt, *Arrian: History of Alexander and Indica*, Vol. I, Cambridge, Mass.
Brunt (1983): Peter A Brunt, *Arrian: History of Alexander and Indica*, Vol. II, Cambridge, Mass.
Burstein (1974): Stanley Mayor Burnstein, *Outpost of Hellenism:The Emergence of Heraclea on the Black Sea*, Berkeley.
Carney (1996): Elizabeth Donnelly Carney, "Alexander and the Persian Women", in: *American Journal of Philology* 117, 563–583.
Carney (2000): Elizabeth Donnelly Carney, *Women and Monarchy in Macedonia*, Norman.
Carney (2017): Elizabeth Donnelly Carney, "Argead Marriage Policy", in: S. Müller et al. (eds.), *The History of the Argeads: New Perspectives*, Wiesbaden, 139–150.
Collard and Cropp (2008): Christopher Collard and Martin Cropp, *Euripides VII Fragments: Augeus-Meleager*, Cambridge, Mass.
Collins (2012): Andrew W. Collins, "The Royal Costume and Insignia of Alexander the Great", in: *American Journal of Philology* 133.3, 371–402.
Collins (2017): Andrew W. Collins, "The Persian Royal Tent and Ceremonial of Alexander the Great", in: *Classical Quarterly* 67.1, 71–76.
Flower (2000): Michael A. Flower, "Alexander the Great and Panhellenism", in A. Brian Bosworth and Elizabeth J. Baynham (eds.), *Alexander the Great in Fact and Fiction*, Oxford, 96–135.
Grainger (1990): John D. Grainger, *Seleukos Nikator*, London.

Hamilton (1987): James R. Hamilton, "Alexander's Iranian Policy", in: Wolfgang Will and Johannes Heinrichs (eds.), *Zu Alexander d. Gr. Festschrift G. Wirth*, Amsterdam, Vol. I, 467–486.
Hamilton (1999): JamesR. Hamilton, *Plutarch* Alexander, 2nd ed., Bristol.
Hampl (1954): Franz Hampl, "Alexander der Grosse und die Beurteilung geschichtlicher Persönlichkeiten", *La Nouvelle Clio* 6, 115–123.
Heckel (1992): Waldemar Heckel, *The Marshals of Alexander's Empire*, London.
Heckel (2006): Waldemar Heckel, *Who's Who in the Age of Alexander the Great*, London.
Heckel (2018): Waldemar Heckel, "Artabazus in the Lands beyond the Caspian", in: *Anabasis* 9, 93–109.
Heckel (2020): Waldemar Heckel, *In the Path of Conquest, Resistance to Alexander the Great*, Oxford.
How and Wells (1912): Walter W. How and J. Wells, *A Commentary on Herodotus*, Vol. I, Oxford.
Lenfant (2007): Dominique Lefant, "Greek Historians of Persia", in: John Maricola (ed.), *Greek and Roman Historiography*, London, 183–191.
Lund (1992): Helen S. Lund, *Lysimachus, A Study in Early Hellenistic Kingship*, London.
Mallory (1991): James P. Mallory, *In Search of the Indo Europeans*, London.
McBee (2000): Randy D. McBee, *Dance Hall Days*, New York.
Meeus (2009): Alexander Meeus, "Alexander's Image in the Age of the Successors", in Waldemar Heckel and Lawrence A. Tritle (eds.), *Alexander the Great: A New History*, London, 235–250.
Müller (2012): Sabine Müller, "Onesikritos und das Achaimenidenreich", in: *Anabasis* 2, 45–66.
Müller (2013): Sabine Müller, "The Female Element of the Political Self-Fashioning of the Diadochi; Ptolemy, Selecucus, Lysimachus and their Iranian Wives", in: Victor Alonso Troncoso and Edward M. Anson (eds.), *After Alexander: The Time of the Diadochi (323–281 BC)*, Oxford, 199–214.
Müller (2014): Sabine Müller, *Alexander, Makedonien und Persien*, Berlin.
Müller (2020): Sabine Müller, "Barsine, Antigone and the Macedonian War", in: Monica D'Agostini *et al.* (eds.), *Affective Relations and Personal Bonds in Hellenistic Antiquity*, Oxford, 81–96.
Müller (2021): Sabine Müller, "Alexander at Naqš-i Rustam? Persia and the Macedonians", in: John Walsh and Elizabeth Baynham (eds.), *Alexander the Great and Propaganda*, London, 107–128.
Mitchell (2007): Lynette Mitchell, *Panhellenism and the Barbarian in Archaic and Classical Greece*, Swansea.
Munson (2009): Rosaria V. Munson, "Who Are Herodotus' Persians?" *Classical World*, 102, 457–470.
Ogden (1999): Daniel Ogden, *Polygamy, Prostitutes and Death*, Swansea.
Ogden (2017): Daniel Ogden, *The Legend of Seleucus*, Cambridge.
Ogilvie (1965): Robert M. Ogilvie, *A Commentary on Livy Books 1–5*, Oxford.
Olbrycht (2011): Marek J. Olbrycht, "Curtius Rufus, the Macedonian Mutiny at Opis and Alexander's Iranian Policy in 324 BC", in: Jakub Pigón (ed.), *The Children of Herodotus*, Newcastle, 231–252.

Olbrycht (2013): Marek J. Olbrycht, "Iranians in the Diadochoi Period", in: Victor Alonso Troncoso and Edward M. Anson (eds.) *After Alexander: The Time of the Diadochi (323–281 BC)*, Oxford, 159–182.

Olbrycht (2014): Marek J. Olbrycht, "'An Admirer of Persian Ways'; Alexander the Great's Reforms in Parthia-Hyrcania and the Iranian Heritage", in: Touraj Daryaee et al. (eds.), *Excavating an Empire, Achaemenid Persia in Longue Durée*, Costa Mesa, Calif., 37–62.

Olbrycht (2015): Marek J. Olbrycht, "The Epigonoi—the Iranian Phalanx of Alexander the Great", in: Waldemar Heckel et al. (eds.), *The Many Faces of War*, Newcastle Upon Tyne, 196–212.

Olbrycht (2016): Marek J. Olbrycht, "Alexander the Great at Susa in 324 B.C.", in: Cinzia Bearzot and Franca Landucci (eds.), *Alexander's Legacy*, Rome, 61–72.

Olbrycht (2017): Marek J. Olbrycht, "Parthia, Bactria and India: The Iranian Policies of Alexander (330–323)", in: Claudia Antonetti and Paolo Biagi (eds.), *With Alexander in India and Central Asia*, Oxford, 194–211.

Piérart (2004): Marcel Piérart, "Argolis", in: Mogens H. Hansen and Thomas H. Nielsen (eds.), *An Inventory of Archaic and Classical Poleis*, Oxford, 599–619.

Roscher (1884–1937): Wilhelm Roscher, *Ausführliches Lexikon der griechischen und römischen Mythologie*, Leipzig.

Schäfer (2002): Christoph Schäfer, *Eumenes von Kardia und der Kampf um die Macht im Alexanderreich*, Frankfurt.

Schäfer (2007): Christoph Schäfer, "Alexander der Große, Pharao und Priester", in: Stefan Pfeiffer (ed.), *Ägypten unter fremden Herrschern zwischen persischer Satrapie und römischer Provinz*, Frankfurt, 54–74.

Stem (2007): Rex Stem, "Exemplary Lessons of Livy's Romulus", in: *Transactions of the American Philological Association* 137, 435–447.

Tomlinson (1972): Richard A. Tomlinson, *Argos and the Argolid*, London.

Tronson (1984): Adrian Tronson, "Satyrus the Peripatetic and the Marriages of Philip II", in: *Journal of Hellenic Studies*, 104, 116–126.

Van Oppen de Ruiter (2014): Branko F. van Oppen de Ruiter, "The Susa Marriages—A Historiographical Note", in: *Ancient Society* 44, 25–41.

Van Oppen de Ruiter (2020): Branko F. van Oppen de Ruiter, "Amastris: The First Hellenistic Queen" *Historia* 69, 17–37.

Waterfield and Dewald (1998): Robin Waterfield and Carolyn Dewald, *Herodotus, The Histories*, Oxford.

Weber (2009): Gregor Weber, "Alexander's Court and Social System", in Waldemar Heckel and Lawrence A. Tritle (eds.), *Alexander the Great: A New History*, London, 83–98.

Yardley and Heckel (1997): John C. Yardley and Waldemar Heckel, *Justin: Epitome of* The Philippic History *of Pompeius Trogus*, Vol. I, Oxford.

Yardley, Wheatley, and Heckel (2011): John C. Yardley, Pat Wheatley, and Waldemar Heckel, *Justin: Epitome of* The Philippic History *of Pompeius Trogus*, Vol. II, Oxford.

Philip Bosman
Two Conceptions of Court at Persepolis

The article considers the two conceptions of court that came face to face over a prolonged period in Persepolis, headquarters of the Persian empire, during the winter of 330 BC. The sojourn started with the looting of the city by the Macedonian soldiers and continued with the huge operation of transporting the contents of the Persepolis treasuries to Susa. It ended, some four months later, with the burning of the royal palaces. This latter event, still there for all to see in the ruins of the ancient citadel, has puzzled both the ancient reports and modern scholarship: why would Alexander have decided to destroy the palaces before leaving the city? One theme dominates the written reports, namely that it formed part, even the capstone, of Alexander's panhellenic revenge war. But as many scholars have argued, the ancient narratives for various reasons should not be seen as presenting the full picture; rather, many factors played a part in the fateful outcome, and the various stakeholders and constituencies would have interpreted it differently. One such factor is the fact that the Macedonian elite encountered a conception of court with an elaborate hierarchy and a notion of distanced kingship they would have found difficult to accept and even threatening to their own brokered positions of power. The royal palaces embodied and supported the Persian court. Their destruction could be read as a show of solidarity by Alexander with his comrades-in-arms and with how the Macedonians negotiated the relationship between king and elites. Alexander soon had second thoughts about this concession and started implementing aspects of the Persian conception of court which, as we know, were unpopular among his companions.

The Burning of Persepolis: A Source Conundrum

The first section of the article is an attempt to organize the ancient source material and scholarship on the burning of Persepolis. This is necessary in order to establish where my argument fits into the picture, and if anything further needs, indeed, can, be said about the reasons for the Macedonian destruction of the ancient palaces. It would require a much more extensive treatment than what I can offer here to properly account for the complexity of the ancient literary sources, archaeological material and the mountain of available scholarship.

Even a cursory glance at the amount of scholarly work on the burning of Persepolis would reveal a lack of consensus on many of the issues it raises.[1] One aspect does currently enjoy general agreement, namely the scholarly repulsion of the overly destructive behavior, exacerbated by an ancient account that this happened as the result of a drunken bout. Maria Brosius expresses the general sentiments of shame, disgust, and sadness about the callousness of the Macedonians responsible for the destruction: "This act of hooliganism on the part of the Macedonian soldiers was a senseless act of unprovoked violence, brutal killing and deliberate destruction of the central capital of the Achaemenid kings".[2] The sentiments are not modern either but are already reflected in the ancient sources, with Diodorus (17.70.1–6) and Curtius (5.6.3–8) dwelling on the frenzied greed and brutality of the invaders. Even the early publicists probably rationalized the events and attempted to deflect some of the blame away from Alexander. It certainly left Plutarch (*Alex.* 38) and Arrian (*Anab.* 3.18.12), both generally favourable towards Alexander, with considerable embarrassment.

Much less consensus can be claimed on how events actually proceeded and whether the burning was a strategic decision or not. Those who wish to extract Alexander's motivations from the source material are confronted with two versions, at first glance hard to reconcile: on the one hand, a premeditated act resulting from deliberation and executed in such a way as to convey a pointed message; on the other hand, a random decision after late-night revelry in which the true culprit was an eloquent Athenian courtesan. To others, the literary source material constitutes a mere distraction from the true reasons, which need to be deduced from a larger political and military context. If we wish to add the notion of clashing conceptions of court as having contributed to what happened at Persepolis, the proper place for such an argument needs to be established in relation to the source material, as well as to the current state of scholarship.

---

[1] Reports on the archaeological records in Schmidt (1953–1970). The incident is naturally dealt with in all histories of Alexander the Great; pointed contributions to the debate include Badian (1967); Wheeler (1968); Borza (1972); Balcer (1978); Hammond (1992); Bloedow and Loube (1997); Sancisi-Weerdenburg (1993); Wirth (1993); Nawotka (2003); Seibert (2004/2005). A recent handy survey of the ancient literary evidence and scholarship in Mousavi (2012), with a bibliography of subsequent archaeological work on p. 9 and full bibliography, pp. 221–231, a description of the remains pp. 9–56, and a discussion of its *Nachleben*; on the latter, see also McAuley (2018).
[2] Brosius (2003) 183.

(i) A premeditated act

The first option is to be found in Arrian's account of the episode (*Anab.* 3.18.10 – 12). Arrian tersely lists a few main points: Alexander hastened to Persepolis and managed to arrive there before the guards could raid the treasuries. He then hauled in the treasure at Pasargadae and appointed Phrasaortes[3] as satrap of Persis before he burned down the royal palaces. Arrian's preferred sources evidently stressed that the major motivation for Alexander to get to Persepolis was to confiscate its riches before anyone else could do the same.[4]

As to the burning, Arrian's account reduces it to a summary of the opposing views of Parmenio and Alexander before it happened (*Anab.* 3.18.11– 12): Parmenio could muster various reasons why the palaces should not be destroyed but only two are explicitly mentioned: that Alexander had no reason to destroy his own property, and that Alexander should rather portray himself to the people of Asia as having obtained the rulership of Asia and not merely as a conqueror passing through (οὐδὲ αὐτῷ ἐγνωκότι κατέχειν τῆς Ἀσίας τὴν ἀρχήν, ἀλλὰ ἐπελθεῖν μόνον νικῶντα).[5] Alexander's wish, however, prevailed, namely that he wanted to punish the Persians for harm done to the Greeks, in particular for their destruction of Athens and the city's temples during Xerxes' invasion a hundred and fifty years previously. Arrian (*Anab.* 3.18.12) ends by expressing his disagreement with what occurred and adds that it made no sense as punishment of the Persians of a distant past.

The problem with Arrian's version, as has been noted,[6] is that it is suspiciously brief considering the magnitude of the event. While Ptolemy may have suppressed a longer account due to his involvement with Thais, it is to be doubted that Arrian's other preferred source, Aristobulus, would have had enough reason to gloss over something of such enormous significance. The same applies to Callisthenes, who is known to have pushed the revenge war agenda and was fond of employing Parmenio as Alexander's counterpoint in policy and strategic matter. Arrian's brevity was by choice, whether for apologetic reasons or for sim-

---

[3] According to Arrian the son of the Persian cavalry commander Rheomithres who fought at the Granicus River and Issus; cf. Arr. *Anab.* 1.12; 2.11; 3.18; cf. Heckel (2006) 223.
[4] Diodorus (17.69.1) rather stresses control of the city.
[5] On Parmenio here playing the part of the "Tragic Warner", cf. Sancisi-Weerdenburg (1993) 178. Lehmann (2015) 61 sees the literary confrontations between Alexander and Parmenio as going through Aristobulus and Ptolemy back to Callisthenes. It should be noted, however, that in Arrian (*Anab.* 3.9.4) Parmenio's advice prevailed over Alexander's own view shortly before at Gaugamela, where it was evidently regarded as the better option.
[6] Sancisi-Weerdenburg (1993) 178.

ply not finding the Thais-version credible. Evidently, his account does not tell the whole story, but it does imply that the destruction was collectively discussed and endorsed, even if the king had the last say.

(ii) An impromptu decision

The second option is the extended version of events occurring at a symposium in which the courtesan Thais was instrumental in the palace burning. The story's basics are often accepted by scholars who find the burnings irreconcilable with Alexander's imperial policy at that stage.[7] The various versions are too long and too varied in the detail to be properly dealt with here, but they all include a banquet held in the palaces shortly before the departure from Persepolis, at the end of which Alexander and his fellow symposiasts formed a κῶμος ("band of revelers") and initiated the arson, soon to be assisted by the Macedonian soldiery. That this version derived from Cleitarchus is virtually settled by a transmitted remark in Athenaeus that this popular author made Thais the cause of the burning.[8]

Diodorus (17.68–72) gives the fullest account of the journey to and sojourn in the Persian royal city, including a description of the site. Diodorus's own depiction is certainly not an attempt to whitewash the Macedonians; on the contrary, he spends considerable time on the greedy frenzy of the Macedonians, and the orgy of pillaging and slaughter that followed. He also notes Alexander's animosity towards the city and its inhabitants. After making a general mention of Alexander's victory games and entertainment offered to the companions, Diodorus turns to the fateful symposium and the speech of the Athenian courtesan Thais. Diodorus' Thais notes the insult that the involvement of women "in a brief moment" (ἐν βραχεῖ καιρῷ) would add to the injury of eradicating the palaces and the famous deeds of the Persians. Someone else at the banquet then raised the call for revenge on the destruction of the Greek temples, and Diodorus in an authorial comment (17.72) dwells on how the impiety of Xerxes on the Athe-

---

7 E.g. Gehrke (1996) 59–60; cf. also Mousavi (2012) 69–70.
8 Ath.13.576d–e (Cleitarchus *BNJ* 137 F 11): ὁ δὲ μέγας Ἀλέξανδρος οὐ Θαίδα εἶχε μεθ' ἑαυτοῦ τὴν Ἀττικὴν ἑταίραν; περὶ ἧς φησι Κλείταρχος ὡς "αἰτίας γενομένης τοῦ ἐμπρησθῆναι τὰ ἐν Περσεπόλει βασίλεια, αὕτη δὲ ἡ Θαῒς μετὰ τὸν Ἀλεξάνδρου θάνατον καὶ Πτολεμαίῳ ἐγαμήθη τῷ πρώτῳ βασιλεύσαντι Αἰγύπτου, "And did not Alexander the Great have with himself Thais, the Athenian *hetaira*, concerning whom Cleitarchus says she was the cause for the burning of the palaces at Persepolis. This same Thais after Alexander's death was also married to Ptolemy, the first king of Egypt."

nian acropolis was repaid by a single woman from that city, and in παιδία ("playfulness") at that.

Quintus Curtius' account (5.7.2–11) frames the episode as a reproach of Alexander's alcohol abuse, which clouded his usual strategic savvy and made him host numerous *convivia* where the presence of prostitutes was condoned. Curtius' Thais promotes the arson as a way of finding favour with the Greeks, a motivation echoed by Alexander (5.7.4). In an acute observation, surely his own, Curtius notes how the Macedonians attempted to rationalize their wanton act, but also that Alexander regretted (*paenituisse*) it the very next day when he sobered up (5.7.11). The main warning for Curtius to be derived from the events, that such a glorious city could so easily lose its glory and could literally be extinguished from the face of the earth, seems ultimately directed at Rome (5.7.8–10).

Plutarch more obviously than the other authors refers to a longer, eloquent speech by Thais at the occasion, and his summary still reflects a highly rhetorical composition (*Alex*. 38.1–2). His Thais notes that the hardships endured by a woman during a military campaign is offset by the pleasures of the current party in the royal palace, but that vengeance of Xerxes' burning of Athens would make the hardships even more worth their while. Her motivation for setting the palaces alight is that it would embarrass the (male) military commanders of the Greeks when even the women in Alexander's company could achieve more than the στρατήγοι ("commanders") of Hellas.[9]

The subtle variations in the versions of these three authors, and the reasons their various Thiases give for the burning, indicate how difficult it would be to reconstruct the Cleitarchan account. From Cleitarchus, of course, we still need to get to the sources he made use of. Wirth suggests that the elements of Dionysiac ritual in the story may go back to Ephippus, but does not rule out that the episode ultimately derives from Callisthenes.[10] The revenge war motif is certainly a favourite of Callisthenes, and we know him to be fond of legend-making embellishment as well.[11] On the other hand, it is to be doubted that the court publicist would have distributed an official version of events along this particular

---

9 Wirth (1993) 201 refers to Thais as representing Greek vengeance, though more justly as personifying the "Ironifisierung des ganzen Perserkrieges" and "die Persiflage seiner ethischen Implikationen".

10 Wirth (1993) 227 n.236, with reference to E. Mederer, *Die Alexanderlegenden bei den ältesten Alexanderhistorikern* (Stuttgart 1936), which I unfortunately could not consult. Wirth sees three sources in the vulgate source—one official, one trivialising, and one religious.

11 Zahrnt (2006) 174 argues that Callisthenes sent reports shortly after the event from Asia to Greece, probably until after the sojourn in Persepolis.

line of apologetics. The rhetorical turn and possible creative elaboration of the story may even point to that famed "steersman of lies" Onesicritus.[12] While this remains in the realm of speculation, what the analysis does make clear, is that the Cleitarchan reworking of older material should not be read as sober historiography. The literary character of the accounts, both that of Cleitarchus and those of his users, is beyond dispute.[13]

(iii) Planned beforehand; executed on impulse

While some scholars see the two options as irreconcilable,[14] others do not regard them as mutually exclusive.[15] It is indeed likely that the issue of what should become of Persepolis and whether it should remain the symbolic headquarters of the incumbent Great King, would have been brought up among the conquerors on a regular basis. Alexander's view and the decision to present its destruction as a revenge-war gesture could well have prevailed, whether at a Macedonian war-council meeting or during the numerous symposia of Curtius' account, and the final execution of the decision could equally well have been initiated on impulse in the dead of night. That said, both options can equally well be rejected altogether as fabricated or trivial, rationalizations or attempts to deflect blame away from Alexander and the Macedonian leadership.

(iv) The truth is elsewhere

It is thus possible that the literary evidence distracts from the true reasons for the burning of Persepolis. A formidable body of data with the potential to undermine the literary evidence are the archaeological reports based on years of painstaking work in the citadel. Michael Zahrnt optimistically expressed the hope that the Persepolis-episode is now once and for all settled as a *damnatio memoriae* of the legacy of Xerxes,[16] as summarised by Sancisi-Weerdenburg from the archaeo-

---

[12] Onesicritus is prone to zooming in on personal interaction, as in the meetings between Alexander and Diogenes and the gymnosophists; as to imaginative elaboration, cf. the anecdote in Plut. *Alex.* 46 on his reading from his history to Lysimachus on the tale of the Amazons.
[13] Sancisi-Weerdenburg (1993) 180 concludes that the analysis of the narrative themes cannot bring us to a solution of the problem why Alexander burned the palaces.
[14] Hammond (1992); Dreyer (2009) 57.
[15] Badian (1967); Bosworth (1988).
[16] Zahrnt (2006) 162 n. 42.

logical reports of Schmidt and Herzfeld and the Chicago Institute of Oriental Studies.[17] Schmidt's reading of the data points to a "methodical" burning of the areas linked to Xerxes, and he is even able to notice a "particularly vindictive thoroughness" in how it was executed.[18] A revision of the data suggests greater complexity, though. Mousavi objects against the view that buildings associated with Xerxes were targeted, because "there is not a single building at Persepolis that does not bear the name of that king."[19] Sancisi-Weerdenburg herself distinguishes between the revenge motive as an official narrative and the true reason for the burning. In her view, Alexander destroyed the palaces "[n]ot from hatred against his Achaemenid predecessors or from ideological prejudice against Xerxes, but mainly…because he did not want to leave behind a supply of items that could be used to propagate various forms of political power, at various echelons."[20] In response, Mousavi notes that the treasures were removed weeks previously, though a "few long curtains and furniture certainly served as combustibles to burn down the palaces."[21]

Historians have also opted to look for explanations in detail barely hinted at, or even completely ignored in the transmitted source material. Both Wirth and Badian treat the transmitted reports as trivial sideshows.[22] In an influential article, Badian argues that the factor really dominating Alexander's mind was the uprising of Agis III in the Peloponnese, and the long stay at Persepolis should be understood as due to delayed information on the outcome and to a misunderstanding of Alexander's location at the time. While waiting in Persepolis for news from Europe, Alexander's error of not pursuing Darius after Gaugamela slowly dawned on him.[23] At the night of the infamous party, "the releasing power of Bacchus" made him come to decide on a final great gesture to the Greeks back home, then to resume the pursuit of Darius. As soon as news of Agis' defeat arrived, he dismissed the allied (Greek) troops and, with them, the farce of the panhellenic effort.[24] Badian's brilliant resort to *Realpolitik* and psychology crumbles, unfortunately, due to miscalculations on the dates of the stay

---

17 Sancisi-Weerdenburg (1993) 180–185; 187 nn. 28 and 32.
18 Schmidt (1953) 262–3 and 241; one can only speculate about the extent of influence from Arrian's version.
19 Mousavi (2012) 68
20 Sancisi-Weerdenburg (1993) 185.
21 Mousavi (2012) 68 n. 60.
22 Badian (1967); Wirth (1993) 173–251.
23 Badian (1967) 188.
24 Badian (1967) 189.

in Persepolis²⁵ and an underestimation of the communication speed along the imperial networks.²⁶ For Briant, also finding the literary evidence not compelling, the real issue was about Alexander's response to Persian politics, about which the transmitted reports (all from the side of the conquerors) were simply not interested. Alexander sought to side publicly for the lineage of Cyrus (associated with Pasargadae) rather than of Darius I (associated with Persepolis). When, however, he failed to gain approval for his attempt from the Persian nobility, and to officially accede the throne, he decided to signal to the "recalcitrant Persians that the age of imperial grandeur was over, unless they turned to him *en masse*."²⁷ While hard evidence for such a specific reason may be lacking, my own consideration of the roles played by the two courts certainly overlaps with Briant's view that friction between Alexander and the Persian nobility could have played a significant part in events.

(v) Multiple motivations and messages

I would further like to side with those scholars who do not search for the silver bullet that solves the problem, but rather see a spectrum of factors that influenced the decision whether to leave the city with the royal palaces intact (but empty) or nor. Such an approach should not be seen as a renewed attempt to construct an apology.²⁸ A decision of such magnitude would have held messages aimed at various constituencies,²⁹ and it seems more productive to consider its effects on these constituencies and stakeholders: from the Greeks and Macedonians back home to the Macedonians and Greeks of the military campaign, from the people of the land in the vast stretches of the Persian empire to the royal courts and nobles of the Persian administrations and elite to Darius himself;

---

25 Mousavi (2012) 66 and n.43; see also Borza (1972) 238–240.
26 In a study on the Achaemenid communication networks, Colburn (2013) 39 describes the Persian Empire as "connected by means of a network of roads, with Persepolis and Susa as major hubs", and offers detailed arguments for estimating the speed of news travel at approximately 230 km per day; similar Borza (1972) 240 n.41.
27 Briant (2002) 852; (2010) 111.
28 Mousavi (2012) seems inclined to view any scholarly attempt to try to figure out what went through Alexander's mind apart from alcohol and barbarism as apologetic. He is correct, however, that whatever the reasons, Alexander's decision was a blow directed at the heart of the empire.
29 Borza (1972) 242 already argued in favour of widening "the range of interpretations accounting for Alexander's activities in the early months of 330 B.C."; more recently Müller (2014) 191–193 and (2019) 144–147.

from the personnel and inner court at Persepolis to Alexander's own court, council and companions.

A Clash of Courts

Hence, a consideration of the contrasting courts at Persepolis does not offer a solution as to why Alexander destroyed the Persepolis citadel, but should add further context and support for the friction that no doubt existed between the invaders and the Persian establishment. While the ancient literary evidence only hints at such tension, the case can be made stronger by analyzing the two courts with the assistance of theoretical work on the notion of "court." Recent studies of the ancient courts of Persia and Macedon take recourse to socio-historical work on the notion, most of which derived from Norbert Elias' groundbreaking study.[30] For present purposes and in a nutshell, "court" may be viewed as consisting of three tightly linked categories—people, institution and space—harnessed for socio-political purposes and undergirded by an encompassing court ideology. Elias' analysis points to court as a mechanism designed to perpetuate existing power structures in a hierarchical society. At its basis lies a mutually benefiting relationship between king and nobility, giving rise to an ideology that aims to maintain the status quo and that finds expression in court ceremonial and etiquette. Studies of the notion of court typically distinguish between an inner court consisting of functionaries and relatives in permanent close vicinity to the monarch, and an outer court consisting of a wider group of nobles and administrative functionaries with an incidental presence in the physical court.[31]

Facets of "court" are present in a very real way in the ancient source material on the Persepolis sojourn. Arrian's version hints at a meeting, or meetings, of a Macedonian war council where arguments on the fate of the Persepolis palaces were deliberated. In military terms, these councils were gatherings of Alexander's senior officers while on campaign;[32] in terms of court, they were specialized meetings of king and high-ranking nobles. Whatever the view on the institutionalization of these gatherings, the context suggests that the fate of the palaces was discussed and a decision eventually taken by a collective in consultation with the king. The version of events stressing an impromptu execution of the de-

---

[30] Elias (1983); cf. Spawforth (2007) 3; Brosius (2007) 18.
[31] Butz and Dannenberg (2004); see discussions on the applicability of court theory to ancient cultures in Spawforth (2007) 1–16; Brosius (2007) 17–18.
[32] Cf. Naiden (2019) 37–8, 41–2, 49–50, 56–7 and Appendix 3.

cision, on the other hand, involves a Macedonian symposium held within the Persepolis palace. As Pownall demonstrates, regardless of the bad press in ancient Greek sources, the Macedonian symposium had an important integrative function in the courts of both Philip and Alexander: it functioned not only as an aristocratic male bonding ritual, but also to secure and consolidate the loyalty of the Macedonian elite to the Argead dynasty and to the ruler personally.[33] On the Persian side, the Achaemenid court was very much present in the form of the physical space, as well as, most probably, parts of the permanent inner court that kept the palaces going in the absence of the Great King and his entourage, and less immediate court members seeking audience to renegotiate their positions with the new regional power. In order to understand the contrast between the two notions of court that met in Persepolis, brief surveys of the Achaemenid and the Argead courts follow.

(i) The Achaemenid court

The courtly groupings, hierarchies and practices of the Achaemenid court were complex, as would inevitably be the case with well-established and highly organized courts.[34] The Persian court evolved partly from tribal origins. Brosius traces the Achaemenid court back to the hierarchy among the leading and six other powerful families, which evolved into a self-perpetuating system of marriage alliances, protocols and ceremonies supporting a strict hierarchical order and aiming at mutual dependence and preservation. The other part of its make-up derived from the adoption of court practices from other ancient West Asian empires such as the Elamites, the Babylonians, Assyrians and Medes. These courts were similarly characterized by systems of social ranking, supported by practices to maintain the status quo. They also displayed typical constituent parts of inner and outer courts, consisting of relatives, attendants and political and administrative functionaries.

A salient feature of many ancient West Asian courts, the Achaemenid included, is controlled access to the monarch. The king deliberately maintained a distance from both his common subjects and, to a lesser extent, the nobility. He was not to be consulted except by an elect few or by specially granted privilege.[35]

---

[33] Pownall (2010) 62–65.
[34] I rely here for the most part on the careful study by Brosius (2007); cf. also Brosius (2003). Naturally, the treatment here must be highly selective.
[35] As noted by Herodotus (1.99) about Deioces of Ecbatana and Xenophon (*Cyr.* 7.5.37, 41) about Cyrus; see Brosius (2007) 22.

This "social distancing" was implemented by means of complex channels of communication, rituals and ceremonies, and entailed a hierarchy of privileges and formalities. For instance, dining with the king was granted as a special privilege, even though the numbers involved were large; it was "a declaration of royal favor, high rank and privilege."[36] Royal banquets and symposia were conducted according to strict protocols, elaborate ceremonies, and the maintenance of social hierarchy.[37]

Various reasons, apart from safety precautions, could be offered for the ideology of the inaccessible monarch. In the first instance, it serves to set him apart from contending members of his own family and of members of other noble families, and so to shield him against challenges of his authority and against the constant pressure to prove his worth.[38] It creates and preserves an aura of dignity and solemnity around his presence (Xen. *Cyr.* 7.5.37–41) and instills the perception that the king, though not seen, sees and knows everything. Probably foremost among these in terms of court theory is the opportunities it offers for positions of brokered power to selected individuals and groups in exchange for loyalty. In the Achaemenid case, these individuals and groups included immediate family members (mother, wife, heir, other children, brothers and sisters), councilors and judges, the King's Eye, satraps, physicians and scholars, to name a few. The mechanism of controlled access invariably gives rise to elaborate systems of intermediaries, guards and personal attendants (messengers, military guards, ointment-bearer, cup-bearer, staff-bearer, stool-bearer, various weapon-bearers, etc). It creates ceremonies for the performance of privileged access, such as dining with the king, having his ear, being declared a friend of the king, and so forth. In an established court aimed at dynastic perpetuation, the monarch virtually slips into a persona firmly established by group hierarchies, institutions and space, regardless of his/her individuality and personal strengths and weaknesses, to establish a suprapersonal and supratemporal institution.

The royal citadel in Persepolis was inextricably entwined with the Achaemenid court. Brosius notes the close relationship in terminology between the physical court (building complex) and the people involved in court activities: as with the word "house," the Old Persian term *viθ-* refers to both.[39] The architecture of

---

36 Brosius (2007) 42.
37 As described by Heracleides of Cumae *BNJ* 689 F 2; Ath. 4.145; Brosius (2007) 42–43.
38 Herodotus (1.99) mentions that Deioces introduced mechanisms to remove him from the sight of his childhood peers so that they would think him to have changed and so not plot against him.
39 Brosius (2007) 25, also noting that in the Greek sources the terms τὰ βασιλεία and τὰ οἰκήματα denote both the physical palaces and the court as an institution.

the Persian royal palaces at Pasargadae, Susa and Persepolis was meant to communicate power, "the visual expression of a monarch's command of resources … a manifestation of the unique position of the king, of his exalted position above all other levels of society, yet at the same time it asserted his presence among his subjects."[40]

The physical terrain of the Persepolis citadel, with its imposing architecture and imagery, was the "theatre of power" of the empire, the physical expression of monarchical power and its concomitant pomp and ceremony. The ideology of the inaccessible king was made manifest by imposing entrance gates, a strong military presence, and a messenger system. Depictions on reliefs within the palace complex were enactments of court ceremony by functionaries within the court system. Space and institution combined as a single manifestation of imperial hierarchy and ideology. In his discussion of Persian customs, Herodotus (1.134.2) mentions that they conceived of the bestowal of honour in spatial terms:

> They honor most of all those who live nearest them, next those who are next nearest, and so going ever onwards they assign honor by this rule: those who dwell farthest off they hold least honorable of all; for they think that they are themselves in all regards by far the best of all men, that the rest have only a proportionate claim to merit, until those who live farthest away have least merit of all.[41]

We may think of the Persian centers of power, in particular the Persepolis palaces, as at the heart of these widening and diminishing circles of esteem. This was the court with all its ostentation and ceremonial intricacies the Macedonians were confronted with on their arrival in the Persian corridors of power, and which they experienced firsthand during their prolonged winter sojourn in Persepolis.

(ii) The Macedonian court

The Argead clan, in turn, were no foreigners to the notion of court. Whereas the Greeks of the later fourth century might not have had a good grasp of the importance of court, the same could not be said of the Macedonians. Various aspects of Macedonian kingship and elite society attracted attention in recent scholarship: the interaction between the kings and prominent Macedonian families, institutions and practices such as religious duties, burials, gift-giving, land grants,

---

40 Brosius (2007) 46–47.
41 Hdt 1.134.2, trans. Godley (1920).

hunting and feasting, symposia; the position of women and the role of the royal pages, to name a few.⁴² Again, my summary of the character of the Macedonian court focuses on only two aspects, namely the more egalitarian nature of the Macedonian court and the consequent pressure on the monarch to (re)assert his leadership.

Current scholarship emphasizes the informal nature of Macedonian royal power, the absence of much in the way of "constitutional" checks and balances, and the conduct of day-to-day politics as a "power game" between the king, the Macedonian elite and the people.⁴³ Though ancient Macedonian society may be described as feudal, it appears that until Philip II its tribal origins were still prominent and its upper echelons had a much flatter structure than the imperial courts of ancient West Asia. This is already hinted at by the designation of the closest circles around the king as ἑταίροι ("companions") and φίλοι ("friends"). As Strootman notes about the situation prior to the middle fourth century BC:

> The king was principally the war leader of the united tribes of the Macedonian people. Although ideology presented the king as an absolute monarch, he was in practice *primus inter pares* of the high nobility. The Argead family, who dominated the coastal plain around the Thermaic Gulf, was merely the most powerful of several powerful clans. The male heads of the mightiest noble families were called the king's *suggeneis*, "relatives", and had the right to greet the king with a kiss. In fact, they often were tied to the king by family relations. Together they formed a war council, that advised the king. Macedonian aristocrats, particularly those ruling the mountainous hinterland, were fervently independent, and the king was entirely dependent on their support in wartime.⁴⁴

While there was a central palace at Pella by at least the late fifth century BC, this aspect of court remained underdeveloped, partly due to the often migratory nature of the Macedonian court.⁴⁵ Elite burial practices seem to corroborate the view of the Macedonian king as first among equals.⁴⁶ Kingship gained in stature with the reign of Philip II, who aimed to bypass the nobility by promoting more personal allegiances, though with varying success. The relationship between king and powerful nobility remained fluid, depending on the persona and strategies of the king. Alexander's own style was still very much that of a comrade-in-arms rather than a lord and master.⁴⁷ The Macedonian court reflected a warrior

---

42 Carney (2010); King (2010); Pownall (2010); Sawada (2010); Palagia (2017).
43 Spawforth (2007) 83.
44 Strootman (2007) 94; cf. Strootman (2014) 112–113.
45 Spawforth (2007) 87.
46 Palagia (2017) 409, 424.
47 King (2010) 380; see also the biographical survey at 390–392.

ethos which gave its institutions an archaic, Homeric feel: it was highly competitive and personal, and the authority of the king resided in his person rather than in the institution.[48] Unlike the protecting ideology of the inaccessible Achaemenid king, the Macedonian leader had to show himself worthy of his position. Ever new military ventures offered the opportunity for the realization of his warrior virtues and for the concomitant claims to honor.

Philip, who probably endeavored to imitate Persian court practices, was not shy of ostentation and self-elevation through court ceremonies.[49] Likewise, Alexander was interested in matters Persian, image-building and lavish consumption even before departing on the Asian campaign and continued with displays of power and prestige before arriving in the heart of Persian territory. But, as Spawforth notes, "there is as yet no hint in the sources that these occasions were particularly marked by pomp."[50]

Major changes in court style were gradually introduced from the latter part of 330 BC, when the Macedonian campaign moved into Hyrcania and Parthyaea. It included a magnificent tent for the purposes of feasting and audiences (Polyaen. *Strat.* 4.3.24), a royal Persian dress for Alexander himself (Plut. *Al.* 45.1), Asian ushers introducing Persian court etiquette and a Persian bodyguard, purple cloaks and Persian harnesses for the horses of the Companions (Curt. 6.6.8) and an εἰσαγγελεύς ("announcer"), one of whom was the early Alexander source, Chares of Mytilene. Many of the changes in court etiquette aimed not simply at portraying grandeur, but at formalizing protocol and at limiting access to Alexander, stressing "the mystique and deference surrounding the king."[51] Subsequent court reforms, including the introduction of *proskynesis*, were obviously modelled on the Achaemenid example.

In comparison to the Achaemenid court, then, Alexander's court was more personal and egalitarian, with freer and more informal access to the king for the high-ranking nobles. The monarch was less institutionalized, and the king's claim to power was less absolute, depending on asserting kingly virtues through action and military success. The physical space of the Argead court was also less developed, as was the concomitant court ceremonial. This would

---

48 Sawada (2010) 406–408 and bibliographical essay 408. Significantly, in an anecdote about the young Alexander interviewing Persian envoys, he asks questions about the infrastructure of the Persian empire, the warrior skills of the king, and the courage and power (ἀλκὴ καὶ δύναμις) of the Persians; Plut. *Alex.* 5.
49 Among these were the introduction of the royal pages as court attendants and a special *thronos* for public occasions; cf. Spawforth (2007) 91, nn. 24 and 25 for source references.
50 Spawforth (2007) 91–93.
51 Spawforth (2007) 93–94

have applied to the moving courts of both groups as well, as reflected in an anecdote on Alexander's reaction to Darius' luxurious tent after the battle of Issus: "This, it seems, is what being a king is like" (Plut. *Alex.* 20).

(iii) The chain of events

Alexander's most thorough encounter with Persian court procedures and ideology must have occurred during the unexpectedly and intriguingly long stay in Persepolis. The Macedonians claimed Babylon some three weeks after Gaugamela, and Susa probably in December of 331 BC. They defeated the resistance at the Persian Gates mid-January and arrived at Persepolis by the end of that month, to leave again for Media, where Darius had dug in at the remaining royal city of Ecbatana, only some 120 days later.[52] Indications are that Alexander's position after Gaugamela was not as secure in his victory as the claimed title "King of Asia" intended to portray, and the entitlements and accessions of Darius' throne seem at least partly to have been directed at the Greeks and Macedonians back home:[53] Persian succession ideology would not allow accession to the throne of the "King of kings" while the incumbent king was still alive. Significantly, Arrian (3.19.4) reports that Darius readied himself to fight it out again with replenished forces (which in the end did not materialize), and Alexander had to subdue the Paraetacae during the twelve days it took them to reach Media.

Thus, when Alexander left Susa five months earlier, two things were prominent in his mind. First, that the effort to defeat the current king was not over and—much similar to the detour to Egypt and the south after Issus—he decided to take his time in mustering his resources. Secondly, the major resource depot of the Persian empire, namely the treasury in Persepolis, was largely unprotected; whoever got there first could claim the spoils.[54] When he did not go straight up north after Darius but through the south exit of Susa hurried to Persa, the Macedonian had loot in mind. And so did his soldiers, presumably after promises along such lines by their commanders. The extraction of the loot must have

---

[52] Curt.5.6.12 mentions a 30 day campaign during this time "to reconnoiter the surrounding countryside", Borza (1972) 237 and n. 28.
[53] Wirth (1993) 174–190, 223–224; see also Borza (1972) 243; Fredricksmeyer (2000). Plutarch's anecdote of Demaratus seeing Alexander on Darius' throne, which he sets in Persepolis (*Alex.* 37) should probably be in Susa (Diod. 17.66.3; Curt. 5.2.13).
[54] Diodorus' (17.69) report of a letter from the κυριεύων of Persepolis, Tiridates, that basically invited him in, explains the lack of local resistance on entry, though, like with Egypt, says little about local sentiment against the conquerors.

taken a considerable time: Diodorus (17.71) mentions that vast numbers of mules, other pack and harness animals and three thousand pack camels were brought from Susa (ca. 800 km), Babylon (ca. 1100 km) and Mesopotamia to Persepolis to carry most of the booty for safekeeping in Susa, an extraction operation that could have lasted the full duration of the Macedonian stay.

As the Macedonian elite settled around and into the palaces of Persepolis, they came into close contact with a court culture that would have been familiar in some respects, but quite alien in others. It differed from their own ideology of an informal court promoting an egalitarian ethos among members of the elite in communal settings, with ease of access to the *primus inter pares*. The Achaemenid court was older, more established, and far more ritualized. The divide between the two conceptions of court may have been aggravated by the fact that the Great King was not dead, so no formal accession ceremony could be performed yet. Alexander and his inner circles of nobles may have felt pressure from the local establishment to conform to customs foreign to them, in particular different sets of rules of access to the king. Resistance to the Macedonian ways of conducting court procedures, and perhaps even contempt among members of the inner court may have triggered the "bitter enmity" and "distrust" that Alexander in the Cleitarchan report held towards the people of Persis.

After the Macedonians stripped the palace terrace of its valuables, an impressive but hollow shell remained. Emptied of what gave the space its dignity, the Persepolis palaces lost much of their *raison d'etre* to the Persian inner court as well. Something of this rejection remained in the Arrian version where Alexander remained unpersuaded by the fact that the palace was now his "possession," and by the idea (uttered by Parmenio) that he should send the message that he was there to stay. The Cleitarchan version similarly contains an element of rejection, in this case of decorum and court etiquette which the Greeks liked to associate with the coarse Macedonian court.[55] The scene is a typically rowdy Macedonian symposium, with the king very much in the thick of things. For the Macedonians this was part and parcel of the way politics was conducted, the arena of raising contentious issues. During the discussion a courtesan spoke—completely out of line from an Achaemenid court perspective. The content of her speech would even for the Greeks have been of less importance than the fact that her counsel—radical as it was—was accepted and implemented with immediate effect.

The message that Alexander ripped out the institutional heart of the Persian empire would have had various reverberations: for the Macedonian soldiers, it

---

55 Pownall (2010) 55–62.

was a sign that the campaign was coming to a close; for the Persian nobility, it marked the end of an era; for the Macedonian elite, it served as reassurance of their relationship with Alexander in the new dispensation.

How does an initial rejection of the Achaemenid conception of court tally with its implementation shortly afterwards? The traditions of regret, or rather of "coming to think differently" that the sources retained as Alexander's reaction,[56] were perhaps partly apologetic, but at least partly they express Alexander's reconsideration of his future role as king of Asia. His second thoughts about the destruction of τὰ βασιλεία (the royal palaces) were not merely about the physical buildings, but also about the court they represented. He soon started his program to rectify this error of judgement.

Conclusion

While both Achaemenid and Argead courts relied on ostentation and conspicuous consumption, the Persian court did so on a much grander scale, even when on the move. In contrast to the established and formalized sophistication of the Achaemenid court ceremonial and etiquette, the Macedonian court functioned more informally, with the king essentially a *primus inter pares*. Ideologies surrounding the monarch also differed: like other ancient West Asian empires, the Achaemenid court implemented various mechanisms to limit access to the king as a way to institutionalize the monarchy and maintain the hierarchies of power in its empire. The Macedonian king, on the other hand, had to continually reassert his authority by way of displays of personal prowess and virtue. The prolonged close encounter of the two courts would have highlighted their contrasting ideologies and styles. With the Persepolis palaces inextricably tied to the Achaemenid court, their destruction was simultaneously a rejection of the court they held and a gesture to the Macedonian nobles that their relationship with Alexander was not in jeopardy. But the ancient sources go on to report that Alexander soon had a μετάνοια ("change of mind", "regret") which applied not only to the physical destruction, and he soon started to implement various

---

56 While the fires were still burning in Plut. *Alex*. 38 (ὅτι δ' οὖν μετενόησε ταχὺ καὶ κατασβέσαι προσέταξεν ὁμολογεῖται, "they agree that he changed his mind quickly and ordered to extinguish the fire"); when Alexander sobered up in Curt. 5.7.10–11 (*ipsum, ut primum gravato ebrietate mentem quies reddidit, paenituisse constat*, "it is certain that Alexander regretted what he had done as soon as sleep restored his senses after getting drunk") and on a subsequent visit to the site in Arr. *Anab*. 6.30 (οὐδ' αὐτὸς Ἀλέξανδρος ἐπανελθὼν ἐπῄνει, "Alexander himself did not condone it when he went back").

court practices by which to narrow the gap between the two conceptions of court.

Bibliography

Badian (1967): Ernst Badian, "Agis III", in: *Hermes* 95.2, 170–192.
Balcer (1978): Jack M. Balcer, "Alexander's burning of Persepolis", in: *Iranica Antiqua* 13, 119–133.
Bloedow and Loube (1997): Edmund F. Bloedow and Heather M. Loube, "Alexander the Great 'under fire' at Persepolis". *Klio* 79.2, 341–353.
Borza (1972): Eugene N. Borza, "Fire from Heaven: Alexander at Persepolis", in: *Classical Philology* 67.4, 233–245.
Bosworth (1988): A. Brian Bosworth, *Conquest and Empire: The Reign of Alexander the Great*, Cambridge.
Briant (2002): Pierre Briant, *From Cyrus to Alexander: A History of the Persian Empire*, Winona Lake, Indiana.
Briant (2010): Pierre Briant, *Alexander the Great and His Empire: A Short Introduction*, Princeton.
Brosius (2003): Maria Brosius, "Alexander and the Persians", in: Joseph Roisman (ed.), *Brill's Companion to Alexander the Great*, 169–193, Leiden and Boston.
Brosius (2007): Maria Brosius, "New out of old? Court and court ceremonies in Achaemenid Persia", in: Anthony J.S. Spawforth (ed.), *The Court and Court Society in Ancient Monarchies*, 82–120, Cambridge.
Butz and Dannenberg (2004): Reinhard Butz and Lars-Arne Dannenberg, "Theoriebildungen des Hofes", in: Reinhard Butz, Jan Hirschbiegel, and Dietmar Willoweit (eds.), *Hof und Theorie: Annäherungen an ein historisches Phänomen*, 1–41, Cologne, Weimar and Vienna.
Carney (2010): Elizabeth D. Carney, "Putting Women in their Place: Women in Public under Philip II and Alexander III and the last Argeads", in: Elizabeth D. Carney and Daniel Ogden (eds.), *Philip II and Alexander the Great: Father and Son, Lives and Afterlives*, Oxford, 43–53.
Colburn (2013): H.P. Colburn, "Connectivity and Communication in the Achaemenid Empire", in: *Journal of the Economic and Social History of the Orient* 56, 29–52.
Dreyer (2009): Boris Dreyer, "Jeder hat Alexander-Bild, das er verdient: The Changing Perceptions of Alexander in Ancient Historiography", in: Pat Wheatley and Robert Hannah (eds.), *Alexander & his Successors. Essays from the Antipodes*, 56–71, Claremont.
Elias (1983): Norbert Elias, *The Court Society*, Oxford.
Fredricksmeyer (2000): Ernst Fredricksmeyer, "Alexander the Great and the Kingship of Asia", in: A. Brian Bosworth and Elizabeth J. Baynham (eds.), *Alexander the Great in Fact and Fiction*, 136–166, Oxford.
Gehrke (1996): Hans-Joachim Gehrke, *Alexander der Grosse*, Munich.
Hammond (1992): Nicholas G.L. Hammond, "The Archaeological and Literary Evidence for the Burning of the Persepolis Palace", in: *The Classical Quarterly* 42.2, 358–364.

Heckel (2006): W. Heckel, *Who's Who in the Age of Alexander the Great. Prosopography of Alexander's Empire,* Malden/Oxford/Victoria.

King (2010): Carol J. King, "Macedonian Kingship and Other Political Institutions," in: Joseph Roisman and Ian Worthington (eds.), *A Companion to Ancient Macedonia,* Malden, MA and Oxford, 373–91.

Lehmann (2015): Gustav Adolph Lehmann, *Alexander der Große und die "Freiheit der Hellenen". Studien zu der antiken historiographischen Überlieferung und den Inschriften der Alexander-Ära,* Berlin/Munich/Boston.

McAuley (2018): Alex McAuley, "The Great Misstep: Aleander the Great, Thais, and the Destruction of Persepolis", in: Ken R. Moore (ed.), *Brill's Companion to the Reception of Alexander the Great,* Leiden, 717–738.

Mousavi (2012): Ali Mousavi, *Persepolis: Discovery and Afterlife of a World Wonder,* Berlin/Munich/Boston.

Müller (2014): Sabine Müller, *Alexander, Makedonien and Persien,* Berlin.

Müller (2019): Sabine Müller, *Alexander der Große. Eroberung—Politik—Rezeption,* Berlin.

Naiden (2019): Fred S. Naiden, *Soldier, Priest, and God: A Life of Alexander the Great,* Oxford.

Nawotka (2003): Krzysztof Nawotka, "Alexander the Great in Persepolis", in: *Acta Antiqua* 43.1–2, 67–76.

Palagia (2017): Olga Palagia, "The Royal Court in Ancient Macedonia: The Evidence for Royal Tombs", in: Andrew Erskine, Lloyd Llewellyn-Jones and Shane Wallace, *The Hellenistic Court: Monarchic Power and Elite Society from Alexander to Cleopatra,* Swansea, 409–432.

Pownall (2010): Frances Pownall, "The Symposia of Philip II and Alexander III of Macedon: The View from Greece", in: Elizabeth D. Carney and Daniel Ogden (eds.), *Philip II and Alexander the Great: Father and Son, Lives and Afterlives,* Oxford, 55–65.

Sancisi-Weerdenburg (1993): Heleen Sancisi-Weerdenburg, "Alexander and Persepolis", in: *Analecta Romana institute Danici, Supplementum* 20, 177–188.

Sawada (2010): Noriko Sawada, "Social Customs and Institutions: Aspects of Macedonian Elite Society," in: Joseph Roisman and Ian Worthington (eds.), *A Companion to Ancient Macedonia,* Malden, MA and Oxford, 392–408.

Schmidt (1953): Erich F. Schmidt, *Persepolis* Vols. 1–3, Chicago.

Seibert (2004/2005): Jakob Seibert, "Alexander der Große in Persepolis (Takht-e Jamšīd)", in: *Iranistik* 3.2, 5–105.

Spawforth (2007): Anthony J.S. Spawforth, "The Court of Alexander the Great between Europe and Asia", in: Anthony J.S. Spawforth (ed.), *The Court and Court Society in Ancient Monarchies,* Cambridge, 82–120.

Strootman (2007): Rolf Strootman, *The Hellenistic Royal Court. Court Culture, Ceremonial and Ideology in Greece, Egypt and the Near East, 336–30 BCE,* PhD thesis, University of Utrecht.

Strootman (2014): Rolf Strootman, *Courts and Elites in the Hellenistic Empires: The Near East After the Achaemenids, c. 330 to 30 BCE,* Edinburgh.

Wheeler (1968): Mortimer Wheeler, *Flames over Persepolis,* London.

Wirth (1993): Gerhard Wirth, *Der Brand von Persepolis. Folgerungen zur Geschichte Alexanders des Großen,* Amsterdam.

Zahrnt (2006): Michael Zahrnt, "Von Siwa bis Persepolis. Überlegungen zur Arbeitsweise des Kallisthenes", in: *Ancient Society* 36, 143–174.

Rolf Strootman
Pothos or Propaganda? Alexander's Longing to Reach the Ocean and Argead Imperial Ideology

According to Arrian, the main trait of Alexander III's personality was his *pothos*, his being possessed by an indomitable yearning to surpass his predecessors and to go where no one had gone before. This specifically concerned his longing to reach the Ocean beyond India—the very limit of the known world. Modern historians have interpreted *pothos* as an actual trait of the king's personal psychology or dismissed it as a later, Roman-era invention or topos. In this paper I will take a different approach and reconsider *pothos* in the light of the royal and imperial ideology of Alexander's own time. On this view, I believe *pothos* to be historical, even though the notion of Alexander's longing for the Ocean probably was not yet called *pothos* at that time.[1] The word and concept *pothos* was Arrian's rendering of genuine Hellenistic imperial cosmography.

I argue that what was later presented as Alexander's personal *pothos* originally was an expression of universalistic ideology, such as it developed at Alexander's court in the wake of Argead military success.[2] Although it can be shown that Arrian's formula πόθος ἔλαβεν αὐτὸν (*Anab.* 1.3.5) is used also in other Greek history writing since the time of Herodotos,[3] the repeated reference to Alexander's insatiability and his eagerness to reach the world's end—present in all the Alexander tradition, including the Alexander romances—prevents us from disqualifying Arrian's use of *pothos* as merely a literary convention.[4]

---

[1] This contribution is based on a Dutch-language article published in *Groniek* (Strootman [2010a]); an expanded version of the argument appeared in 2013, also in incomprehensible Dutch. I would like to thank Frances Pownall for inviting me to Edmonton and giving me the opportunity to present these thoughts to an audience of acclaimed Alexander scholars. The present article has benefited much from discussions at the conference.
[2] See Arr. *Ind.* 20.2, citing Nearchos on Alexander's ἐπιθυμία ("desire," "yearning") "to always do something new and extraordinary"; cf. Arr. *Anab.* 5.25.2. Curtius independently from Arrian speaks of Alexander's *ingens cupido*, probably another representation of the longing that Arrian calls *pothos* (the mythological figure Pothos in Greek thought was one of the Erotes, see below; cf. Curt. 4.7.8, cf. 4.8.3; 7.11.4); cf. Montgomery (1965) 208–210.
[3] See Montgomery (1965).
[4] But allow me to repeat that I *do not* endorse the view expressed by Ehrenberg that Alexander himself used the term; what I am saying, is that expressions of world conquest in Argead ideology later became his *pothos*.

https://doi.org/10.1515/9783110622942-011

Universalistic imperial ideology was common in the eastern Mediterranean and Near East at the time of the Argead expansion into these regions; in a well-established and widespread tradition, the desire to reach the edges of the known world, in particular the Ocean encircling the world, was embodied by the king, who was expected to achieve that aim either ritually or actually (and preferably both).[5] Universalism was an important ideological tool to create cohesion within empires characterized by internal cultural and political diversity. The idea that the world was, or should be, a political unity under a single king was central to the ideologies of both Alexander's predecessors, the Achaemenids, and his successors, the Seleucids and Ptolemies. Roman leaders of the Late Republic later introduced in the western Mediterranean a "Romanized" version of an already "Hellenized" universalistic ideology. In the Roman Empire, however, historians associated the idea of world empire with Alexander, whose imperial ideology offered a more acceptable model for the Roman *imperium sine fine* than the Achaemenid, Seleucid, or Ptolemaic rulers.[6] It does not follow, however, that Roman-era notions of world rule were simply projected upon Alexander. Like Alexander and his successors, Augustus and his successors stood in an age-old tradition of universal empire, but covered up their tracks.[7] This may account for "the lack of knowledge (or deliberate misrepresentation) among ancient Greek and Roman sources about Achaemenid traditions regarding boundaries."[8]

Alexander's *Pothos*

In ancient Greek thought, Pothos was the personification of passionate longing. Nonnus wrote in the fifth century CE that Pothos was the son of Zephyrus (the west wind) and Iris (the rainbow);[9] in Classical art, he was often depicted

---

[5] On the Near Eastern notion of the Ocean as an imperial boundary see Miltner (1952); Haubold (2012); Rollinger (2020). Also see Kosmin (2014) 59–76, on the significance of the Ocean in Seleucid imperial ideology.
[6] See Bichler (2016).
[7] On the other hand, the notion of *translatio imperii* was of course present in several Hellenistic and Roman historians, e.g., in Diodorus, Trogus/Justin, and Velleius Paterculus; see Van Wickevoort Crommelin (1993) 223–227; Stronk (2016) 535; Hofmann (2018) 165–222; Gotter (2019). In this outline of history, however, the present empire is normally presented as the last, eternal one in an almost eschatological manner; this was a pivotal aspect of Hellenistic imperial ideologies, see Hazzard (2000); Strootman (2014a); Kosmin (2018).
[8] Howe/Müller (2012) 38.
[9] Nonnus, *Dion.* 31.110–111; 47.341–342.

with Eros and Himeros as one of the winged Erotes. Himeros, too, personified desire; Plato explains the difference between Himeros and Pothos by saying that "the word *pothos* signifies that it pertains not to that which is present, but to that which is elsewhere or gone, and therefore the same feeling which is called *himeros* when its object is present, is called *pothos* when it is absent."[10] So Himeros and Pothos represented respectively longing to what was at hand and what was out of reach or unknown. They were figures of the artistic and poetic imagination, however, with no mythology or religious cult of their own.

It was Arrian who in the second century CE introduced *pothos* as an outstanding aspect of Alexander's personality. The theme of Alexander's insatiability is omnipresent in the *Anabasis*; Alexander is described e.g., as "zealous for honor" and "insatiable of glory alone".[11] This can only partly be understood from Arrian's ambition to create "a new Alexander" for audiences in his own time.[12] Arrian did not invent the notion of an urge to reach the Ocean and other ideas associated with Alexander's *pothos*; all that Arrian did, was to present these in fact commonplace ideas as a character trait unique to Alexander, using the word *pothos*.

In the *Anabasis*, Alexander's *pothos* first appears in the context of the Argead campaign in the Balkans in 335: when Alexander had reached the banks of the Ister (Danube), Arrian writes that "he was suddenly seized with a longing (πόθος) to go beyond the river," which indeed he did.[13] After driving off the opposing barbarians (the Getai, a Thracian people) altars were built to bring thank offerings to Zeus Soter and Heracles.[14]

The term reoccurs several times in the *Anabasis*, typically in the contexts of the symbolic borders of Alexander's empire, especially the Ocean. With regards to the Caspian Sea, Alexander famously longed to prove that this sea was indeed a gulf of the encircling Ocean:

> He was seized by a longing (*pothos*) to discover what other sea is joined by this sea, called both Caspian and Hyrcanian, whether it joins the Euxine [Black Sea], or whether on the east side towards India the great sea circling round pours into a gulf, the Hyrcanian, just as he

---

10 Pl. *Cra.* 419e–420b; transl. Lamb.
11 Arr. *Anab.* 28.2. On the close association of *pothos* with *aretē* and *philotimia*, see Goukowsky (1978) 173–174.
12 Arrian's literary aspirations and his wish to create a "new" Alexander are highlighted by Burliga (2014); on the *Anabasis* as a literary work, see now also Liotsakis (2019).
13 Arr. *Anab.* 1.3.5.
14 Arr. *Anab.* 1.4.1–5.

had discovered the Persian Sea or, to use its actual name, the Red Sea, to be only a gulf of the Ocean.[15]

The significance of the Ocean as the ultimate boundary of Alexander's imagined empire is well known, although Alexander's longing for it is rarely understood as a borrowing from previous imperial ideologies.[16] It is associated above all with India. In a speech delivered at the Hyphasis (Beas)—the farthest extent of the actual Macedonian campaign in India—Arrian has Alexander say the following:

> If anyone longs to hear what will be the limit of the actual fighting, he should understand that there remains no great stretch of land before us up the river Ganges and the eastern sea. This sea, I assure you, will prove to be joined to the Hyrcanian Sea; for the Great Sea encircles all the land. And it will be for me to show Macedonians and allies alike that the Indian gulf [Arabian Sea] forms but one stretch of water with the Persian Gulf. From the Persian Gulf our fleet shall sail round Libya, and as far as the Pillars of Heracles; from the Pillars all the interior of Libya then becomes ours, just as Asia is in fact becoming ours in its entirety, and the boundaries of empire (*archē*) here are becoming those which God set for the whole continent.[17]

Both Arrian and Curtius refer to Heracles and Dionysus, the figures Alexander allegedly wanted to emulate and surpass.[18] Of course, these words are not what Alexander actually said; but they may nonetheless represent Argead ideology created after the campaigns in Bactria, Sogdia, and India. It is at any rate hardly credible that the stories about Heracles' exploits in these regions predated the campaigns of Alexander. While the references to Dionysus may go back to a Ptolemaic invention, the centrality of Heracles seems to have been genuinely Argead.[19] As a "culture hero," Heracles provided a model for imperial expansion. Like his descendant Alexander, he had been a prolific builder of altars, an act that announced the defeat of chaos and the introduction of civilization in Greek mythology.

The final empire-related mentioning of *pothos* relates to Babylonia, where Alexander was possessed by a *pothos* to sail down the Euphrates and Tigris to the Persian Gulf.[20] He aimed, Arrian writes at the beginning of Book 7, to see how these two rivers indirectly gave access to the Ocean, and were thus connect-

---

15 Arr. *Anab.* 7.16.2; transl. Brunt.
16 For this interpretation, see Howe/Müller (2012); cf. Strootman (2014b).
17 Arr. *Anab.* 5.26.1–2; transl. Brunt.
18 Arr. *Anab.* 5.26.5; Curt. 9.2.29.
19 Heckel (2015).
20 Arr. *Anab.* 7.1.1.

ed to the mouth of the Indus. That of course was known since millennia, also Alexander and his courtiers knew this well. Immediately after this passage, Arrian adds that Alexander wanted to use the several supposed inlets of the Ocean that he controlled to sail around Asia and Africa to demarcate the extent of his world empire and claim control of both continents:

> Some have also recorded that Alexander was planning to sail round Arabia, Ethiopia, Libya and the Nomads beyond Mount Atlas, Gadeira [Cadiz] and into our sea [the Mediterranean, Rome's *Mare Nostrum*] and, after subduing Libya and Carthage, finally to earn the title of king of all Asia; as for the Persian and Median kings, in his view they had not ruled even a fraction of Asia, and so had no right to call themselves Great Kings.[21]

With a totally anachronistic reference to the Roman Empire, Arrian then claims that Alexander may have aimed at conquering Europe, too:

> Thereafter, in some accounts, he planned to sail into the Euxine [Black Sea] to Scythia and Lake Maiotis [Sea of Azov], in others to make for Sicily [...] as he was already rather disturbed that Rome's fame was advancing to a great height.[22]

These two passages from the opening of Book 7 repeat more extensively Arrian's earlier remark that Alexander planned to conquer Asia, Africa, and Europe, and to sail round these continents.[23] They are followed by the much-discussed passage on Alexander's final aims; though the word *pothos* is not mentioned, it reads almost as a definition of it:

> Although I might not dare to guess what thoughts exactly went on in Alexander's head, I think I can safely say [...] that he would never have been satisfied with whatever he might have conquered, even if he had extended his empire from Asia to Europe and from Europe to the British Isles. He would certainly have gone even further, looking for unknown lands beyond them, and would have competed with himself if not other rival was left.[24]

Arrian refers three more times to Alexander's *pothos* in the context of imperial conquest; these references are all set in India. First, his longing to surpass Heracles by seizing the rock Aornus, which according to a legend (presumably constructed or manipulated at the Argead court) Heracles had failed to capture.[25]

---

21 Arr. *Anab*. 7.1.2–3; transl. Brunt.
22 *Ibid*.
23 Arr. *Anab*. 4.7.5.
24 Arr. *Anab*. 7.1.4; translation adapted from Brunt. On the symbolic significance of Britain in Roman imperial cosmology, see Gambash (2016).
25 *Anab*. 4.28.4. On the possible "Near Eastern" antecedents of the image of the "birdless rock" Aornus (Plut. *De Alex. fort*. 1.3 = *Mor*. 327c), see Rollinger (2014).

Second, his longing to see the place in India where allegedly "certain memorials" of Dionysus were displayed.²⁶ Third, his wish that one of the Indian sophists should accompany him—a remark that with some caution can be understood from the typical imperial urge to accumulate at the imperial center marvelous persons, fauna and things from the presumed periphery of the world, to make the court, or the capital, into a symbolic center were the world converges.²⁷

Pothos and the Ideology of Empire

Modern historians often take Alexander's pothic personality for granted. Victor Ehrenberg not only understood *pothos* as an almost mystical form of inspiration—which in fact it is, though demonic possession would perhaps be a better description—but also that Alexander's yearning after the unknown was the main driving force of his career.²⁸ William Woodthorpe Tarn believed that the "ecumenical" ideal of later Christianity through Stoicism and Roman imperial ideology originated with the genius of Alexander the Great, specifically his allegedly revolutionary dream of a "Unity of Mankind."²⁹ As I have argued elsewhere, Tarn was not wrong to recognize in Alexander's self-presentation the expressed aim of uniting the whole of mankind within a single, peaceful world empire—he was mistaken only in his conviction that this was exceptional and innovative. The idea in fact was common in the ideologies of Near Eastern empires, including Alexander's, and would remain the foundation of the ideologies of subsequent universalistic empires of the Ancient World, including the Seleucid, Ptolemaic, Roman, Sasanian, and Umayyad empires.³⁰ Imperial polities almost as a rule

---

26 *Anab.* 7.2.2.
27 *Anab.* 5.2.5; compare e. g., Persepolis as a *palais des nations* (Root [1979]), where also animals and material tribute were kept and displayed (see Llewellyn-Jones [2017]); or the display at the Grand Procession of Ptolemy II Philadelphus at Alexandria of people, animals and objects from India, Ethiopia and elsewhere (Kallixeinos of Rhodes *BNJ* 627 F 2 *ap*. Athenaios 5.196–203; cf. Strootman [2014d] 254–261). A last mention of *pothos* (3.1.5) concerns Alexander's "longing" to begin the building of Alexandria-by-Egypt, a statement that likely stems from Ptolemaic, not Argead propaganda (on Ptolemaic uses of the memory of Alexander in the foundation myths of Alexandria, see Howe [2014]).
28 Ehrenberg (1965). Not many scholars today would still endorse this view, though the belief that Alexander was driven by a personal motivation to reach the outer Ocean pervades many textbooks; for a list of examples, see Anson (2009) 983.
29 Tarn (1933), cf. Tarn (1948).
30 Strootman (forthcoming); *pace* Badian (1958). On Tarn's Alexander image and its influence on later scholarship, see Bichler (2018) 656–660.

claim to create worldwide peace. To be sure, the false belief that empire exists for the benefit of mankind was not unknown in Tarn's own Britain either.

Closer to Alexander's own lifetime was the common presentation of Achaemenid imperial rule as both universal and peaceful. One only has to think of the art and architecture of Persepolis to see how central the idea of a Unity of Mankind was to Achaemenid imperial ideology; the reliefs on the ceremonial staircases of the Great Apadana abundantly show how the peoples of the earth—out of their own free will and wearing their best dresses—solemnly climb up the stairs to present gifts to the one who sits enthroned in his great hall. Harmony is the key sentiment expressed by the Apadana reliefs.[31] The image of the Persian king as the creator and protector of peace meanwhile was also disseminated empire-wide through seal images showing him in the act of slaying barbarians and beasts.[32]

The Symbolic Attainment of the World Border

The ideology of worldwide conquest has deep roots in the Ancient World, going back to the third millennium. In the first millennium BCE, the ideal of conquest as far as the earth's edge had become a core element in the public image of Assyrian, Babylonian, and Persian kings.[33] For the kings of the Neo-Assyrian Empire, the expansion of the empire's territory through conquest was a divinely ordained duty.[34]

Mesopotamian royal propaganda divided the world in two: a peaceful, civilized core governed by the true king was surrounded by a barbaric periphery populated by dangerous barbarians who posed a constant threat.[35] In this simple scheme, the monarch played a pivotal role as the protector of a divinely ordained Order. Because the "true" king enjoyed the support of the gods, he was always victorious. The theme of world conquest was further expressed by monarchical titles such as Great King, King of All, King of the Four Regions, King of the Lands, or King of the Peoples. In addition to the prestige it generated, claiming world dominion had a very practical function: it was a powerful tool to create a

---

31 See Root (1979).
32 On the pervasiveness of war and peace in Achaemenid imperial ideology, see Tuplin (2017).
33 Liverani (2001) 23–28; Galter (2014); Rollinger (2020).
34 Tadmor (2011).
35 Liverani (2001) 17–22.

sense of unity in empires characterized by their internal cultural, linguistic, and political diversity.[36]

The opposition between a freedom-loving Greece and a despotic Near East, needless to say, is a modern invention.[37] The Greek world had been integrated into a wider Achaemenid world since c. 500 BCE, and Greeks and Macedonians were well-acquainted with this type of ideology. The Argeads participated in a West Achaemenid *koine* of interconnected royal and satrapal courts, a pan-Aegean system of elite interaction and exchange.[38] It is no surprise that the Argeads, too, would adopt such an ideology after the conquest of the Achaemenid Empire—a stance that not only was expected from imperial leaders but had proven its worth as an instrument of imperial integration. Universalistic ideology would continue under Alexander's successors, in particular the Seleucids and Ptolemies.[39]

The key to understanding Alexander's *pothos* is his construction of altars, and his sacrificing upon them, to demarcate the extent of his dominion. He did so at the Ister/Danube, Jaxartes/Syr Darya, and Hyphasis/Beas—rivers that could be seen as the symbolic borders of the civilized world. Pliny mentions "Altars of Alexander" on a promontory along the coast of Carmania, near a new settlement he calls Portus Macedonum.[40] The precise location is unknown. Boucharlat and Salles suggest the altars were established on the Iranian side of the Strait of Hormuz, the narrow channel between the Persian Gulf and the Ocean.[41] Eggermont identified the Altars of Alexander with the altars for Tethys and Oceanus that according to Diodorus were built on an island in the Indian Ocean in the Summer of 325:

> [Alexander] resumed his voyage down the river (Indus) and sailed out into the Ocean with his Friends. There he discovered two islands and on them performed rich sacrifices. He threw many large cups of gold into the sea following the libations which he poured from

---

[36] For this function of imperial universalism, see Strootman (2010b); Bang (2011). On ancient imperial universalism in general, see Bang/Kołodziejczyk (2012); Strootman (2014a); Lavan/Payne/Weisweiler (2016); Bichler/Rollinger (2017); Rollinger (2020).
[37] See Van Dongen (2014); cf. Rollinger/Luther/ Wiesehöfer (2007).
[38] On this West-Achaemenid *koine* and its visibility in Aegean dynastic art and iconography, see *i.a.* Dusinberre (2003); Kaptan (2013), and most recently the excellent study by Poggio (2020); for the Argeads' participation in it, see Howe/Müller (2012) 26–27, and most recently Müller (2021).
[39] On the adoption of universalistic ideology by Alexander's successors, see Strootman (2014b) and (2014c).
[40] Plin. *NH* 6.28.
[41] Boucharlat/Salles (1981) 67–68.

them. He erected altars to Tethys and Oceanus and judged that his projected campaign was at an end.[42]

Plutarch mentions only one island opposite the mouth of the Indus; he writes that on that island,

> [Alexander] sacrificed to the gods, and studied the nature of the sea and of all the sea-coast that was accessible. Then, after praying that no man after him might pass beyond the bounds of his expedition, he turned to go back.[43]

These passages, too, strongly suggest an image of the Ocean as an imperial boundary, rather than a personal longing on the part of Alexander.

The construction of monuments and other memorials at the world's periphery has a long tradition in western Eurasia. Assyrian, Babylonian, and Persian kings regularly undertook campaigns of imperial expansion to the supposed peripheries of the earth; these campaigns were motivated by a mixture of military, economic, and political considerations, but also had a profound ritual significance.[44] Mario Liverani has called this "the symbolic attainment of the world border."[45] The extension of the frontier was marked by the erection of steles, statues and, altars—in the mountains, on the edge of desolate deserts, on riverbanks, on the shores of the High and Low Seas (sc. the Mediterranean and the Persian Gulf, both inlets of the world-encircling Ocean)—and the performance of rituals, such as sacrificing to the gods or the ritually cleaning of the king's weapons in the Ocean's water.[46] The latter ritual clearly was not only intended to demarcate conquests but also to stress that universal peace had been estab-

---

42 Diod. 17.104.1, cf. Curt. 9.9.27; Just. 12.10.4; Eggermont (1975) 37–41, 134–137. According to Arr. *Anab*. 6.19.3–4, one island was in the Indus, the other just outside of it; before marching to coast, Alexander poured a libation into the Hydaspes and offered the gold libation *phiale* to the river god; he moreover called upon the rivers Acesines and Indus, and made offerings "to his ancestor Heracles and Ammon and all the other gods" (*Anab*. 6.3.2); on these sacrifices, see Bucciantini (2009), emphasizing their "multicultural" imperial nature. Compare Hdt. 7.54.2, where Xerxes pours a libation into the Hellespont, and afterwards deposits in the water the libation *phiale*, a golden bowl, and a Persian sword (*akinakes*); on these offerings and their imperial connotations, see Rollinger (2013b) 102–107.
43 Plut., *Alex*. 66.1; transl. Perrin.
44 Rivaroli (2015); Melville (2016).
45 Liverani (2001) 34–37, cf. id. (1979).
46 Several examples of the performance of this ritual by Babylonian and Assyrian kings are discussed by Rollinger (2012) 725–730.

lished. The construction of steles announcing the conquest of the world often were part of this form of symbolic attainment of the world border.[47]

Alexander and Three Rivers

At the Danube, where *pothos* first manifested itself, Alexander's longing to *cross* that river (which indeed he did) is significant. The crossing of rivers belonged to the imagery of world conquest in pre-Hellenistic Afro-Eurasia.[48] Crossing a river, or even attempting to cross it, "would have been sufficient to propagate the accomplishment of a mission", as Timothy Howe and Sabine Müller stated in the context of Alexander's withdrawal from the Hyphasis (see below).[49]

Arrian describes the Danube in terms that strongly suggest a boundary between civilization and barbarity (and he may have been thinking of the river's function as symbolic border of the Roman Empire as well): "the Ister [is] the greatest river of Europe, [...] a barrier to the most warlike tribes."[50] The Danube had also been a symbolic frontier of the Achaemenid Empire.[51] In ca. 513 BCE, Darius I erected steles there before crossing the river and attacking the "nomadic" Scythians.[52]

The difficult crossing that Alexander longed for was indeed made by him and part of the army, using boats; the opposing barbarians "fled into uninhabited country, as far from the river as they could go."[53] As we already saw, Alexander then sacrificed on the banks of the Danube to Zeus Soter and Heracles.[54] The latter probably not only appears here as Alexander's ancestor, but also in his capacity of a culture hero who fights "Chaos" and spreads order and civilization to the edges of the earth. After crossing back, envoys of a number of barbaric tribes visited the Macedonian camp to make peace with Alexander.[55] Note that the altars that Alexander built were not safely on the river's south

---

47 On the construction of monuments at the periphery, see Liverani (1979); Shafer (1998); Rollinger (2012); Bichler/Rollinger (2017).
48 Lang/Rollinger (2010). Rollinger (2013a), a book-length study of Alexander's river crossings, was unfortunately not available to me while writing this chapter.
49 Howe/Müller (2012) 31.
50 *Anab.* 1.3.1.
51 Deinon *BNJ* 690 F 23b *ap.* Plut., *Alex.* 36.4; cf. Kuhrt (2007), 203; Müller (2014).
52 Hdt. 4.89–91.
53 *Anab.* 1.4.1–4.
54 *Anab.* 1.4.5.
55 *Anab.* 1.4.6.

side, but were located, from the Macedonian perspective, *across* the river, in Getae territory; I will return to that remarkable fact at the end of this section.

In 329 BCE the Macedonian army was at the Syr Darya in Sogdia, the ancient river Jaxartes. Arrian calls this river Tanais (today's Don), presenting it as a boundary running all the way from the Pamir Mountains to the Black Sea (instead of the Aral Sea).⁵⁶ Beyond that river was the steppe inhabited by the "Scythians," the generic Greek name for nomadic peoples. Being challenged by the Scythians from across the Jaxartes with insults and arrows, Alexander crossed the river with part of his army and put them to flight.⁵⁷ As on the Danube, envoys of the barbarians then came to the Macedonians camp to make peace.⁵⁸ Pliny in his *Natural History* writes about the place where all this took place (and where Alexander founded Alexandreia Eschate ("the Furthest"), perhaps modern Khojend):

> At this spot are the altars which were raised by Hercules and Father Liber (Dionysus), as also by Cyrus, Semiramis, and Alexander; for the expeditions of all these conquerors stopped short at this region, bounded as it is by the river Jaxartes, by the Scythians known as the Silis, and by Alexander and his officers supposed to have been the Tanais. This river was crossed by Demodamas, a general of kings Seleucus and Antiochus. [...] He also consecrated certain altars here to Apollo Didymaeus.⁵⁹

In the context of India, the word that Arrian uses for Alexander's desire to advance beyond the Hyphasis (Beas) is not πόθος but ἐπιθυμία, a word also used in a similar context in the *Indica* of Nearchos, Alexander's Greek admiral,⁶⁰ which strongly suggests that the association of Greek notions of "longing" with imperial ideology indeed originated at the Argead court.

A mutiny of his troops, who refused to go on, prevented Alexander from continuing his march along the Ganges to the "Outer Ocean" in the east, and forced him to return to the west.⁶¹ When this decision had been made,

> [Alexander] divided the army into twelve parts and ordered each to set up an altar as high as the greatest towers [...] as thank-offerings to the gods who had brought him so far as a

---

56 The identification was probably propagated by Alexander's own court, see Plin. *NH* 6.18, cited below.
57 *Anab.* 4.4.
58 *Anab.* 4.5.1.
59 Plin. *NH* 6.18 (16).
60 Cited by Arr. *Ind.* 20.2.
61 See Arr. *Anab.* 5.29.1–2, cf. Plut. *Alex.* 62.7–8; Curt. 9.3.19; Diod. 17.95.1–2.

conqueror, and as memorials of his own exertions. When the altars had been built for him, he performed the customary sacrifices on them and held athletic and equestrian games.[62]

The building of altars at the Hyphasis has been recorded by all the ancient Alexander historians.[63] The twelve altars on the Hyphasis mirror the twelve altars that according to Justin Alexander built on the Hellespont before he invaded Asia.[64] The Hellespont, too had been associated with the Ocean in Achaemenid imperial cosmology, and crossing it (though in the other direction) could be seen as a form of symbolic attainment of the world border.[65]

Philip Spann and Waldemar Heckel have argued that Alexander did not really aim to conquer the whole of India, and that the famous "mutiny" on the Hyphasis may in reality have been staged by Alexander himself to save face.[66] Pierre Briant suggested that Alexander's aim was to conquer "only" the Achaemenid Empire, and that he did not intend to move beyond its boundaries, which in India were the Hyphasis and the Indus.[67]

Briant's suggestion is problematic however because it assumes that the Achaemenid Empire had official borders and that these borders could be rivers. A universal empire however is an empire whose political borders are identical with the borders of the world. There is no evidence that the Achaemenids saw their empire as limited.[68] The ideological value of rivers like the Danube, Jaxartes, Hyphasis, or Indus is that they *symbolized* the edges of the world. Rivers in fact are rarely obstacles. They can be crossed, and normally served as means on transportation rather than as barriers. Timothy Howe and Sabine Müller recently argued that in India Alexander was "not forging his own new path to World's End," but was following Near Eastern tradition in marking the limits of his empire by erecting altars on the banks of the Hyphasis.[69] But if he really was following those traditions, the building must have signaled the completion of world conquest, not the admittance of failure to conquer. Indeed, while Arrian says nothing about the precise location of the altars, Pliny places them on the

---

62 Arr. *Anab.* 5.29.1–2.
63 Diod. 17.95.1–2; Curt. 9.3.19; Plut. *Alex.* 62.7–8; Just. 12.8.16; *Metz Epitome* 69.
64 Just. 1.5.4; Arrian says that offerings were made to Zeus, Athena, and Heracles (*Anab.* 1.11.7).
65 Haubold (2012); Rollinger (2013b).
66 Spann (1999); Heckel (2003). Holt (1982), too, doubts the historicity of the "mutiny." Against this interpretation, and in favor of the mutiny's historicity, see Anson (2015).
67 Briant (2010 [1974]) 37–38.
68 See Rollinger/Degen 2021.
69 Howe/Müller (2012) 23–24.

east bank of the Hyphasis.⁷⁰ The altars that Alexander built on the banks of the Danube, too, were built *across* that river—and indeed that would have been the most effective way of imprinting conquest on the frontier.⁷¹

The lands beyond these rivers needed not to be brought under direct administrative control as they could be imagined as "unhabitable" lands where—not quite as paradoxical as it may seem—the only inhabitants were "barbarians" or "nomads." Launching punitive raids across these rivers to drive off the barbarians sufficed to claim that the lands beyond the pale had been pacified. Both the Getae and the Scythians are said to have retreated to a "desolate land" (ἐρῆμος).⁷² Indeed, in the speech at the Hyphasis, in the passage that enumerates the countries and peoples Alexander had conquered (in a manner reminiscent of Achaemenid imperial rhetoric, e. g. in the Bīsotūn Inscription of Darius I), Arrian has Alexander boast to have subdued, "all the nations who were subject to Persia and Media, *and* those who were not, [and] the regions *beyond* the Caspian Gates, *beyond* the Caucasus, *on the other side of* the Tanais (Jaxartes) [and] the Hyrcanian Sea."⁷³ The list of conquered territories, as Bosworth has noted, culminates at the Ocean: "Alexander's men have already reached the Ocean in the north [the Caspian]; [...] now they are on the verge of doing so in the east" (with the Ocean in the south, we may add, already attained through possession of the Indus river).⁷⁴

Conclusion

It is hard to believe that Alexander's longing for the Ocean was a myth constructed by later, Roman-era sources. It is too commonplace a notion in the imperial ideologies of premodern Afro-Eurasia. Actively participating in a wider Achaemenid koine for about two centuries, the Argead dynasty was well-acquainted with Persian concepts of monarchy and empire, and it is more likely that this myth was constructed at Alexander's court. *Pothos* was a later rendering of the common duty of the king to conquer the world and reach its final frontier, the Ocean.

---

70 Plin. *NH* 6.62.
71 See however Plut. *Alex.* 62.2, perhaps suggesting that the local rulers who later made regular offerings at Alexander's altars "in the Greek manner" had to cross the river from the east in order to do so.
72 Arr. *Anab.* 1.4.5 and 5.25.5.
73 Arr. *Anab.* 5.25.5; italics added, of course.
74 Bosworth (1995) 346.

To be sure, our sources offer much more that reflects Argead universalistic ideology. For instance, Alexander's refusal of an offer by Darius III to share power (but with Alexander in a subordinate position as Darius' son-in-law and vice-ruler). The famous incident took place between the battles of Issus and Gaugamela and has been recorded by all Alexander historians in comparable form. In Diodorus' version, Alexander allegedly said that just as the universe (*kosmos*) cannot be held together by two suns, so too the world of men (*oikoumenē*) cannot be ruled by two kings. And he allegedly added that the verdict of battle would decide "which of them would be the only and universal ruler of the world."[75]

These traditions of world conquest and universal rule did not disappear after Alexander: the Seleucids and Ptolemies, too, asserted universal rule by various means.[76] India featured prominently in Seleucid and Ptolemaic imperial cosmologies. Both dynasties had direct access to India and they both claimed sovereignty there.[77] In Hellenistic times, then, India was both a marvelous land of wonders *and* an area that was well-integrated, by land and sea routes, in the international system of connectivity and exchange now known as the Hellenistic World. Indeed, though the interpretation of Alexander's longing for the Ocean may be safely decoded as common Afro-Eurasian imperial cosmography, we perhaps must take into consideration the possibility, *not* that Roman world views were retrospectively projected on Alexander (in Roman imperial ideology, the symbolic value of the Ocean as frontier was associated primarily with the Atlantic, not the Indian Ocean),[78] but that the "Hellenized" Greco-Roman image of a world empire encircled by the Ocean was to a significant degree a Seleucid construction.

Be that as it may, Alexander had an important intermediate place in the development of imperialism in western Afro-Eurasia. He propagated a universalist ideology to create unity within his multicultural empire. His role moreover was symbolic. Like Aristotle, Alexander served as a vessel through which "oriental" ideas about kingship and empire could be safely transmitted to the Greco-Roman and Medieval west.[79] In fact, the Seleucid and Ptolemaic empires did more for the *interpretatio graeca* and further development of so-called "Near Eastern"

---

75 Diod. 17.54.5–6.
76 Strootman (2014b).
77 For the Seleucid Empire's presentation of India as a region it controlled, see Kosmin (2013), cf. Wiesehöfer (1998). For Ptolemaic claims to India, see Strootman (2010b) and (2014d), 258–261; cf. Kuttner (2005).
78 Gambash (2016); Lightfoot (2020).
79 Campopiano (2013).

concepts of kingship and empire than the Argeads, ensuring their transmission to the Roman Empire.[80] For Roman leaders however, Hellenistic-style universalism was more conveniently ascribed to an idealized and long-dead Alexander than to the Hellenistic successor dynasties they had fought and defeated.[81]

Bibliography

Anson (2009): Edward M. Anson, "Alexander the Great in current scholarship", in: *History Compass* 7.3, 981–992.
Anson (2015): Edward M. Anson, "Alexander at the Beas", in: Pat Wheatley and Elizabeth Baynham (eds.), *East and West in the World Empire of Alexander: Essays in Honour of Brian Bosworth*, Oxford and New York, 65–74.
Badian (1958): Ernst Badian, "Alexander the Great and the Unity of Mankind", in: *Historia* 7.4, 425–444.
Bang (2011): Peter F. Bang, "Lords of all the world: The state, heterogeneous power and hegemony in the Roman and Mughal empires", in: C. A. Bayley and Peter F. Bang (eds.), *Tributary Empires in Global History*, London and New York, 171–192.
Bang/Kołodziejczyk (2012): Peter F. Bang and Dariusz Kołodziejczyk, "'Elephant of India': Universal empire through time and across culture", in: *id.* (eds.), *Universal Empire: A Comparative Approach to Imperial Culture and Representation in Eurasian History*, Cambridge, 1–40.
Bichler (2016): Reinhold Bichler, "Die Wahrnehmung des Alexanderreiches: Ein Imperium der Imagination", in: *id.*, *Historiographie—Ethnographie—Utopie. Gesammelte Schriften, Teil 4: Studien zur griechischen Historiographie*, Wiesbaden, 183–218.
Bichler (2018): Reinhold Bichler, "Alexander's image in German, Anglo-American and French scholarship from the aftermath of World War I to the Cold War", in: Ken Moore (ed.), *Brill's Companion to the Reception of Alexander the Great*, Leiden and Boston, 640–674.
Bichler/Rollinger (2017): Reinhold Bichler and Robert Rollinger, "Universale Weltherrschaft und die Monumente an ihren Grenzen. Die Idee unbegrenzter Herrschaft und deren Brechung im diskursiven Wechselspiel (vom Alten Orient bis zum Imperium Romanum)", in: Robert Rollinger (ed.), *Die Sicht auf die Welt zwischen Ost und West (750 v. Chr.–550 n. Chr.) / Looking at the World From the East and the West (750 BCE–550 CE)*, Wiesbaden, 1–30.
Bosworth (1995): A. Brian Bosworth, *A Historical Commentary on Arrian's History of Alexander*, Vol. 2, Oxford.
Boucharlat/Salles (1981): Rémy Boucharlat and Jean-François Salles, "The history and archaeology of the Gulf from the 5th cent. B.C. to the 7th cent. A.D.", *Proceedings of the Seminar on Arabian Studies* 11 (1981) 65–94.
Briant (2010 [1974]): Pierre Briant, *Alexandre le Grand*, Paris = *Alexander the Great and his Empire*, Princeton, NJ.

---

80 Strootman (in press).
81 Bichler (2016).

Bucciantini (2009): Veronica Bucciantini, "Überlegungen zu den Opfern Alexanders des Großen auf seiner Indischen Expedition", in: *Das Altertum* 54, 269–282.
Burliga (2014): Bogdan Burliga, *Arrian's Anabasis: An Intellectual and Cultural Story*, Gdańsk.
Campopiano (2013): Michele Campopiano, "A philosopher between East and West: Aristotle and the Secret of Secrets", in: Rolf Strootman and Michele Campopiano (eds.), *De klassieke oudheid in de islamitische wereld* (Lampas 46.3), Hilversum, 282–289.
Dusinberre (2003): Elspeth Dusinberre, *Aspects of Empire in Achaemenid Sardis*, Cambridge.
Eggermont (1975): Pierre Herman Leonard Eggermont, *Alexander's Campaign in Sind and Baluchistan and the Siege of the Brahmin Town of Harmatelia*, Leuven.
Ehrenberg (1965): Victor Ehrenberg, "Pothos", in: *id., Polis und Imperium*, Zürich and Stuttgart, 458–465.
Galter (2014): Hannes D. Galter, "Sargon II. und die Eroberung der Welt", in: H. Neumann, R. Dittmann, S. Paulus, G. Neumann, and A. Schuster-Brandis (eds.), *Krieg und Frieden im Alten Vorderasien*, Münster, 329–344.
Gambash (2016): Gil Gambash, "Estranging the familiar—Rome's ambivalent approach to Britain", in: D. Slootjes and Michael Peachin (eds.), *Rome and the Worlds Beyond its Frontiers*, Leiden and Boston, 20–32.
Gotter (2019): Ulrich Gotter, "The succession of empires and the Augustan Res Publica", in: I. Gildenhard, U. Gotter, W. Havener, and L. Hodgson (eds.), *Augustus and the Destruction of History: The Politics of the Past in Early Imperial Rome*, Cambridge, 97–109.
Goukowsky (1978): Paul Goukowsky, *Essai sur les origines de mythe d'Alexandre (336–270 av.J.-C.). I: Les origines politiques*, Nancy.
Haubold (2012): Johannes Haubold, "The Achaemenid Empire and the sea", in: *Mediterranean Historical Review* 27.1, 5–24.
Hazzard (2000): Richard A. Hazzard, "The Soter Era", in: *id., Imagination of a Monarchy: Studies in Ptolemaic Propaganda*, Toronto/Buffalo/London, 25–46.
Heckel (2003): Waldemar Heckel, "Alexander the Great and the 'limits of the civilized world'", in: Waldemar Heckel and Lawrence A. Tritle (eds.), *Crossroads of History: The Age of Alexander*, Claremont, CA, 147–174.
Heckel (2015): Waldemar Heckel, "Alexander, Achilles, and Heracles: Between myth and history", in: Pat Wheatley and Elizabeth Baynham (eds.), *East and West in the World Empire of Alexander: Essays in Honour of Brian Bosworth*, Oxford and New York, 21–34.
Hofmann (2018): Dagmar Hofmann, *Griechische Weltgeschichte auf Latein. Iustins "Epitoma historiarum Pompei Trogi" und die Geschichtskonzeption des Pompeius Trogus*, Stuttgart.
Holt (1982): Frank L. Holt, "The Hyphasis 'Mutiny': A source Study", in: *Ancient World* 5.1/2, 33–59.
Howe/Müller (2012): Timothy Howe and Sabine Müller, "Mission accomplished: Alexander at the Hyphasis", in: *Ancient History Bulletin* 26, 21–38.
Howe (2014): Timothy Howe, "Founding Alexandria: Alexander the Great and the politics of memory", in: P. Bosman (ed.), *Alexander in Africa*, Pretoria, 72–91.
Kaptan (2013): Deniz Kaptan, "Déjà vu? Visual culture in western Asia Minor at the beginning of Hellenistic rule", in: Eftychia Stavrianopoulou (ed.), *Shifting Social Imaginaries in the Hellenistic Period: Narrations, Practices, and Images*, Leiden and Boston, 25–49.

Kosmin (2013): Paul J. Kosmin, "Apologetic ethnography: Megasthenes' Indica and the Seleucid elephant", in: Eran Almagor and Joseph Skinner (eds.), *Ancient Ethnography. New Approaches*, London, New York, Sydney, 97–115.

Kosmin (2014): Paul J. Kosmin, *The Land of the Elephant Kings: Space, Territory, and Ideology in the Seleucid Empire*, Cambridge, MA.

Kosmin (2018): Paul J. Kosmin, *Time and Its Adversaries in the Seleucid Empire*, Cambridge, MA.

Kuhrt (2007): Amélie Kuhrt, *The Persian Empire: A Corpus of Sources from the Achaemenid Period*, London and New York.

Kuttner (2005): Ann Kuttner, "Cabinet fit for a queen: The Λιθικά as Posidippus' gem museum", in: Kathryn Gutzwiller (ed.), *The New Posidippus: A Hellenistic Poetry Book*, Oxford and New York, 141–163.

Lang/Rollinger (2010): Martin Lang and Robert Rollinger, "Im Herzen der Meere und in der Mitte des Meeres. Das Buch Ezechiel und die in assyrischer Zeit fassbaren Vorstellungen von den Grenzen der Welt", in: Robert Rollinger et al. (eds.), *Interkulturalität in der Alten Welt. Vorderasien, Hellas Ägypten und die vielfältigen Ebenen des Kontakts*, Wiesbaden, 207–264.

Lavan/Payne/Weisweiler (2016): Myles Lavan, Richard Payne, and John Weisweiler, "Cosmopolitan politics: The assimilation and subordination of elite cultures", in: *id.* (eds.), *Cosmopolitanism and Empire: Universal Rulers, Local Elites, and Cultural Integration in the Ancient Near East and Mediterranean*, Oxford, 1–28.

Lightfoot (2020): Jessica Lightfoot, "Tacitus' *Germania* and the limits of fantastic geography", in: *Histos* 14, 116–151.

Liotsakis (2019): Vasileios Liotsakis, *Alexander the Great in Arrian's 'Anabasis': A Literary Portrait*, Berlin and Boston.

Liverani (1979): Mario Liverani, "The ideology of the Assyrian Empire", in: M. T. Larsen (ed.), *Power and Propaganda: A Symposium on Ancient Empires*, Copenhagen, 297–317.

Liverani (1990): Mario Liverani, *Prestige and Interest. International Relations in the Near East ca. 1600–1100*, Padua.

Liverani (2001): Mario Liverani, *International Relations in the Ancient Near East, 1600–1100 BC*, London.

Llewellyn-Jones (2017): Lloyd Llewellyn-Jones, "Keeping and displaying royal tribute animals in Ancient Persia and the Near East", in: T. Fögen and E. Thomas (eds.), *Interactions between Animals and Humans in Graeco-Roman Antiquity*, Berlin and Boston, 305–338.

Melville (2016): Sarah C. Melville, "The role of rituals in warfare during the Neo-Assyrian period", in: *Religion Compass* 10.9, 219–229.

Miltner (1952): Franz Miltner, "Der Okeanos in der persischen Weltreichsidee", in: *Saeculum* 3, 542–554.

Montgomery (1965): Hugo Montgomery, *Gedanke und Tat. Zur Erzählungstechnik bei Herodot, Thukydides, Xenophon und Arrian*, Lund.

Müller (2014): Sabine Müller, "Alexanders indischer Schnee, Achaimenidische Wassersouvenirs und 'mental mind mapping'", in: *Anabasis* 5, 47–52.

Müller (2021): Sabine Müller, "Alexander at Naqsh-e Rostam? Persia and the Macedonians", in: J. Walsh and E. Baynham (eds.), *Alexander the Great and Propaganda*, London and New York, 107–128.

Poggio (2020): Alessandro Poggio, *Dynastic Deeds: Hunt Scenes in the Funerary Imagery of the Achaemenid Eastern Mediterranean* (BAR International Series 2974), Oxford.

Rivaroli (2015): Marta Rivaroli, "The ritualization of war: The phases of bellum and their sacred implications", in: Claus Ambos and Lorenzo Verderame (eds.), *Questioni di Rito: Rituali come Fonte di Conoscenza delle Religioni e delle Concenzioni del Mondo nelle Culture Antiche*, Pisa, 261–286.

Rollinger/Luther/Wiesehöfer (2007): Robert Rollinger, Andreas Luther, and Josef Wiesehöfer (eds.), *Getrennte Wege? Kommunikation, Raum und Wahrnehmung in der Alten Welt*, Frankfurt.

Rollinger (2012): Robert Rollinger, "From Sargon of Agade and the Assyrian kings to Khusrau I and beyond: On the persistence of Ancient Near Eastern Traditions", in: Giovanni Lanfranchi et al. (eds.), *LEGGO! Studies presented to Prof. Frederick Mario Fales on the Occasion of his 65th Birthday*, Wiesbaden, 725–743.

Rollinger (2013a): Robert Rollinger, *Alexander und die großen Ströme. Die Flussüberquerungen im Lichte altorientalischer Pioniertechniken (Schwimmschläuche, Keleks und Pontonbrücken*, Wiesbaden.

Rollinger (2013b): Robert Rollinger, "Dareios und Xerxes an den Rändern der Welt und die Inszenierung von Weltherrschaft. Altorientalisches bei Herodot", in: Boris Dunsch and Kai Ruffing (eds.), *Herodots Quellen*, Wiesbaden 2013, 95–116.

Rollinger (2014): Robert Rollinger, "Aornos and the mountains of the east: The Assyrian kings and Alexander the Great", in: S. Gaspa, A. Greco, D. Morandi Bonacossi, S. Ponchia, and R. Rollinger (eds.), *From Source to History: Studies on Ancient Near Eastern Worlds and Beyond*, Münster, 597–635.

Rollinger (2020): Robert Rollinger, "Some considerations on empire and mental mapping: Conceptualizing the ends of the world in the First Millennium BCE", in: Michele Cammarosano, Elena Devecchi, Maurizio Viano (eds.), *Talugaeš Witteš: Ancient Near Eastern Studies Presented to Stefano de Martino on the Occasion of his 65th Birthday*, Münster, 383–398.

Rollinger/Degen (2021): Robert Rollinger and Julian Degen, "Conceptualizing universal rulership: Considerations on the Persian Achaemenid worldview and the Saka at the 'end of the world'", in: Hilmar Klinkott, Andreas Luther, and Josef Wiesehöfer (eds.), *Beiträge zur Geschichte und Kultur des alten Iran und benachbarter Gebiete*, Stuttgart, 187–224.

Root (1979): Margaret Cool Root, *The King and Kingship in Achaemenid Art. Essays on the Creation of an Iconography of Empire*, Leiden.

Shafer (1998): Ann Taylor Shafer, *The Carving of an Empire: Neo-Assyrian Monuments on the Periphery*, PhD dissertation, Harvard University.

Spann (1999): Philip Spann, "Alexander at the Beas: Fox in a lion's skin", in: Frances B. Titchener and Robert F. Moorton, Jr. (eds.), *The Eye Expanded: Life and the Arts in Greco-Roman Antiquity*, Berkeley, 62–74.

Stronk (2016): Jan P. Stronk, *Semiramis' Legacy: The History of Persia According to Diodorus of Sicily*, Edinburgh.

Strootman (2010a): Rolf Strootman, "Het verlangen van Alexander de Grote: pothos of propaganda?", in: *Groniek* 186, 5–20.

Strootman (2010b): Rolf Strootman, "Queen of Kings: Cleopatra VII and the Donations of Alexandria", in: Margherita Facella and Ted Kaizer (eds.), *Kingdoms and Principalities in the Roman Near East*, Stuttgart, 139–158.

Strootman (2013): Rolf Strootman, "Alexander de Grote en het oosterse koningschap", in: Diederik Burgersdijk, Wouter Henkelman, and Willemijn Waal (eds.), *Alexander en Darius. De Macedoniër in de spiegel van het Nabije Oosten*, Hilversum, 101–114.

Strootman (2014a): Rolf Strootman, "The dawning of a Golden Age: Images of peace and abundance in Alexandrian court poetry in the context of Ptolemaic imperial ideology", in: Annette Harder, Remco Regtuit, and Gerry Wakker (eds.), *Hellenistic Poetry in Context*, Leuven, 325–341.

Strootman (2014b): Rolf Strootman, "Hellenistic imperialism and the idea of world unity", in: Claudia Rapp and Hal Drake (eds.), *The City in the Classical and Post-Classical World: Changing Contexts of Power and Identity*, Cambridge, 38–61.

Strootman (2014c): Rolf Strootman, "'Men to whose rapacity neither sea nor mountain sets a limit': The aims of the Diadochs", in: Hans Hauben and Alexander Meeus (eds.), *The Age of the Successors and the Creation of the Hellenistic Kingdoms (323–276 B.C)*, Leuven, 307–322.

Strootman (2014d): Rolf Strootman, *Courts and Elites in the Hellenistic Empires: The Near East After the Achaemenids, 330–30 BCE*, Edinburgh.

Strootman (in press): Rolf Strootman, "Hellenistic influences on Roman court culture", in: Ben Kelly *et al.* (eds.), *The Roman Emperor and his Court, ca. 31 BC–ca. AD 300*, Cambridge.

Strootman (forthcoming): Rolf Strootman, "Cosmopolitan empire in Arrian's *Anabasis*: Achaemenid, Hellenistic, or Roman?", in: Julian Degen and Robert Rollinger (eds.), *The World of Alexander in Perspective: Contextualizing Arrian 6*, Wiesbaden.

Tadmor (2011): Hayim Tadmor, "World dominion: The expanding horizon of the Assyrian Empire", in: *id. "With My Many Chariots I Have Gone Up the Heights of the Mountains": Historical and Literary Studies on Ancient Mesopotamia and Israel*, Vol. I, Jerusalem, 55–62.

Tarn (1933): William Woodthorpe Tarn, *Alexander the Great and the Unity of Mankind*, Oxford and New York.

Tarn (1948): William Woodthorpe Tarn, "Brotherhood and unity", in: *id., Alexander the Great*, Vol. II, Cambridge, 399–449.

Tuplin (2017): Christopher J. Tuplin, "War and peace in Achaemenid imperial ideology", *Electrum* 24, 31–54.

Van Dongen (2014): Eric van Dongen, "The concept of 'the Near East': A reconsideration", in: Robert Rollinger and Kordula Schnegg (eds.), *Kulturkontakte in antiken Welten: Vom Denkmodell zum Fallbeispiel*, Leuven, 253–268.

Van Wickevoort Crommelin (1993): Bernard Rymond van Wickevoort Crommelin, *Die Universalgeschichte des Pompeius Trogus: Herculea audacia orbem terrarum adgressus*, Hagen.

Wiesehöfer (1998): Josef Wiesehöfer, "Geschenke, Gewürze und Gedanken. Überlegungen zu den Beziehungen zwischen Seleukiden und Mauryas", in: E. Dąbrowa (ed.), *Ancient Iran and the Mediterranean World: Studies in Ancient History*, Cracow, 225–236.

IV Raising a Prince in the Macedonian Court: Stories of Alexander's Birth and Education

Daniel Ogden
The Serpent Sire of Alexander the Great: A Palinode

Introduction

In previous publications I reviewed the evidence for the tradition of Alexander's divine sire, which features both Zeus and Ammon, closely identified with each other and, strikingly, a serpent. In attempting to contextualise a serpent that could also be a Zeus, I turned to the sometimes anguiform figure of Zeus Meilichios and hesitantly concluded that the serpent sire may have had an identity of this sort in origin. I now argue that this was (diametrically!) the wrong approach to take to the tradition, which should not be aggregated but rather disaggregated: we are dealing not with a single messy tradition but rather with two cleaner and originally quite distinct ones—on the one hand the Zeus-Ammon tradition; on the other the divine-serpent tradition—which have, occasionally, been contaminated with each other. The identity of the serpent sire, now liberated from any original association with Zeus(-Ammon), may accordingly be sought elsewhere entirely.

I Catalogue A: The Divine Sire of Alexander the Great: The Principal Testimonies

The following list catalogues the principal references extant in the Alexander tradition to Alexander's divine sire (simple references to Philip himself as Alexander's sire are excluded).

1. The coinage of Alexander.[1]
DATE: 336–323 BC.
CONTENT: Alexander's association of himself with the traditional Argead eagle-and-thunderbolt imagery potentially offers a context for the generation of the

---

[1] Mørkholm (1991) figs. 5–6 (cf. also fig. 202); Le Rider (1996) plate 9, nos. 10, 11 and 12 (the reverse is paired with obverses of both Zeus' head and of Alexander's). Note also that Callisthenes, who died in 327 BC, described Alexander as a thunderbolt-bearer before whom even waves did obeisance: *FGrH / BNJ* 124 F40 (*apud* Pol. 12.12b3).

tale known from Plutarch (A, 12, below) in accordance with which Zeus sires Alexander by striking his mother Olympias' womb with his thunderbolt (the eagle being Zeus' thunderbolt-bearer).
SIRE: **Zeus (?).**

2. Ephorus *FGrH / BNJ* **70 F 217** *apud* **Tertullian,** *De anima* **46.**
DATE: Before ca. 330 BC.
CONTENT: Philip has a vision of himself sealing Olympias' womb with a lion-emblazoned signet-ring. On the assumption that the lion represents (the lion-skin wearing) Heracles, the vision could suggest either that Zeus is siring Alexander as a second Heracles, or that Heracles is siring a son for himself.
SIRE: **Zeus / Heracles.**

3. Inscribed pedestal from the temple of Ammon at Bahariya, near Siwah[2]
DATE: 332–331 BC (?)
CONTENT: The pedestal carries bilingual dedications supposedly by Alexander himself, the Greek one reading "King Alex(a)nder to Ammon, his father" (Βασιλεὺς Ἀλέξ(α)νδρος Ἄμμωνι τ[ῷ]ι πατρί).
SIRE: **Ammon**

4. Callisthenes *FGrH / BNJ* **124 F14** *apud* **Strabo C814 (= 17.1.43).**
DATE: 331–327 BC.
CONTENT: Ammon addresses Alexander as his own son at Siwah.
SIRE: **Ammon.**

5. Eratosthenes *FGrH / BNJ* **241 F28** *apud* **Plutarch,** *Alexander* **2.**
DATE: Later 3rd c. BC (?), 1st c. AD (?).
CONTENT: As Olympias sends Alexander off on campaign she tells him the secret of the way in which he was sired. The analogy, for what it is worth, with the Scipio tradition may imply that the secret consisted of his siring by a serpent. According to Silius Italicus, when the ghost of Pomponia tells Scipio that he had been serpent-sired, the information is similarly presented as the final revelation from mother to son of a long-kept secret (see B, 10, below).[3]
SIRE: ***drakōn* (???).**

---

[2] Published by Bosch-Puche (2008).
[3] Silius Italicus, *Punica* 13.634–649.

6. Cicero, *On Divination* 2.135.
DATE: 45–44 BC.
CONTENT: Cicero in effect identifies the *drakōn* that tells Alexander how to heal the dying Ptolemy at Harmatelia with Alexander's own sire: "When Ptolemy, Alexander's associate, had been struck in battle by a poisoned arrow and was dying from that wound in the greatest pain, Alexander, sitting by him, fell asleep. Then, in his slumbers, he saw a vision of that serpent [*draco*] that his mother Olympias used to keep carrying a root in its mouth and at the same time telling him where it grew (nor was it far from that place)." Although Cicero does not directly specify that Olympias' *drakōn* is Alexander's sire, his characterisation of it as her pet is surely a gentle rationalisation of such a serpent sire.[4]
SIRE: ***drakōn***.

7. Diodorus 17.51.
DATE: Ca. 30 BC.
CONTENT: The priest of Ammon addresses Alexander as "son."
SIRE: **Ammon.**

8. Virgil, *Aeneid* 4.196–210.
DATE: Before 19 BC.
CONTENT: Iarbas, the Gaetulian king hostile to Dido and Aeneas, is sired by (H)Ammon when the latter rapes a Garamantian nymph. He is a devoted worshipper of Jupiter in his role as lord of the lightning bolt. It is difficult not to see an allusion to the Alexander tradition in this imagery, and if Alexander does indeed lurk behind it then the passage will constitute the first indication of an assimilation between Ammon and Zeus-Jupiter in the role of Alexander's sire.
SIRE: **Ammon = Zeus.**

9. Livy 26.19.7–8.
DATE: After 19 BC.[5]
CONTENT: Scipio's habit of sitting alone in the temple of Jupiter on the Capitol "revived the rumour formerly spread about Alexander the Great, which was comparable in its emptiness and fantasy, that he was conceived by sex with a huge snake [*anguis*]." (See B, 6, below for the full text.)
SIRE: ***drakōn***.

---

[4] Lucian (as catalogued below) evidently inverts the chronological order of the generation of this myth and its subsequent rationalisation for satirical purposes.

[5] Dating of Livy's third decad: Fusillo and Schmidt (2005) 750.

10. Antipater of Thessalonica at *Greek Anthology* 9.241.
DATE: Turn of the eras.
CONTENT: In a brief list of gods that transformed themselves into animals: "The famous Ammon was a snake ['Άμμων δ' ώμφιβόητος ὄφις]." This can only entail the tale that Ammon sired Alexander in the form of a serpent.
SIRE: **Ammon** = *drakōn*.

11. Trogus at Justin 11.11.
DATE: Ca. AD 9 (Trogus).
CONTENT: "Then Alexander made his way to Hammon to ask about the future and about his own origin. For his mother Olympias had confessed to her husband Philip that she had conceived Alexander not from him but from a serpent [*serpens*] of great size.... As Alexander entered the temple the priests greeted him at once as the son of Hammon." The text is ambiguous rather than truly disjunctive: it may imply a tradition that the siring serpent was itself Ammon, but need not do so.
SIRE: **Ammon** OR *drakōn*.

12. Curtius 4.7.8.25–7.
DATE: Mid–late 1st c. AD.
CONTENT: Jupiter-Ammon's eldest priest addresses Alexander as his son.
SIRE: **Zeus = Ammon.**

13. Plutarch, *Alexander* 2–3.
DATE: Ca. AD 100.
CONTENT: (A) Alexander is sired by a thunderbolt, i.e. Zeus; OR (B) by a lion-emblazoned signet ring (cf. Ephorus, above); OR (C) by a gigantic *drakōn*, revealed to be Ammon: "And once too a serpent [*drakōn*] was seen stretched out beside Olympias' body as she slept. And they say that this most of all blunted Philip's desire for and fond feelings towards his wife, so that he no longer visited her frequently to sleep with her.... Anyway, after the manifestation Philip sent Chaeron of Megalopolis to Delphi, and they say that he brought an oracle from the god that bade him sacrifice to Ammon and honour this god most of all. And it said that he would lose the eye that he had applied to the hinge-gap in the door when he saw the god sleeping with his wife in the form of a serpent [*drakōn*]."
SIRE: **Zeus** OR *drakōn* = **Ammon.**

14. Plutarch, *Alexander* 27.
DATE: Ca. AD 100.

CONTENT: Ammon's prophet greets Alexander as "son".
SIRE: **Ammon**.

15. Ptolemy Chennus *apud* Photius cod. 190, §148a.
DATE: Ca. AD 98–138.
CONTENT: Alexander is sired by a man called Drakon (a self-evident rationalisation of the *drakōn*-proper tradition).
SIRE: *drakōn*.

16. Alexandrian choliambic epitaph.[6]
DATE: 2nd c. AD.
CONTENT: "Alexander the Macedonian king, whom Ammon sired in the form of a snake [*ophis*]."
SIRE: **Ammon** = *drakōn*.

17. Aulus Gellius, *Attic Nights* 6.1.1.
DATE: Later 2nd c. AD.
CONTENT: "That which has been written in Greek history of Olympias, the wife of king Philip and mother of Alexander, has similarly been handed down in tradition in relation to the mother of the first Publius Scipio..." i.e., the tradition that he was sired by snake (*anguis*).
SIRE: *Drakōn*.

18. Pausanias 4.14.7.
DATE: Later 2nd c. AD.
CONTENT: "The Messenians hold that Aristomenes of Messene's birth was rather splendid, for they say that a demon [*daimōn*] or a god took on the form of a serpent [*drakōn*] and had sex with his mother Nicoteleia. I am aware that the Macedonians have said similar things in the case of Olympias and the Sicyonians in the case of Aristodama, but these differ to the following extent. For the Messenians do not make of Aristomenes a son of Heracles or Zeus as the Macedonians make Alexander the son of Ammon and the Sicyonians make Aratus the son of Asclepius."
SIRE: **Ammon** = *drakōn*.

19. Lucian, *Dialogues of the Dead* 13.
DATE: Ca. AD 170s.

---

[6] Reproduced at Fraser (1972) 2.950.

CONTENT: A fast-paced dialogue between the ghosts of Alexander and Diogenes in the underworld:

> DIOGENES: So Ammon was lying when he said that you were his own son, when you were really Philip's son all along? ALEXANDER: Yes, obviously I was Philip's son, for if I was Ammon's son, I wouldn't have died. DIOGENES: And the same was true of the things said about Olympias, to the effect that a *drakōn* had sex with her and was seen in her bed, and that that was the way in which you were sired, whilst Philip was deceived into thinking that he was your father?

The dialogue ostensibly indicates that the *drakōn* and Ammon were sires to Alexander in alternative traditions, as opposed to constituting variant expressions of the same sire: the text is seemingly disjunctive.
SIRE: **Ammon** OR ***drakōn***.

20. Lucian, *Alexander* 7; cf. 15.
DATE: After AD 181.
CONTENT: "There [in Macedon] Alexander [of Abonutichus] and Cocconas saw huge serpents [*drakontes*], so completely tame and harmless that women keep them as pets, they sleep alongside babies and they tolerate being walked over and don't get angry when squeezed, and drink milk from the breast, just like babies. (They have many snakes of this sort, and this was no doubt the origin of the tale that was bruited abroad about Olympias, to the effect that she conceived Alexander when a serpent of this sort, I suppose, slept with her.) The story of Alexander the Great being sired by a *drakōn* is said to have arisen from the custom of Macedonian women of keeping large, tame serpents as pets." Alexander of Abonutichus takes one of these serpents to turn into his famous 'New Asclepius' or 'Glycon.'
 SIRE: ***Drakōn***.

21. *Alexander Romance* (A) 1.6–8, 10, 12, 14, 24, 30, 35, 2.13, 21, 3.33.
DATE: Early 3rd c. AD.
CONTENT: Nectanebo sleeps with Olympias whilst dressed as Ammon and also deploying a magically manufactured *drakōn*. He subsequently transforms himself into a huge *drakōn* before Philip, coils on Olympias' lap, and kisses her. Ammon sends Alexander a dream of himself embracing Olympias, to confirm his own fatherhood. The tradition that Ammon sired Alexander in the form of a *drakōn*, *inter multa alia*, evidently lies behind this complex and contradictory tale.
SIRE: **Ammon** = ***drakōn***.

22. Solinus 9.18.
DATE: Mid 3rd c. AD.
CONTENT: Olympias professed that Alexander was sired when she had sex with a *draco*.
SIRE: ***Drakōn***.

II The dating of the tradition of the serpent sire

How far back can we take the tradition of Alexander having a serpent sire? It is hard to say. The tradition surely did exist by 45–44 BC when Cicero offers us in passing what is evidently a rationalised version of the tale (A, 6).

Beyond this, we enter the realm of speculation. For reasons given above (the comparison of Silius Italicus' words on Scipio), it is quite possible that the secret of Alexander's birth referred to in the Eratosthenes fragment consisted of a serpent sire (and the fact that the secret is focused upon Olympias herself and indeed herself alone seemingly points in the same direction—contrast the non-serpent stories in Plutarch's collection). But the difficulty here is the dating of the fragment: is it genuinely Eratosthenic (as Frances Pownall holds in her *BNJ* commentary), or does it belong to the pseudo-Eratosthenes of the *Catasterisms?* One can imagine the story being told, for example, in connection with the *Catasterisms*' treatment of the constellation of Draco.[7] The developmental tradition of the *Catasterisms* text was complex, and material in it need not be earlier than the first century AD.

Beyond this again we can only construct a circumstantial case that the tradition of the serpent sire originated in or close to Alexander's own age by pointing to the proliferation of serpents in the early tradition for Alexander. First, the Agathos Daimon serpent, the presiding hero of the city of Alexandria, is first attested iconographically as early as ca. 320–300 BC (he is integrated into statues of Alexander Aegiochus), and his cult was tightly associated with that of Alexander's own, but we have to wait until the early third-century AD *Alexander Romance* for the literary justification of this association. This tells how Alexander had the original great Agathos Daimon serpent slain and then heroized at the site of Alexandria as the city was initially being built, and how the serpent's body was then somehow transmogrified into the smaller Agathos Daimon snakes

---

7 As found at [Eratosth.] *Cat.* epitome 1.3.

that served the historical Alexandrians as protective house-snakes.[8] Secondly, Clitarchus (as we can tell from the coincidence between Diodorus and Curtius), writing probably ca. 310 BC, spoke of the *drakōn* that appeared to Alexander in a dream and gave him instructions for the healing of Ptolemy at Harmatelia.[9] Thirdly, Onesicritus of Astypalaea, who wrote before 309 BC, had the Indian king Abisares tell Alexander that he kept a pair of pet *drakontes*, one of 140 cubits in length, the other of 80 cubits.[10] Fourthly, Ptolemy, writing before 282 BC, spoke of a pair of *drakontes* endowed with human voice that rescued Alexander and his army from the Libyan desert when lost en route to Siwah.[11]

III The original identity of the serpent sire: "Ogden I"[12]

I have written on Alexander's serpent sire on several previous occasions.[13] In these contributions I approached the above catalogue of sources aggregatively. I looked for an Ammon or a Zeus that could also have been a *drakōn*, a great serpent, and that we could expect either to have had some purchase in the Macedon of Alexander or to have been imagined have done so by the later tradition. Nothing could be done with "Ammon": there was no basis for thinking that he ever possessed an identity as a serpent in his own right beyond the realm of the actual traditions under discussion here.[14] But one kind of "Zeus" seemed

---

8 *Alexander Romance* (A) 1.32.5–13 ≈ (Arm.) §§86–87 Wolohojian; cf. also Phylarchus *FGrH / BNJ* F27 (*apud* Ael. *NA* 17.5), F28 (*apud* Plin. *HN* 10.208); Dio Cass. 51.17.4–5; *The Oracle of the Potter* at *P.Oxy.* 2332 lines 51–3; [Epiph.] *De prophetarum et obitu* first recension p.9 Schermann, second recension pp.62 Schermann; *Chronicon Paschale* p.293 Dindorf. Discussion at Dunand (1969) and (1981); Stewart (1993) 246–253, 421–422, with figs. 82–83; Hillard (1998), (2010); Ogden (2012), (2013a) 286–309, (2013b), (2014); Barbantani (2014); Djurslev and Ogden (2018).
9 Clitarchus *apud* Diod. Sic. 17.103 and Curt. 9.8.22–28 (not in *FGrH / BNJ*); cf. also Strab. C723 (= 15.2.7). I continue to prefer the traditional date of *ca.* 310 BC for Clitarchus as opposed to the late third-century BC date for him that some believe they can extrapolate from *P.Oxy.* lxxi 4808.
10 Onesicritus of Astypalaea *FGrH / BNJ* 134 16a–c.
11 Ptolemy *FGrH / BNJ* 138 F8, *apud* Arr. *Anab.*3.3.4–6; contrast Aristobulus *FGrH / BNJ* 139 F14.
12 A pretentious calque on the two phases of Wittgenstein's thought, with 'Wittgenstein II' discarding the work of 'Wittgenstein I.'
13 Ogden (2009a), (2009b), (2011) 7–56, (2013a) 330–342, (2015). These items may be turned to for more detailed and more nuanced justifications of the points perforce made more telegraphically in this piece.
14 The only text that might be thought significantly to suggest so is a passage of Herodotus in which the historian tells us that sacred horned snakes lived near Egyptian Thebes, and that

to offer some promise: Zeus Meilichios and the more minor Zeus deities of a similar sort, Zeus Ktesios and Zeus Philios.[15]

Zeus Meilichios himself had a well-established profile in his iconography (where the bulk of the evidence for him resides), particularly that of fourth-century BC Athens, both as a humanoid Zeus figure in the standard paternal mould and, at the same time, as a great serpent. He is shown in the latter guise most notably in a particularly fine series of relief stelae from the Piraeus. His anguiform nature has led to him being much misunderstood, one might almost say maligned, in the past: he has been considered a terrible deity, with his epithet, Meilichios, "The Gentle One," "The Propitiated One," being taken as sinisterly propitiatory in its significance. But there is simply no evidence for this supposed terrible nature, and no citable example of this god behaving in dreadful fashion towards anyone. Rather it was without irony that he was "gentle," "readily propitiated," or even perhaps "already propitiated." His iconography and the (limited) literary sources for him reveal him to have been a god devoted to the promotion of wealth and success, above all in the context of the household and its nuclear family. The Piraeus stelae typically depict daddy, mummy and a pair of children approaching the great coiling serpent as he towers over them—not threateningly: protectively, perhaps—and as they give thanks for the benefits he has conferred. Indeed, he evinces the sweet and harmless nature that is common to all the anguiform deities of the ancient Greek world, notably Agathos Daimon, to whom we have already referred, and of course the famous Asclepius, no harmer but actually a healer of harm, of whom more anon.

Secondly, there was vestigial evidence for a cult of Zeus Meilichios in Macedon, under the Antigonids at any rate. Philip V made a dedication to him at Pella.[16] If the remains of the colossal marble coiling-serpent statue found in a deposit in the antechamber of Temple II in the Eucleia sanctuary at Vergina did not represent Zeus Meilichios himself, then they must have represented one of the closely allied deities. The remains are dated to some point before the mid second century BC.[17] Thirdly, a Zeus Meilichios-like deity featured in

---

when they died they were buried in the temple of Zeus (i.e. Ammon) there, to whom they were sacred (2.74). But the significance of this gesture is made clear in context: Ammon is not given horned snakes because he is a snake but rather because, as actually a ram, he is himself horned. *Pace* Bosworth (1980) 272 (on Arr. *Anab*.3.3.2).

15 For Zeus Meilichios in the round, and the more minor Zeus deities of similar type, see Ogden (2013a) 272–286, with further references; for his iconography and his cult at Athens, see Lalonde (2006).
16 Gauthier and Hatzopoulos (1993) 146 n. 3; Le Bohec (2002) 47.
17 Saatsoglou-Paliadeli (2000) 12–21.

the Macedonian myth of the eponymous Pindus. Aelian records at some length the tale in which the wholesome Pindus' hunting—his wealth, of a sort—in the country around the river that was to bear his name is prospered by a gigantic *drakōn* he encounters there, endowed with human voice. The *drakōn* arrives too late, alas, to prevent the young man's murder at the hands of his envious brothers, but it avenges him by crushing them to death, and then guards his body until his better relatives can retrieve it.[18]

IV The original identity of the serpent sire: "Ogden II"

However, on further consideration of Catalogue A, I have come to see this approach as profoundly misguided. It is now apparent to me that the Catalogue should not be taken to preserve the different facets of a unitary identity, but rather to preserve two contrasting traditions that were in origin wholly separate from each other, and that over the course of time became contaminated and merged, as follows:

- **The Zeus-Ammon tradition:** (1) the Neisos gem and the coinage, (2) Ephorus, (3) the Bahariya pedestal, (4) Callisthenes, (7) Diodorus, (8) Virgil, (11) Trogus-Justin, (12) Curtius, (13) Plutarch, (14) Plutarch, (19) Lucian.
- **The serpent sire tradition:** (5) Eratosthenes (???), (6) Cicero, (9) Livy, (11) Trogus-Justin, (15) Ptolemy Chennus, (17) Aulus Gellius, (19) Lucian, (20) Lucian, (22) Solinus.
- **The contaminated tradition:** (10) Antipater, (13) Plutarch, (16) the Alexandrian cholimabic epitaph, (18) Pausanias, (21) the *Alexander Romance*.

Of particular interest in this regard are Trogus-Justin (A, 11) and especially Lucian (A, 19), both of whom indeed present Ammon and the *drakōn* less as a unitary sire for Alexander, or as different aspects of the same one, but more as paradigmatic alternatives to each other. The contaminated tradition begins—for us at any rate—with Antipater of Thessalonica (A, 10), who wrote around the turn of the eras.[19]

---

[18] Ael. *NA* 10.48.
[19] This raises the mild possibility that it is a reflex of the potentially earlier Roman tradition in accordance with which Scipio Africanus was sired by Jupiter in the form of a serpent (see B, 5–6 below). However, the contaminated tradition always ties Alexander's *drakōn*-sire to "Ammon" as opposed to "Zeus" or "Jupiter."

V Catalogue B: The serpent sires of the Graeco-Roman world

With Alexander's serpent sire now dissociated from Zeus-Ammon in its original incarnation, we are left to renew our enquiry as to what its original identity might have been. The method of investigation that commends itself is to survey the phenomenon of Graeco-Roman serpent sires in the round and to determine their typical profile. Accordingly, the following catalogue charts all the evidence known to me for individuals being sired by serpents in antiquity, in rough chronological order. For clarity and convenience, the relevant evidence bearing upon Alexander the Great from Catalogue A is interleaved at the appropriate points.

1. The two children of Nicasibula: *EMI* (B) 42 = *IG* iv^2 122.42 = Edelstein and Edelstein 1945 no. 423.
DATE: 4th c. BC.
CONTENT: A record from the Epidaurian miracle inscriptions. The barren Nicasibula incubates at Epidaurus. In her dream, Asclepius visits her and his serpent avatar has sex with her, siring two male children.
SIRE: *drakōn* = Asclepius.

2. Alexander: Eratosthenes *FGrH* / *BNJ* 241 F28 (*apud* Plutarch *Alexander* 2).
DATE: Later 3rd c. BC (?), 1st c. AD (?).
CONTENT: See above (A, 5).
SIRE: *drakōn* (???) = unspecified.

3. Aratus of Sicyon: Statue base, Epidaurus, *IG* iv^2 622.
DATE: 3rd c.–2nd c. BC.
CONTENT: The Sicyonians set up an offertory in the form of a *drakōn*, to salute the form of Aratus of Sicyon's father Asclepius.
SIRE: *drakōn* = Asclepius.

4. Alexander: Cicero, *On Divination* 2.135.
DATE: 45–44 BC.
CONTENT: See above (A, 6).
SIRE: *drakōn* (in strongly **Asclepian** context).

5. Scipio Africanus: Caius Oppius, *apud* Aulus Gellius, *Attic Nights* 6.1.1.
DATE: 43–33 BC.

CONTENT: "That which has been written in Greek history of Olympias, the wife of king Philip and mother of Alexander, has similarly been handed down in tradition in relation to the mother of the first Publius Scipio to acquire the surname Africanus. For both Gaius Oppius and Julius Hyginus, and others who have written of the life and achievements of Africanus, relate that his mother had long been held barren. They say too that Scipio, to whom she was married, had given up hope of children. But subsequently, when she was lying down alone and had fallen asleep in her bedroom in the absence of her husband, a huge snake [*anguis*] was suddenly seen lying by her side in the bed. The people that saw it were terrified and shouted out, whereupon it slipped away and they were unable to find it. Publius Scipio himself referred the matter to the soothsayers and they, after making sacrifice, replied that children would be born to him. And indeed a few days after that snake was seen in the bed, his wife began to perceive the signs and feelings of pregnancy. In the tenth month thereafter she gave birth and that Publius Scipio was born who defeated Hannibal and the Carthaginians in Africa in the Second Punic War. But he too was believed to be a man of divine excellence because of his achievements rather more than because of that portent. I do not hesitate to relate this too, which the same writers I mentioned above have entrusted to writing. This Scipio had the custom of frequenting the Capitol during the last part of the night, just before dawn, ordering the temple of Jupiter to be opened and staying there for some time, as if he were consulting with the god about affairs of state. The shrine's temple-wardens would often wonder that he was the only person that came on to the Capitol at that time without the dogs barking at him or running at him, although they would attack all others." (Hyginus is Augustan in date.)
SIRE: ***drakōn*** = **Jupiter (?)** – but with broadly **Asclepian** imagery: cf. Nicasibula, above (B, 1).

6. Scipio Africanus: Livy 26.19.7–8.
DATE: After 19 BC.
CONTENT: "This habit [of Scipio's of sitting alone in the temple of Jupiter on the Capitol before performing any business], maintained through the entirety of his life, brought about for certain men belief in the notion bruited abroad, be it advisedly or rashly, that he was a man of divine stock, and it revived the rumour formerly spread about Alexander the Great, which was comparable in its emptiness and fantasy, that he was conceived by sex with a huge snake [*anguis*], and that the manifestation of that prodigy had been seen often in his mother's bedroom, and that, when people came across it, it suddenly shot off and slithered from view. He himself never did anything to compromise belief in these miracles.

Nay rather, this belief was enhanced by the variety of artfulness he deployed in neither denying nor openly confirming any such thing.'
SIRE: *drakōn* = **Jupiter**.

7. Alexander: Livy 26.19.7–8.
DATE: After 19 BC.
CONTENT: A passing reference in the discussion of Scipio, as above.
SIRE: *drakōn* = **unspecified**.

8. Alexander: Trogus at Justin 11.11.
DATE: Ca. AD 9.
CONTENT: See above (A, 11).
SIRE: *drakōn* = **unspecified** OR = **Ammon**.

9. Augustus: Asclepiades of Mendes *FGrH* / *BNJ* 617 F2 (*apud* Suetonius, *Augustus* 94).
DATE: Later 1st c. BC – 2nd c. AD.
CONTENT: "Atia came in the middle of the night for a solemn rite of Apollo. She had her litter set down in the temple and fell asleep, the other matrons sleeping likewise. A serpent suddenly insinuated itself into her and exited a little later [*draconem repente irrepsisse ad eam pauloque post egressum*]. When she woke up, she purified herself as she would after the embrace of her husband. And at once there manifested itself on her body a mark as of a painted serpent [*draco*], and she could never expunge it."
SIRE: *drakōn* = **Apollo**—but the imagery of incubation is again strongly **Asclepian:** cf. Nicasibula again, above (B, 1).

10. Scipio Africanus: Silius Italicus, *Punica* 13.634–49.
DATE: Ca. AD 100.
CONTENT: Having slept, Scipio's mother Pomponia awakes at midday in a brilliant light, to find herself embraced by Jupiter in the form of a giant serpent.
SIRE: *drakōn* = **Jupiter**.

11. Alexander: Plutarch, *Alexander* 2–3.
DATE: Ca. AD 100.
CONTENT: See above (A, 13).
SIRE: *drakōn* = **Ammon**.

12. Alexander: Ptolemy Chennus *apud* Photius cod. 190, §148a.
DATE: Ca. AD 98–138.

CONTENT: Alexander is sired by a man called Drakon.
SIRE: *drakōn* = **unspecified.**

13. Miletus: Inscription of Caesarea Troketta, *IGROM* iv.1498.
DATE: Ca. AD 160.
CONTENT: Miletus, the priest of Apollo Soter, is declared to be the son of "Paphlagonian Glykon."
SIRE: *drakōn* = **Glykon = Asclepius.**

14. Alexander: Aulus Gellius, *Attic Nights* 6.1.1.
DATE: Later 2nd c. AD.
CONTENT: See above (A, 17, B, 5).
SIRE: *drakōn* = **unspecified.**

15. Aratus of Sicyon: Pausanias 2.10.3 and 4.14.7.
DATE: Later 2nd c, AD.
CONTENT: Aratus' mother Aristodama was represented "on" a *drakōn*, his sire, in a mobile hanging from the roof of the temple of Asclepius in Sicyon.
SIRE: *drakōn* = **Asclepius.**

16. Aristomenes of Messene: Pausanias 4.14.7.
DATE: Later 2nd c. AD.
CONTENT: A *daimōn* or a god took the form of a *drakōn* and had sex with Aristomenes' mother Nicoteleia (see above for the full passage: A, 18). This tale is seemingly derived from the late-3rd c. BC *Messeniaca* of Rhianus of Bene, which also mentioned Nicoteleia (see *FGrH* / *BNJ* 265 F39 / 50 Powell).
SIRE: *drakōn* = **a daimon or a god.**

17. Alexander: Pausanias 4.14.7.
DATE: Later 2nd c. AD.
CONTENT: See above (A, 18).
SIRE: *drakōn* = **Ammon.**

18. Alexander: Lucian, *Dialogues of the Dead* 13.
DATE: Ca. AD 170s.
CONTENT: See above (A, 19).
SIRE: *drakōn* = **unspecified.**

19. Alexander: Lucian, *Alexander* 7; cf. 15.
DATE: After AD 181.

CONTENT: See above (A, 20).
SIRE: *drakōn* = **unspecified.**

20. Alexander of Abonutichus: Lucian, *Alexander* **11.**
DATE: After 181 AD.
CONTENT: Alexander of Abonutichus claims to have been sired by Podalirius of Tricca, the son of Asclepius.[20]
SIRE: (*drakōn?*) = **Podalirius, son of Asclepius.**

21. Augustus: Cassius Dio 45.1.2–3.
DATE: ca. AD 229.
CONTENT: Caesar chooses to adopt Octavian-Augustus on the basis of Atia's claim that he had been sired by Apollo; cf. *Epigrammata Bobiensia* 39 (text at Speyer 1963) and the Portland Vase (?).
SIRE: *drakōn* = **Apollo.**

22. Scipio Africanus: Cassius Dio 16.7.39; cf. 17.57.63.
DATE: Ca. AD 229.
CONTENT: Jupiter takes the form of a serpent to have sex with Scipio's mother.
SIRE: *drakōn* = **Jupiter.**

23. Alexander: *Alexander Romance* **(A) 1.6–8, 10, 12, 14, 24, 30, 35, 2.13, 21, 3.33.**
DATE: Early 3rd c. AD.
CONTENT: See above (A, 21).
SIRE: *drakōn* = **Nectanebo, Ammon (Zeus, Heracles, Dionysus).**

VI The serpent sires of the Graeco-Roman world: their identity-profile

If we bracket off the Alexander examples under discussion, the identity-profile of the remaining serpent sires can be characterised as more coherent than is initially apparent. The dominant trend is emphatically Asclepian:[21]

---

[20] The slightly tricky case for understanding that Podalirius performed this act of siring in the form of a *drakōn* is laid out at Ogden (2009c).
[21] For Asclepius in general see Edelstein and Edelstein (1945) (incorporating a vast collection of sources), and LiDonnici (1995) (for the Epidaurian miracle inscriptions). For his iconography see

- Asclepius: (B, 1) Nicasibula's children, (B, 3) Aratus, (B, 13) Miletus, (B, 15) Aratus,
- Apollo, the father of Asclepius: (B, 9) Augustus, (B, 21) Augustus,
- Podalirius (?), the son of Asclepius: (B, 20) Alexander of Abonutichus
- Zeus-Jupiter: (B, 10) Scipio Africanus, (B, 22) Scipio Africanus
- Mysterious *drakōn:* (B, 16) Aristomenes

Three individuals (in four contexts) are directly given Asclepius as father. Augustus is (twice) given as his father Apollo, who is the father of Asclepius, and in one of these contexts his siring is of an emphatically Asclepian nature: Asclepiades of Mendes has his mother Atia incubating in a temple of Apollo, just as one might more normally do in a temple of Asclepius, where she is penetrated by a sacred snake, just as the barren Nicasibula is penetrated by a sacred snake in the sanctuary of Asclepius at Epidaurus. Alexander of Abonutichus is given as his father Podalirius, who is the son of Asclepius (if indeed he is given a serpent sire at all). It becomes apparent that the stand-out anomaly here is Scipio Africanus, who is twice given Zeus-Jupiter as his father. And yet even so Asclepianism lurks in his tradition too. First, it is noteworthy that the earlier account of this Scipio tradition, that of Oppius, whilst (so far as we can tell from Aulus Gellius' report) suggesting that the serpent's identity is Jupiter rather than directly declaring it, imbues the tale of the serpent-siring with strongly Asclepian imagery: again, a barren woman is impregnated by a snake as she sleeps, like Asclepius' own Nicasibula. Secondly, it is a strong possibility that the tradition of Scipio's serpent sire was a secondary development of the tradition of Augustus' own serpent sire as the incipient emperor sought to fashion a typological precedent for himself: the switch to Jupiter may have been occasioned either by Scipio's own established relationship with that god, or indeed simply for reasons of *variatio.*[22]

VII Alexander and the Asclepian

When we return to Alexander it is noteworthy again that the earliest certain mention of Alexander's serpent sire, Cicero's (B, 4), is also emphatically Asclepian in its context: Cicero connects the serpent sire with the serpent that manifests itself

---

LIMC Asklepios *passim.* For his shrines see Riethmüller (2005) (a monumental catalogue), and for incubation in his sanctuaries see now Renberg (2017) esp.1: 115–270, 634–649, 689–713. For the god's serpentine affinities see Ogden (2013a) 310–317.
22 For Augustus' serpent sire see Becher (1996); Lorsch (1997).

in a dream to Alexander at Harmatelia to show him the herb to use to heal the wound dealt to Ptolemy with a poison arrow (an arrow imbued with snake venom in turn, as it happens).[23] There is enough here to raise the possibility that the Alexander tradition had originally conceptualised his serpent sire as Asclepius or at any rate Asclepian.

Could such thinking have had any root in Alexander's own lifetime or close to it? We know at least that Asclepius in the aspect of a giant serpent was of interest to Ptolemy Philadelphus a generation later. Aelian tells that two gigantic snakes were brought for Philadelphus from Ethiopia, and that three similar creatures were brought also for his successor Euergetes; these were then carefully maintained in the Alexandrian Asclepieion. A vestige of this tradition is already found in Diodorus, who tells that Philadelphus was given a serpent of the length of 30 cubits by some hunters, and that he kept it as a pet.[24]

The pickings from Alexander's own biographical tradition are not rich, and such as they are indicate an ambivalent attitude towards the god on the king's part: he made offerings to Asclepius in his in temples at Soli, Epidaurus and Gortys in Arcadia,[25] but then he also supposedly burned down his temples because he failed to save the life of Hephaestion.[26]

But the star witness in this connection is a piece of contemporary evidence that stands outside Alexander's biographical tradition. In frustratingly allusive *obiter dicta* Hyperides, writing in the early 320s BC, remarks that "[Euxenippus] behaved abominably over the *phiale* [a *patera*, a shallow dish], in having allowed Olympias to dedicate it to the image of Hygieia."[27] It is suggestive indeed, from a historical perspective, to learn that Alexander's mother was in actual fact a devotee of Asclepius' daughter.[28]

Hyperides' words also direct our attention to the iconographic traditions for Hygieia and Olympias alike. Hygieia (and subsequently her Roman reflex Salus) had a simple and consistent iconography in her statuary and on coins (perhaps because she had no mythology of her own to inspire experimentation in it): she is shown either seated and cradling a great serpent on her lap, or standing, with the serpent winding itself around her body; in both cases she feeds the serpent from a *phiale*. We can see, therefore, that Olympias' gift was a very appropriate one. The serpent represented at once the alternative form of Hygieia's manifesta-

---

23 Cf. again Clitarchus [not in *FGrH / BNJ*] apud Diod. Sic. 17.103 and Curt. 9.8.22–28.
24 Ael. *NA* 16.39; Diod. Sic. 3.36–7.
25 Soli: Arr. *Anab.* 2.5.8. Epidaurus: Arr. *Anab.* 7.14.5. Gortys: Paus. 8.28.1.
26 Arr. *Epict. diss.* 2.22.17 and *Anab.* 7.14.5–6.
27 Hyp. 4.19.
28 Discussion at Carney (2006) 95–96.

tion, or her avatar, just as the serpent that wound itself around her father Asclepius' staff did in his case.[29] We have to wait until late antiquity before we find images of Olympias with Alexander's siring serpent, but when we do, they are strikingly reminiscent of the iconography of Hygieia. On a series of fourth-century AD Roman contorniates Olympias ("*Olympias regina*") reclines on a bed and the serpent coils vertically by her side as she feeds it from a *phiale*.[30] Enough remains of a fragmentary mosaic from Baalbek to show that a serpent once similarly coiled on the lap of its seated Olympias. Whether she also fed it from a *phiale* is less clear. Perhaps not: the left hand in which she would have had to have held it seems wrongly positioned for it.[31] The convergence of Olympias and Hygieia's iconography cannot be better demonstrated than by the confusion surrounding a fragment of a marble relief from Palatitsa in Macedon: the body of a large serpent coils vertically on a woman's lap: scholars dispute, precisely, whether it belonged to a Hygieia or an Olympias.[32]

Is it conceivable that the tradition of Olympias' impregnation by a serpent originated in the association of her name with a serpent-toting statue of Hygieia on the Athenian acropolis?

VIII An alternative possibility: ostentatious mystery

The one non-Alexander entry in our catalogue of serpent sires we have yet to address is that of Aristomenes of Messene (B, 16). Pausanias declares that his serpent sire was either "a *daimōn* or a god" but asserts the mysteriousness of his identity beyond this in a positive way; indeed, far from seeking to identify Aristomenes' sire further, he pours scorn on the attempts of others to identify the serpent sires of both Alexander and Aratus of Sicyon. Whilst Asclepius is hardly excluded as a potential sire for Aristomenes by these words, they do raise the possibility of an alternative syndrome of a *drakōn*-sire that is ostentatiously mysterious and designedly not tied to any one nameable god. This potential syndrome is worth mentioning because it is possible that—*pace* Pausanias' own

---

[29] For Hygieia and her iconography see Croissant (1990), Saladino (1994), Ogden (2013a) 317–321.
[30] See Ross (1963) 17–21, Vermeule (1982), Stewart (2003) 62–65, Carney (2006) 122–123; cf. also the coins at Dahmen (2007) 140–141, 154.
[31] See Chéhab (1958–9), Ross (1963) 3–5.
[32] Louvre M. A. 2550; discussion at Simon (1957) 25–26.

words here—two of the Alexander texts conform with it. If the Eratosthenic passage (A, 5 = B, 2) is indeed serpent-related (irrespective of whether or not it is penned by the actual Eratosthenes), then it might well, given its ostentatious obfuscation, constitute another example of a "mysterious *drakōn*" tendency. It is also possible that Ptolemy Chennus' more ludic, euhemerising treatment of the theme (A, 13 = B, 12), in apparently excluding reference to any further deity (but we do depend on Photius' summary for his words), points to an underlying tradition of a similar "mysterious *drakōn*," beyond which one is simply not supposed not look.

Conclusion

Such, then, has been my palinode. Careful scrutiny of the tradition for Alexander's divine sire encourages us to disaggregate it into two principal strands or sub-traditions: a strand in accordance with which Alexander was sired by Zeus-Ammon; and a strand in accordance with which he was sired by serpent. By the turn of the eras there had developed an occasional tendency to knot these strands together, to contaminate the two sub-traditions, and so it was that Zeus-Ammon and the serpent-sire came to be identified with each other. But when we consider both the evidence for the original identity of Alexander's serpent sire in its own context, and also the (not inconsiderable) comparative evidence for other serpent sires in the Graeco-Roman world, we are brought to conclude that, whilst the identity of Alexander's serpent may (or may not) have remained (contrivedly) mysterious, its affinities were emphatically Asclepian.

Abbreviations

BNJ   Worthington (2007–).
EMI   LiDonnici (1995).
FGrH   Jacoby (1923–).
IG   *Inscriptiones Graecae* (1903–).
IGROM Cagnat *et al.* (1906–27).
LIMC   Kahil *et al.* (1981–99).
P.Oxy.   Grenfell *et al.* (1898–).

Bibliography

Barbantani (2014): Silvia Barbantani, "Mother of snakes and kings: Apollonius Rhodius' *Foundation of Alexandria*", in: *Histos* 8, 209–245.
Becher (1996): Ilse Becher, "Atia, die Mutter des Augustus—Legende und Politik", in: Ernst G. Schmidt *et al.* (eds.) *Griechenland und Rom*, Tbilissi, 95–116.
Bosch-Puche (2008): Francisco Bosch-Puche, "L'ʽautel' du temple d'Alexandre le Grand à Bahariya retrouvé", in: *Bulletin de l'Institut français d'archéologie orientale* 108, 29–44.
Bosworth (1980): A. Brian Bosworth, *A Historical Commentary on Arrian's* History of Alexander, vol. 1, Oxford.
Cagnat *et al.* (1906–27): René Cagnat *et al.* (eds.), *Inscriptiones Graecae ad res Romanas pertinentes*, 3 vols., Paris.
Carney (2006): Elizabeth D. Carney, *Olympias. Mother of Alexander the Great*, London.
Chéhab (1958–9): Maurice Chéhab, "Mosaiques de Liban", in: *Bulletin du Musée de Beyrouth* 15, 46–50, with plates 22–5.
Croissant (1990): François Croissant, "Hygieia", in: *LIMC* v.1, 554–572.
Dahmen (2007): Karsten Dahmen, *The Legend of Alexander the Great on Greek and Roman Coins*, London.
Dindorf (1832): Ludwig A. Dindorf (ed.), *Chronicon Paschale*, 2 vols., Bonn.
Djurslev and Ogden (2018): Christian T. Djurslev and Daniel Ogden, "Alexander, Agathoi Daimones, Argives and Armenians", in: *Karanos* 1, 11–21.
Dunand (1969): Françoise Dunand, "Les representations de l'Agathodémon; à propos de quelques bas-reliefs du Musée d'Alexandrie", in: *Bulletin de l'Institut français d'archéologie orientale* 67, 9–48.
Dunand (1981): Françoise Dunand "Agathodaimon", in: *LIMC* i.1, 277–282.
Edelstein and Edelstein (1945): Emma J. L. and Ludwig Edelstein, *Asclepius: A Collection and Interpretation of the Testimonies*, 2 vols., Baltimore. Reprinted in 1998 with a new introduction.
Fraser (1972): Peter M. Fraser, *Ptolemaic Alexandria*, 3 vols., Oxford.
Fusillo and Schmidt (2005): Massimo Fusillo and Peter L. Schmidt, "Livius, T.", in: *Brill's New Pauly*, Leiden, vii, 749–754.
Gauthier and Hatzopoulos (1993): Philippe Gauthier and Miltiades B. Hatzopoulos, *La loi gymnasiarchique de Beroia*, Athens.
Grenfell *et al.* (1898–), Bernard P. Grenfell *et al.* (eds.), *The Oxyrhynchus Papyri*, London.
Hillard (1998): Tom W. Hillard, "The *Agathos Daimon* abandons Alexandria: the Potter's Oracle and possible Roman allusions", in: Tom W. Hillard *et al.* (eds.), *Ancient History in a Modern University. 1. The Ancient Near East, Greece and Rome*, Grand Rapids, 160–172.
Hillard (2010). Tom W. Hillard, "The god abandons Antony: Egyptian street theatre in 30 BC" in: Naguib Kanawati (hon.), Alexandra Woods, Ann McFarlane and Susanne Binder (eds.), *Egyptian Culture and Society. Studies in Honour of Naguib Kanawati*, 2 vols., Cairo, i, 201–217.
Jacoby *et al.* (1923–): Felix Jacoby *et al.* (eds.), *Die Fragmente der griechischen Historiker*, Berlin and Leiden.
Kahil *et al.* (1981–99): Lily Kahil *et al.* (eds.), *Lexicon iconographicum mythologiae classicae.* 9 vols. in 18 pts., Zurich and Munich.

Lalonde (2006): Gerald V. Lalonde, *Horos Dios: An Athenian Shrine and Cult*, Leiden.
Le Bohec (2002): Sylvie Le Bohec, "The kings of Macedon and the cult of Zeus in the Hellenistic Period", in: Daniel Ogden (ed.) *The Hellenistic World. New Perspectives*, London, 41–57.
Le Rider (1996): Georges Le Rider, *Monayage et finances de Philippe II. Un état de question*, Athens.
LiDonnici (1995): Lynn R. LiDonnici, *The Epidaurian Miracle Inscriptions. Text, Translation and Commentary*, Atlanta.
Lorsch (1997): Robin S. Lorsch, "Augustus' conception and heroic tradition" in: *Latomus* 56, 790–799.
Mørkholm (1991): Otto Mørkholm: *Early Hellenistic Coinage from the Accession of Alexander to the Peace of Apamea (336–186 AD)*, Cambridge.
Ogden (2009a): Daniel Ogden, "Alexander's snake sire", in: Pat Wheatley and Robert Hannah (eds.), *Alexander and his Successors: Essays from the Antipodes*, Claremont, CA, 136–178.
Ogden (2009b): Daniel Ogden, "Alexander, Scipio and Octavian: serpent-siring in Macedon and Rome", in: *Syllecta Classica* 20, 31–52.
Ogden (2009c): Daniel Ogden, "Lucianus, Glycon and the two Alexanders", in: Mustafa Çevik (ed.) *International Symposium on Lucianus of Samosata*, Adiyaman, 279–300.
Ogden (2011): Daniel Ogden, *Alexander the Great: Myth, Genesis and Sexuality*, Exeter.
Ogden (2012): Daniel Ogden, "Sekandar, Dragon-Slayer", in: Richard Stoneman, Kyle Erickson and Ian Netton (eds.), *The Alexander Romance in Persia and the East*, Ancient Narrative Supplementum 15, Groningen, 277–294.
Ogden (2013a): Daniel Ogden, *Drakōn: Dragon Myth and Serpent Cult in the Greek and Roman Worlds*, Oxford.
Ogden (2013b): Daniel Ogden, "The Alexandrian foundation myth: Alexander, Ptolemy, the *agathoi daimones* and the *argolaoi*", in: Victor Alonso Troncoso and Edward Anson (eds.), *After Alexander: The Time of the Diadochoi*, Oxford, 241–252.
Ogden (2014): Daniel Ogden, "Alexander, Agathos Daimon and Ptolemy: the Alexandrian foundation myth in dialogue", in: Naoíse Mac Sweeney (ed.), *Foundation Myths in Ancient Societies: Dialogues and Discourses*, Philadelphia, 129–150.
Ogden (2015): Daniel Ogden, "Nectanebo's seduction of Olympias and the benign anguiform deities of the ancient Greek world", in: A. Brian Bosworth (hon.), Pat Wheatley and Elizabeth Baynham (eds.), *East and West in the World Empire of Alexander. Essays in Honour of Brian Bosworth*, Oxford, 117–132.
Powell (1925): John U. Powell (ed.), *Collectanea Alexandrina*, Oxford.
Pownall (n.d.): Frances Pownall, "241 Eratosthenes", in: *BNJ*.
Riethmüller (2005): Jürgen W. Riethmüller, *Asklepios: Heiligtümer und Kulte*, 2 vols., Heidelberg.
Renberg (2017): Gil H. Renberg, *Where Dreams May Come: Incubation Sanctuaries in the Greco-Roman World*, 2 vols. (continuous pagination), Leiden.
Ross (1963): David J. A. Ross, "Olympias and the serpent: the interpretation of Baalbek mosaic and the date of the illustrated Pseudo-Callisthenes", in: *Journal of the Warburg and Courtauld Institutes* 26, 1–23.

Saatsoglou-Paliadeli (2000): Chryssoula Saatsoglou-Paliadeli, "Queenly appearances at Vergina-Aegae: old and new epigraphic and literary evidence", in: *Archäologischer Anzeiger* 3, 387–403.

Saladino (1994): Vincenzo Saladino, "Salus", in: *LIMC* vii.1, 656–661.

Schermann (1907): Theodor Schermann, *Prophetarum vitae fabulosae*, Leipzig.

Simon (1957): Erika Simon, *Die Portlandvase*, Mainz.

Speyer (1963): Wolfgang Speyer (ed.), *Epigrammata Bobiensia*, Leipzig.

Stewart (1993): Andrew Stewart, *Faces of Power: Alexander's Image and Hellenistic Politics*, Berkeley.

Vermeule (1982): Cornelius Vermeule, "Alexander the Great, the Emperor Severus Alexander and the Aboukir Medallions", in: *Revue suisse de numismatique/Schweizerische numismatische Rundschau* 61, 61–79.

Wolohojian (1969): Albert M. Wolohojian (trans.), *The Romance of Alexander the Great by Pseudo-Callisthenes. Translated from the Armenian Version*, New York.

Worthington (2007–): Ian Worthington (ed.), *Brill's New Jacoby* [online resource], Leiden.

Christian Thrue Djurslev
Educating Alexander: High Culture in the Argead Court through Ancient Texts

I Introduction

In Aleksandra Klęczar's presentation at a 2018 conference in Edmonton, Canada —the *fons et origo* of this volume—she argued that scholars should take a more sympathetic view of the literary traditions about the Macedonian royal court than is typically held in scholarship.[1] Indeed, the non-Macedonian origin of our source material and the widely scattered nature of the scarce evidence demand that we evaluate what is still available in a thoroughgoing fashion.[2]

Accordingly, in this chapter, I adopt an inclusive approach to what remains in the Greek and Roman texts, showing how they provide not only early evidence of the Temenid dynasty of Macedon, the so-called "Argeads", but also a rich literary discourse that was renewed throughout antiquity. Since the scope is broad, I take Argead education as my theme, focusing on the pre-campaign episodes of Alexander's upbringing in Macedon.[3] The "evidence" for the princeling's education is wholly literary in nature, as ever, and so poses similar problems as the familiar narrative accounts of the eastern campaign.[4] The present investigation is therefore an important reminder that we need to pay due attention to the literary games in texts before any historical reconstruction of Argead court culture may occur.[5]

---

[1] Similarly, in one of Brian Bosworth's last lectures, he argued that there was more to the many anecdotes about Philip and Alexander outside the principal histories. For the written version of his Trendall lecture, see Bosworth (2011).

[2] Howe and Pownall (2018). Cf. Asirvatham (2017).

[3] Although a staple subject of modern biographies, the topic is often relegated to a prefatory section named "the Macedonian background," *vel sim.* For a sober account, see Müller (2016) 278–282.

[4] Consider literary accounts of Aristotle's tutelage of the young prince at the precinct of the Nymphs in Mieza at Mt. Bermium (c. 343–340 BC; from age 13 to 16), discussed in Djurslev (2020) 43–50. For an overview of modern scholarship until 2015, see Marín (2018) 78–79. Cf. Seibert (1972) 72–73.

[5] See e.g. Ogden (2011). Ogden (forthcoming) will treat the evidence for Alexander's life from childhood to accession to the throne, and I thank him for making an early draft available to me. For the education theme, see e.g. Billows (2018) 52 (the historical dimension). Cf. Peltonen (2019) 93–99 (reception in later literature).

In the first section, I argue against the notion that Plutarch's *Life of Alexander* represents the only valuable account of Alexander's youth by comparing Plutarch's account with that of the *Alexander Romance*, as well as a range of other texts (Aeschines, Aelian, and Plutarch's other works). In the second section, I collate the various stories about Alexander's teachers, demonstrating that there existed many alternatives to Alexander's Aristotle. I suggest that these kinds of stories developed early in the crown prince's literary tradition, reflecting the agendas of intellectuals at the Argead court and their later followers.[6] In the third and final section, I conduct three case studies of minor topics that corroborate the key tendencies traced throughout this chapter: the early origin of tales, the historical importance of less frequent topics, and the innovations in later periods.

II Alexander's education beyond Plutarch's *Life*

The principal literary account of Alexander's upbringing comes from approximately ten chapters of Plutarch's famous biography.[7] A part of this *Life* has often been regarded as a reworking of the writings by Onesicritus of Astypalea,[8] one among many elusive figures from the first generation of Alexander historiographers. Some ancient writers considered Onesicritus a Cynic philosopher and credited him with an *Education of Alexander*, but we are no longer certain about the nature, or even the title, of this lost work.[9] This casts Plutarch's assumed engagement with it into doubt. Moreover, Marsyas of Pella offers the only other known account of an *Education of Alexander* before Plutarch, but the existence of such a work is now also called into question.[10] Our major narrative histories from the Roman period, from Diodorus Siculus to Arrian, avoid the topic of Alexander's upbringing.[11]

---

6 Cf. Pownall (2020) 260–261.
7 Plut. *Mor.* 179d–e contains other references to activities, while Alexander was young, some of which appear in the *Life*.
8 See e.g. Hamilton (2001) lxiii, who holds Onesicritus responsible for the early parts of the *Life*, although he stresses that Plutarch follows Onesicritus much more fully in *De Alex. fort.*, a conclusion accepted by Whitmarsh (2002) 179.
9 Onesicritus of Astypalea *BNJ* 134 T 1 *ap.* D.L. 6.84, with commentary by Whitby (2011).
10 Marsyas of Pella/Philippi *BNJ* 135–136 T 1 *ap.* Suda s.v. Μαρσύας 227 Adler, with Howe's commentary: "it seems unlikely that Marsyas of Pella wrote a separate work on Alexander's education."
11 Nep. *Praef.* 1 provides a clue for this omission, saying that the sort of content about educational or artistic details might be too trifling and inappropriate for Roman taste. He uses the ex-

The Greek *Alexander Romance* (hereafter *AR*) does not often enter scholarly discussions in company with these texts, perhaps because it contains a rather fanciful account of Alexander's early years.[12] At a structural level, however, it is clear that the *AR* operates in much the same way as the *Life*. For instance, Plutarch ends Alexander's upbringing with the Attalus incident at the wedding of Philip and Cleopatra (9),[13] the Pixodarus affair (10), and Pausanias' killing of Philip (10.6–8),[14] whereas the anonymous author of the *AR* selects the Attalus incident (§§ 56–59), Alexander's hosting of the Persian envoys (§§ 64–65),[15] and Philip's murder by Pausanias (§§ 67–70). Plutarch places Alexander's visit to Delphi after the sack of Thebes,[16] but the *AR* records the visit before the Attalus incident (§ 55). In fact, a longer look at Plutarch and the *AR* reveals that the authors have much in common. Both narratives feature set pieces on Alexander's birth,[17] looks,[18] athletics,[19] teachers,[20] taming of Bucephalas,[21] other educational activities,[22] and interactions with members of the court. On the whole, the two accounts actually agree.[23]

The main takeaway from my structural comparison of Plutarch and the *AR* is that by the early imperial period, if not before, the set of stories concerning Alexander's pre-campaign life feels fairly consistent. It is difficult to ascertain

---

ample of Epaminondas of Thebes' music teacher, the general's dancing ability and his skill with the pipes, *tibia*. For the *topos* of an artistic king/commander, see Müller (2017a).
12 Against this trend, see Landucci (2018).
13 A story on early authority: Satyrus F 21 Kumaniecki from Ath. 13.557b–e. Cf. Just. *Epit.* 9.7.3–7.
14 Also known to Arist. *Pol.* 1311ab. Cf. Diod. Sic. 16.93–5, Just. *Epit.* 9.6–7.
15 Cf. Plut. *Alex.* 5.1–3.
16 Plut. *Alex.* 14.5–6.
17 Plut. *Alex* 2–3; *AR* Armenian §§ 6–27.
18 Plut. *Alex.* 4.1–7; *AR* Armenian § 28.
19 Plut. *Alex.* 4.8–11; *AR* Armenian § 30 (changing sides help his friends win in play), §§ 49–54 (games at Pisa).
20 Plut. *Alex.* 5.7 (Leonides the tutor), 5.8 (Lysimachus), 7 (Aristotle); *AR* Armenian § 29 (list of teachers), § 37 (Aristotle).
21 Bucephalas: Plut. *Alex.* 6; *AR* Armenian § 31 (part I), § 36 (part II), §§ 47–8 (part III).
22 Plut. *Alex.* 7.6–8 (exchange with Aristotle); *AR* Armenian §§ 39–46 (exchange with Zeuxis).
23 It is noteworthy, however, that the frame of reference in Plutarch's biography and the *AR* is so similar. For instance, as Nawotka (2017) 78–9 notes, Plutarch (*Alex.* 4.10, *Mor.* 331b. Cf. *Mor.* 179d) has Alexander make the complaint that he will not compete in the Olympic Games unless kings compete with him and, in the *AR* (1.18–19), we find Alexander competing against three other kings in the chariot races. Moreover, Plutarch claims that Alexander took no interest in sport, boxing and pancratium (4.11), whereas the *AR* has Philip reminding Alexander that he never trained in sport, also referring specifically to the pancratium (1.18.3–4). Of course, Plutarch leaves out a number of episodes known from the *AR*, primarily relating to the tales of Nectanebus (1.1–14).

whether we should credit this consistency to a single source, like Onesicritus, or see it as a general agreement on how one wrote about Alexander's upbringing. For this, we must consult some of the less organized snippets of information about the education of Alexander.

Alexander's earliest appearance in the historical record comes in a short section of Aeschines' oration, *Against Timarchus* (1.166–9, delivered c. 346/5 BC). Alongside Demosthenes, Aeschines had been part of a three-month peace embassy to Philip's court in the spring of 346, when Alexander was not yet ten years old. Of course, we have to be cautious about Aeschines' accuracy,[24] but the encounter does not seem farfetched. Aeschines (1.168) reports what Demosthenes had said during a symposium in which the princeling performed:

> αὐτὸς [...] ὑπὲρ τοῦ παιδὸς Ἀλεξάνδρου διεξῄει, ὡς ἔν τῳ πότῳ ἡμῶν κιθαρίζοι καὶ λέγοι ῥήσεις τινὰς καὶ ἀντικρούσεις πρὸς ἕτερον παῖδα[.]
>
> [...] when he (i.e. Demosthenes) was talking in detail about the boy Alexander, how he played the cithara at a drinking party, and recited some speeches and made some sallies against another boy[.] (trans. Fisher, adapted)

The chief academic interest in this passage is Aeschines' perspective on Greek pederasty, because Aeschines is defending himself against Demosthenes' accusation that he had taken too strong an interest in the youth.[25] Sabine Müller links Demosthenes' anti-Macedonian rhetoric with sexual innuendo,[26] specifically because of Alexander's cithara, which Aristotle would later consider inappropriate for aristocrats (*Pol.* 1341a). However, as Müller also recognizes, to play the cithara was a standard element of Greek education. For example, in the Platonic dialogue *Theages* (122e), Demodocus takes his son Theages to Socrates, and we learn that the boy had already learned basic education: cithara practice is listed specifically, alongside other worthwhile pursuits, such as reading and writing.

---

[24] One test case is Aeschin. *Or.* 2.28–9 (*On the False Embassy*), discussed at Billows (2018) 53–54. Claiming to be an eyewitness, Aeschines speaks of Philip and his brother Perdiccas as "children", *paidia*, when they were in fact teenagers. The orator goes on to say that the two could be placed in the arms and sit on the knee of the Athenian general Iphicrates, as he sorted the conflict over the succession. Moreover, Philip was not even present in Macedon at the time (mid-368 BC), as he was kept hostage in Thebes.

[25] For an overview of scholarship, see Koulakiotis (2006) 35–38. No sexual undertones detected in Hamilton (1973) 32; Fisher (2001) 313; Carney (2015) 192.

[26] Müller (2017a) 254. Cf. Müller (2016) 281. I am, however, not persuaded by the suggestion that Demosthenes is harsh on Alexander because he was the pupil of a Greek philosopher. Aristotle did not begin teaching Alexander until three years *after* the embassy in question.

Whatever the intent of Demosthenes or Aeschines, the reference to the instrument has resonated the most in the literary tradition. Nick Fisher proposes in his commentary on *Against Timarchus* that Alexander's playing can be connected to a story in Aelian (*VH* 3.32).[27] The story goes that a musician was instructing Alexander as a boy, παῖς ὤν, in playing the cithara, when the student asked for the importance of striking a different string than the one he struck. The instructor responded that a king needed not trouble himself; that was the concern only of the musician. He said this to save his own neck, remembering that Heracles killed Linus when the poet corrected the hero's playing—Alexander's instructor feared the same treatment if he ever had to correct the prince.

Aelian's anecdote may carry historical significance in that the reference to Heracles and Linus stands out.[28] While the young Heracles' slaying of Linus was well known across the Greek and Roman worlds,[29] Gary Vos has argued for a strong link between Linus and the Argead court based on a story in Pausanias.[30] He relates that Philip brought back Linus' bones to Macedon after Chaeronea and later returned them (Paus. 9.29.8–9). Although this transference of local heroes had been a fairly familiar literary motif since Herodotus' tale of the bones of Orestes,[31] there is no reason to doubt that Philip would have done this action or circulated a story to that effect,[32] given the Macedonian associations of Linus and Orpheus. As Vos proposes, it is immensely fitting that an anecdote about a music teacher and Alexander, recalling Linus and Heracles, should appear during the early 330s, especially now that we have seen that Alexander had musical training and was known outside Macedon for it.

Plutarch also takes interest in Alexander's music practice, preserving anecdotal material contemporary with the historical Alexander's time. For instance, in the biography of Pericles (*Per*.1.6), Philip rebukes his young son for playing the lyre too skillfully (τεχνικῶς)—a king should spend his leisure listening to other good artists play, with the implication that a ruler required the ability to deter-

---

27 Fisher (2001) 313.
28 Scholarship is currently reassessing the historical value of Aelian's anecdotes, see e.g. Kuin (2019).
29 See e.g. the passing remark remark in Plaut. *Bacch.* 155–7. A fuller version is preserved in Apollod. *Bibl.* 2.4.9.
30 The following builds on Vos (2018) 68, 161, 444. I thank the author for making the relevant sections of his dissertation available for perusal.
31 Hdt. 1.67–8. Cf. Paus. 7.1.8.
32 This event may have been celebrated into Hellenistic times: the Thespians, an anti-Theban city restored by Philip, held Mouseia festivals at Mt. Helicon (Paus. 9.31.3), presumably at the behest of Ptolemaic patrons like Arsinoë II, whose statue stood at Mt. Helicon (cf. Paus. 9.31.1).

mine the skill of artists, not to play well themselves.[33] Plutarch has probably taken the sentiment from Aristotle, who makes the very same point.[34] It follows that Plutarch has applied this sentiment to a Philip-Alexander anecdote with an indeterminable context. Furthermore, I must stress how strongly Plutarch's two representations of the young prince diverge from the vignette of the disinterested student in Aelian's account.

Given the evidence of Aeschines and the two separate anecdotes, it becomes crucial that neither Plutarch's *Alexander* nor the *AR* include any of the three tales. In fact, Plutarch does not include the Philip-Alexander anecdote from the *Life of Pericles* anywhere else in his works.[35] Of course, I recognize that both Plutarch's *Life of Alexander* and the *AR* contain passages that fit well with Aeschines in terms of thematic parallels: (1) Alexander hosting an embassy of Persians in Philip's stead;[36] and (2) the symposium setting of the wedding of Philip and Cleopatra. However, these parallels fail to convince. The two episodes serve very different narrative functions in the biographical sources than Alexander's performance in Aeschines. The former episode suggests the young Alexander's antagonism against Persia and his suitability to rule in Philip's place, whereas the latter indicates drunken disorderliness during Philip's symposia, again pointing to Alexander's superiority as the eventual ruler.[37] Moreover, the specificity of the historical situations in Aeschines and Plutarch/*AR* signal that they were referring to unrelated events. This difference again expresses dif-

---

[33] I note that, in the second Plutarchan Alexander speech, Alexander has learned this lesson already, see Plut. *De Alex. fort.* 2.2 (*Mor.* 334d). This is important not only because of the contrast to the anecdote in the *Life of Pericles*, but also because the whole oration is concerned with Alexander's patronage of the arts. Plutarch thus follows the Aristotelian principle of representing Alexander as a better patron when the king himself is a poorer musician.
[34] Arist. *Pol.* 1340b with Griffiths (2015) 43. Cf. Müller (2017a) 255.
[35] Plutarch mentions other anecdotes about Alexander and musical instruments, but none of them refers to events prior to the campaign. See e.g. the anecdote about Achilles'/Paris' lyre offered to Alexander at Troy, Plut. *Alex.* 15.9, *De Alex. fort.* 10 (331d–e); cf. Ael. *VH* 9.38. For divergent stories of Alexander across Plutarch's works, see Asirvatham (2018).
[36] Cf. Plut. *Mor.* 342b–c. Cf. Heinrichs (2020) 55–60. Ogden (forthcoming) proposes a convincing parallel in Herodotus' account (Hdt. 5.18–22: Alexander I hosting a Persian embassy after he has sent his father away to sleep). Ogden argues that the tale shows how Alexander III pursued "the long-game war against the Persians with rather greater subtlety and effectiveness than his namesake predecessor". This interpretation meshes well with Alexander's general policy for his Persian war, now revisited in Yates (2019) 214–228. Cf. Yates (2019) 93–96 (Philip's contemporaries' use of Alexander I), 109–112 (Alexander I's own policies).
[37] For these two passages, see Beneker (2009) 194–6. Alexander will eventually fail at one of his own symposia (Clitus' murder at Samarkand in 328 BC), but not for the same reasons as Philip fell over his couch.

ferent literary origins, despite the common settings. After all, embassies and symposia were frequent occurrences at the Argead court, as well as a topic of discourse in the Greek south.[38]

Based on these examples of Alexander's musical ability, our initial impression of the education theme's coherence from Plutarch's biography and the *AR* needs modification.[39] The theme consisted of episodes that could be picked up, rearranged, and reworked, while other stories floated around in a great "ocean of story."[40] Plutarch used freely from this boundless resource, and it is important to bear in mind that his aim was not to be exhaustive (Plut. *Alex.* 1.1). Indeed, Plutarch must have had knowledge of many other stories about Alexander's education that he omitted in the biography or learned after its publication. The anecdotes in the *Moral Essays* would suggest that he knew much more than he let on in the biography.[41]

The key takeaway from this discussion is not the truism that Plutarch's *Life of Alexander* and the *AR* are not telling the whole story of Alexander's youth. That was not their purpose. But we need to realize that their biographical framework poses some limitations which put our engagement with the topic into a certain frame of thinking. This is undesirable because it makes scholars overlook some equally important historical material in the process, like the testimonies of Aeschines and Aelian, who bring us somewhat closer to a historical context. This is not to dismiss Plutarch or the *AR*—two essential sources—but simply to appreciate that the discourse on Alexander's education at court was much richer than normally assumed.

III Teaching and teachers beyond Aristotle

Anton-Hermann Chroust once made a provocative argument that the historical Aristotle had not taught Alexander.[42] Other scholars have shown that most stories about the pair are indeed of romantic nature and rather late.[43] On this reading, Chroust held that other intellectuals, like Xenocrates, had instructed the

---

38 Pownall (2010).
39 Depending on how one dates the *AR*, it is possible that either Plutarch provided the primary model for the author of the *AR* or that Plutarch was revising the account found therein. The question of priority would be an engaging topic to explore elsewhere.
40 Stoneman (2012) 17.
41 Asirvatham (2018).
42 Chroust (1973) 127.
43 Düring (1957); Brocker (1966). Cf. Koulakiotis (2006) 74–84.

young Alexander in various ways, primarily through written works. It is certainly true that we have many names connected to the education of Alexander and, in this section, I shall review some of the alternatives to Aristotle. Just as in the previous section, I propose that the stories of the imperial period are mainly refractions of tales circulated during Alexander's lifetime or very early on in the Hellenistic period. On this principle, I contend that the great Aristotelian smoke in the texts from the imperial period does not make sense without an underlying fire.[44]

Prosopographical references to individual teachers in the histories

The most common point of reference is passing remarks to Alexander's teachers, mostly in the form of brief anecdotal material of the sort studied above. Even the major histories preserve such references, however laconic, and they are often explicitly linked to specific characters or historical events that took place during the campaign. We can therefore presume an early date. For instance, the historians acknowledge Alexander's rearing by the wet nurse Hellanice (Lanice, Alcrinis) when they narrate the death of her brother Clitus.[45] Plutarch makes a similar sort of reference to the two chief tutors (*paidagōgoi*), Leonides of Epirus and Lysimachus of Acarnania, whom he remembers for the former's austerity and the latter's Homeric flattery (Lysimachus styled himself a Phoenix to Alexander's Achilles).[46]

There exist separate passing remarks that detail Alexander's attempts to invite intellectuals along on the campaign, no doubt with origin in the tradition of Callisthenes of Olynthus.[47] Evidently, Callisthenes did join the campaign, and so

---

[44] See e.g. Luc. *Dial. Mort.* 25.3, *AR* 1.16, Phot. *Bibl.* cod. 190 (Ptolemy Chennus 147a). Ptolemy Chennus has a penchant for Alexander and Aristotle, studied by Rebecca Frank. I am grateful to her for making available to me a written version of her paper "The Apocryphal Alexander: Alexander the Great in Ptolemy the Quail" (CAMWS 114th meeting, 2018).
[45] Curt. 8.1.21, 8.2.8. Cf. Arr. *Anab.* 4.9; Just. *Epit.* 12.6; Ael. *VH* 12.26; Athen. 129a; *AR* 1.13; *AR* Armenian §29 Wolohojian. For Lanice, see Alonso Troncoso (2007), Asirvatham (2020).
[46] For the former, see the three anecdotes in Plut. *Alex.* 5, 22, 25. Cf Plut. *Mor.* 179E–F; Plin. *NH* 12.62; Quint. 1.1.9 (after Diogenes of Babylon). Further discussion at Djurslev (2020) 41–42. Further information on Leonides at Heckel (2006) s.v. Leonides [1] (146–7). For Lysimachus, see Plut. *Alex.* 5 and 24 for the Phoenix parallel (citing Chares of Mytilene *BNJ* 125 F 7 Müller) with Heckel (2006) s.v. Lysimachus [1] (153).
[47] See e.g. Plut. *Adv. Stoic.* 20 (*Mor.* 1043), who commends Ephorus, Xenocrates, and Menedemus for not agreeing to go on the campaign with Alexander, whereas Callisthenes is ridiculed for

did Lysimachus, Alexander's erstwhile tutor, who like the king found fault with Callisthenes' conduct at court (Plut. *Alex.* 55.2).

Letters

Letters supply the second most common type of information. For instance, Plutarch cites collections of Alexander's letter multiple times.[48] The *AR* contains more than thirty cited letters, some of which deal with matters of education.[49] As far as we know, Isocrates' *Letter to Alexander* (*Ep.* 5), if genuine, seems to be the very first letter sent to the historical Alexander.[50] Its preface suggests that the personal letter was appended to another letter addressed to Philip, now lost, and the missives reached the Argead court when Alexander was about 14 or 15 (c. 342/1 BC). Based on Isocrates' brief criticism of eristic teaching, or argumentative wrangling (5.3), rather much has been made of the fact that Isocrates was not chosen to teach Alexander, whereas Aristotle was, because he was former student of Plato.[51] Be that as it may, it is central to the present discussion that Isocrates associates Alexander so effortlessly with Greek *paideia*, 'the learning about the letters', τὴν παιδείαν τὴν περὶ τοὺς λόγους, presumably rhetoric.[52] I do not interpret it as evidence for Alexander's own level of learning at the time, but rather as an appeal to the Macedonian royalty's Panhellenic identity through Greek education.

Other letters attributed to Alexander or his teachers indicate that they were written in post-Alexander times. For example, the most important one appears in two sources. In Plutarch's version (Plut. *Alex.* 7.6–9),[53] Alexander wrote Aristotle to tell his teacher that he was disappointed to learn that Aristotle had published secret doctrines that might otherwise have given him an advantage over others. The Roman miscellanist Aulus Gellius (*NA* 20.5.11) preserves the same letter with Aristotle's full response (*NA* 20.5.12). Although both Plutarch and Gellius were

---

doing so. A fourth-century AD tradition arose about Aristotle partaking in Alexander's campaign, as evidenced by e.g. Himer. *Or.* 40.8.
48 Monti (2016).
49 Arthur-Montaigne (2014).
50 Sullivan (2007) 15–16 argues persuasively for the letter's authenticity.
51 Codoñer (2005) 8–14.
52 Note also the impressive tricolon of *Ep.* 5.2, [...] φιλάνθρωπος εἶ καὶ φιλαθήναιος καὶ φιλόσοφος [...] "You are a philanthropist, a lover of Athens, and a philosopher, Alexander" (trans. Djurslev).
53 Hamilton (2001) 19–20.

active in the second century AD, this correspondence has a pre-imperial date. Gellius comments (*NA* 20.5.10) that the Alexander-Aristotle correspondence came from a collection by Andronicus of Rhodes, the leader of Aristotle's Peripatetic school (fittingly) in the age of Cicero. The frequency of such letter compositions intensified during the imperial period.[54]

Dialogues

A large amount of data comes in the form of engaging dialogues between the young Alexander and his superiors. Perhaps the most well-known example is a pair of orations by Dio Chrysostom. In them, Alexander discourses on the best of Greek culture with his father Philip (*Or.* 2) and on power with the Cynic philosopher, Diogenes of Sinope (*Or.* 4).[55] Such elaborate texts are rife with educational details, including Dio's stunning claim that Alexander knew the entirety of Homer's *Iliad* by heart.[56]

At first glance, the number of dialogues by key imperial writers, including Dio, may indicate that this is a late phenomenon. Indeed, scholars have mainly studied them for imperial-period agendas, such as promoting the leaders of the relevant regime.[57] However, we have it on good authority that the Philip-Alexander dialogue is in fact a Hellenistic construct. According to the church historian Eusebius of Caesarea (*Praep. Evang.* 15.2.4), Alexinus of Elis (fl. c. 300 BC) had seemingly invented such a dialogue in which Alexander "spat upon the doctrines of Aristotle", διαπτύοντα μὲν τοὺς τοῦ Ἀριστοτέλους λόγους.[58] Moreover, according to Alexinus, the student preferred instead the teachings of Nicagoras of Zeleia (near Cyzicus on the Propontis), a tyrant who had styled himself as the

---

54 D.L. 5.27 claims that Aristotle wrote four books of letters to Alexander. Cf. Ael. *VH* 12.54.
55 See also *Or.* 47.9 and *Or.* 49.4–5 for Dio's thoughts on the recruitment of Aristotle. Cf. D.L. 5.10. Furthermore, the dialogue's existence evinces that the topics discussed, and the interlocutors themselves, are well-established *topoi* in the imperial period. One needs only consider that Lucian of Samosata wrote dialogues between Alexander and Philip (*Dial. Mort.* 12) and Alexander and Diogenes (*Dial. Mort.* 13). Lucian's choice of location—the underworld—is striking, seeing that Dio sets his version of these encounters in a vibrant, youthful setting, namely, the period prior to Alexander's campaign.
56 Dio Chrys. *Or.* 4.39; the claim is accepted by Carney (2015) 192.
57 See e.g. Asirvatham (2010) 196–199.
58 For Alexinus, see D.L. 2.109 and Athen. 15.696, who specifically refers to a paean written by the philosopher for Craterus, thus establishing Alexinus' ties to the Macedonians post Alexander.

god Hermes.⁵⁹ Therefore, just one generation after Aristotle, detractors could use Aristotle's best-known student to criticize the philosopher's tenets.

Catalogues of Alexander's teachers

Lists of Alexander's boyhood teachers rarely appear in the surviving corpus of Greek and Roman texts, but they did exist. The list format is significant because lists are the sort of documentary evidence that does not depend on the teacher's relevance in the campaign narrative. According to Alan Samuel, a notable chapter of the *AR* preserves an example of such an early list.⁶⁰ It is clear that the list was once a separate document because the information contained in it goes against the grain of the *AR*'s narrative. Helpfully, the Armenian and Latin versions say explicitly that they have the list on the authority of Plutarch's contemporary Favorinus of Arles.⁶¹ Of course, the list itself could have roots in earlier times. Anyway, the reference to Favorinus is significant because it shows us that, when Plutarch inserts a story about the taming of Bucephalas in the middle of his "listing" of Alexander's teachers from Leonides and Lysimachus to Aristotle (Plut. *Alex.* 5–7), he is reworking this format to fit his biographical ends.

Sayings of individual teachers

Quotable lines from any of Alexander's teachers are uncommon and difficult to date, but the literary tradition remembers some. For instance, the *Suda* refers to the Cynic philosopher Philiscus of Aegina as Alexander's master of letters, *grammatodidaskalos*.⁶² Aelian (*VH* 14.11) supplies us with the story that Philiscus told Alexander that he should study glory, δόξα, to bring peace and health (preserva-

---

59 I note with interest that tradition also remembers Alexander for dressing up as Hermes, for which see Koulakiotis (2006) 227–33. For the historical Nicagoras, see Heckel (2006) s.v. Nicagoras (175–6). The historical Alexander may have firsthand knowledge of this individual since the Macedonians "liberated" the Zeleians from Nicogoras' tyranny after the Battle of the Granicus (334 BC): Arr. *Anab.* 1.17.2.
60 Samuel (1986) 429–433.
61 *AR* 1.13.4–5. Cf. *AR* Armenian § 29 (list of teachers, citing Favorinus), Jul. Val. 1.13 (list of teachers, citing Favorinus at length), with commentary in Stoneman (2007) 498. In the Latin *AR*, Favorinus also offers a genealogy of Alexander that agrees with Plut. *Alex.* 2 rather than the *AR*'s engaging tale of Nectanebus' siring of Alexander.
62 *Suda*, s.v. Philiskos φ 359 Adler. Cf. Heckel (2006) s.v. Philiscus (215) for the issues this attribution poses.

tion of his subjects) rather than plague (governing tyrannically by sacking cities and depopulating countries). The irony is, of course, that Alexander went on to do the exact opposite of what Philiscus had advised. Unlike Aelian's previous lyre story, which may originate close to the historical Alexander's time, the Philiscus anecdote seems to recall Cynic ideals specific to the imperial period.[63]

Books

A limited number of books on matters of education expressly dedicated to Alexander appear in the literary tradition. For instance, Aristotle may have written his now lost works *On Kingship* and *Alexander* or *On behalf of the Colonies* for the boy-prince.[64] According to Diogenes Laertius (4.14),[65] the philosopher Xenocrates also wrote an *Elementary Principles of Kingship, Addressed to Alexander* in four books.[66] If Aristotle and Xenocrates, both students of Plato, did indeed write books on kingship for Alexander, it is not entirely impossible that there was a kind of agonistic element between them, since Aristotle was passed over for the chair at the Academy that was won by Xenocrates in 339.[67] It is also possible that the two works on kingship were really just a single one and that the literary tradition attributed them to two different authors.

Another instance of such contested works, perhaps the most widely known since it survives, is a manual of rhetoric, the *Rhetoric to Alexander*.[68] In antiquity, it was famously attributed to Aristotle, as the work was prefaced with a letter from Aristotle to his student, which unfortunately seems to be an invention of the third century AD (at the earliest). The *Rhetoric* is now regarded as the genuine work of Anaximenes of Lampsacus, an intellectual who formed part of Alexander's entourage on the expedition,[69] and so confirms the tendency that much of the later material can be shown to have early origins if evaluated properly.

---

[63] Koulakiotis (2006) 121.
[64] Hamilton (1973) 33. These works are in the lists of (e. g.) D.L. 5.22, Anon. *Vita Aristotelis* § 21. For a full view of the works relating to Alexander attributed to Aristotle, see Koulakiotis (2006) 75 n. 280.
[65] Cf. Plut. *Adv. Col.* 32 (*Mor.* 1126d).
[66] For Xenocrates, see Heckel (2006) s.v. Xenocrates (271).
[67] D.L. 5.2.
[68] Chiron (2011) argues that Aristotle wrote his *On Rhetoric* in engagement with the *Rh. Al.*
[69] For him, see Heckel (2006) s.v. Anaximenes (27).

To sum up, evidence of Alexander's various teachers comes from many types of texts, illustrating the rich variety and divergent formats in which information was presented to readers. Many intellectuals were involved in the academic education of the historical Alexander, as the Greek literati at court vied for favor from the Macedonian overlords. In this regard, the picture presented here fits well with the efforts of recent scholarship in showing how much Greek knowledge was actually financed by Argead patronage, and so incurred the criticism of those who did not enjoy this sponsorship.[70] If we consider the large amount of correspondents and interested parties during Alexander's upbringing, it would appear that Philip's court was probably greater than that of his son, at least with a view to the quality of the intellectuals.[71]

IV Training for the Argead art of war

So far, tales of Alexander's training have had an overwhelmingly early dating and an extremely academic theme, which is perhaps not surprising given the intellectual pursuits of the authors that preserve the information. Our evidence is thus skewed towards the academe in its very nature. In this section, I provide brief case studies of less frequent and therefore overlooked topics, namely, physical education, warfare, and medicine.

1. Like Aelian (*NA* 6.44), I do not have much to add on the principal component of Alexander's physical education: horseback riding. It is well illustrated by Plutarch's episode of the taming of Bucephalas (*Alex.* 6). Elizabeth Carney argues that Plutarch's story demonstrates that Alexander took up riding, hunting, and cavalry training early in life as preparation for war.[72] Even if the Plutarchan set piece is a highly literary episode,[73] there is no reason to doubt Carney's deduction. In general, the tradition of Bucephalas originates in the time of the historical Alexander, since most of the relevant material is supplied by Chares of Mytilene.[74] Of course, the horse quickly rode into legends as vivid as those of his master, the only rider ever to mount the valiant charger.[75]

---

[70] Pownall (2020) 250.
[71] Consider only names such as Aeschines, Aristotle, Demosthenes, Isocrates of Athens, Theopompus of Chios and Speusippus, Plato's successor at the Academy. Evidence at Moloney (2015) 63–71.
[72] Carney (2015) 192.
[73] Stadter (1996) 291–296. Cf. Whitmarsh (2002) 180–181.
[74] Chares of Mytilene *FGrH/BNJ* 125 F 18 via Gell. *NA*. 5.2.1–5, with Müller's commentary.

2. Considering Alexander's fame for military excellence, it is perplexing that almost no source relates how this ability came about. Plutarch's passing references to physical education by Leonides, for example, primarily focus on inculcating moral qualities rather than training for war. Indeed, Plutarch (*Alex.* 9.1–2) presents Alexander as a full-fledged commander in Philip's absence and at the Battle of Chaeronea he takes Alexander's military training for granted.[76] Dio Chrysostom (*Or.* 2.1–2) presents a different view. He opens one of his Alexander dialogues with an anecdote that has the young Alexander longing for war so badly—as if a dog for hunting—that his father could not hold him back. Dio claims that it was Alexander's youth and enthusiasm that led to the victory at Chaeronea, not his training.

Dio's story was expanded by the fourth-century AD orator Himerius, Emperor Julian's teacher of rhetoric at Athens. The elaboration is worth quoting in all its rich texture (Himer. *Or.* 54.4):

> They say that Alexander the Great, son of Philip—Alexander is known to all Greeks, I think, from books; we hear that he had a noble nature and was reared in a manner that matched his nature, for ⟨he grew up⟩ in the midst of military trophies, victories, and glorious deeds—anyway, we hear that, whenever he learned that his father was marching off to war, his desire was not to lag behind the battle line, but to follow his father, despite the fact that he was still young and just at the beginning of his adolescence and not yet mature enough for battle. His father was anxious about his son and bade him stay home, but Alexander would have none of this. Instead, he offered his father the same object lesson that I just offered you about the puppies—namely, that noble bitches are trained right from the time they are puppies and when just on the verge of hunting. He persuaded his father to let him engage in battle; and so, with this military experience acquired in his youth, he went on to put all lands under the sun in the palm of his own hand. (trans. Penella)

The passage stems from an extempore speech delivered in Himerius' own home at Athens to welcome new students, εἰς νεήλυδας. Older students were also present, and Himerius was encouraging them to train the latest arrivals. Like Philip's training of Alexander from youth, students would be trained at a young age, on the assumption that Himerius would give them the rhetorical skills to conquer the world. Himerius highlights experience, ἐμπειρία, as the key to success, whereas Dio in the similar anecdote had emphasized youth and enthusiasm, διὰ τὴν νεότητα καὶ τὴν ἐπιθυμίαν. It follows that Himerius' audience of

---

[75] Ogden (2020), but I wish to single out the often-overlooked testimony of Oppian of Apamea *On Hunting* 1.229–35, which brings Bucephalas into company befitting his majestic stature: Achilles' horses, Pegasus, and the horse that made Darius I king of Persia. Cf. Lib. *Ep.* 1332, Himer. *Or.* 47.11.

[76] Neither Frontinus nor Polyaenus (*Strat.* 4.3) pay heed to Alexander's education.

pepaideumenoi and specific performative context prompted him to rework the anecdote. Himerius' delivery to such an audience also helps to explain some of the more curious information, such as the novel idea that everyone knew about Alexander *from books*, ἐκ τῶν βιβλίων.

To my knowledge, the earliest extant reference to Alexander's experience in military training appears in Polybius' scathing criticism of Callisthenes.[77] To expose Callisthenes' incompetence, Polybius recounts at length the technical mistakes that Alexander's historian makes in the account of the battle at Issus (333 BC). One last fault in the catalogue is an error in describing troop movements that "should not be attributed to Alexander, because there is no doubting his *experience* and expertise at warfare, τὴν ἐν τοῖς πολεμικοῖς ἐμπειρίαν καὶ τριβήν, gained since childhood, ἐκ παιδός" (12.22.5, trans. Waterfield).[78]

3. In the *Life of Alexander* (8.1), Plutarch tells the remarkable story that Aristotle taught Alexander medicine,[79] noting that this subject was the prince's favorite. Plutarch says that Alexander used his knowledge to heal his Macedonian soldiers during the campaign. At the end of the second Alexander speech, the king even guides his soldiers to operate on his own body, thus saving his life.[80] The literary tradition also acknowledges Alexander's healing hands, especially in the case of curing Ptolemy's poisoned wound at Harmatelia,[81] but it attributes this ability to a divine serpent rather than Aristotle's instruction. Besides Plutarch, only Diogenes Laertius associates Alexander, Aristotle, and healing. In Laertius' biography of Aristotle, he preserves the story that Aristotle joined Alexander on daily walks while the prince was recovering from an illness, and these walks gave rise to the term "peripatetic".[82] Naturally, the king was cured in the process of conversing with the philosopher. But these stories are exceptions to the rule. The notion that Alexander had Aristotelian training in medicine thus appears apocryphal.

---

[77] Callisthenes of Olynthus *BNJ* 124 T 29 *ap.* Polybius 12.17–22.
[78] Cf. *Rhet. Her.* 4.31.
[79] This is a startling claim considering Aristotle does not have a reputation for being a medical thinker. His father Nicomachus, however, had been a doctor to Philip's father, Amyntas III. Like father, like son? Cf. Pownall (2020) 245.
[80] Plut. *De Alex. fort.* 2.13 (*Mor.* 344f–335b).
[81] Full discussion at Ogden (2011) 30–32, citing Cic. *Div.* 25, Diod. Sic. 17.103.4–8, Curt. 9.8.22–8, Strabo 15.2.7 (C723).
[82] D.L. 5.2, *contra* Plut. *De Alex. fort.* 1.4 (*Mor.* 328a), who argues that Alexander never set foot in the Lyceum.

V Conclusion

The three case studies of section IV corroborate the literary tendencies traced throughout this chapter. The first study indicates that most relevant content comes from the time of the historical Alexander or just after, with later elaborations. The second signifies that less mainstream topics, like the catalogues of Alexander's teachers in section III, nevertheless were useful for historians and rhetoricians throughout antiquity. The third suggests that some writers took great liberties in altering existing content for their own purposes and because of contemporary circumstances, to the point of innovating Alexander's tradition.

Sections III and IV provide illumination of the point of section II, namely, the need to read the biographical accounts of Plutarch and the Greek *Alexander Romance* critically and in a wider context, because their selection criteria and idiosyncrasies oftentimes diverge from other ancient discourses on Alexander's education. For historical reconstruction, we cannot rely on any single account.

The inclusive approach to Greek and Roman texts has enabled the detection and analysis of these major patterns in the ancient discourse on the Argead court. These patterns offer some key insights into the nature of the sources, primarily the complexity when viewed from a bird's-eye perspective and at a grand scale. I believe that employing this inclusive approach would be a productive way forward for investigating other aspects of the high culture at the Argead court before, under, and after Alexander.

To illustrate this potential, I end with a rare a testimony to the higher education among the other members of the Argead court. In the Plutarchan essay *On the Education of Children*,[83] we learn of a brief quotation of a poem by Queen Eurydice I of Macedon, mother of three Argead rulers, including Philip II, and the paternal grandmother of Alexander himself.[84]

> Εὐρυδίκη Ἴρρα πολιήτισι τόνδ' ἀνέθηκε / Μούσαις εὔιστον ψυχῇ ἑλοῦσα πόθον. / γράμματα γὰρ μνημεῖα λόγων μήτηρ γεγαυῖα / παίδων ἡβώντων ἐξεπόνησε μαθεῖν.
>
> Eurydice, daughter of Sierras, dedicated this to the Muses upon fulfilling her soul's desire for knowledge. For, as the mother of young sons, she laboured to learn letters, records of words (trans. Djurslev).

This powerful dedicatory epigram may once have had a different material context, perhaps adorning a Hellenistic statue base. Although the Plutarchan author

---

83 [Plut.] *De Lib. Educ.* 20 (*Mor.* 14b–c), cf. Plant (2004) 43–44.
84 Carney (2000) 28–29.

contextualizes the poem to mean that Eurydice took up letters to teach her children, it is clear that the cited text makes no such claim. It is a proclamation of Eurydice's own achievement in acquiring literacy *after* the rearing of her sons, which was something clearly worth celebrating, even among the Greek aristocracy of the fourth century BC.[85]

Bibliography

Alonso Troncoso (2007): Victor Alonso Troncoso, "Alexander, Cleitus and Lanice: Upbringing and Maintenance", in: Waldemar Heckel and Pat Wheatley (eds.), *Alexander's Empire: Formulation to Decay*, Claremont, CA, 109–123.

Arthur-Montaigne (2014): Jacqueline Arthur-Montaigne, "Persuasion, Emotion, and the Letters of the Greek *Alexander Romance*", in: *Ancient Narrative* 11, 159–189.

Asirvatham (2010): Sulochana Asirvatham, "His Son's Father? Philip II in the Second Sophistic", in: Elizabeth Carney and Daniel Ogden (eds.) *Philip and Alexander the Great: Father and Son, Lives and Afterlives*, Oxford, 193–204.

Asirvatham (2017): Sulochana Asirvatham, "The Argeads and the Second Sophistic", in: Sabine Müller *et al.* (eds.), *The History of the Argeads: New Perspectives*, Wiesbaden, 281–295.

Asirvatham (2018): Sulochana Asirvatham, "Plutarch's Alexander", in Kenneth Royce Moore (ed.) *Brill's Companion to the Reception of Alexander the Great*, Leiden, 335–376.

Asirvatham (2020): Sulochana Asirvatham, "Alexander's Wet-nurse Lanice and Her Sons", in: in: Monica D'Agostini *et al.* (eds.), *Affective Relations and Personal Bonds in Hellenistic Antiquity*, Oxford, 37–50.

Beneker (2009): Jeffrey Beneker, "Drunken violence and the transition to power in Plutarch's *Alexander*", in: José Ribeiro Ferreira *et al.* (eds.), *Symposion and Philanthropia in Plutarch*, Coimbra, 193–200.

Billows (2018): Richard A. Billows, *Before and After Alexander: The Legend and Legacy of Alexander the Great*, New York.

Bosworth (2011): Albert Brian Bosworth, "Anecdote, apophthegm and the "real" Alexander", in: *Humanities Australia* 2, 44–52.

Brocker (1966): Max Brocker, *Aristoteles als Alexanders Lehrer in der Legende*, Ph.D. diss., Bonn.

Carney (2000): Elizabeth D. Carney, *Women and Monarchy in Macedonia*, Norman, OK.

Carney (2015): Elizabeth D. Carney, *King and Court in Ancient Macedonia: Rivalry, Treason and Conspiracy*, Swansea.

---

[85] I would like to thank Frances Pownall for organizing a wonderful conference at the University of Alberta. The paper took a turn in the writing process, and the editors have provided much insightful feedback, for which I am thankful to all three. Thanks are also due to Daniel Ogden. I would like to express my gratitude to my colleagues at Aarhus University, Erich Pracht and Lavinia Cerioni, for commenting on a late draft of this paper. A personal note of affection and appreciation to Taylor FitzGerald for all her assistance.

Chiron (2011): Pierre Chiron, "Relative Dating of the *Rhetoric to Alexander* and Aristotle's *Rhetoric:* A Methodology and Hypothesis", in: *Rhetorica* 29, 236–262.
Chroust (1973): Anton-Hermann Chroust, *Aristotle: New Light on his Life and on Some of his Lost Works. Some Novel Interpretations of the Man and his Life*, London and New York, vol. 1, 125–132 [republished in 2016].
Codoñer (2005): Juan Signes Codoñer, "The *Panathenaicus* of Isocrates and the Letters to the Macedonians", *Emerita* 69, 7–53 [English translation by Tony Natoli and Thomas Pill].
Djurslev (2020): Christian Thrue Djurslev, *Alexander the Great in the Early Christian Tradition: Classical Reception and Patristic Literature*, London.
Düring (1957): Ingemar Düring, *Aristotle in the Ancient Biographical Tradition*, Stockholm.
Fisher (2001): Nick Fisher, *Aeschines: Against Timarchos*, Oxford.
Griffith (2015): Mark Griffith, "The Earliest Greek Systems of Education", in: W. Martin Bloomer (ed.), *A Companion to Ancient Education*, Malden, MA, 26–60.
Hamilton (1973): John R. Hamilton, *Alexander the Great*, London.
Hamilton (2001): John R. Hamilton, *Plutarch. Alexander.* 2nd ed., Bristol.
Heckel (2006): Waldemar Heckel, *Who's Who in the Age of Alexander the Great*, Malden, MA and Oxford.
Heinrichs (2020): Johannes Heinrichs, "Alexander I", in: Waldemar Heckel *et al.* (eds.), *Lexicon of Argead Makedonia*, Berlin 2020, 55–60.
Howe (2018): Tim Howe, "Masyas of Pella", in: Ian Worthington (ed.), *Brill's New Jacoby* nos. 135–136, online.
Howe and Pownall (2018): Tim Howe and Frances Pownall (eds.), *Ancient Macedonians in Greek and Roman Sources: From History to Historiography*, Swansea.
Koulakiotis (2006): Elias Koulakiotis, *Genese und Metamorphosen des Alexandermythos im Spiegel der griechischen nichthistoriographischen Überlieferung bis zum 3. Jh. n. Chr.*, Konstanz.
Kuin (2019): Inger N. I. Kuin, "Sulla and the Philosophers: the Cultural History of the Sack of Athens", in: Alexandra Eckert and Alexander Thein (eds.), *Sulla. Politics and Reception*, Berlin and Boston, 143–158.
Landucci (2018): Franca Landucci, "Alexander, the Crown Prince", in: *Anabasis* 9, 9–20.
Marín (2018): Antonio Ignacio Molina Marín, *Alejandro Magno (1916–2015). Un siglo de estudios sobre Macedonia Antigua*, Zaragoza.
Moloney (2015): Eoghan Moloney, "Neither Agamemnon nor Thersites, Achilles nor Margites: The Heraclid Kings of Argead Macedon", in: *Antichthon* 49, 50–72.
Monti (2016): Giustina Monti, "Le lettere di Alessandro: storia degli studi", in: *Histos* 10, 17–33.
Müller (2016): Sabine Müller, *Die Argeaden. Geschichte Makedoniens bis zum Zeitalter Alexanders des Großen*, Paderborn.
Müller (2017a): Sabine Müller, "The Artistic King: Reflections on a *topos* in Second Sophistic Historiography", in: Tim Howe *et al.* (eds.), *Ancient Historiography on War and Empire*, Philadelphia, PA, 250–261.
Müller (2017b): Sabine Müller, "Chares of Mytilene", in: Ian Worthington (ed.), *Brill's New Jacoby* no. 125, online.
Nawotka (2017): Krzysztof Nawotka, *The Alexander Romance by Ps.-Callisthenes. A Historical Commentary*, Leiden.
Ogden (2011): Daniel Ogden, *Alexander the Great: Myth, Genesis and Sexuality*, Exeter.

Ogden (2020): Daniel Ogden, "The Theft of Bucephalas", in: Monica D'Agostini et al. (eds.), *Affective Relations and Personal Bonds in Hellenistic Antiquity*, Oxford, 143–161.

Ogden (forthcoming): Daniel Ogden, "Birth and Childhood", in: Daniel Ogden (ed.), *Cambridge Companion to Alexander the Great*, Cambridge.

Peltonen (2019): Jaakojuhani Peltonen, *Alexander the Great in the Roman Empire*, London.

Plant (2004): Ian M. Plant, *Women Writers of Ancient Greece and Rome*, London.

Pownall (2010): Frances Pownall, "The Symposia of Philip II and Alexander III of Macedon: The View from Greece", in: Elizabeth Carney and Daniel Ogden (eds.), *Philip and Alexander the Great: Father and Son, Lives and Afterlives*, Oxford and New York, 55–65.

Pownall (2020): Frances Pownall, "Sophists and Flatterers: Greek Intellectuals at Alexander's Court", in: Monica D'Agostini et al. (eds.), *Affective Relations and Personal Bonds in Hellenistic Antiquity*, Oxford, 243–265.

Samuel (1986): Alan E. Samuel, "The Earliest Elements in the *Alexander Romance*", in: *Historia* 35, 427–437.

Seibert (1972): Jakob Seibert, *Alexander der Grosse*, Darmstadt.

Stadter (1996): Philip A. Stadter, "Anecdotes and the Thematic structure of Plutarchean Biography", in: José Antonio Fernández Delgado and Francisca Pordomingo Pardo (eds.), *Estudios sobre Plutarco: Aspectos formales*, Madrid, 291–304.

Stoneman (2007): Richard Stoneman, *Il Romanzo di Alessandro*, vol. 1, Milan.

Stoneman (2012): Richard Stoneman, "Persian Aspects of the Romance Tradition", in: Richard Stoneman et al. (eds.), *The Alexander Romance in Persia and the East*, Groningen, 3–18.

Sullivan (2007): Robert G. Sullivan, "Classical Epistolary Theory and the Letters of Isocrates", in: Carol Poster and Linda C. Mitchell (eds.), *Letter-writing Manuals and Instruction from Antiquity to the Present*, Columbia, SC, 7–20.

Vos (2018): Gary Patrick Vos, *Linus Songs: Time, Narrative, and Intertextuality in Greek and Roman Poetry*, Ph.D. diss., Edinburgh.

Whitby (2011): Michael Whitby, "Onesikritos", in: Ian Worthington (ed.), *Brill's New Jacoby* no. 134, online.

Whitmarsh (2002): Tim Whitmarsh, "Alexander's Hellenism and Plutarch's Textualism", in: *CQ* 52.1, 174–192.

Yates (2019): David C. Yates, *States of Memory: The Polis, Panhellenism, and the Persian War*, Oxford.

V Alexander's Court in Retrospective

Rebecca Frank

"The Best Man Among the Dead:" Alexander son of Ammon in an Alexandrian Inscription

I Greek Text and Translation

Alexandria, ca. 1st or 2nd c. CE, 38 × 43.8 cm.
ed. pr. Cagnat *Rev. Arch.* 40 (1880):166–70 = *SEG* 8 372 = Peek *GVI* 1935 = Milne *IG* 9224 = Bernand 71

[σχές, ξεῖνε, παρ]ιών ἴχνος, εἰ θέλεις γνῶναι   1
[τίς ἐσθ' ὑποταφε]ὶς τῇδε λαΐνῃ στήλῃ.
[ἐνταῦθα κεῖται] χρηστὸς ἐν φθίτοις ἀνήρ,
[ἄωρος, ὃς] λέλοιπεν ἡλίου φέγγος
[ὅλον δρόμον ἐτ]ῶν μηδέπω τελειώσας.   5
[πολλοῖς ἀρέσ]αι δέδοκτο, μοῦνος ἀνθρώπων,
[ὃς πάντας] ἀρετῇ τοὺς ὁμήλικας προῦχεν
[εὔνους, δί]καιος, θεοσεβής, φιλάνθρωπος.
[πᾶς οὖν ἑτ]αίρων τὸν τεὸν μόρον κλαίει·
[πολὺς] μὲν ὄχλος οἰκετῶν σε δακρύει,   10
[ἄθλιε·] τί δ' ἦσθα σεμνὸς ὡς δοκεῖν εἶναι
[κἂν ὄν]τα παῖδα τοῖς νοήμασιν πρέσβυν;
[δεινὸ]ν, ποθητὴ μῆτερ, εὔνασον θρῆνον
[πέ]νθους τιθηνόν, ὃς μάτην σε πημαίνει·
οὐδεὶς γὰρ ἐξήλυξε τὸν μίτον Μοιρῶν,   15
οὐ θνητός, οὐκ ἀθάνατος, οὐδ' ὁ δεσμώτης
οὐδ' αὖ τύραννος βασιλικὴν λαχὼν τιμὴν
θεσμοὺς ἀτρέπτους διαφυγεῖν ποτ' ᾠήθη.
Φαέθοντα Τιτὰν οὐκ ἔκλαυσ' ὅτ' ἐκ δίφρων
ἀπ' οὐρανοῦ κατέπεσεν εἰς πέδον γαίης;   20
Ἑρμῆς δ' ὁ Μαίας οὐκ ἔκλαυσ' ἑὸν παῖδα
Μύρτιλον ἀπὸ δίφρων κύμασιν φορούμενον;
οὐδ' αὖ Θέτις τὸν στεναρὸν ἔστενεν παῖδα
ὅτ' ἐκ βελέμνων θνῆσκε τῶν Ἀπόλλωνος;
ὁ(ὐ)δ' αὖ βροτῶν τε καὶ θεῶν πάντων ἄναξ   25
Σαρπηδόν' οὐκ ἔκλαυσεν, οὐκ ἐκώκυσεν,

οὐδ' αὖ Μακηδὼν ὁ βασιλεὺς Ἀλέξανδρος
ὃν τίκτεν Ἄμμων θέμενος εἰς ὄφιν μορφήν;

[Stranger, check your step,] if you wish to know   1
[who is buried under] this marble stele.
[Here lies] the best man among the dead,
[an untimely dead, who] left behind the light of the sun
not yet having finished [the whole race of (his) years.]   5
He had seemed [pleasing to many,] he alone of men,
[who] surpassed [all his comrades] in virtue,
[friendly,] just, pious, tender-hearted.
[Therefore each of your companions] cries your fate;
[a great] crowd of your household mourns you,   10
[wretched;] why were you grave, so as to seem to be
an elder in your thoughts [even though you were] still a child?
Beloved mother, cease your [wretched] lament,
nursing your [grief], which only pains you;
for no one has escaped the thread of the Fates,   15
no mortal, no immortal, neither the prisoner
nor even the tyrant, having obtained by lot kingly honor,
thought to escape the unchangeable laws.
Did Titan not weep for Phaethon when he fell
from the sky out of the chariot onto the plain of the earth?   20
Did Hermes son of Maia not weep for his son
Myrtilos, borne by waves from the chariot?
Or did Thetis not lament her gruff son
when he met death from the arrows of Apollo?
Or did the lord of all mortals and of gods   25
not weep for Sarpedon? Did he not lament?
Or the Macedonian King Alexander,
whom Ammon sired while in serpent form?[1]

1 [σχές, ξεῖνε, παρ]ίων Frank : [ξεῖν' ἔπεχε παρ]ίων Cagnat : [ξεῖν' ἔπεχε παρέρ]πων Peek² : [στῆ-σον, ξένε, παρ]ίων Peek³ || **2** [τίς ἐσθ' ὑποταφε]ὶς τῇδε Cagnat : [τίς ἐστι κρυφθε]ὶς τῇδε Peek² : ΛΑΙΝΗ lapis || **3** [ἐνταῦθα κεῖται] Cagnat : [Ἀγάθων ὕπεστι] Peek² : [Ἀγάθων ὅδ' ἐστι] Peek³ || **4** [ἄωρος, ὅς] Frank : [γλύκιστον ὅς] Cagnat : [πανάωρος ὅς] Peek² : [ὃς ἄωρος ὤν] Peek³ || **5** [ὅλον δρόμον ἐτ]ῶν Cagnat : [δρόμον γὰρ ἐτ]έων Peek² : [εἰκάδα γὰρ ἐτ]έων Peek³ || **6** [πολλοῖς ἀρέσ]αι δέ(δ)οκτο Cagnat : [- - - κ]αὶ δέ(δ)οκτο (?) Miller : [ὅλοις ἀρέσ]αι δέ(δ)οκτο Peek² : ΔΕΧΟΚΤΟ lapis || **7** [ὃς πάντας] Cagnat : [καὶ πάντας] Peek³ || **8** [εὔνους] Cagnat : [ἐών]

---

1 This translation, and all following, are my own.

Peek¹ : [ἀγαθός] *Peek³* : [χρηστός] *Lavagnini¹* : [σώρφρων] *Lavagnini²* : [εἰς πᾶν δί]καιος *Knox* ǁ 9 [πᾶς οὖν] *Cagnat* : [χορὸς δ'] *Miller* : [πᾶς τις ἑ]ταίρων *Lavagnini¹* : [πᾶς τις δ'ἑ]ταίρων *Peek³* : [τίς οὐχ] *Knox* ǁ 10 [πολύς] *Cagnat* : [ὅλος] *Peek¹* : [πάντων] *Peek²* : [ἅπας] *Knox* ǁ 11 [ἄθλιε] · τί δ' ἦσθα *Cagnat* : [ἐν παν]τί *Miller* ǁ 12 [κἂν ὄ]ντα *Cagnat* : [τὸν ὄ]ντα *Miller* : [ἔτ' ὄ]ντα *Milne* ǁ 13 [δειν]όν *Cagnat* : [κοιν]όν *Miller* : [λυγρ]όν *Peek¹* : [δει]γόν *Peek²* : [σύρ]ον *Peek³* : [δειλ]όν *Lavagnini¹* : [κεν]όν *Lavagnini²* : [πικρ]όν *Lavagnini²* ǁ 14 [π]ένθους *Cagnat.* ǁ 15 ἐξήλξε *Cagnat* : ΕΖΗΛΥΖΕ *lapis* ǁ 18 ᾠήθη *Cagnat* : ΩΗΘΗ *lapis* ǁ 21 ἔκαυσ' ἑόν *Miller* : ἔκλαυσε ὅν *Cagnat* ǁ 25 ο(ὐ)δ' αὖ *Cougny* : ὁ δ' αὖ *Cagnat* : ΟΔΑΥ *lapis* : θεῶν ἄναξ πάντων *Weil ap. Miller*

II Introduction

Alexander the Great is known to history in many different guises: Macedonian king, military commander, world conqueror, son of a god, and even a god himself. These last two characteristics caused considerable controversy during Alexander's own lifetime and continued to be a subject of debate for generations. Questions such as how Alexander could be both the son of a god and the son of Philip II of Macedon appear in the extant literature on Alexander as early as the first generation of Alexander historians and persist well into the Roman Imperial period.[2] Alexander's filiation was exploited throughout antiquity by those seeking to use Alexander and his image to further their own political ends. Claims that Alexander was sired by Philip II, Zeus, Ammon, or even the Egyptian pharaoh Nectanebo tap into different aspects of Alexander's rule and images of his reign that could be exploited for their political as well as cultural capital.[3] Through his various filiations, Alexander could be transformed from simply a Macedonian king into a Greek hero or an Egyptian pharaoh. He could be a mortal, or he could be divine.

Alexander's dual status as both mortal and divine is on display in an Alexandrian funerary tablet commemorating the premature death of a young man. The text ends with a *consolatio* containing a reference to Alexander, calling him the son of Ammon whom the god sired while in the form of a snake. Alexander's presence in this inscription has only recently begun to receive attention from scholars, who have hitherto been concerned primarily with supple-

---

2 See n. 36 below.
3 This can be seen especially clearly in Egypt, where Alexander was used by the Ptolemies and the Roman emperors alike to promote the legitimacy of the reigns. See below, especially nn. 30, 31, 46.

menting the opening of the poem.⁴ Those who do comment on the contents have argued that the reference to Alexander is an ill-fitting and jarring end to the poem.⁵ In this paper, I argue that the epitaph's reference to Alexander the Great provides the interpretive linchpin of the poem and that his representation in the text engages directly with key themes of the popular literary portrayals of Alexander in the Hellenistic and Roman worlds, in particular with regard to his filiation and divinity.

In what follows, I present first a discussion of the tablet and how it has been interpreted historically. Next, I argue that Alexander is not an afterthought in this inscription as has previously been suggested but instead represents the climax of the *consolatio* addressed to the deceased's mother. I show that his presence is not ill-fitting to the context, but represents a natural progression from what proceeds it and serves as an effective cap to the emotional plea of the poem. I also demonstrate that this inscription is closely connected to the popular Alexander tales known collectively as the *Alexander Romance*, tapping into the themes, language, and even meter of the *Romance* tradition. In so doing, I argue that the use of Alexander's filiation in the poem reflects popular views of Alexander and his status as a ruler in Roman Egypt. Finally, by situating this inscription within its historical context in first or second century CE Egypt, I reveal a connection between inscribed and literary texts during this era and the importance of place in interpreting the funerary monument and understanding the community that erected it.

III The inscription

The inscription was discovered in 1879 in Alexandria, although nothing further is known about its original context.⁶ The epitaph is comprised of twenty-eight verses of choliambic trimeters. It is carved onto a rectangular marble plaque measuring 38 centimeters tall and 43 centimeters wide, engraved with letters measuring 8 to 9 millimeters. Cagnat originally proposed a post-Augustan date for the inscription based on the letter forms. While the exact date is disputed, it likely

---

4 This has been undertaken primarily by Milne (1905) 50–51; Peek (1931) 334, (1932) 61, (1955) 598; and Knox (1967) 278–281. This was also the focus of Cagnat (1880), who published the *editio princeps* of this inscription.
5 See, for example, Lavagnini (1937) 375–376 and Lavagnini (1947) 84–86.
6 Cagnat (1880) 466, Bernand (1969) 285.

belongs to the first or second century CE.⁷ Maspero records traces of plaster on the reverse, indicating that it was a plaque, though the surface into or onto which it was installed is unknown.⁸ The upper left corner of the inscription has been lost, resulting in lacunas of all or part of the first foot in verses 1–14. There are substantial margins on the upper, left, and right sides of the engraved surface, but the text continues to the very bottom of the face. Nevertheless, the bottom edge is straight, and no letters or parts thereof are missing. Additionally, Bernand notes that there is no physical evidence that the stone has been broken off along this edge.⁹

Nevertheless, the continuation of the text to the edge of the stone, together with the contents of the final couplet, has produced considerable disagreement over the completeness of the text.

The epitaph opens with an address to the viewer (vv. 1–2), and goes on to praise the deceased for having been an exemplary youth (v. 3: χρηστός, v. 8: [δί]-καιος, θεοσεβής, φιλάνθρωπος) whose early passing was lamented by all who knew him (vv. 9–10). The stone then addresses the man's mother, bidding her to put aside her grief (vv. 13–14) since death is universal (vv. 15–18).¹⁰ The mother should not weep excessively over the loss of her child, the text argues, for others have suffered a similar grief and no one is able to live beyond the time allotted to them by the Fates (v. 15: οὐδεὶς γὰρ ἐξήλυξε τὸν μίτον Μοιρῶν). To prove this point, the epitaph includes a catalogue of divine parents who, like the deceased's mother, were also left distraught over the premature death of a child: Titan over Phaethon's death (vv. 19–20), Hermes over Myrtilos' (vv. 21–22), The-

---

7 Cagnat (1880) 170 initially argued for a post-Augustan date based on the letter forms of the alpha, delta, lambda, mu, and xi, proposing a first century CE date for the inscription. Against this, Miller (Miller *et al.* (1883) 196) suggested the third century CE, and Milne (1905) 51 the second century CE. Lavagnini's (1937) 376 proposal of the late Hellenistic age ignores the physical characteristics of the inscription. While it is possible that the text may originate from the Hellenistic period, it is unlikely that the inscription itself was produced then. See also Bernand (1969) 286: "haute époque impériale, d'après la gravure et le contenu du texte."
8 Maspero suggests, not implausibly, that the plaque was affixed to the tomb, sarcophagus, or crypt of the deceased. See Miller *et al.* (1883) 193.
9 Bernand (1969) 292.
10 While the text is highly corrupt due to the preservation of the left side of the stone, the contents of the first 18 lines are standard features of epitaphs, particularly those of the untimely dead (ἄωροι): praising the deceased for his virtues, claiming his passing was greatly lamented, and reflecting on the universality of death. See, for example, *EG* 191; *EG* 567; *IG* 12, 2, 384; *IG* 14, 819; *IG* 14, 1806. Additionally, as Lattimore (1962) 250–255 demonstrates, these themes are not unique to funerary inscriptions, but are found throughout Greek literature as well.

tis over Achilles' (vv. 23–24), and Zeus over Sarpedon's (vv. 25–26).[11] The catalogue concludes with a final parent-child pairing: "Or Alexander, king of the Macedonians, whom Ammon sired while in serpent form?" (vv. 27–28: οὐδ' αὖ Μακηδὼν ὁ βασιλεὺς Ἀλέξανδρος / ὃν τίκτεν Ἄμμων θέμενος εἰς ὄφιν μορφήν;).

This ending couplet has led scholars to propose that the text here is incomplete or corrupt. For example, Miller assumed that the inscription was broken and that the end of the poem has been lost, in which view he was followed by Knox.[12] But although the text does continue to the edge of the stone, the stone does not appear to have been broken after the text was engraved, nor does the edge of the stone appear smooth enough for the inscription to have continued on another register. Lavagnini proposed that there is a lengthy lacuna between verses 26 and 27, claiming that the inscription was "incompletamente transcritto sulla pietra," both because of the shift from mythological heroes to a historical figure and because of the lack of a verb in the final couplet.[13] This argument hinges on the assumption that the poem as it is carved on the stone was not the original version of the text. The length of the inscription, and the care with which the stone was prepared and the letters carved, make it unlikely that such a careless mistake would have been made on such an expensive project. Barring evidence of physical damage to the stone, arguments for a lacuna are only called for if the text is unintelligible as it stands. In reaching to supplement the text in this way, assuming a lacuna to explain the presence of the Alexander couplet, scholars have overlooked the message of the text as it exists on the stone. In what follows, I analyze the poem's *consolatio*, and the Alexander couplet in particular, demonstrating the effect on the poem of reading as a completed work that ends with verse 28.

In the epitaph, the poet elevates the deceased and his mother by comparing their misfortune to that of gods and heroes. These mythical exempla are connected one to the next by thematic or verbal parallels, culminating in Alexander and his father Ammon. First the poet names Phaethon, son of Titan, who tumbled to earth from Helios's chariot (v. 19: ἐκ δίφρων). Next comes Hermes's son Myrtilos who, we are told, also met his fate over the edge of a chariot (v. 22: ἀπὸ δίφρων). Following Myrtilos is Achilles, son of Thetis, whom the poet refers to as with Myrtilos as a παῖς (vv. 21, 23) continuing the pattern of using verbal repetition to link

---

11 The motif of comparing the deceased to gods and heroes is amply attested in other contemporary inscriptions and serves to elevate both the deceased and his parents, as Vérilhac (1982) 26–27 argues persuasively.
12 Miller *et al.* (1883) 197, Knox (1946) 281.
13 Lavagnini (1937) 376, Lavagnini (1947) 85–86.

the figures.¹⁴ In the remaining verses there is a combination of both verbal and thematic pairings. The repetition of οὐδ' αὖ at the opening of verses 23, 25, and 27 binds together the couplets referencing Achilles, Sarpedon, and Alexander respectively, connecting Alexander to the two Trojan war heroes.¹⁵ The continuation of this pattern in verse 27 with οὐδ' αὖ Μακηδὼν ὁ βασιλεὺς Ἀλέξανδρος makes this final example the third repetition of the phrase and thematically the climax of the series. The close grammatical connection between the final three examples in the *consolatio* matches the closeness of the figures themselves to each other. Achilles and Sarpedon were the famed children of gods fighting for the Greeks and Trojans respectively during the Trojan war. The astute reader will also remember that it is the arrows of Apollo that slay Achilles (v. 24), and it is also Apollo who in the *Iliad* rescues Sarpedon's body after he was slain by Achilles's cousin, Patroclus.¹⁶ Furthermore, Patroclus did so while wearing Achilles's armor and leading the Myrmidons in Achilles's place.¹⁷ Alexander, while not himself a Trojan war hero, is nonetheless not an inappropriate figure to come next in the *consolatio*. He is, as the text notes explicitly, the son of Ammon, who was widely associated in the Greek world with Zeus.¹⁸ Seen in this light, Alexander follows naturally after Sarpedon, bound by this shared identity as children of Zeus. Alexander was also compared directly with Achilles in the imperial era and indeed throughout much of the historiographical tradition.¹⁹ Thus, there is no clear break in theme or in sense between the first four

---

14 On this designation as παῖς see also v. 12 of the inscription.
15 I follow Cougny's reading ο⟨ὐ⟩δ' for the stone's ΟΔΑΥ based on logic and symmetry.
16 Hom. *Il.* 16.64–154.
17 Hom. *Il.* 16.419–683. The Homeric connection between Achilles and Sarpedon creates a thematic pairing for the two heroes.
18 The connection between Zeus and Ammon goes back at least to the fifth century BCE. See, for example, Pind. *Pyth.* 4.16 (Διὸς ἐν Ἄμμωνος θεμέθλιος) and Pind. fr. 36 (Ἄμμων Ὀλύμπου δέσποτα). Bosworth (1977) 52 has collected a representative sample of the evidence, which includes also *SEG* 8.551.25–26, and Luc. 9.511–514. Caneva (2012) traces the development of the association between Theban Amun, Lybian Ammon, and the Greek Zeus, demonstrating in particular how the god's image was manipulated and exploited by Alexander and the Ptolemies to strengthen their control over Egypt.
19 See, for example, Diod. Sic. 17.1.4, 17.97.3; Strabo 13.1.27; Dio Chrys. *Or.* 4.39; Plut. *Alex.* 8, 26, 72; Arr. *Anab.* 1.12.1; 7.14.4. As Bowden (2018) 163–164 notes, it is difficult to ascertain exactly when the connections between Alexander and Achilles that are so prevalent throughout the source tradition were first made. While Alexander is compared explicitly with Achilles throughout the extant Imperial era sources, it is likely, as Heckel (2015) argues, that this association was a later construct and not a reflection of how Alexander saw himself—or was seen—in his own day. On the connections made between Alexander and Achilles made both during Alexander's

examples of ἀπόγονοι θεῶν and the example of Alexander that would support the argument for a lacuna between verses 26 and 27.

It is undeniable, however, that the two Alexander scazons represent a structural break from what proceeds them in both the grammatical case of the hero and the lack of a verb for the couplet. In the proceeding examples, the youthful heroes are named in the accusative case, the ones being lamented by the parents who are listed in the nominative. Grammatically, verse 27 (οὐδ' αὖ Μακηδὼν ὁ βασιλεὺς Ἀλέξανδρος) matches closely verse 25 (ο⟨ὐ⟩δ' αὖ βροτῶν τε καὶ θεῶν πάντων ἄναξ), placing Alexander, "the king of the Macedonians," in direct parallelism with Zeus, "lord of all mortals and gods," rather than with Sarpedon. It is only with the second line of the couplet, the final line of the poem, that the reader realizes that the poet has inverted the structure used for the preceding verses, referencing the son first, and the father second. De Sanctis has suggested that Alexander is named in the place of the parent in the nominative case because the poet was positioning him among those who lamented a prematurely-lost loved one, supplying Hephaestion as a candidate for such a figure.[20] This reading would produce with an even starker contrast from the proceeding examples, with the mourner a young man and identified as the son of a god who is also named, but lacking a heroic child to be the object of his grief. Although Alexander's excessive mourning of Hephaestion was a common motif in Alexandrography during the imperial era, such a pairing is incongruous with the preceding examples, and difficult to justify given Hephaestion's absence from the stone.[21] While I do not agree with De Sanctis's interpretation that the deceased should be understood to be Hephaestion, his proposal does help indicate what I believe was an intentional ambiguity on the part of the poet that serves to highlight different aspects of Alexander's image that were popular in Egypt during this era.

As with the four preceding examples of deceased young men and their divine parents, Alexander too is given a single couplet in the text. Just as Phaethon, Myrtilos, Achilles, and Sarpedon were the heroic sons of gods whose youthful passing was lamented by their parents, so too was Alexander son of

---

lifetime as well as after his death, see Edmunds (1971) 372–373, Mossman (1988), Stewart (1993) 78–86, Müller (2006), and Vorhis (2017).

20 De Sanctis *apud* Lavagnini (1947) 86.

21 Additionally, the poet's choice to cite in verses 23–24 Thetis's grief at the death of Achilles, rather than Achilles' at the death of Patroclus, stands as further evidence against De Sanctis's reading. For comparisons of Alexander's grief over the death of Hephaestion to that of Achilles over Patroclus, see, for example, Arr. *Anab.* 7.14.3–8, Diod. Sic. 17.110.8; Just. 12.12.12; Plut. *Alex.* 72.5, Ael. *VH* 7.8.

Ammon. But the structure of the final couplet also invokes Alexander's dual identity as both the child of a god and someone who was also divinized.[22] That is to say, the anacoluthon is deliberate and meaningful: unlike the other young men named in the *consolatio*, Alexander was accepted as more than a hero, receiving divine honors and rituals appropriate for a god. In naming Alexander first, and in a way that mirrors how Zeus appears in the epitaph, the poet plays with the status of Alexander: he is a child of the god Ammon, but also a god himself. Reading Alexander in the role of the child produces a meaning akin to the previous lines: he, like the young man whose epitaph this is, was a child whose premature death was mourned by a parent.[23] Reading Alexander as a god elevates the *consolatio* to a new level: not only heroes, but even gods could also meet the same fate suffered by the unnamed youth and his distraught mother. The omission of a verb and the structure of the concluding couplet allows for and indeed suggests both readings, calling to mind different aspects of Alexander simultaneously.

By ending the poem with Alexander in this way, the emphasis shifts from the grief of the mother which has been the focus of the inscription since verse 13, turning the focus back to the child. Stylistically, Alexander serves as an effective bridge between the mythological figures and the deceased child through their historical closeness (at least in comparison with the other figures named), and their shared connection to Alexandria, the city where both the unnamed youth and Alexander were laid to rest.

But for the Alexandrians, Alexander was more than just another young hero whose premature passing was lamented. Alexander was the founder of Alexandria, where this inscription was displayed and which was presumably the home of the youth honored in the epitaph.[24] The link in this inscription between Alexander and Alexandria, or Greek Egypt more broadly, is strengthened further through Alexander's paternity as given here. Instead of Zeus, Alexander's father is listed as Ammon, presenting Alexander as the son of an Egyptian god. This choice is perhaps more obvious when seen in contrast to how other writers discussed Alexander's divine heritage. Callisthenes, for example, writing for a Greek

---

[22] Although when Alexander's divinity became widely accepted is a much fraught issue, it is clear that by the early Hellenistic era Alexander was worshiped as a god. On the question of Alexander's divinity, see Fraser (1972) 215–219, Badian (1996) 24–26, Bosworth (1996) 140–166, Anson (2003) 117–130, Fredricksmeyer (2003) 253–278, Worthington (2004) 83–92, Dreyer (2009) 218–234, Collins (2009) 179–205, Collins (2012) 1–2.

[23] This is, in effect, reading Alexander as another subject of ᾠήθη (v. 18), another youth who was unable to escape the μίτρον of the Fates.

[24] On Alexander's purported foundation of Alexandria, see Howe (2014) 72–84.

audience, was consistent in referring to Alexander's father not as Ammon, but as Zeus.[25] In contrast, Ptolemy's choice to describe Alexander's father as Ammon is in line with Ptolemy's other efforts to strengthen his position in Egypt by binding Alexander more closely to Egyptian religion and tradition.[26] While Ammon was associated with Zeus, in this context, the name the author of the inscription has chosen to use is indicative of the perspective and interests of the author and of his audience.

Alexander's identification as the son of Ammon presents him in terms used by the Egyptians themselves in Alexander's titulary as well as in his birth name, both of which linked the Macedonian king closely to the Egyptian god.[27] In identifying Alexander as the son of Ammon, the epitaph emphasizes the local aspect of Alexander as well as Alexandria's claim to him: he was both their founder and the son of a local god.[28] Furthermore, the Alexandrians worshipped Alexander himself as a god, a fact to which the grammatical structure of the poem nods.[29] In this way, the poet uplifts the child of the epigram through this direct comparison of the young man with Alexander. The end of the epitaph thus need not be assumed to be corrupt, since Alexander, far from being inappropriate, serves as a uniquely fitting figure to end the poem.

Through the *consolatio*, the poem elevates the deceased youth and his mother by comparing directly their situations with those heroes and gods.[30] In this context, Alexander plays a multifaceted role. By concluding the list of wide-ranging heroes with Alexander, the poet closes the epitaph with a figure who held particular importance at a local level and in so doing comparing the fate of the deceased to that of Alexander the Great. The Alexander couplet thus binds the poem together, returning the reader to Alexandria and uplifting the epitaph's

---

25 As Bosworth (1988) 52 notes, nowhere in the extant fragments does Callisthenes call the god Ammon. See, for example, *BNJ* 124 F 14 (Strabo 17.1.43), and F 36 (Plut. *Alex.* 33.1). By emphasizing Alexander's status as a child of Zeus, Callisthenes appears to have portrayed Alexander as directly competing with his heroic ancestors, Heracles and Perseus, in also being a child of Zeus and possibly even outshining them by having this divine patrimony revealed by Zeus's oracle (Arr. *Anab.* 4.14.1–2, Plut. *Alex.* 55.6, Curt. 8.6.24). For this argument, see Howe (2013) 61–62.
26 As argued by Howe (2013) 62, n. 22. For Ptolemy's account of Alexander's paternity, see in particular Arr. *Anab.* 3.3.1–3.4.5.
27 On the different royal titularies given to Alexander, see Burstein (1991). On the importance of Ammon to Alexander's Egyptian titulary, see Bosch-Puche (2015) and Bianchi (2018).
28 As Bernand (1969) 292 notes, "L'épigramme s'achève non sans habileté sur le souvenir du fondateur de la ville."
29 On the cult worship of Alexander in Egypt, see Dreyer (2009) 218–223, Habicht (2017) 26.
30 For a discussion of the heroization of individuals in funerary epigrams, see Vérilhac (1982) 26–28 and Wypustek (2013) 79.

subject through comparison with Alexander, the king of the Macedonians, the son of Ammon, and the divine founder of Alexandria.

IV Alexander's divine birth

Whether Alexander was the son of Ammon, a claim central to Alexander's inclusion in this epitaph, was debated by a vast array of Alexandrographers. Through their writings they grappled with questions such as, was Alexander actually the son of a god? If Alexander was Ammon's son, was he not Philip's? and, how exactly did Ammon sire Alexander?[31] Several competing narratives of Alexander's conception and paternity emerge from the extant literary, epigraphic, and numismatic sources, including the one given in this epitaph: that the god Ammon, having assumed the form of a snake, lay with Alexander's mother Olympias. As Collins and Ogden have noted, conception through copulation with a god in the form of a snake is not unique to the case of Alexander, nor is it by any means limited to Ammon or Zeus.[32] How the snake-siring made its way into the tradition is difficult to trace with certainty, whether it pre-dated Alexander's visit to Siwah or came about in the Ptolemaic period in Egypt, and whether the god was originally Ammon or was another such as Dionysus or Asclepius.[33] However, in spite of this ambiguity of how or when the snake entered into the tradition, once Alexander's status as Ammon's son was spread and became accepted, this birth narrative became a key element in the Alexander tradition, explaining how he was able to be a son of Ammon. But while Alexander as the son of

---

[31] These questions are also connected by later sources to the nature of polygamy in the Macedonian court, and used to explain why Philip took on other wives after Olympias. See, for example, Plut. *Alex.* 2.6 (below), Just. *Epit.* 9.7.2. For Ammon alone being Alexander's father, see, for example, Diod. Sic. 17.51; Curt. 4.7.8, 25 – 27; Plut. *Alex.* 27.6 – 7 (below); Just. *Epit.* 11.11.9 (below). See also Lucian *Dial. mort.* 13. Cf. Ogden (2011) 22.

[32] See, for example, a 4th c. BC *iama* from Epidaurus (*IG* IV^2 1.122 42) describing a woman being healed of infertility by Asclepius, who instructed a snake to have intercourse with her in an epiphanic dream. For a discussion of this *iama*, see Ogden (2011) 44 – 45; Collins (2012) 10 – 11.

[33] Ogden (2011) 41 – 52, Collins (2012) 11 – 13. Stoneman (2008) 7 claims that because Heracles as an infant fought the snakes sent by Hera, "it is no surprise to find snakes involved in Alexander's birth too." However, given the other, stronger reasons for the snake being involved, this seems to be more a case of coincidence rather than causation. The ambiguity as to which god the snake represented is preserved in a speech of Philip given by Pseudo-Callisthenes 1.10: "for he seemed to me the shape of the god Ammon and of Apollo and of Asclepius" (ἔδειξε γὰρ ἡμῖν καὶ θεοῦ Ἄμμωνος μορφὴν καὶ Ἀπόλλωνος καὶ Ἀσκληπίου). On this passage see Ogden (2009) 166.

Ammon is found throughout the extant sources, the combination of Ammon and a snake-siring, while present, is decidedly less common.[34]

In one of the earliest extant narratives associating Alexander's conception with snakes, the Augustan historian Pompeius Trogus, "epitomized" by Justin, declares that, according to Olympias, Alexander was conceived by a giant snake and Alexander bribed the priests of Ammon to declare the god his father.[35] Plutarch, in his discussion of Alexander's conception, notes both that Olympias was seen sleeping with a snake, and that the Delphic oracle informed Philip that this snake was Ammon.[36] It is this tale to which Lucian also alludes in the *Dialogues of the Dead*. Alexander appears there in two separate dialogues, both of which address—and mock—the debate over Alexander's true paternity. While

---

[34] For a complete assessment of the different accounts of Alexander's snake-siring and the origins of the snake-siring motif, see Ogden (this volume).

[35] Just. *Epit.* 11.11.3–8: "For his mother, Olympias, had confessed to her husband, Philip, that Alexander was not his son, but that he had been conceived from a giant serpent. Moreover, Philip, at the end of his life, had declared openly that Alexander was not his son, on which grounds he had repudiated Olympias for adultery. Therefore Alexander, desiring to acquire divine parentage and at the same time free his mother from infamy, through emissaries bribed the priests to say what he wished. When he entered the temple, immediately the priests greeted him as the son of Ammon" (*Namque mater eius Olympias confessa viro suo Philippo fuerat, Alexandrum non ex eo se, sed ex serpente ingentis magnitudinis concepisse. Denique Philippus ultimo prope vitae suae tempore filium suum non esse palam praedicaverat. Qua ex causa Olympiada velut stupri conpertam repudio dimiserat. Igitur Alexander cupiens originem divinitatis adquirere, simul et matrem infamia liberare, per praemissos subornat antistites, quid sibi responderi vellet. Ingredientem templum statim antistites ut Hammonis filium salutant*). For an overview of the nature and trustworthiness of Justin's work based upon Trogus's *Philippica*, see Yardley (1997) 15–19. On the presentation of Olympias within the work, see Frank (2018).

[36] Plut. *Alex.* 2.6, 3.2: "Once also a snake was seen stretched out next to Olympias while she was sleeping, and this most of all, they say, cooled his love and his kindliness towards her, either fearing some magic in it and enchantment of his wife, or eschewing intercourse on religious grounds because she had lain with a superior being... [but the oracle in Delphi] ordered [Philip] to sacrifice to Ammon and to be especially pious to this god; and that he would lose one of his eyes, the one with which looking through a crack in the door he had cast his eye upon the god in the form of a snake lying with his wife" (ὤφθη δέ ποτε καὶ δράκων κοιμωμένης τῆς Ὀλυμπιάδος παρεκτεταμένος τῷ σώματι, καὶ τοῦτο μάλιστα τοῦ Φιλίππου τὸν ἔρωτα καὶ τὰς φιλοφροσύνας ἀμαυρῶσαι λέγουσιν, ὡς μηδὲ φοιτᾶν ἔτι πολλάκις παρ' αὐτὴν ἀναπαυσόμενον, εἴτε δείσαντά τινας μαγείας ἐπ' αὐτῷ καὶ φάρμακα τῆς γυναικός, εἴτε τὴν ὁμιλίαν ὡς κρείττονι συνούσης ἀφοσιούμενον... κελεύοντος Ἄμμωνι θύειν καὶ σέβεσθαι μάλιστα τοῦτον τὸν θεόν· ἀποβαλεῖν δὲ τῶν ὄψεων αὐτὸν τὴν ἑτέραν, ἣν τῷ τῆς θύρας ἁρμῷ προσβαλών, κατώπτευσεν ἐν μορφῇ δράκοντος συνευναζόμενον τῇ γυναικὶ τὸν θεόν). Asirvatham (2001) argues that Plutarch presents the tale of Olympias and the snake in a way that discredits both Olympias herself and the notion of Alexander's divine parentage. On the question of Olympias's association with snakes, see Carney (2006) 88–103.

in dialogue 12 (Philip and Alexander) Lucian does not mention the manner in which Alexander was conceived, this matter features prominently in dialogue 13 (Diogenes and Alexander). There, the philosopher Diogenes taunts Alexander for appearing as a shade in the underworld,[37] recounting the tale of how Olympias was impregnated by a serpent[38] and ridiculing those who worshipped the son of a snake (δράκοντος υἱῷ) as a god.[39] In each case, it is clear that Justin/Trogus, Plutarch, and Lucian respectively were aware of, and expected their readers to be familiar with, the tradition of Alexander's snake-siring by Ammon, as is evidenced by the ways in which they each modify the tale, either by explaining how it came about or mocking Alexander and those who promoted his divine filiation. But by far the most complete and elaborate account of Alexander's snake siring is found in the Greek *Alexander Romance*.

In the *Romance*, instead of Ammon, it is the exiled Egyptian pharaoh Nectanebo who sires Alexander. After deceiving Olympias into sleeping with him through false dreams and a disguise, Nectanebo then shape-shifts into a snake to convince Philip that it was a god who impregnated his wife.[40] Although in this version Alexander is not in fact the son of Ammon, but rather the son of Nectanebo, in varying from the theme the *Romance* tacitly acknowledges the existence of the other version.[41] Furthermore, in a move that disregardes internal cohesion, while the opening of the *Romance* leaves no room for doubt that Nectanebo is Alexander's true father, later, when Alexander is about to face Darius, Ammon himself appears to Alexander in a vision addressing him as τέκνον.[42]

---

37 Lucian *Dial. mort.* 13.1: "then Ammon lied saying that you were his, it seems you were Philip's" (οὐκοῦν ὁ Ἄμμων ἐψεύδετο λέγων ἑαυτοῦ σε εἶναι, σὺ δὲ Φιλίππου ἄρα ἦσθα).
38 Lucian *Dial. mort.* 13.1: "concerning Olympias also similar things were said, that a serpent consorted with her and was seen in her bed, and because you were conceived in this way, that Philip was deceived thinking that he was your father" (καὶ μὴν καὶ περὶ τῆς Ὀλυμπιάδος ὅμοια ἐλέγετο, δράκοντα ὁμιλεῖν αὐτῇ καὶ βλέπεσθαι ἐν τῇ εὐνῇ, εἶτα οὕτω σε τεχθῆναι, τὸν δὲ Φίλιππον ἐξηπατῆσθαι οἰόμενον πατέρα σου εἶναι).
39 Lucian *Dial. mort.* 13.2: "...and some even placing you in the twelve gods and building temples to you and making sacrifices a serpent's son" (ἔνιοι δὲ καὶ τοῖς δώδεκα θεοῖς προστιθέντες καὶ οἰκοδομοῦντές σοι νεὼς καὶ θύοντες ὡς δράκοντος υἱῷ). See also Paus. 4.14.7–8, where Pausanias claims that it is the Macedonians who tell the story of Olympias conceiving Alexander by uniting with Ammon in the form of a serpent, a claim which is supported by the tale's appearance on Macedonian coinage. For a discussion of these coins see Dahmen (2007) 32–33.
40 Ps-Call. 1.4–7 (Stoneman (2007) 476–479). See also Fraser (1996) 212 and Stoneman (2008) 6–24.
41 Stephens (2003) 64–73 argues that the conflicting filiations given to Alexander in the *Romance* serve to legitimize Alexander's rule in Egypt, the one by presenting him as a descendant of a pharaoh, and the other by inserting him into Egyptian theology.
42 Ps.-Call. 2.13.5.

This slip, as well as Nectanebo's deceit, using the form of a snake to trick everyone into believing Alexander to be the child of Ammon, indicates the *Romance* tradition's clear knowledge of the tale of Ammon as Alexander's snake-sire.

The *Alexander Romance* enjoyed widespread reception throughout the Greek world and well beyond it. The Greek version of the story reflects in particular Egyptian as well as Ptolemaic themes, emphasizing the legitimacy and the excellence of Alexander, and consequently of the Ptolemies, as rulers of Egypt.[43] Indeed, rather than a history, the *Romance* is a glorification and celebration of Alexander as an unmatched youth, a hero as great as any lauded by Homer. While this portrayal alone reveals parallels between the *Romance* tradition and the inscription at hand—emphasizing Alexander's divine connection, his snake-siring, and his heroic spirit—there is a further similarity as regards the poetic elements of these texts to justify viewing them as a product of a shared tradition.

The inscription under discussion here is composed in choliambic trimeter, which is unusual for sepulchral epigrams, whether from Greece or Egypt.[44] This choice of meter has a parallel, however, in the *Romance*. As Knox and Merkelbach have noted, there is evidence that behind the predominantly prose *Alexander Romance*, there lay a choliambic "Life of Alexander," or at the very least, a series of fables concerning Alexander.[45] Evidence of this survives in hints in the *Romance*, in both iambic and choliambic lines scattered throughout.[46] For example, in Book 1 of the α-recension of the *Romance* Ammon speaks to Alexander in a dream, delivering a prophecy composed in a mix of iambic and choliambic verses. In the midst of this prophecy, Ammon makes the following declaration:

> πολλοὶ δὲ διὰ βίου σε πάντῃ πάντοτε
> καθὼς θεὸν γεγονότα προσκυνήσουσιν.
> σὺ δ' ἀποθεωθεὶς προσκυνηθήσῃ θανών
> καὶ δῶρα λήψῃ βασιλέων. σὺ πάντοτε
> οἰκήσεις αὐτὴν καὶ θανὼν καὶ μὴ θανών·
> τάφον γὰρ ἕξεις αὐτὸς ἣν κτίζεις πόλιν.

---

43 See, for example, Stoneman (2008) 8.
44 On this point see Cagnat (1880) 168–169, Miller *et al.* (1883) 196. For other examples of choliambic fragments from sepulchral epigrams, see Knox (1946) 256–259, 264–265, and 278–279. For other examples of epigrams containing reference to Alexander from this period, see Barbantani (2017) 105–114.
45 Knox (1946) 287–289, Fraser (1996) 218, Adrados (1999) 546–547.
46 For a rather optimistic list, see Knox (1946) 291–333.

> Many people, from everywhere, will worship you at all times during your life even as a god. And after your death, you will be deified and worshiped, and will receive gifts from kings. You will dwell for all time in [Alexandria], both dead and not dead; for you will have as a tomb the city which you will found.[47]

This poem in the *Romance*, together with similar ones like it, led Knox, and to a lesser extent Fraser, to ask whether there is any connection between the poetic elements in the *Romance* and this inscription given the parallels both in meter and in sense between the two works: both glorify Alexander and emphasize his divine ties, all in the context of Alexander's death.[48] The lines quoted above identify Alexander as one who would be buried in Alexandria, while also being deified and receiving honors proper for a god. Similarities such as these prompted Knox to go so far as to claim that the poems may have been the product of the same poet. Given the extraordinarily difficult task of attempting to date elements in the *Romance* as well as the lack of a clear date for this inscription, I do not believe that it is possible to support a claim to the same authorship for both texts.[49] But as Ross argues concerning a mosaic depicting scenes evocative of the *Alexander Romance*, the presence of a theme does not prove that the *Romance* text must have existed before the object; it merely demonstrates that a version of the tale—written or oral—was known at the time of the object's creation.[50] The overlap in themes and content between the *Romance* and this inscription suggest a shared tradition of Alexander-*laudatio* and a recognition of Alexander's divine parentage and his divinity that is reflected in these two works. That it is these aspects of Alexander shared by both the inscription

---

47 Ps.-Call. recension α 1.33.11. This is a six-verse excerpt of the 40-verse section. Of the verses quoted here, all are iambic except the second (καθὼς θεὸν γεγονότα προσκυνήσουσιν).
48 Knox (1946) 278–281; Fraser (1996) 218–221. See also a similar oracle by Serapis delivered to the Egyptians prophesying Alexander's return as the descendant of Nectanebo. Ps.-Call. 1.3.4: "The strong and brave elder fleeing Egypt / a king, a ruler, will come after a time, young / having put aside the old appearance of his features, / having drawn the world around Egypt's plain / giving the submission of all our enemies to us" (Αἴγυπτον ὁ φυγὼν κρατερὸς ἄλκιμος πρέσβυς / βασιλεὺς δυνάστης †ἥξει† μετὰ χρόνον νέος, / τὸ γηράλαιον ἀποβαλὼν τύπων εἶδος, / κόσμον κυκλεύσας ἐπὶ τὸ πεδίον Αἰγύπτου, / ἐχθρῶν ⟨ἁπάντων⟩ ὑποταγὴν διδοὺς ἡμῖν).
49 For attempts to date the *Romance* tradition, see Merkelbach (1954), Stoneman (2003) 601–612, Selden (2012) 34, Nawotka (2017) 1–5. Although, as Ross (1988) 5 notes, even if the date of the *Romance* as we have it may be fixed, "probably even the original text was not the earliest romanticized biography of Alexander to be composed." As regards the authorial claim for this inscription see Knox (1946) 281.
50 Ross (1963) 20–21.

and the *Romance* is perhaps not surprising given the inscription's provenance, as it is generally accepted that the Greek *Romance* originated in Egypt.⁵¹

This would not be the only example of themes or even text from the *Romance* making the leap between literary text and engraved monuments. The *Tabulae Iliacae,* discovered in Roman Italy and dating to the first century CE, contain depictions of scenes from the Trojan War, the *Thebaid*, and from tales of Heracles and of Alexander the Great.⁵² On one of these tablets, the so-called Vasek Polak Chronicle, is carved the middle verses of a four-line inscription containing parts of a letter purportedly from Alexander to Darius that is also found in the *Alexander Romance*.⁵³ In this tablet, as with the inscription at hand, we see elements of the *Alexander Romance* tradition excerpted and combined with tales of mythical heroes and events. The *Tabulae Iliacae* and the epitaph do not present the same aspects of the *Romance*, nor do the *Tabuae Iliacae* reference Ammon. Nevertheless, the *Tabulae Iliacae* do demonstrate that by the early imperial era, long before the *Alexander Romance* itself is generally accepted to have been assembled from its various constituent parts, aspects of the *Romance* were not only in circulation, but were also being excerpted and incorporated into monuments in Rome.⁵⁴ It is not surprising, then, to find similar monuments present in Roman Egypt, nor is it surprising that Alexandrians would in commemorating the premature death of a young man tap into the narratives and language used to praise their city's divine founder.

IV Conclusion

In commemorating the death of a young man, the anonymous poet of the epitaph engages directly with the popular tradition and mythos surrounding Alexander the Great. The resulting image of Alexander that emerges is that of a complex and multifaceted figure. In 1ˢᵗ–2ⁿᵈ century CE Egypt, Alexander represented a young man who died before his time, a hero on par with any of those who fought at Troy, the founder of Alexandria, and a god worthy of receiving the

---

51 For a discussion of the evidence of the *Romance* author's origins, see Nawotka (2017) 25–27.
52 Sadurska (1964) 7.
53 *SEG* 33.802. On the tablet, see Burstein (1989) 275–276 and Merkelbach (1989) 279–280. See Sadurska (1964) for a discussion of the *Tabulae Iliacae* more broadly, and Petrain (2012) 598–614 on Alexander's appearance in the *Tabula Chigi* (*IG* 14.1296)
54 While scholars disagree on the exact date of the text's compilation, the *Romance* is generally situated around the third century CE. For a discussion of the problems associated with dating the work, see Nawotka (2017) 1–5.

divine honors bestowed upon him. What is the subject of rationalization by Plutarch and a topic for mockery by Lucian, is for those behind the tales in the Greek *Alexander Romance* a means to celebrate Alexander, and through him, Alexandria and the Alexandrians. The author of this sepulchral inscription, in employing the language of the *Romance* tradition, celebrates also the deceased young Alexandrian. In a period in which Alexander's paternity was a hotly contested matter for debate by Greek authors throughout the Mediterranean world, the author of this inscription has chosen to leave no room for debate or disagreement: in the epitaph, Alexander was the son of Ammon, just as Sarpedon was the child of Zeus. Ultimately the text glorifies both the deceased young Alexandrian as well as Alexander himself, to whom all of the named characteristics of the deceased could conceivably be applied and with whom the poem ends. This epigram, while certainly peculiar, is not truly unique. It engages directly in both its contents and meter with the ongoing popularization and romanticization of Alexander and his rule. In Roman Egypt, Alexander was not only a Macedonian king. As seen in this sepulchral inscription, Alexander was a hero, the son of the god Ammon, and a god himself.

Bibliography

Adrados (1999): Francisco Rodríguez Adrados (L. A. Ray, trans.), *History of the Graeco-Latin Fable*, vol. 1, Leiden.
Anson (2003): Edward M. Anson, "Alexander and Siwah", in: *The Ancient World* 34.2, 117–130.
Asirvatham (2001): Sulochana R. Asirvatham, "Olympias' Snake and Callisthenes' Stand: Religion and Politics in Plutarch's *Life of Alexander*", in Sulochana R. Asirvatham, Corinne Ondine Pache, and John Watrous (eds.) *Between Magic and Religion: Interdisciplinary Studies in Ancient Mediterranean Religion and Society*, New York, 93–125.
Badian (1996): Ernst Badian, "Alexander the Great between two thrones and Heaven: variations on an old theme", in Alastair Small (ed.) *Subject and Ruler: The Cult of the Ruling Power in Classical Antiquity*, Ann Arbor, 11–26.
Barbantani (2017): Siliva Barbantani, "'His σῆμα are both continents'. Alexander the Great in Hellenistic Poetry", in: *Studi Ellenistici* 31, 51–127.
Bernand (1969): Étienne Bernand, *Inscriptions Métriques de l'Égypte Gréco-Romaine: Recherches Sur la Poésie Épigrammatique des Grecs en Égypte*, PhD. Université de Paris.
Bianchi (2018): Robert Steven Bianchi, "Alexander, Son of Amun: The Interaction Between the Egyptian Priesthood and Alexander's Policy Makers", in: *Chronique d'Égypte* 93.185, 86–97.
Bosch-Puche (2015): Francisco Bosch-Puche, "The Egyptian Royal Titularies of the Roman Emperors: A Local Version of the *Imitatio Alexandri?*", in: *Chronique d'Égypte* 90.180, 276–305.

Bosworth (1977): A.B. Bosworth, "Alexander and Ammon", in: Konrad H. Kinzl (ed.), *Greece and the Eastern Mediterranean in Ancient History and Prehistory*, Berlin, 51–75.

Bosworth (1988): A.B. Bosworth, *Conquest and Empire: The reign of Alexander the Great*, Cambridge.

Bosworth (1996): A.B. Bosworth, *Alexander and the East: The Tragedy of Triumph*, Oxford.

Bowden (2018): Hugh Bowden, "Alexander as Achilles: Arrian's Use of Homer from Troy to the Granikos", in: Timothy Howe and Frances Pownall (eds.), *Ancient Macedonians in the Greek and Roman Sources: From History to Historiography*, Swansea, 163–179.

Burstein (1989): Stanley M. Burstein, "'SEG 33.802' and the Alexander Romance", in: *ZPE* 77, 275–276.

Burstein (1991): Stanley M. Burstein, "Pharaoh Alexander: A Scholarly Myth", in: *Ancient Society* 22, 139–145.

Cagnat (1880): R. Cagnat, "Inscription Funéraire d'Alexandrie", in: *Revue Archélogique* 40, 166–170.

Caneva (2012): Stefano Giovanni Caneva, "D'Hérodote à Alexandre: l'appropriation Gréco-macédonienne d'Ammon de Siwa, entre pratique oracular et légitimation du pouvoir", in: Corinne Bonnet, Amandine Declercq, and Iwo Slobodzianek (eds.), *Les représentations des dieux des autres*, Palermo, 193–219.

Carney (2006): Elizabeth Carney, *Olympias: Mother of Alexander the Great*, New York.

Collins (2009): Andrew Collins, "The Divinity of Alexander in Egypt: A Reassessment", in: Pat Wheatley and Robert Hannah (eds.), *Alexander and his Successors: Essays from the Antipodes*, Claremont, 179–205.

Collins (2012): Andrew Collins, "Callisthenes on Olympias and Alexander's Divine Birth", in: *AHB* 26, 1–14.

Dahmen (2007): Karsten Dahmen, *The Legend of Alexander the Great on Greek and Roman Coins*, New York.

Dreyer (2009): Boris Dreyer, "Heroes, Cults, and Divinity", in: Waldemar Heckel and Lawrence A. Tritle (eds.), *Alexander the Great: A New History*, Malden, 218–234.

Edmunds (1971): Lowell Edmunds, "The Religiosity of Alexander", in: *Greek, Roman, and Byzantine Studies* 12.3, 363–391.

Frank (2018): Rebecca Frank, "A Roman Olympias: Powerful Women in the *Historiae Philippicae* of Pompeius Trogus", in: Timothy Howe and Frances Pownall (eds.), *Power, Kingship, and Memory in Ancient Macedonia: Sources and Context*, Swansea, 41–58.

Fraser (1972): Peter M. Fraser, *Ptolemaic Alexandria*, Oxford.

Fraser (1996): Peter M. Fraser, *Cities of Alexander the Great*, Oxford.

Fredricksmeyer (2003): Ernst Fredricksmeyer, "Alexander's Religion and Divinity", in: Joseph Roisman (ed.), *Brill's Companion to Alexander the Great*, Leiden, 251–278.

Habicht (2017): Christian Habicht (J.N. Dillon, trans.), *Divine Honors for Mortal Men in Greek Cities: The Early Cases*. Dexter.

Heckel (2015): Waldemar Heckel, "Alexander, Achilles, and Heracles: Between Myth and History", in: Pat Wheatley and Elizabeth Baynham (eds.), *East and West in the World Empire of Alexander: Essays in Honour of Brian Bosworth*, Oxford, 21–33.

Howe (2013): Timothy Howe, "The Diadochi, Invented Tradition, and Alexander's Expedition to Siwah", in: Victor Alonso Troncoso and Edward M. Anson (eds.), *After Alexander: The Time of the Diadochi (323–281 BC)*, Oxford, 57–70.

Howe (2014): Timothy Howe, "Founding Alexandria: Alexander the Great and the Politics of Memory", in: Philip Bosman (ed.), *Alexander in Africa*, Pretoria, 72–91.
Knox (1946): Alfred D. Knox, *Herodes, Cercidas, and the Greek choliambic poets*, Cambridge, MA.
Knox (1967): Alfred D. Knox, *Herodes, Cercidas, and the Greek choliambic poets*, Cambridge, MA.
Lattimore (1962): Richmond Lattimore, *Themes in Greek and Latin Epitaphs*, Urbana.
Lavagnini (1937) / Lavagnini[1]: Bruno Lavagnini, "Miscellanea", in: *Rivista di Filologia e d'Istruzione Classica* 16, 372–376.
Lavagnini (1947) / Lavagnini[2]: Bruno Lavagnini, "Motivi Diatribici in Lucrezio e in Giovenale", in: *Athenaeum: Studii Periodici di Letteratura e Storia dell'Antichità* 25, 83–88.
Miller *et al.* (1883): E. Miller, G. Maspero, and Henri Weil, "Inscriptions Greques Découvertes en Égypte", in: *Revue Archéologique* 1, 193–208.
Merkelbach (1954): Reinhold Merkelbach, *Die Quellen des griechischen Alexanderroman*, Munich.
Merkelbach (1989): Reinhold Merkelbach, "Der Brief des Dareios im Getty-Museum und Alexanders Wortwechsel mit Parmenion", in: *ZPE* 77, 277–80.
Milne (1905): J.G. Milne, *Greek Inscriptions*, Oxford.
Mossman (1988): Judith M. Mossman, "Tragedy and Epic in Plutarch's Alexander", in: *Journal of Hellenic Studies* 108, 83–93.
Müller (2006): Sabine Müller, "Alexander der Große als neuer Achilles. Die panhellenische und makedonische Repräsentation des Persienkrieges in den Medien der königlichen Propaganda", in: Stefan Jaeger and Christer Peterson (eds.), *Zeichen des Krieges in Literatur, Film und den Medien II: Ideologisierungen und Entideologisierungen*, Kiel, 263–294.
Nawotka (2017): Krzysztof Nawotka, *The Alexander Romance by Ps.-Callisthenes: A Historical Commentary*, Leiden.
Ogden (2009): Daniel Ogden, "Alexander's Snake Sire", in: Pat Wheatley and Robert Hannah (eds.), *Alexander and his Successors: Essays from the Antipodes*, Claremont, 136–178.
Ogden (2011): Daniel Ogden, *Alexander the Great: Myth, Genesis and Sexuality*, Exeter.
Peek (1931) / Peek[1]: Werner Peek, "Zu griechischen Epigrammen aus Ägypten", in: *Hermes* 66.4, 317–3.
Peek (1932) / Peek[2]: Werner Peek, "Griechische Epigramme aus Aegypten", in: *BSA Alex.* 27, 61–62.
Peek (1955) / Peek[3]: Werner Peek, *Griechische Vers-Inschriften: Grab-Epigramme*, Berlin.
Petrain (2012): David Petrain, "The Archaeology of the Epigrams from the *Tabulae Iliacae*: Adaptation, Allusion, Alteration", in: *Mnemosyne* 65, 597–635.
Ross (1963): David J.A. Ross, "Olympias and the Serpent: The Interpretation of a Baalbek Mosaic and the Date of the Illustrated Pseudo-Callisthenes", in: *Journal of the Warburg and Courtauld Institutes* 26.1–2, 1–21.
Ross (1988): David J.A. Ross, *Alexander Historiatus: A Guide to Medieval Illustrated Alexander Literature*, Frankfurt.
Sadurska (1964): Anna Sadurska, *Les Tables Iliaques*, Warsaw.
Selden (2012): Daniel L. Selden, "Mapping the Alexander Romance", in: Richard Stoneman, Kyle Erickson, and Ian Netton (eds.), *The 'Alexander Romance' in Persia and the East*, Groningen, 19–59.

Stephens (2003): Susan A. Stephens, *Seeing Double: Intercultural Poetics in Ptolemaic Alexandria*. Berkeley.
Stewart (1993): Andrew Stewart, *Faces of Power: Alexander's Image and Hellenistic Politics*, Berkeley.
Stoneman (2003): Richard Stoneman, "The Metamorphoses of the *Alexander Romance*", in: Gareth Schmeling (ed.), *The Novel in the Ancient World*, Leiden, 601–612.
Stoneman (2007): Richard Stoneman, *Il Romanzo di Alessandro*, vol. 1, Milan.
Stoneman (2008): Richard Stoneman, *Alexander the Great: A Life in Legend*, New Haven.
Vérilhac (1982): Anne-Marie Vérilhac, *ΠΑΙΔΕΣ ΑΩΡΟΙ: Poésie Funéraire*, vol. 2, Athens.
Vorhis (2017): Justin Vorhis, *The Best of the Macedonians: Alexander as Achilles in Arrian, Curtius, and Plutarch*, University of California Los Angeles diss.
Worthington (2004): Ian Worthington, *Alexander the Great: Man and God*, London.
Wypustek (2013): Andrzej Wypustek, *Images of Eternal Beauty in Funerary Verse Inscriptions of the Hellenistic and Greco-Roman Periods*, Leiden.
Yardley (1997): John C. Yardley, *Justin:* Epitome of the Philippic History of Pompeius Trogus Books 11–12: Alexander the Great, Oxford.

Steven E. Hijmans
Alexander or not? The Problem of Alexander-like Portraits in Roman Art

Ancient sources agree that Alexander was very particular about how artists were to portray him. In fact, they suggest that he had it made known that only Apelles (painting), Lysippus (sculpture) and Pyrgoteles (gem/coin-engraving) were to make portraits of him.[1] Whether this was ever a formal decree is difficult to say, but seems unlikely. The implication that Alexander carefully managed the way he was depicted in public is nonetheless interesting. Studying the state-approved portraits could shed a fascinating light on how Alexander and his court hoped to (re)present him in the far-flung corners of the Empire that he was in the process of conquering—making it all the more unfortunate that none of these early portraits survive. This lends added interest to recent art-historical attempts to deduce original portrait types of Alexander through formal analytical study of later portraits.[2] But the early portraits of Alexander are not the topic of this paper, nor will we discuss attempts to rediscover them. We will actually focus on the viability of the central premise of such research, namely that we can recognize Roman portraits of Alexander. Can we?

That Alexander and his portraits influenced Rome is beyond dispute, of course.[3] It was not uncommon for an orator to compare a Roman general or Emperor to Alexander. Pompey was not "the Great" by chance, and both he and others extended those comparisons to include their portraits, in which they incorporated elements of Alexander's portrait, such as the *anastole*.[4] Plutarch, who mentions this, seems to take for granted that this kind of borrowing from Alexander's portrait was recognizable to contemporary viewers, but in truth, for us it is not. We cannot know, of course, whether we would have recognized the short upturned lock or two about Pompey's pudgy face as a direct reference to Alexander's *anastole*, if we hadn't had Plutarch to guide us. What we do know is that there is not a single surviving sculptural portrait of Alexander of Roman date, in which the identity of the depicted person is uncontested in today's schol-

---

[1] Plin. *HN* 7.125; Plut. *Mor.* 335a–b (= *De Alex. fort.* 2.2); Arr. *Anab.* 1.16.4; Plut. *Alex.* 4.1–3; Plin. *HN* 34.64–66; 35.93–99; 37.8. Bieber (1964) discusses the ancient sources for Alexander's appearance at length; see also the recent studies of Kiilerich (2017) and Dorka Moreno (2019).
[2] Mihalopoulos (2009).
[3] Green (1978); Spencer (2002); O'Sullivan (2016); Peltonen (2019).
[4] Plut. *Pomp.* 2. See Marshall (2016).

arship. We have many Alexander-*like* images of Roman date, but there is no consensus which ones, if any, actually depict Alexander himself. They simply defy easy identification and categorization.

Obviously we cannot study the impact of Alexander on Roman portraits, if we cannot be certain that any of the portraits we are studying depict Alexander.[5] More importantly, if Romans could readily identify a portrait as Alexander while we cannot, we must be doing something wrong. To proceed, then, we must take a step back, and look anew at images that have traditionally been identified as Alexander. What is more, we must attempt to do so with "Roman" eyes; we must try to look at these images in the way that a Roman would. To that purpose, the first part of this essay will be slightly unconventional. To help us take a Roman perspective, we turn first to Philostratus maior (ca. 170 – 250), author of one of the most fascinating ancient collections of ecphrases to survive. Philostratus does not describe real images, but evokes virtual pictures in the mind's eye of his audience, because he was not asking his audience to study pictures, but to ponder the act of viewing. Likewise we will not be dealing with real images, suitably illustrated in this article, but also with virtual images evoked in our mind's eye, and based on our past knowledge and experience. My hope is that this will help us focus on how these images were viewed, without the ballast of past and current interpretations of particular pictures getting in the way.

So taking our cue from Philostratus, we begin by imagining ourselves in Naples. Our goal is not the multi-level portico-complex supposedly housing the paintings which Philostratus so brilliantly expounds for the ten-year-old child of his host. We turn instead to a small, unassuming structure which, we should imagine, was fitted into one of the vaulted spaces of the terraced substructures supporting Philostratus' portico.[6] Upon entry we find ourselves in a very dimly

---

[5] Nielsen (1993) 140 puts it, one gets "the unpleasant feeling that the criteria for identification (sc. of Alexander) vary according to individual taste." Cf. Blum (1914) (cf. Hijmans (in press), catalogue A3.9); L'Orange (1947) 34; Kleiner (1957) 101; Hölscher (1971) 43 – 45; Stewart (1993); Schörner (2001); Stewart (2004).

[6] The best introduction to Philostratus' *Imagines* is probably Squire (2013). The portico that Philostratus uses as the setting for his *Imagines* is wholly fictitious but easy to imagine as a building type. In the *praefatio* of his *Imagines*, Philostratus is studiously vague about the whereabouts of the portico (with its "four or five" levels) that purportedly housed the paintings he describes to the unnamed child of his unidentified host in an unspecified suburb of Naples. Clearly his *Imagines* were not a guide to a gallery, for one does not write guidebooks to "some collection somewhere." The portico is in Philostratus' head, rather than at Naples, as are the paintings. The "descriptions" he gives of them could be considered exercises in rhetoric—the art of describing was one of the *progymnasmata* in a rhetor's education— designed perhaps to stimulate philosophical discussion about the nature and practice of viewing and modes of visual signification.

lit, vaulted space, in which hardly anything can be seen clearly. Along the walls to either side are low platforms covered with spreads and the odd pillow. Guests could recline here, one assumes, but not very many; perhaps as few as four or five. There does not appear to be any furniture, but wherever the gloom is lifted a bit by a filtered beam of light, one catches glimpses of richly frescoed walls. Furthermore, the rear of the room is occupied by shadowy sculptures of life-size figures who seem to move in the faint, flickering rays of light that barely penetrate the deep gloom, accentuating rather than lifting the darkness in which these statues stand.

But none of us entering the room sees any of this. Our eyes are drawn immediately to the brilliantly illuminated marble bust of a young man in the upper left hand corner of the rear wall. A small, artfully hidden opening in the ceiling allows a shaft of daylight to beam in, bathing only this head in light, and leaving all else dark. It is with a description of this image in its particular setting that we open this discussion of the portrayal of Alexander the Great in Roman art.[7]

To get some sense of how a Roman may have described it, we will first eavesdrop on a conversation that I imagine Philostratus and his ten-year-old disciple might have had about this bust.[8] So let us mingle with the youngsters[9] accompanying the two in that dark chamber and observe, as Philostratus asks the child to give a description of the bust. Hesitatingly the child begins:

> "We see the sculpted head of a handsome, beardless young man; it is turned to the left and his gaze appears to be upwards towards the hidden source of light. The sculptor has beautifully rendered his long, curly hair, a riot of unruly locks falling down towards his shoulders and framing his face, except above, where it is brushed upwards and back to reveal his powerful forehead. His lips are slightly parted, though not enough to reveal his teeth, and

---

As my article intends to contribute, in a small way, to precisely those philosophical issues, I have no qualms about expanding Philostratus' fictional portico to include an equally fictional structure of my own, in which the first part of this paper is set. It too is of an easily recognizable type.
7 While both the setting and, therefore, the image are figments of my imagination (see previous footnote), the type of setting and the type of image are not, as we will see.
8 The following dialogue is not modelled directly on anything Philostratus wrote. On the contrary, he does not really engage in a dialogue at all in his *Imagines*. But it would be hubris indeed to present an ecphrasis of my own with the *auctoritas* of Philostratus. In both ancient painting and the art of rhetoric, he is master and I am but a tyro. I have chosen the (open-ended) dialogue-form accordingly.
9 In the *praefatio*, Philostratus mentions a constant stream of μειράκια (youths) dogging his steps even when he had no intention to teach.

his nostrils are flaring as if he is breathing hard, giving a sense of power and passion to the image."[10]

The lad stops for a moment, gathering his thoughts, and then continues:

"It is clear that this is Alexander the Great. His youth, his flowing hair, the wild curls brushed back from the forehead into an *anastole*, and below a pronounced brow his hypnotizing, unmatched eyes whose deceptively limpid gaze masks a hidden force, all point to the same conclusion: this is a magnificent portrait of the great Macedonian conqueror!"[11]

Stuttering with enthusiasm, lad continues,

"Perhaps this is a work of Pyrgoteles—but no, he was an engraver of gems only.[12] This must then be a copy of a bronze by Lysippus, for the king was very protective of his image and only Lysippus was allowed to sculpt it. Likewise Apelles alone was allowed to paint his portrait and in that is said to have been as inimitable as Alexander was invincible."[13]

As the child pauses again, Philostratus steps in.

"Well done, my pupil; unorthodox and very rough at the edges—you clearly have not yet mastered rhetorical skill of ecphrasis—yet effective nonetheless, as you leave us in no doubt whom, you think, this bust portrays. I noticed, though, that you did not mention the location of this bust, nor the effect of the staged beam of light striking his features only. Do they not factor into its identity? Have you taken stock of where we stand?"

The student looks rather blankly at his instructor and ventures: "It's too dark to tell," but Philostratus shakes his head.

"Nonsense! Your eyes are used to the gloom by now, even though you have only gazed at the single bright bust up high. Look at the statues at the back. What do you see?"

"Mithras—it is Mithras killing the bull", the child whispers. "But I am not ... —We must leave..."

"We must nothing! I am *Pater*, and if I say we may stay, all will obey. So you now recognize that this is a shrine of Mithras.[14] And yet you identify this bust as the great Macedonian king and conqueror, Alexander. Tell me, what role is there for Alexander in a Mithraeum? And look also to the corresponding bust in the upper right-hand corner. Do you not see that here we have the moon goddess Luna, she who, as the poets sing, is

---

10 The description is (very) loosely based on the way Philostratus describes Amphion (*Imag.* 1.10), *mutatis mutandis*, of course.
11 It is not uncommon for Philostratus to identify the image early in his ecphrasis, and only then explain how he arrives at that conclusion; cf. *Imagines* 1.7 (Memnon). In the course of his explanations, he regularly quotes other works without attribution, trusting (or challenging) the erudition of his audience. In this passage I have drawn terms to describe the portrait's features from Plut. *Alex.* 4,1 and Plut. *Mor.* 335a–b (*De Alex. fort.* 2.2). The "unmatched" eyes of Alexander are only mentioned in Pseudo Callisthenes 1.13; the *anastole* is associated with Alexander only indirectly (Plut. *Pomp.* 2.1).
12 On Pyrgoteles as preferred engraver of Alexander, see Plin. *HN* 7.125 & 37.8.
13 Sources in n. 1.
14 On temples of Mithras see Hensen (2017); much has been written about the cult of Mithras, but we know little about its day to day routine. I have taken the position that access to the shrine was restricted because it was a mystery cult, but there is no direct evidence to support this. Philostratus may well have been affronted by my suggestion that he was a Pater (highest priest) in the cult. In both class and education he was far ahead of most Mithraists; cf. Clauss (1992).

none other than Artemis the arrow-pourer, who co-nursed at Leto's breast with her brother, Phoebus Apollo?[15] Tell me, do you still believe our bust to portray Alexander?"

"No, I do not; he is undoubtedly Sol, so commonly paired with Luna in a wide range of religious settings."[16]

"Nonetheless, if you had not recognized the particularity of this location and the pairing of the Sol and Luna images, you would have maintained that this was undoubtedly a portrait of Alexander?"

"Yes."

"Are Alexander and Helios then so akin to each other that their portraits are interchangeable?"

"No, but normally Sol would be depicted with rays, confirming his identity."

"True, but ..."

"... but Sol can be depicted without rays as well! I remember you teaching me that rays are not essential to his image, especially if the context leaves no doubt regarding his identity."[17]

"If not the rays, is there then any part or aspect of Sol's iconography that clearly differentiates a head or bust of Sol from one of Alexander?"

"No, there is not."

"And is only Sol so closely akin in his features to Alexander?"

"I think so."

"Come with me to the statue of Mithras, here, and let us study his head closely. Do you not see that it too portrays a young man with slightly parted lips, flaring nostrils, and wild curls of gilded hair, brushed back from his powerful forehead? Do you see the tension of his neck as he directs his gaze not towards the bull and his deadly dagger, but up and away towards the sun behind him? Does he not remind you of Alexander?"

"He resembles him, perhaps, but nobody could ever mistake Mithras the bull-slayer for Alexander, if only because Mithras always wears his Persian cap and is dressed in full Persian attire."

"True, but I ask again: are there no others whose heads or busts, like Sol and Mithras, share the traits and features of Alexander?"

"Possibly, but I have not seen any myself."

"It is more than likely that you have seen, but never observed the likeness. I myself remember being struck by the Alexander-like traits of a statue of Meleager in Mediolanum, one of Apollo in Italica, another of Apollo in Catana, a number of busts of Sol from Mithraic shrines in Ostia and Rome, Aeneas in an old wall-painting in a villa not far from here, and in fact at another villa, near Tarraco, I have even seen an Antinous with features that seemed to me remarkably akin to Alexander's, and we should not forget the Alexander-like images of Achilles, Hercules, the Dioscuri, and Dionysus.[18] So let us examine how we view these busts and statues, identify them, and determine their true meaning."

---

15 For "arrow-pourer" see Hom. *Il.* 5.53, *Od.* 6.102.
16 For an extensive analysis of Sol-and-Luna imagery in Roman art cf. the relevant section of chapter 3 in Hijmans (in press).
17 On the iconography of Sol, see Hijmans (in press) chapter 2.
18 These examples of other Greek gods and heroes with Alexander-like images are drawn from Strocka (2006); Vout (2005); Kiilerich (2017); and in particular Dorka Moreno (2019).

Here we must leave Philostratus and his pupil, if only because we do not know *his* answer to that crucial question: how did he and his fellow Romans distinguish the sculpted portrait of one individual from that of another?[19] For that matter, how do we ourselves do that, where Roman art is concerned?[20] Indeed, when is a Roman portrait a portrait, and did the Romans wrestle with that question as we do?[21] The answers are elusive, in particular where Alexander is concerned. That is troubling, because to say that an image is *Alexander-like* implies a clear understanding of that to which the image is likened, i.e. of how Alexander himself was portrayed; and precisely that understanding we appear not to have.

In a recent article, Palagia surveys a fairly extensive range of presumed portraits of Alexander and discusses their impact on Hellenistic art.[22] She does not offer clear criteria, however, for determining whether an image is actually a portrait of Alexander or not. That this is a problem can be illustrated with the first image she discusses, a fresco in the House of the Vettii at Pompeii. That painting, Palagia claims, is "generally thought" to be a copy of the famous portrait of Alexander *keraunophoros* by Apelles.[23] Actually, that suggestion, first made by De Lorenzo,[24] was rejected by Sogliano, Mau, Petersen, Bernoulli, Schreiber and Rumpf,[25] and although it was resurrected by Mingazzini,[26] it was rejected again by Schwarzenberg,[27] Stewart,[28] and others, who all point out that the theme of the room containing the painting is the *lovers of gods in their youth:* Leda and Danae with Zeus, Ariadne with Dionysus and Kyparissos with Apollo.[29]

Similar doubts have been expressed about many of the images that, in Palagia's view, are clearly portraits of Alexander. This brings us right to the crux of the problem with Alexander's portraits. There are no criteria to determine conclu-

---

19 On the nature of Roman portraits see: Squire (2016).
20 Vout (2005) 80.
21 A good introduction to portraiture is West (2004). A recent review of the current definitions of portraiture can be found in Maes (2015). Still popular is Panofsky's definition of a portrait, quoted by West (2004) 24, and many others. Whether these modern definitions can be applied to Roman art is doubtful.
22 Palagia (2015).
23 Palagia (2015) 2.
24 De Lorenzo (1900).
25 Mingazzini (1961) 6 n.2.
26 Mingazzini (1961).
27 Schwarzenberg (1976) 263.
28 Stewart (1993) 198–199.
29 Some still accept the identification of this fresco as a copy of Apelles' painting. Cf. Childs (2018) 94, citing only Mingazzini (1961); Mihalopoulos (2009) 289, remains non-committal. For a different, but similar disputed Alexander in Pompeii, cf. Strocka (2006).

sively whether a given head or bust depicts Alexander or not. In the context of Roman art in particular that should give us pause, because if an identity mattered, Roman art developed the prerequisite iconographic rules to render that identity unambiguous, and Roman artists scrupulously adhered to those precepts.[30] The contrast between this clarity of iconography, one of the hallmarks of Roman art, and the ambiguity and uncertainty surrounding most presumed Roman portraits of Alexander could not be greater. It is this contrast that makes the whole group of Alexander- and Alexander-like images an interesting problem in Roman art.[31]

We can illustrate this with the issues that arise when dealing with Alexander-like images of Helios/Sol in imperial Rome.[32] In Roman art the iconographic rules for the depiction of Sol were crystal clear. Three basic "image-types" of a beardless young man—as charioteer of a *quadriga*, as a standing figure, and as a bust—are rendered readily recognizable as Sol through the addition of one or more select attributes: rays around the head, a globe, a whip, a *chlamys*, a *quadriga* or four horses, and a raised right arm are the most common ones. None of these attributes is indispensable, although Sol without a *chlamys* is exceedingly rare. Even the rays can be omitted, in particular if the context was one in which Sol could easily be recognized regardless. At the same time these attributes are irreplaceable in the sense that the list of acceptable attributes is quite short. The addition of any attribute not on that list immediately obliges the viewer to revise the identity of the figure as a whole. Sol cannot be depicted driving a *biga*, for example, or wearing a toga, or holding a phoenix, and so however Sol-like a figure may appear to be, if he deviates from the norm in some such manner, the viewer is forced to seek an alternative identity for him.[33]

---

30 Hijmans (in press) chapters 1 & 2.
31 Such ambiguity is not restricted to Roman portraits of Alexander. As my colleague, Frances Pownall, points out, we already see comparable ambiguity in Alexander's Heracles coinage, for example.
32 On Sol-Alexander, see also Dorka Moreno (2019) 168–175. His discussion reviews a far larger number of images, but as most are unambiguously Sol, I do not include them here. His conclusions concerning Alexander and Sol are quite similar to mine. The main difference is that he considers Roman-era statuettes that are of the Sol-type, but fully armed, to be depictions of Alexander-Sol, while I consider them to be Romanized images of Near Eastern sun gods (who were warriors); Hijmans (in press).
33 Hijmans (in press) chapter 2. Note in particular the strict rules pertaining to acceptable and unacceptable modes of indicating Sol's radiant light. It was acceptable to depict Sol without any form of radiance at all, but this was rare. He is mostly depicted radiate, subject to strict rules. Of the four major Roman conventions for the depiction of divine light or radiance, only two are acceptable for Sol: rays emanating directly from his head (depicted with or without an accompa-

The consistency with which Roman art maintained such detailed iconographic rules over centuries, throughout the Empire, is truly remarkable. Of the more than two thousand images of Sol that I have documented for my research, all are instantly identifiable without reservation, with the exception of one fairly small and quite homogenous group of images: busts (mostly marble) of Sol in a "baroque" Hellenistic style with all the Alexander-like traits described above. In my study of Sol I have catalogued 22 such busts[34] of which only six can be unequivocally identified as Sol.[35] All six busts share a similar style, that is clearly inspired by Hellenistic conventions, and depict a beardless young man with long, wavy hair and, in varying degrees, other traits such as the *anastole* and sometimes the upward tilting of the head and gaze that we have been taught to associate with Alexander (*supra*, n. 1). Five are radiate, one is not.

None of these busts can be securely identified as either Sol or anyone else on the basis of these iconographic elements alone. In three cases, their provenances are the decisive factor, as these were found in temples of Mithras.[36] The presence of Sol is essential there. He is invariably included in the main cult icon in the upper left corner, with his counterpart Luna invariably in the opposite corner. The presence of Alexander in a Mithraeum, on the other hand, would be unprecedented and inexplicable, making it a foregone conclusion that these three busts represented Sol and were viewed as such.

In the other three cases it is some additional element of the iconography itself which is decisive. The radiate bust from Schloss Fasanerie near Fulda rests on four very small horses drawing a chariot of which only the pole is visible. As the *quadriga* is a standard part of the iconography of Sol, this additional iconographic element establishes beyond reasonable doubt that this bust too repre-

---

nying nimbus), or rays attached to a fillet without ribbons and placed on the head as a radiate crown. A figure depicted with one of the other two conventions—a nimbus without rays or a radiate crown with a ribbon at the back—cannot be Sol. The differentiation between these conventions was fully in place by the first century BC and remained so into the fifth century AD. I am not aware of any exceptions over this long period of use. This is particularly remarkable in the case of the radiate crown which, without a ribbon, is exclusive to Sol, while with a ribbon it is exclusively worn by mortals (in most cases the emperor during his lifetime), never by Sol. Although the only formal difference between the two is the ribbon, they are never confused, even on coins, in the more than 300 years that both were in use simultaneously. Cf. Hijmans (in press) fig. 2.1.

34 Hijmans (in press) catalogue A3.1–22.
35 Hijmans (in press) catalogue A3.2, 7, 8, 11, 14 & 16.
36 Hijmans (in press) catalogue A3.7 (Ostia, mitreo degli animali), A3.8 (Ostia, mitreo del palazzo imperiale) and A3.14 (Rome, Mithraeum of S. Clemente).

sents Sol.³⁷ The busts in Venice and Madrid have such an elaborate radiate nimbus that their identification as Sol also seems beyond dispute.³⁸

The other sixteen busts in the catalogue, as well as many not included in it, share the general Alexander-like iconography, but are without provenance and lack any additional identifiers. All of them *could* be Sol; they could also be Alexander, Achilles, Castor, etc., and do not have to be any of these. As Smith states:³⁹

> The Alexander-like appearance of a head, especially one of evident Roman date, is not a sufficient criterion for detecting an Alexander—not even a Roman Alexander, still less a copy of a fourth-century or Hellenistic Alexander. More of its context and function must be known, but they rarely are. In other words, unless a head has unmistakable portrait features, one can never be sure whether a given Alexander-like head is actually an Alexander or merely a mythological or ideal figure borrowing from the Alexander iconography.

This perfectly sums up the problem, but offers no solution, because whether portrait features are *unmistakable* or not is in the eye of the beholder. Hence it is not surprising that opinions on what constitutes an unmistakable portrait of Alexander continue to differ, ranging from Nielsen,⁴⁰ who believes that we have no extant portraits of Alexander and that we would not recognize him if we came face-to-face with him, to Trofimova who sees Alexander's portrait features in an astonishing array of extant busts and statues.⁴¹ Even the three busts known to be from mithraea in Ostia and Rome are variously interpreted. According to Hannestad, for example, the non-radiate bust from the Mitreo del Palazzo Imperiale in Ostia is a fine portrait of Alexander, while the S. Clemente bust is a portrait of Alexander that was later reworked to transform it into a bust of Sol.⁴² Only the radiate bust from the Mitreo degli Animali in Ostia is actually Sol, he states. Hannestad does not explain how a Mithraic adept would identify the bust in the Mitreo degli Animali as Sol, yet recognize Alexander in the bust from the Mitreo del Palazzo Imperiale, and Alexander-Sol in the S. Clemente Mithraeum. Surely he would see Sol in all three, even though the bust from the Mitreo del Palazzo Imperiale was not radiate.⁴³

---

37 Hijmans (in press) catalogue A3.16.
38 Hijmans (in press) catalogue A3.2 & 11.
39 Smith (1988) 59.
40 Nielsen (1993) 137.
41 Trofimova (2012).
42 Hannestad (1993) 66–68.
43 One must remember that the bust need not have had metal rays of some sort to "shine"; it could have been placed in front of some hidden source of light coming from above, for instance.

Faced with our inability to identify Roman images of Alexander conclusively, the solution has been to buckle down and try twice as hard to find that elusive criterion by which we can determine without a doubt whether a given bust depicts Alexander himself or an Alexander-like other. Unfortunately, there is no reason to think that we are getting any closer to establishing criteria for the recognition of "unmistakable portrait features" of Alexander in the context of Roman portraiture. In fact, what makes a (Roman) portrait a portrait in general is becoming more debated today, not less so.[44]

Fortunately, we do not have to grapple with that issue here, because all the Roman images of young men with Alexander-like features depict deities or heroes. There was no tradition of "portraits" for these deities; their identities were invariably established by a synergy of factors, including art (style, aesthetics, quality), long established iconographical cues (Persian cap of Mithras, whip or globe of Sol, lyre of Apollo, etc.), and context, all working to render a given figure identifiable. Thus an Alexander-like head can belong to a statue of Sol if that statue holds, say, a whip or a globe and is nude except for a *chlamys*. The same head can be used for other figures by varying the attributes, as Trofimova well illustrates.[45] We have already seen that these include the Dioscuri, Achilles, Aeneas, and other youthful heroes, as well as the gods Dionysus, Apollo, even Mithras, and quite a few more. For some of these deities the headgear would need to be modified (Mithras, Castores), but there is no intrinsic reason why that should be a problem.

It is worth noting that in all these cases it is not the bust or head alone that establishes the identity of the deity or hero. That explains why, in most cases, rendering their heads with Alexander-like features was optional. In Mithraea, for example, the variety of styles in which Sol could be depicted was remarkable, and we should point out that this was not a matter of provincial versus imperial styles. In fact, the range of styles near Hadrian's wall in Britain was almost as large as it was in the city of Rome itself. The Alexander-like heads of Sol from Mithraic temples discussed above, for example, blend in seamlessly with the classicizing style of other sculpture in higher class Mithraea, whether in Rome or Sidon, but would stand out as a sore thumb in most other Mithras temples, not because of their identity or religious meaning, which does not change

---

On the extensive use of special light-effects in Mithraic shrines see Clauss (2000) 127–130. Cf. Hijmans (in press) C2c.62.

44 Boschung/Queyrel (2019).
45 Trofimova (2012).

with the style, but because of the socio-political connotations associated with the style in which they are depicted.⁴⁶

That explains why Sol can sometimes have Alexander-like features, other times not. It is not his head, far less the style of his head that identifies him, but his attributes and context. Hence we may assume that in the case of Alexander as well, the decisive iconographic identifiers could be found elsewhere than the head, or at least elsewhere than the head alone. Whether this is true for the Roman period only, or was also the case with some, or even all early Hellenistic portraits of Alexander is difficult to say, but appears very likely. We know that archaic statues made no attempt at individualization, but were deemed to portray individuals nonetheless, named in accompanying inscriptions. The lack of individualization remains a characteristic of the Classical era (even while the styles changed markedly). It is true that when more "personal" traits appear in the later Classical period, they do render portraits more lifelike, but this does not mean they were truer to life.⁴⁷ We simply do not know at which point, if ever, Greek portraits took on the distinctly mimetic character that modern definitions of portraiture assume. A strong case can be made against Greek portraits ever undergoing such a change.⁴⁸ That is in line with the consideration that the earliest portraits of Alexander's were sculptures and paintings by Late Classical Greek artists. As far as we know those artists did not reduce portraits to depictions of a head or bust only.⁴⁹ They preferred full-body portraits, such as Alexander seated, Zeus-like, wielding a thunderbolt (Apelles),⁵⁰ or Alexander on horseback as part of a group of some 25 equestrian statues (Granicus monument),⁵¹ or again on horseback in an immense painting depicting a turning point in battle and the rout of Darius (Philoxenus); many believe the Alexander Mosaic from the House of the Faun in Pompeii, currently in Naples, to be to be copy of

---

46 Cf. CIMRM 1, 352, 353, and 354—all three from the Esquiline, but 352 on the one hand, and 353–354 on the other are not very likely to come from the same Mithraeum. Cf. also Hijmans (in press) catalogue C2a.14 (found in the area of the Forum Transitorium in Rome). Similarly wide ranges of styles can be found at the edges of the Empire. See Hijmans (in press) catalogue C2c.106 and catalogue C2j.1, the former discovered recently on the outskirts of Edinburgh at Inveresk, see Hunter et al. (2016), the latter a component of a rather nicely set up shrine just outside the Roman Camp at Whitley Castle, see Went & Ainsworth (2013), 115–116, for an image see: https://collectionssearchtwmuseums.org.uk/#details=ecatalogue.1017.
47 Childs (2018) 284–286; Vorster (2017) 9, 19–22, 40–41; Keesling (2018).
48 Vorster (2017) 41–42 and *passim*.
49 On Greek sculptural portraits, Dillon (2008); Ferris (2007); Vorster (2017); Keesling (2018).
50 Plut. *Mor.* 335a; Plut. *Alex.* 4.2; Plin. *HN.* 35.93.
51 Arr. *Anab.* 1.16.2; Just. 11.6.13.

this painting.[52] Certainly I am not aware of any literary evidence for portraits of Alexander, made during his lifetime, that were restricted to his head or bust alone.[53]

Why, then, should we expect to be able to recognize Alexander by his head or bust alone?

In fact, it is much easier to argue that we should not expect that. It seems likely that Greek portraits were not intended to give a true likeness, but were instead windows on an individual's ethos and character. In that case the characteristic traits of Alexander's head were never intended to be likeness enough to identify him, but rather informative enough to "qualify" him. That makes it much easier to explain why we can find the very same traits deployed on Rhodian coins depicting Helios, minted a generation before Alexander. By the middle of the fourth century BC, the sun god on these coins could be depicted with head slightly turned (3/4 facing), long wavy hair, powerful forehead with pronounced ridges above the eyes, enigmatic gaze away over the shoulder of the viewer, flaring nostrils, and slightly parted lips.[54] This means that we can agree with Dorka Moreno that Alexander's portrait did not play a role in determining the iconography of Helios or Sol.[55] In fact, we can go much further and contend that portraits of Alexander did not play a definitive role in establishing the iconography of any of the gods and heroes referred to above, and that to describe them as "Alexander-like" because they have in common the set of features under discussion misstates the issue. Indeed, these features are insufficient to identify any of these gods and heroes, *including Alexander*. In all cases additional information—attributes, setting, context—is needed. Whenever that additional information is lost, and we are left with an unadorned

---

[52] Plin. *HN* 35.110. Andreae (2012) 65–78; on the mosaic in general: Cohen (1997); Cavalieri (2019).

[53] Almost all are full-body images. Plin. *HN* 34.63–65, mentions an Alexander Hunting, for example. Numerous other examples: Plin. *HN* 35.93–96. The issue of the emergence of portraits in prehellenistic Greek art is becoming, anything, more confused according to Vorster (2017) 15. Her article gives a *status quaestionis* of the issue.

[54] See, for example, a gold stater (?) in the Calouste Gulbenkian Museum inv. 775 (image at Wikimedia: File: Moneta di rodi, 350–330 BC, inv. 775.jpg 1 June 2020); a didrachm sold by UBS (www.ubs.com) in auction 69, 27.01.2004, lot 5714; a didrachm sold by Leu Numismatik AG auction 81 16.05.2001, lot 295 (= Ashton 1990, plate 3E, but the auction image is much better). Note that the identity of Helios is established by the context: Rhodian coin with the rose of Rhodes on the reverse. Viewed in isolation it would not be possible to identify the head—without rays—as Helios.

[55] Dorka Moreno (2019) 155.

head or bust only, the viewer—whether ancient or modern—is no longer able to recognize the god or hero depicted.

I should stress that this is as true for Alexander as it is for any of the others. We have no trouble recognizing him in the Alexander mosaic (context, composition), and the Azara herm helpfully supplies an inscription confirming the bust's identity, but without that additional, crucial information we would be unable to identify either head conclusively as an Alexander. Why? It is not for lack of artists' ability, for by the late classical period artists were well able to produce recognizable "portraits" of Homer, for example, or Socrates—although it can sometimes be difficult to distinguish the latter from Silenus, which was the whole point, of course.[56] These portraits are recognizable, but not life-like. There can be no direct connection between portrait and appearance, if simply because neither in Homer nor Socrates' time such portraits existed.

Dorka Moreno is right to stress that there is the same "disconnect" between "portraits" of Alexander and his actual appearance. He rejects Palagia's conclusion that the image of Alexander on the so-called "elephant medallions" shows that in 327 BC, when the medallions were minted, Alexander wore his hair long.[57] The problem, Dorka Moreno argues, is that she concludes this without questioning what "long hair" signifies in the particular pictorial context. The notion that there was a referential connection between portrayed length and actual length of Alexander's hair at the time of portrayal rests on the unfounded postulate that there should be such a connection. He stresses that from a semiotic, practicable perspective on portraiture, the question to what extent and whether Alexander's portraits provide information about his real appearance proves to be unfruitful. For Dorka Moreno, portraits of Alexander are *Zeichenkomplexe*, semantic units composed of multiple semiotic signs construing a coherent and comprehensible image. If he is depicted wearing his hair long it is not because it was fashionable, or because there was a dearth of barbers in his court in 327 BC, but because the iconographic sign "long hair" imbues the portrait with meanings the artist desires.

That principle, that in Greek as well as in Roman art meaning always trumped mimetic accuracy, is entirely clear, but applying it has been less than straightforward. The problem is in part the anachronistic use of the word "portrait" which, in western art, has traditionally been used for works of art which render the physiognomy of the individual(s) portrayed with sufficient mimetic accuracy that it should be possible to securely recognize the individual portrayed in the

---

[56] For a useful overview of portraits of Homer see Wallis (2014); for Socrates, see Smith (2003).
[57] Dorka Moreno (2019) 29.

portrayal itself. From that perspective it is logical to seek the personal features of Alexander in what survives of his portraits, even if that is a head only. But if a portrait is a "complex of signs" (an ugly term for what can be a perfectly attractive work of art) then there is no reason to assume that the signs identifying the individual are incorporated in his face or head alone. In fact, it is in many respects the last place where we should expect such identity-clinching semiotic markers, because it is relatively speaking the most difficult place to include them. It is far easier to differentiate between Zeus and Poseidon by equipping them with a thunderbolt or trident respectively, than it is to consistently give them recognizably distinct facial features. This remained the case throughout antiquity. There are invariably specific attributes and/or contexts by which a given figure can be recognized unequivocally—a set of Persian clothes and cap (Mithras), a lance, horse, and twin (Dioscuri), whip or globe, *chlamys*, rays (Sol), etc. We have no trouble recognizing any of these figures as long as they are reasonably complete and/or in a recognized setting. The Romans did not need any of them to have distinct facial features to render their identity secure, and so they do not. In fact, two of the best preserved full-length statues of Sol can be securely identified even though in both cases they have lost their head.[58]

Against this backdrop, it is inherently more likely that Alexander's portrait, too, is a "complex of (generic) signs" rather than a mimetic approximation of Alexander's actual facial physiognomy. Nonetheless, Dorka Moreno makes a valiant attempt to identify physiognomy unique to Alexander in certain surviving marble heads by exploring *Traditionslinien*—lines of tradition—which he seeks to follow back to some early and securely identifiable Alexander portrait.[59] This "lineage" of images goes some way towards resolving the identity crisis we face with Alexander portraits, he feels, but he also warns that in many individual cases it will remain difficult to determine whether the image should be deemed to be active in a *Traditionslinie* or independent of it. This is ultimately quite similar to Smith's suggestion that we begin with those portraits of which we are absolutely certain that they depict Alexander and then add a circle of those which we are almost certain and another circle of those of which we are somewhat certain, then uncertain, and finally those which we now confidently reject.[60]

Even with these lines of tradition we are left with very few "secure" Alexander-portraits and Dorka Moreno warns that in most cases we only have *Ähnlich-*

---

[58] Hijmans (in press) catalogue A1a.1, A1a.2.
[59] Dorka Moreno (2019) 39.
[60] Smith (1988) 60–61.

keitsrelationen (almost "web of similarities") to work with, rather than direct copies of earlier originals. A major exception, he feels, is the relationship between the Schwarzenberg Alexander and the Alexander mosaic in Naples. Citing von den Hoff, he argues that locks of hair in the right side of the Schwarzenberg bust are arranged in exactly the same way as (*exakt entsprechen*) the locks of Alexander's hair in the mosaic. He accepts von den Hoff's conclusion that the Schwarzenberg Alexander type is derived from an original portrait produced in the late fourth century BC, which in turn was a copy of the Alexander painting, now lost, but preserved for us in a mosaic-copy now in Naples.[61]

I find this unconvincing, primarily because the locks of hair are not arranged in precisely the same manner at all, *pace* von den Hoff.[62] On the bust some locks partially cover the ear, while on the mosaic they leave the ear free, and while some locks could be of the same shape and position in both portraits, the majority are not. It is not unthinkable, furthermore, that Alexander is depicted with sideburns on the mosaic, although this feature could simply be interpreted as a deep shadow. The Schwarzenberg Alexander certainly does not have sideburns.

The problem with such studies is that they are searching for something that is not there. Convinced, and probably rightly so, that there must be a fair number of Alexanders among the surviving ancient "Alexanderish" busts and heads in museum collections across Europe, the Near East, North Africa, and beyond, they aim to find criteria to identify, *zweifelsfrei*, at least some of these elusive portraits of that great Macedonian hero, working from the unspoken assumption that traits enabling us to do so are there to be found *in the head or bust alone*, if only we look hard enough. I do not share this assumption. In my opinion, all figures depicted with the generic "Alexander-like" traits were eminently distinguishable from each other by their particular attributes, actions and/or contexts, even if their facial features were all roughly similar. This does not mean that the facial features did not matter. They go a long way towards identifying the figure portrayed insofar as one could never depict Alexander bald with a long, flowing beard, for example. But the head was not the deciding factor in the decoding of the identity of Alexander-like figures, including Alexander himself. We do not need to examine the precise positioning of the curls on the side of his head to recognize Alexander in the mosaic in Naples. Nor do those curls, however they may be arranged, make it impossible to place a marble Schwarzenberg head, suitably drilled for rays, atop one of the headless Sol-statues mentioned

---

61 Dorka Moreno (2019) 39.
62 Von den Hoff (2014) 221; Dorka Moreno (2019) 39–42, 56–61.

above. This means that when we have only the head or bust of some Alexander-like figure, without provenance and without a trace of the original context, then we must abandon all hope of securely identifying the image.

This conclusion is predicated on the understanding that Roman art was powerfully communicative thanks to its remarkably durable and highly comprehensive semantic system. Within this system, following the basic rules of semiotics, images provide the detailed semiotic signs required for actual communication. The more sophisticated the system, the wider the array of signs it requires, and the more important their durability. A crucial measure of a successful semantic system is the care those availing themselves of that system take to deploy its signs coherently. Such a system does not take kindly to ambiguous images.

The Roman visual semiotic system was by any measure one of the most elaborate, longstanding and far-reaching of such systems that we know. Perhaps one of the starkest examples with which to illustrate this are some mosaic floors of synagogues in third and fourth century AD Palestine, which had a large, central panel depicting the sun within a zodiac circle. In the majority of these synagogues, the sun was depicted in his purely Greco-Roman iconography (albeit in wildly different styles) as the youthful charioteer of a *quadriga*, for the simple reason that this was how one depicted the sun in Roman art. But at one or possibly two synagogues this was apparently felt to be too "pagan" for a Jewish place of worship and the sun was depicted as a large, radiant orb instead.[63] It is striking that these are virtually the only depictions in the Roman Empire of the sun as an orb with rays, a manner of depiction that today seems self-evident to us even in our earliest childhood drawings. Even more striking is the fact that the orb alone was not deemed to be enough. In order to make clear that it was the sun, the artists felt obliged placed it atop a high post standing in a chariot drawn by four horses!

Characterized as it was by its large set of durable and widely recognized signs, Roman art features another key characteristic of sophisticated semiotic systems. Despite its visuality, Roman art developed many signs that were indexical or even arbitrary in their connection of signifier and signified. We recognize a picture of a tree by the way it is drawn, an iconic sign in which the signifier (the drawing) resembles the signified (the tree). But we would not recognize the sun in the youth driving a *quadriga* before we were taught that this was how one depicted the sun in Roman art. And even the knowledge that this indexical/arbitrary sign is the way to depict the sun in *any* context has not prevented scholars from interpreting the image as one depicting the Sun *god*, even in con-

---

63 See Hijmans (in press) catalogue D1a.2–8.

texts, such as synagogues, in which the sun as god had no place. These scholars forget that just as the Latin word *sol* was used for every mention of the sun—religious, scientific, casual—so the youthful charioteer depicted the sun in its full range of meanings as well.

The fluidity of the "Alexander-like" traits that we have been focusing on is at odds with such a strictly regimented system of visual communication, and there would have been little patience with such fluidity, if recognizing Alexander on the basis of portrait-features of his head alone had been important. As we have seen, however, recognition of the specific individual within the longish list of deities and heroes with such features was not established by their head or facial features alone. The artist simply equipped them with specific, defining attributes and/or deployed them in specific contexts or scenes in a way that left no doubt as to their identity.

Our first mistake, then, has been to seek proof of identity in the fragments preserved for us—the Alexander-like heads and busts—rather than accept what a Roman viewer would have deemed obvious, that the identity is not established there. This is important for the issues at hand, because if we accept that a head or bust alone lacks the iconographical information needed to securely identify an Alexander, that means that the heads and busts of figures other than Alexander *could not render their own image "Alexander-like" using only those inconclusive features.*

But why, then, do all these statues share such strikingly similar traits, if not to unite them in some manner? Can we replace "Alexander" with a more workable bond that holds them together? One aspect to consider, particularly in the Roman era, is style. The images deemed to be "Alexander-like" inevitably share late Classical or Hellenistic stylistic characteristics. That may have seemed unremarkable when Alexander was deemed to be the binding factor. Obviously the portraits which were thought to have given rise to the Alexander-like traits were themselves late Classical or Hellenistic in style. Taking Alexander out of the equation, however, as we must, increases the importance of the stylistic unity, the more so because style was itself a powerful actor in Roman visual communication. Roman art deployed the full array of Greek and Italic styles, imbuing specific styles with particular connotations of mood, class and theme.[64]

The particular style, then, can be added to the other common elements—the unruly hair, the brow, the gaze, the flaring nostrils, the slightly opened mouth and the turn of the neck—as a determinant factor in establishing this group—if "group" is the correct term. Is the intent of these elements, or, if intent is

---

64 Hölscher (1987) is still fundamental.

too strong, their effect really to establish the group as a specific, defined collection of images? To answer this question we must make sure to approach it on visual terms. We are not—or at least not necessarily—establishing which deities or heroes did or did not belong to it. We must understand the group dynamics along the visual lines by which it was instantiated, which can be difficult to articulate verbally.[65] Indeed, to be honest, it is often in their ineffability that images can be most effective communicators. This goes far beyond such obvious ineffables as style. Time is another key factor. The immediacy of art stands in stark contrast to the sequenced precision of verbality. Verbal meanings evolve diachronically, as words form sentences, and sentences become paragraphs and chapters. Visual meanings are apprehended instantaneously, or at least without chronological or sequential control over the interpretative process.[66]

The inability to verbally express key visual meanings does not mean that we cannot map or trace them. Taking a page from literary studies we could, for example, explore the *intericonicity* of a group of images and discuss the degree to which that sets them apart. One could certainly argue that the combination of traits and style shared by this large group of figures is an example of what we could call the visual counterpart of intertextuality. But that is too facile, insofar as it does not allow sufficiently for the fundamental differences between the visual and the verbal in their modes of communication.[67]

Rather than pursue the study of this group through some sort of visual intertextuality, I think we need a more "visuality-friendly" approach, and propose that we explore the possibility of referring to the traits and style as *anchoring* elements. In doing so, I am using the term anchoring to describe a quite specific

---

[65] Style is a good example of a visual element of great importance that is impossible to render in words, and hence is often granted too little weight in our academic studies.

[66] The issues of verbality, visuality and translation are, or at least should be, at the forefront of any attempts to decode or derive meanings from the visual. Dorka Moreno's discussion of the roles of "intericonicity" or "interpictoriality" partially addresses this, insofar as it emphasizes that one cannot simply "intertextualise" imagery, but it does not really broach the fundamental problem of the ineffability of much that is visually communicated and apprehended. Kahneman (2012) offers useful insights, but his approach is primarily verbal. Most epic similes draw on strikingly visual comparisons, but are all but impossible to successfully render in a visual medium. Inability to express images in words should not be taken as proof of the superiority of the verbal over the visual. Each has its own strengths. The dense and detailed theology around the crucifixion of Christ cannot possibly be transmitted visually. Conversely there is no text that can define a space as quickly and effectively as a crucifix hung on the wall.

[67] The differences can also be explored in terms of what Kahneman (2012) calls fast and slow thinking, fast thinking being the more visual and un- or subconscious mode of understanding, while slow thinking is verbal and conscious.

heuristic concept, introduced to Classics recently by a ten-year research project "Anchoring Innovation" that is currently underway in the Netherlands.[68] As I understand the term here, anchoring refers to any strategies that allow or enable phenomena to cohere as, or belong to, a group where without the anchoring there would be no cohesion or belonging. Anchoring strategies are found in many different fields: intertextuality can be considered an anchoring force; memory, and especially group memory is another; ritual can also sometimes serve an important anchoring purpose, as can myth. Anchoring can function vertically, i.e. over time, or horizontally.[69]

In this essay, the style and traits we have been discussing are understood to be the "anchors" that position a given image within this specific sphere or context for reasons that are not necessarily self-evident. As anchors, these elements do not necessarily have an elaborate meaning themselves, but visually they form a very effective tool, ordering images into particular, visual categories to which they would not otherwise evidently belong. We must take care, however, not to confuse the shared anchors of a group with its shared meanings. Having established the existence of an anchored group, our task as students of Roman visual culture is to determine why this particular set of images is constituted in the way that it is. We know that a specific combination of style and traits characterizes the group, but we do not know (yet) what the shared visual concepts or purposes were that made this group cohere.

Further research is needed—far beyond what is feasible here. We must first strengthen our grasp of the anchoring elements and other means used determine membership of the group. Next we must gauge the group's range of visual meanings or functions, establishing their sphere of operation or impact zone. This could revolve around understandings of style (elite, Greek, skilled, expensive), shared identity/ies (youth, divine/heroic, Greek/mythic, masculine) and inclusion/exclusion (are there any heroes or deities whose presence one would expect and whose absence is therefore remarkable?). It would involve studying intericonicities that are beyond the shared traits and style, as well as cross-medium intertextualities, i.e. between the verbal and the visual, insofar as they can be established. A stronger understanding of neurological and psychological aspects of seeing and viewing will be important here, not least because we should not expect outcomes to take the form of a carefully defined set of (verbal) meanings embedded in images of this group. Rather, we should seek research outcomes

---

68 The easiest way to access this project is through its website: https://www.ru.nl/oikos/anchoring-innovation/.
69 Sluiter (2017).

that equip us to better recognize visually series of connotations or understandings that were associated with images belonging to this group, associations which may not be readily apparent to the modern viewer, but were ingrained in the minds of ancient viewers. Gaining a better understanding of these anchored connotations can give us insight into the social forces shaping visual understanding in the Roman world, or more broadly, into the social life of things. Where would a given image have been "proper," and where out-of-place? What class of persons can readily be associated with this or that group or set of cultural objects? What types of functions do the members have in common and what does that tell us about how images were deployed, and how that evolved over time? By the same measure, we may find unsuspected commonalities of meaning or connotation. Thus we can, with some confidence, expect that after abandoning the focus on Alexander, and by studying the images as anchored along the lines sketched here, we will add a significant new layer of meaning to statues of the Dioscuri, or Sol, Achilles and, yes, likely Alexander himself, arising from their anchored collectivity.

In conclusion, this article has examined the longstanding practice to describe a specific set of facial traits and hairstyles as "Alexander-like," the suggestion being that the adoption of such traits by other figures in some manner recalled Alexander. This is problematic because we are not able to identify portrait heads and busts of Alexander with certainty. We have a substantial number of sculpted heads and busts that could potentially portray Alexander, but there is absolutely no consensus among scholars on how many of these actually do, with opinions ranging widely. Such inconclusiveness would be unacceptable to the visual semiotic system of Roman art, particularly in the imperial period. In this case the ambiguity is a modern problem, however, rooted as it is in the assumption that a portrait head must be mimetic, or at least individualistic enough to be an individual. The Roman viewers did not share that expectation because in Roman art the precise identity would have been established by other means, such as attributes or context, lost with the separation of the head from its body. This is as true of Alexander as it is of any other in the group of sculptures with the same facial traits and hairstyles. Hence there is no reason to connect these generic traits with Alexander specifically. They did not originate with his portraits—Helios was already depicted with most of the traits before Alexander was born—and they are not in any way especially connected to him. We must conclude, then, that to label these traits as Alexander-like expresses a false confidence in our ability to recognize portraits of Alexander conclusively, based on features of the face and head alone, and imputes to these traits a major role in that recognition which they simply do not have. That said, while "Alexander-like" is a misnomer with regards to these traits, the fact that this group of deities and heroes shares them does create a certain degree of cohesion. It is by their joint usage that these traits act as the anchors which keep the various members connected. A closer analysis of the group is needed to determine why these traits play their anchoring role and what various meanings or connotations the group members consequently have in common. Such an analysis is far beyond the scope of this paper, and where it will leave Alexander in all this is impossible to predict. One thing we can state with some confidence, however; the notion of a pervasive *imitatio Alexandri* in Roman art rests on untenable assumptions and circular arguments. It cannot stand.

We return to Naples where we catch up with teacher and pupil just as they emerge from the Mithraeum. Philostratus[70] is saying:

> "So you see that art conveys so much more than merely the identity of the image. That is why whosoever scorns painting and the other visual arts does injustice to Truth,[71] as well as to all the insight that has been gifted to poets. For poets and painters in equal measure help us to understand both the appearance and the drive of heroes like Mithras or Alexander. Art does not merely imitate, it allows us to perceive from its gaze whether it is a madman we see, or one who is happy, or filled with sorrow. But you must not seek all this in the painting alone. Look away! Only then will you be able to see in your mind's eye all that gave rise to the image. And with that I am not just referring to the character, *paideia* and class of the patron, but to the nature and essence of the image as mediated by the skill of the artist. Much of this you can learn from a work of art at a glance. It is simply a matter of adding a little discipline to your gaze. A ten-year old can do it."
>
> The child, with a wondering look, responds:
> "I can't believe it's that simple, professor!"

Bibliography

Andreae (2012): Bernard Andreae, *Antike Bildmosaiken*, Darmstadt.
Ashton (1990): Richard Ashton, "The solar disk drachms of Caria", in: *NumChron* 150: 27–38.
Bieber (1964): Margarete Bieber, *Alexander the Great in Greek and Roman Art*, Chicago.
Blum (1914): Gustave Blum, Alexandre Hélios, in: *RA* 24, 94–101.
Boschung/Queyrel (2019): Dietrich Boschung and François Queyrel, *Das Porträt als Massenphänomen / Le Portrait comme Phénomène de Masse*, Paderborn.
Cavalieri (2019): Marco Cavalieri, "Le mythe d'Alexandre au pied du Vésuve: une étude historico-critique de la mosaïque de Gaugamèles retrouvée dans la Maison du Faune à

---

[70] The following draws freely on the first few lines of the introduction to Philostratus' *Imagines* as well as the first *imago* (Scamander) in which the very first command directed to his young disciple is: ἀποβλέψον ("look away") from the painting.
[71] Here Philostratus appears to foreshadow Plotinus (5.8.1), Cf. Zovko (2018) 153.

Pompéi", lecture given at l'Association culturelle Belgo-Hellénique de Charleroi " Alexandre le Grand " (Charleroi, 22/02/2019).
Childs (2018): William A.P. Childs, *Greek art and aesthetics in the fourth century B.C.*, Princeton.
Clauss (1992): Manfred Clauss, *Cultores Mithrae*, Stuttgart.
Clauss (2000): Manfred Clauss, *The Roman cult of Mithras: the god and his mysteries*, Edinburgh.
Cohen (1997): Ada Cohen, *The Alexander Mosaic. Stories of Victory and Defeat*, Cambridge.
De Lorenzo (1900): Giuseppe De Lorenzo, *Una probabile copia pompeiana del ritratto di Alessandro Magno dipinto da Apelle*, Naples.
Dillon (2008): Sheila Dillon, review of Dirk Piekarski, *Anonyme griechische Porträts des 4. Jhs. v. Chr.* (2004), in: *Gnomon* 80.3, 248–250.
Dorka Moreno (2019): Martin Dorka Moreno, *Imitatio Alexandri? Ähnlichkeitsrelationen zwischen Götter- sowie Heroenbildern und Porträts Alexanders des Großen in der griechisch-römischen Antike*, Leidorf.
Ferris (2007): I. Ferris, "A Severed Head. Prolegomena to a Study of the Fragmented Body", in: *Roman Archaeology and Art. Roman finds: context and theory*, 116–127.
Green (1978): Peter Green, "Caesar and Alexander: Aemulatio, Imitatio, Comparatio", *American Journal of Ancient History* 3.1, 1–26.
Hannestad (1993): Niels Hannestad, "Imitatio Alexandri in Roman Art", in: *Alexander the Great. Reality and myth* (Analecta Romana Instituti Danici. Supplementa, 20), 61–69.
Hensen 2017: Andreas Hensen, "*Templa et spelaea Mithrae*. Unity and Diversity in the Topography, Architecture and Design of Sanctuaries in the Cult of Mithras", in: Svenja Nagel, Joachim Friedrich Quack, and Christian Witschel (eds.), *Entangled Worlds: Religious Confluences between East and West in the Roman Empire. The Cults of Isis, Mithras, and Jupiter Dolichenus*, Tübingen, 384–412.
Hijmans (in press): Steven E. Hijmans, *Sol: Image and Meaning of the Sun in Roman Art and Religion*, Leiden.
Hölscher (1971): T. Hölscher, *Ideal Und Wirklichkeit in den Bildnissen Alexanders des Grossen*, Heidelberg.
Hölscher (1987): T. Hölscher. *Römische Bildsprache als semantisches System*, Heidelberg.
von den Hoff (2014): R von den Hoff, "Neues im 'Alexanderland': Ein frühhellenistisches Bildnis Alexanders des Großen", in: *Göttinger Forum für Altertumswissenschaft* 17, 209–245.
Hunter et al. (2016): F. Hunter, M. Henig, E. Sauer, & J. Gooder, "Mithras in Scotland: A Mithraeum at Inveresk (East Lothian)", in: *Britannia* 47, 119–168.
Kahneman (2012): Daniel Kahneman, *Thinking fast and slow*, New York.
Keesling (2018): Catherine M. Keesling. *Early Greek Portraiture: Monuments and Histories.* Cambridge.
Kiilerich (2017): Bente Kiilerich, "The head posture of Alexander the Great", in: *Acta ad Archaeologiam et Artium Historiam Pertinentia* 29, 1–23.
Kleiner (1957): G. Kleiner, "Helios und Sol", in: *Charites*, 101–104.
Maes (2015): Hans Maes, "What is a portrait?", in: *British Journal of Aesthetics* 55, 303–322.
Marshall (2016): Bruce Marshall, "An Aureus of Pompeius Magnus", in: *Antichthon* 50, 107–133.

Mihalopoulos (2009): Catie Mihalopoulos, "The construction of a new ideal: the official portraiture of Alexander the Great", in: Waldemar Heckel and Lawrence A. Tritle (eds.), *Alexander the Great: A New History*, Oxford, 275–293.

Mingazzini (1961): Paolino Mingazzini, "Una copia dell'Alexandros Keraunophoros di Apelle", in: *Jahrbuch der Berliner Museen* 3, 6–17.

Nielsen (1993): Anne Marie Nielsen, "The Mirage of Alexander—A Minimalist View," in: Jesper Carlsen et al. (eds.), *Alexander the Great. Reality and Myth*, Rome, 137–144.

L'Orange (1947): H. P. L'Orange, *Apotheosis in Ancient Portraiture*, Oslo.

O'Sullivan (2016): Lara O'Sullivan, "Augustus and Alexander the Great at Athens", in: *Phoenix* 70.3–4, 339–360.

Palagia (2015): Olga Palagia, "The Impact of Alexander on the Arts of Greece", the ninth BABesch Byvanck Lecture, BABesch Foundation, Leiden.

Peltonen (2019): J. Peltonen, *Alexander the Great in the Roman Empire, 150 BC to AD 600*, London and New York.

Schörner (2001): G. Schörner, "Helios und Alexander. Zum Einfluß der Herrscherikonographie auf das Götterbild", in: *Archäologischer Anzeiger* 1, 59–68.

Schwarzenberg (1976): Erkinger von Schwarzenberg, "The portraiture of Alexander," in: Ernst Badian (ed.), *Alexandre le Grand: Image et Réalité*, Geneva, 223–267.

Sluiter (2017): Ineke Sluiter, "Anchoring Innovation: A Classical Research Agenda", in: *European Review* 25, 20–38.

Smith (2003): Amy C. Smith, "Athenian Political Art from the fifth and fourth centuries BCE: Images of Historical Individuals", in: in C.W. Blackwell (ed.), *Dēmos: Classical Athenian Democracy* (A. Mahoney and R. Scaife, edd., T*he Stoa: a consortium for electronic publication in the humanities* [www.stoa.org]) edition of January 18 2003.

Smith (1988): Roland R.R. Smith, *Hellenistic Royal Portraits*, Oxford.

Spencer (2002): D. Spencer, *The Roman Alexander; Reading a Cultural Myth*, Exeter.

Squire (2013): M. Squire, "Apparitions apparent: Ekphrasis and the parameters of vision in the Elder Philostratus's *Imagines*", in: *Helios* 40.1, 97–140.

Stewart (1993): Andrew Stewart, *Faces of Power: Alexander's Image and Hellenistic Politics*, Berkeley.

Stewart (2004): Andrew Stewart, *Roman Art*, Oxford.

Strocka (2006): Volker M. Strocka, "Aeneas, nicht Alexander! Zur Ikonographie des römischen Helden in der pompejanischen Wandmalerei", in: *Jahrbuch des Deutschen Archäologischen Instituts* 121, 269–315.

Trofimova (2012): Anna Trofimova, *Imitatio Alexandri in the Hellenistic Art*. Rome.

Vorster (2017): C. Vorster, "Das Porträt im vorhellenistischen Griechenland—eine Standortbestimmung", in: Dietrich Boschung and François Queyrel (eds.), *Bilder der Macht. Das griechische Porträt und seine Verwendung in der antiken Welt*, Leiden, 15–47.

Vout (2005): Caroline Vout, "Antinous, Archaeology and History", in: *JRS* 95, 80–96.

Wallis (2014): William Wallis, "Homer: a Guide to Sculptural Types," *Living Poets*, Durham 2014; https://livingpoets.dur.ac.uk/w/Homer:_A_Guide_to_Sculptural_Types (seen 01.06.2020).

Went & Ainsworth (2013): D. Went and S. Ainsworth, "Whitley Castle, Northumberland: An Analytical Survey of the Fort and its Setting", in: *Britannia* 44, 93–143.

West (2004): Shearer West, *Portraiture*, Oxford.

Zovko (2018): Jure Zovko, "Mimesis in Plotinus's Philosophy of Art", in: Heather L. Reid and Jeremy C. De Long (eds.), *The Many Faces of Mimesis*, Sioux City, Iowa, 149–158.

Index

Abisares 218
Achaemenid/Achaemenids 1, 4f., 8–10, 28, 130, 150f., 157f., 161f., 164, 170, 175f., 178f., 182, 184f., 190, 195f., 198, 200f.
Achilles 138, 238, 240, 246, 260–262, 279, 283f., 294
Adaeus 132f.
Aegae 60, 62, 65
Aelian 156, 220, 227, 234, 237–239, 243–245
Aeneas 213, 279, 284
Aeschines 6, 57–65, 68–75, 85, 87f., 91f., 135f., 234, 236–239, 245
Aeschylus 137
Aetolia, Aetolians 111, 114f.
Agathocles, son of Lysimachus 36–47, 50f., 119
Agathon 127f.
Agis III 175
Alexander I 1, 19, 72, 74, 238
Alexander II 19Alexander III (the Great), portraits of 1, 8, 17, 19, 34, 125, 131, 137, 189, 238
Alexander-like images 276, 279, 281
Alexander Numenius 85
Alexander of Abonutichus 216, 225, 226
Alexander of Epirus 58
Alexander Romance (Pseudo-Callisthenes) 10, 189, 216–218, 220, 225, 234f., 248, 258, 267–271
Alexandria 5, 10f., 37, 40f., 49f., 194, 215, 217, 220, 227, 255, 257f., 263–265, 269–271
Alexinus of Elis 242
Alexis 139f.
Amastris, daughter of Oxyathres 43, 51, 158, 161
Amestris, Persian queen 164
Ammon 10f., 197, 211–216, 218–221, 223–225, 229, 255–257, 260f., 263–268, 270f.
Amphipolis 61, 83f., 90, 135

Amyntas III 3, 57, 247
anastole 275, 278, 282
Anaximenes of Lampsacus 244
anchor, anchoring 292f., 295
Andromeda, mythological princess 153
Andronicus of Rhodes 242
Antigonus Gonatas 45, 46, 105
Antigonus Monophthalmus 35, 42, 46, 50, 100, 106, 107, 108, 109
Antipater, regent of Macedonia 5, 34f., 40, 51, 63, 99, 105f., 119, 161f., 214, 220
Antiphanes 132, 140
Aornus Mountain/Rock 193
Apama/Apame, daughter of Spitamenes 159, 161, 165
Apelles 275, 278, 280, 285
Apollo 199, 223–226, 256, 261, 265, 279f., 284
Aratus of Sicyon 221, 224, 228
Archelaus 19f., 57, 74
Argeads/Argead monarchy 1, 9, 29, 33, 131, 196, 203, 233
Aristobulus of Cassandria, historian of Alexander the Great 152, 158, 160, 171, 218
Aristomenes of Messene 215, 224, 228
Aristophanes 126–128, 135
Aristotle 4, 10, 92, 202, 233–236, 238–245, 247
Arrian of Nicomedia, historian of Alexander the Great 9, 21, 22, 26, 149–165, 170, 171, 175, 177, 183, 184, 189, 191, 192, 193, 198–201, 234
Arses, Persian king 151
Arsinoë 6, 33f., 36–39, 41, 43–48, 50f., 237
Artabazus, Persian satrap 154, 158
Artacama/Apama, daughter of Artabazus 158
Artaxerxes II, Persian king 151, 154, 164
Artemis 279
Artonis, daughter of Artabazus 158
Asclepiades of Mendes 223, 226
Asclepius 215f., 219, 221, 224–228, 265

assassination 3, 6, 25, 151, 162
Assyria, Assyrians 178, 195, 197
Athenaeus 65, 125, 127, 130, 133, 136, 156, 172
Athens, Athenians 6–8, 19, 21, 40, 57–64, 67–76, 79–84, 86f., 89f., 92f., 97–102, 104–120, 125–127, 130–138, 140f., 171, 173, 219, 241, 245f.
Atossa, Persian queen 137, 164
Atrestidas of Arcadia 68
Atropates, Persian satrap 153f., 158, 162
Attalus 24, 65, 235
Augustus 22, 190, 223, 225f.
aulos 136
Aulus Gellius 215, 220f., 224, 226, 241
Autophradates, Persian noble 153

Babylon 50, 137, 154, 160–162, 183f., 240
Babylonia, Babylonians 4, 149, 178, 192, 195, 197
Bactria, Bactrians 154f., 159, 192
Bagoas, Persian vizier 151
banquet: *see* symposium (*symposion*)
Barsine, daughter of Artabazus 154, 158, 161
Baryaxes, Persian noble 153
beard 138, 289
Behistun 152
Bessus, satrap of Bactria 152, 154
Bodyguards: *see* Somatophylakes
Boeotia, Boeotians 8, 63, 75, 101, 105f., 108, 110f., 114–119
bribe, bribery 69, 72, 102, 136f.
Bucephalas 235, 243, 245f.

Caecilius Caleacte 79
Callias of Chalcis 73
Callias of Sphettus 117
Callisthenes of Olynthus 240, 247
Cambyses, Persian king 157
Caranus, Brahmin sage 156
Carmania 153f., 196
Cassander 7, 35–37, 44, 48, 51, 99–101, 105f., 108–112
Cassius Dio 225
Cepheus, mythological king 153

Chaeronea, Battle of 22, 66, 101, 111, 114, 119, 132, 140f., 237, 246
Chares, Athenian general 80f., 132f., 156
Chares of Mytilene, chamberlain of Alexander and historian 156, 182, 240, 245
Cicero 213, 217, 220f., 226, 242
Cimon, fifth-century Athenian general 61, 72
Cimon, fourth-century Athenian envoy 61, 72
Cleitarchus 172–174
Cleitus, general of Alexander III 24f., 157
Cleomenes of Naucratis 152
Cleopatra, Alexander's sister 24, 58, 63, 65, 162, 235, 238
Cleopatra, last wife of Philip II 24, 58, 63, 65, 162, 235, 238
Comedy, Greek 8, 103, 112, 125, 128, 131f., 137, 139f.
Companions: *see* hetairos, hetairoi
Cornelius Nepos 44
Corupedium, Battle of 6, 41, 43–46, 50
Craterus, marshal of Alexander 35, 153, 158, 161, 242
Curtius Rufus, Roman historian of Alexander the Great 26, 154, 156, 170, 173, 174, 189, 192, 214, 218, 220,
Cyrus II, the Great, Persian king 151, 152, 153, 157, 160, 176, 178, 199
Cyrus the Younger, Persian prince 160, 164

Danube (Ister) 191, 196, 198–201
Darius III, Persian king 151f., 157f., 164, 202
Darius I, Persian king 9, 137, 152, 157, 164, 176, 198, 201, 246
Delian League 131
Demades 72
Demaratus of Corinth 73
Demetrius of Phalerum 7, 98–100, 107f., 112, 114, 117, 134
Demetrius Poliorcetes 7, 36, 49, 97, 99, 108
Demochares of Leuconoe 7, 97, 99, 102
Demosthenes, Attic orator 6–8, 18–20, 27, 57–65, 67–75, 79–93, 97, 99–102, 105, 114, 116–120, 128, 134–138, 140f., 236f., 245

Dio Chrysostom 242, 246
Diodorus Siculus 26, 62, 63, 66, 67, 73, 75, 91, 100, 102, 105, 106, 115, 116, 156, 170–172, 183–184, 190, 196, 202, 213, 218, 220, 227, 234
Diogenes Laertius 112, 244, 247
Diogenes of Sinope 242
Dionysius of Halicarnassus 21, 79
Dionysius of Heraclea Pontica 161
Dionysus 110 f., 113, 192, 194, 199, 225, 265, 279 f., 284
Dioscuri 64, 279, 284, 288, 294
Dorion 136 f.
Drakōn 212–218, 220–226, 228 f.
drink, drinking 23 f., 63–69, 74, 91 f., 133, 151, 216, 236
Droysen, J. G. 38 f., 51, 97 f., 149
Drypetis, daughter of Darius III 162, 164
dynastic strife 34

Ecbatana 165, 178, 183
ecphrasis 277 f.
Egypt, Egyptians 5 f., 10 f., 28 f., 33–36, 38, 40 f., 44, 52, 100, 126, 152, 158, 162, 172, 183, 194, 257 f., 261–265, 267–271
Ephippus of Athens 128
Ephippus of Olynthus 165
Ephorus 212, 214, 220, 240
Eratosthenes; [Eratosthenes] 212, 217, 220 f., 229
Erigon River Valley, Battle of 22
Euchares of Conthyle 100, 107
Eumenes of Cardia, Alexander's Secretary 75
Euphrates 151, 159, 192
Eusebius of Caesarea 242

Favorinus of Arles 243
feasting 156, 181 f.
fish, fish-eater 126, 128–131, 136–139, 141, 236 f.
Four Years' War 97 f., 100, 105, 112

Gaugamela, Battle of 26, 151, 171, 175, 183, 202
gifts/gift-giving 8, 66–72, 76, 119, 180, 195, 269

Glaucias, physician 44, 139
Glycera 137
Glycon 216
Gorgus of Iasos 72

Hadrian's Wall 284
Halonnesus 140
Halus 135
Harmatelia 213, 218, 227, 247
Harpalus 102, 137 f.
Helios: *see* Sol
Hellanice, sister of Cleitus 240
Hellespont 43, 64, 126, 197, 200
Heniochus 131
Hephaestion, Alexander's chiliarch 139, 158, 162, 164 f., 227, 262
Heracles, Alexander's son by Barsine 154, 158, 161
Heracles (Hercules), mythological hero 129 f., 138, 191–193, 197 f., 200, 212, 215, 225, 237, 264 f., 270, 279, 281
Heraclides 132 f.
Hermippus 125–127
Hermolaus 20, 27
Herodotus 57, 74, 88, 153, 157, 162, 178–180, 218, 237 f.
hetairos, hetairoi (Companions) 3–6, 17–28, 63, 66, 73 f., 76, 91, 133, 139, 154, 157, 159, 169, 172, 177, 181 f., 256
Himerius of Athens
Homer 242, 268, 287
Hygieia 227 f.
hypaspists 21, 25, 158
Hyperides 138–140, 227
Hyphasis (Beas) 26, 192, 196, 198–201
Hyrcanian (Caspian) Sea 191 f., 201

Illyria, Illyrians 3, 47, 76, 87, 111, 115
India 26, 153 f., 159, 189, 191–194, 196, 199 f., 202, 218
intericonicity 292
Ipsus, Battle of 35–37, 40, 104 f., 107, 109 f., 117, 161
Isocrates 62, 75, 241, 245
Issus, Battle of 151, 162, 171, 183, 202, 247

Jaxartes (Syr Darya) 196, 199–201

Julian, Roman emperor 246
Jupiter 213f., 220, 222f., 225f.
Justin, Epitome of Pompeius Trogus 26, 33, 46–48, 51, 115, 156, 163, 190, 200, 214, 220, 223, 266f.

Laches 98f., 105, 114, 118f.
Leonides of Epirus 240
Leonnatus, Alexander's bodyguard 35, 159
Leosthenes, exiled Athenian general 75
Linus 237
Livy 111, 155, 213, 220, 222f.
Lucian 34, 213, 215f., 220, 224f., 242, 265–267, 271
Luna 278f., 282
Luxor 152
Lysandra, daughter of Ptolemy I 36–38, 41f., 44f., 50f.
Lysimachea 36, 38–41, 43–45, 50f.
Lysimachus, Alexander's bodyguard, later king of Thrace 5f., 35–48, 50f., 97, 102, 107, 118f., 159, 161, 174, 235, 240f., 243
Lysippus 84, 86, 275, 278

Macedonia, Macedonians 1–12, 17–29, 33, 35, 40, 44–48, 50–52, 57–62, 64–66, 69, 71–76, 79, 82f., 89, 91, 97, 99, 102, 105, 108, 114f., 118f., 125–141, 149f., 152, 154–156, 158f., 162f., 169f., 172–174, 176–178, 180–185, 192, 196, 198f., 215f., 220, 233, 236f., 241–243, 245, 247, 256f., 260, 262, 264f., 267, 271, 278, 289
Maracanda 25, 157
marriage: see weddings, royal
Marsyas of Pella 234
Media, Medes 153f., 158, 183, 193, 201
Meleager 42, 161, 279
Mesopotamia 184, 195
Methone 84, 89
Miletus (priest of Caesarea Troketta) 224, 226
Mithraeum 278f., 282f., 285, 295
Mithras 278f., 282, 284, 288, 295
Mnesimachus 133–136

monarchy, general 4, 10, 17, 22, 66, 185, 201
Mygdonia, Mygdonians 128, 130f.

Naqš-i Rustam 152
Nearchus of Crete, Alexander's admiral 158, 161
Nectanebo 216, 225, 257, 267–269
Neisos gem 220
Neoptolemus II, king of Epirus 37
Neoptolemus of Olynthus, actor 73
Nicagoras of Zeleia 242
Nicanor 25
Nicasibula 221–223, 226
Nicomachus, doctor 247

Olympias 212–217, 222, 227f., 265–267
Olympiodorus 112f., 115, 117f.
Olynthus, Olynthians 7, 59, 67–69, 73, 79f., 82–84, 86–90, 93
Onesicritus of Astypalaea 218
Opis 18, 21, 25–28, 155f., 163
Oppius, Caius 221f., 226
Orestes, son of Agamemnon 237
Orpheus 237
Orsines, Persian noble 153
Otanes, Persian noble 157
Oxyartes, Alexander's father in law 153f.
Oxyathres, brother of Darius III 157f.

Paeonia, Paeonians 3
Pages (*basilikoi paides*) 3, 5, 22–24, 27, 33, 181f.
Palace 9, 60, 65, 152, 169, 171–181, 184f.
panhellenism 152
Parmenio 25, 63, 171, 184
Parysatis, Persian queen 162, 164
Pasargardae 151
Pater (priest of Mithras) 278
patronage 5, 18, 23, 75, 119, 238, 245
Pausanias, assassin of Philip II 24, 235,
Pausanias, life-partner of Agathon 127–128
Pausanias, travel writer 36, 39, 42, 51, 100, 215, 220, 224, 228, 237, 267
Peithon, Alexander's bodyguard 159
Pella 47, 58, 60, 64, 69, 73, 75f., 111, 133, 135, 181, 219

Peloponnesian War   8, 126
Perdiccas, Alexander's marshal   8, 34f., 44, 57, 126f., 158f., 162, 236
Perdiccas II   8, 125
Persepolis   9, 152, 169–180, 183–185, 194f.
Perses, Greek mythological founder of Persian Empire   150f., 153
Perseus, Argive mythological hero   150–153, 264
Persian Gulf   192, 196f.
Persian king   89, 130, 157, 195, 197
Persia, Persians   1, 8f., 22f., 27, 57–59, 62, 66, 74, 76, 89, 130, 149–159, 161–165, 169, 171f., 176–180, 182–185, 192f., 197, 201, 235, 238, 246, 279, 284, 288
Peucestas, Alexander's marshal   159
pezhetairoi   18–22, 27
Pharsalians   135f.
Phila, daughter of Antipater   35, 161
Philemon   137
philia/philos/friendship   57, 67, 70f., 108, 118, 158
Philip II   1f., 6, 8, 11, 17, 19f., 22–24, 34, 57, 79, 99, 111, 125, 133, 159, 181, 248, 257
Philippides of Cephale   112
Philiscus of Aegina   243
Philocrates   68f., 72
Philocrates, Peace of   6, 58f., 74f., 92, 133, 140
Philostratus   276–278, 280, 295
Philotas   25
Phrasaortes   171
Phrataphernes, Persian satrap   153f.
Phrynon of Athens   73
Pixodarus Affair   235
Plato   127, 191, 241, 244f.
Pliny   196, 199f.
Plutarch of Chaeronea, biographer   7, 8, 10, 36, 58, 65, 66, 98–104, 107, 109, 110, 111, 113, 114, 115, 116, 117, 119, 149, 155, 156, 161, 170, 173, 183, 197, 212, 214, 217, 220, 221, 223, 234–235, 237–241, 243, 245–248, 266–267, 271, 275
Podalirius   225f.
„Policy of Fusion"   149

Polybius   247
Pompey   275
portrait, Greek   11, 118, 275f., 278–280, 283–289, 291, 294
portrait, Roman   11, 118, 275f., 278–280, 283–289, 291, 294
pothos   9, 189–194, 196, 198, 201
Potidaea   84, 90
proskynesis   24, 27, 62, 182
Ptolemies   10, 33, 190, 196, 202, 257, 261, 268
Ptolemy I Soter   5, 6, 10, 33–52, 97, 100, 101, 118–119, 158–159, 161, 171–172, 213, 218, 227, 247, 264
Ptolemy II Philadelphus   5, 41, 194, 227
Ptolemy III Euergetes   227
Ptolemy Ceraunus   5f., 33, 36–42, 44, 47
Ptolemy Chennus   215, 220, 223, 229, 240
Pydna   84
Pyrgoteles   275, 278
Pythionice   137
Pythocles of Athens   73
Python of Byzantium   75, 137

rhetoric   7, 79, 81, 84, 88, 201, 236, 241, 244, 246, 276f.
Rome, Romans   155, 173, 193, 270, 275, 279, 281–285
Romulus   155
Roxane, Alexander's wife   153, 155, 159, 162

Sabines   155
Salus   227
Satyrus, actor   69
Satyrus, biographer   3, 58, 235
Scipio Africanus   220–223, 225f.
Scythia, Scythians   193
Seleucids   10, 165, 190, 196, 202
Seleucus I Nicator   6, 9, 33, 36, 37, 39, 40–45, 47, 49–50, 52, 158–161, 165, 199
serpent   10, 211–221, 223, 225–229, 247, 256, 260, 266f.
Silius Italicus   212, 217, 223
Sisygambis, Persian Queen Mother   151, 164
Sitalces   126
Smerdis (Bardiya) brother of Cambyses   157

snake 10f., 213–219, 222, 226f., 257, 265–268
snake-sire 10–11, 211–229, 256, 257, 260, 267, 268
Socrates 236, 287
Sogdiana 153f.
Sol (Helios) 71, 161, 260, 279, 281–286, 288f., 291, 294
Solinus 217, 220
Solon 85
Somatophylakes (bodyguards) 5, 23f., 62, 158, 159
Speusippus 75, 245
Spitamenes, Sogdianian chieftain 159, 161
Stateira, daughter of Darius III 161f., 164
Strabo of Amaseia, geographer 152, 153, 159, 161, 212, 247, 261
Stratocles of Diomeia 101
Strattis 127f.
style 4f., 21, 27, 49, 62, 76, 81, 85, 134, 181f., 185, 203, 282, 284f., 290–293
Susa 5, 9, 149f., 153–159, 161–165, 169, 176, 180, 183f.
symposium (*symposion*) 23, 25, 63, 65–67, 69, 74, 130, 133, 136, 141, 157, 172, 178f., 184, 236, 238

Temenid 233
Tent 4, 62, 75, 156, 182f.
Thais 171–173
Thebes, Thebans 21, 63, 67, 72, 100, 102, 108, 111, 114–116, 119, 128, 130, 218, 235f.
Theopompus 17, 19–21, 62, 65f., 73, 91f., 133, 138f., 245
Thessaly, Thessalians 18, 64, 73, 80, 85, 89f., 104, 111
Thrace, Thracians 3, 18, 37, 43–46, 48, 52, 62, 64, 66, 73, 89, 131, 161
Timarchus 85, 87, 91, 236f.

Trogus, Pompeius 47, 190, 214, 220, 223, 266f.
tyrant, tyranny 7, 33, 74, 79, 82, 87–91, 93, 110, 117, 136, 242f., 256

Virgil 213, 220
visual meanings, ineffability of 292f.

weddings, royal 3, 5f., 9, 12, 24, 33–37, 40f., 45, 47–49, 51, 58, 149–151, 153–159, 161–165, 178

xenia/xenos/guest-friendship 57, 69–71
Xenoclides of Athens 74
Xenocrates 239f., 244
Xenodicus 74
Xenophon 22, 115, 157, 160, 178
Xenophron [Athenian exile] 74
Xerxes, Persian king 153, 164, 171–175, 197

Zeus 10, 33f., 101, 135, 191, 198, 200, 211–215, 218–221, 225f., 229, 257, 260–265, 271, 280, 285, 288
Zeus Ktesios 219
Zeus Meilichios 10, 211, 219
Zeus Philios 219

www.ingramcontent.com/pod-product-compliance
Lightning Source LLC
Chambersburg PA
CBHW020221170426
43201CB00007B/283